The Language Arts in Childhood Education

The Language Arts in Childhood Education

THIRD EDITION

WRITING LISTENING WRITING LISTENING LISTENING WRITING WRITING READING READING READING SPELLING SPELLING SPELLING READING

Paul C. Burns
THE UNIVERSITY OF TENNESSEE

Betty L. Broman
THE UNIVERSITY OF TENNESSEE

RITING

PELLING

LISTENING

NG READING

Rand McNally College Publishing Company • Chicago

ART CREDITS

Larry Frederick: *pages 402, 416.* Robert W. Jay: *pages 200, 231, 258, 404–405, 408, 413–414, 420, 421, 429–431.* Bette LaPorte: *pages 45, 101, 248, 274, 276, 336, 337, 362, 475.* Jerry Warshaw: *pages 16, 29, 54, 67, 100, 171, 185, 229, 241, 300, 307, 309, 339, 343, 347, 349, 369, 395, 437, 441, 468, 489.*

PHOTO CREDITS

All photos by Barbara Van Cleve except those listed below.

Bil Keane's *Family Circus* cartoon, reprinted courtesy of *The Register and Tribune Syndicate, Inc.: page 190.* Dan Miller: *pages 329, 332.* Courtesy of the Newberry Library, Chicago: *page 317.*

Current printing (last digit)

15   14   13   12   11   10   9   8   7   6   5   4   3   2   1

Library of Congress Catalog Card Number 74–27276

Preface

The Language Arts in Childhood Education, *Third Edition, is commit-*
ted to the premise that learning can best be facilitated when teachers
and pupils take a balanced approach—exploratory and systematic—to
the study of language and its uses. The proposed instructional ideas
and strategies are an attempt to awaken that spirit of inquiry inherent
in the best teaching and learning situations.

Well-received features of the second edition have been main-
tained, such as: (1) a separate chapter for the child five and under, (2)
extensive development of oral and written expression, (3) careful de-
tail to language differences and difficulties, and (4) up-to-date bib-
liographies and references to language arts materials. Also main-
tained is attention to the nature of language; close reading and study
of literature; early creative writing of prose and poetry; and ways to
differentiate instruction for pupils of varying abilities.

This third edition represents another major rewriting and revi-
sion with these features:

1. Each chapter is introduced with a set of Objectives and Per-
formance Responses.

2. Chapters provide numerous examples of both exploratory
(introductory) and systematic (mastery) instruction. Activity (task)
cards, worksheets, games, and learning packets are presented as
instructional strategies. In addition, the learning-center concept is
illustrated for various language arts topics.

3. The special role of literature as a tool as well as a content
subject is recognized, and the many possible interrelationships be-
tween it and other language experiences are utilized throughout the
text.

4. Written composition focuses heavily on "process" as well as
"product."

5. Expanded presentation is made for various language arts
topics, such as sensory experiences, the drama process, second lan-
guage learning techniques, oral and written reporting, semantic
elements of language, classroom examples of grammar concepts,
and proofreading. Though topically organized, the chapters indicate
the interrelatedness of the language arts components and discuss
implementation of language arts skills through the various content
areas.

6. In addition to the chapter entitled "Provisions for Individual Differences," each chapter presents ways to individualize instruction.

Three completely new chapters have been prepared: chapter 1, "An Introduction to the Language Arts Program"; chapter 13, "Classroom Organization and Management"; and chapter 14, "Reading." More extensive use of classroom teaching examples and worksheets is provided for chapter topics, and specific suggestions are offered for the implementation of theory. Pupil attitude and self-concept are recognized as important facilitators for learning. Evaluation suggestions applicable to a particular language arts topic are placed within the appropriate chapter. Other reorganization of material has been made in an attempt to improve the presentation (for example, cross references appear at various places throughout the text).

During the preparation of the manuscript, the authors became keenly aware of their indebtedness to many people. Grateful acknowledgment is made of the inspiration of many teachers and children who must go unnamed but whose influences have been great.

Appreciation is due reviewers of the preliminary outline for the third edition: Dr. Lowell Eberwein, University of Kentucky; Dr. Judith Meagher, University of New Hampshire; Dr. Margaret A. Natarella, University of Georgia; Dr. Esther Schatz, Ohio State University; and Dr. Ann M. Whiddon, University of Florida. Drs. Schatz and Whiddon also read the manuscript for this edition, providing further ideas and suggestions.

The authors acknowledge appreciation to Dr. J. Estill Alexander for his advice and counsel in the preparation of chapter 14.

Finally, grateful acknowledgment is given to Carlyle Carter for her creative contributions and editorial assistance through every stage of production of the book.

As was true of the second edition, the preparation of this third edition was the exclusive responsibility of those whose names appear with this preface.

Paul C. Burns

Betty L. Broman

The University of Tennessee
Knoxville, Tennessee

Contents

1

**AN INTRODUCTION
TO THE LANGUAGE
ARTS PROGRAM**

1

2

**CHILDREN'S
LANGUAGE AND
LANGUAGE STUDY**

27

3

**LANGUAGE ARTS
EXPERIENCES FOR
CHILDREN
FIVE AND UNDER**

61

4

LISTENING

95

5

ORAL COMPOSITION

129

6

LITERATURE

183

7

**WRITTEN
COMPOSITION**

227

8

**VOCABULARY
DEVELOPMENT AND
REFERENCE SKILLS**

293

11
HANDWRITING

393

12
**PROVISIONS FOR
INDIVIDUAL
DIFFERENCES**

435

An Introduction to the Language Arts Program

**AN INTRODUCTION TO
THE LANGUAGE ARTS PROGRAM**

This chapter and each of the following chapters are preceded by a set of Objectives and parallel Performance Responses. The Objectives are suggested goals to be attained while studying the chapter; the Performance Responses are guides to methods of attaining the goals and applying the information and ideas acquired in meaningful ways. In other words, the Objectives suggest the major topics of the chapter and the Performance Responses—things you should be able to do as a result of studying the chapter—can be used to help you accomplish the Objectives.

OBJECTIVES	PERFORMANCE RESPONSES
1. **To identify major experiences and related abilities/skills appropriate to the elementary school language arts program**	1. Suggest one experience and list a number of specific abilities/skills related to it. (Examine a language arts textbook for one grade level.)
2. **To describe desirable materials for a language arts program**	2. Begin one type of file described in this chapter.
3. **To apply a major instructional strategy for language arts instruction**	3. Formulate an inductive teaching situation for some aspect of language arts.
4. **To illustrate use of performance (behavioral) objectives.**	4. Formulate a "systematic" lesson for some specific language arts ability or skill.
5. **To examine ways to measure the affective domain**	5. If feasible, use one of the affective domain devices with a child, small group, or class.

THE LANGUAGE ARTS PROGRAM
IN THE ELEMENTARY SCHOOL

While recognizing that the language arts program is developmental in the elementary school years, the following discussion focuses upon two levels within the elementary school.

Primary years

The language arts program in the primary grades (grades K–3) naturally lends itself to a correlated program: the strands of language study are so interwoven that speaking, listening, reading, and writing activities are almost indistinguishable, except for times when they may be artificially separated for particular attention. Literature is a core component of the primary program—teachers and children tell or read aloud stories and poems that develop the child's vocabulary and his[1] feeling for language—its rhythms, patterns, intonations, and meanings.

In turn, stories and poems furnish material for oral expression, providing considerable practice in such activities as conversation, discussion, and creative drama. Naturally, listening is a corollary of the speaking experiences.

From oral activities, the act of composing begins to develop. In giving form to composition, the child draws mainly upon direct experiences and to a lesser extent upon the ideas he gains in sharing and planning activities with other children. Short compositions result—first oral, then dictated to the teacher, and finally written. In this manner, the need for spelling and handwriting occurs, as does the choice of words (vocabulary) and usage patterns.

Intermediate (middle) years

While individual elements of the language arts are more clearly delineated at the intermediate level (grades 4–6), an interrelated program is still important. For example, oral reading of prose and poetry to and by children continues to relate language and composition. Awareness of the "crafts" of the author in a story or a poem begins to have meaning as the learner recounts his own real or imaginary events and ideas.

Dramatization continues, helping to establish a sounder basis

---

1. In order to avoid the awkward usage of *he or she* and *his or her*, we shall use only the masculine form.

for judgments about people and ideas. Dialectal differences appear in historical or regional fiction; and from interests aroused by differing vocabulary and syntax, the teacher can promote principles of usage more effectively than from weeks spent on isolated workbook drills. Dialogue, discussion, and "group talk" provide material for more sophisticated statements—ways of manipulating sentences by adding, deleting, and changing elements. Acts of speech provide a functional need to listen. In undertaking the study of written composition, the child (and teacher) will sense that while the first concern should be with substantive matters, communication necessitates proofreading for spelling, capitalization, punctuation, and handwriting. Such practical application of the conventions gives meaning to the instruction.

SPECIAL EXPERIENCES AND ABILITIES IN LANGUAGE

As a means of presenting a view of the language experiences and some desired abilities/skills related to these experiences, the following topics (listening, speaking, reading, and writing), while not definitive, should provide a clue to the language arts curriculum at the elementary school level. While the experiences mentioned occur at most grade levels, some are given greater emphasis at one level than another.

Listening

Listening to sounds
Listening to stories and poems
Listening to group discussion
Listening to group instruction
Listening to the radio or television
Listening to records (story, music)
Listening to reports
Listening to others in conversation

As children need to develop competence in a variety of reading skills, they must also develop competence in specific listening skills. While listening can best be developed indirectly in a total oral language program, there are times, for most efficient teaching and learning, when the teacher and child should consciously focus on listening skills: listening attitudes toward individuals and in group situations

Listening to story and music records can enhance appreciative listening attitudes and skills.

of all types; listening for directions and instructions; listening for explanations; listening for information; listening for appreciation; and listening for analysis. Each of these skills may be further divided into subskills, as discussed in chapter 4.

Speaking

Sharing
Telling or creating a story
Planning and discussing class activities
Dictating (story, letter, poem, experience)
Conversing and questioning (small informal group and larger group)
Speaking-improvement activities
Giving directions for a game or an activity

Taking part in a discussion
Giving reports (books, current events, science, etc.)
Telling jokes or riddles
Telling about an incident or a personal experience
Choric speaking and dramatizing
Taking part in a telephone conversation
Introducing people
Interviewing
Participating in and conducting class meetings

Through these functional activities, the teacher and learner have a natural need to focus upon such related abilities and skills as: voice and diction; vocabulary and language patterns; courtesies; ideas for a story, report, or discussion; logical sequence; or simple parliamentary procedures. Further elaboration of these experiences and skills can be found in chapter 5.

Reading

Pictures and cartoons
Bulletin boards, charts, labels, signs
Notices and announcements
Captioned films and filmstrips
Stories and poems for enjoyment
Audience reading and choric reading
Songs and musical notation
Graphic materials
Informative (content) materials
Reference materials
Work pages and worksheets
Magazines and newspapers

Elaboration of these experiences is found in later chapters, particularly chapter 14, where the major reading skills are discussed (word recognition, vocabulary development, comprehension, and audience reading) as well as reading and study skills. Also treated in chapter 14 are reading approaches, content area reading, and teaching strategies.

Writing

Dictating ideas to be written by the teacher
Writing a caption for a picture, label, or sign

Writing a simple story
Writing about an experience
Writing a poem
Writing a play
Writing a diary
Writing a friendly or business letter
Writing a report or review
Writing a note
Writing an invitation
Writing for a class or school newspaper

Again, many abilities and skills will be involved in these experiences: sentence and paragraph construction, letter structure, using a variety of expressive words, bibliography development, dictionary study, proofreading, legible handwriting, correct spelling, and neat and attractive papers. These and other abilities and skills are further delineated in later chapters.

Two important writing stimuli are time for the children to write and the knowledge that someone will be interested in what they write.

Summary

In considering the above-mentioned abilities and skills, it is obvious that there are numerous components of the language arts (listening, oral composition, literature, written composition, grammar, spelling, handwriting, etc.). Many of these function as "tools" rather than "knowledge" and, of course, there is an interrelationship of the components themselves. The language arts must be seen in some sort of perspective within the curriculum of the elementary school, and the relationship of the language arts to other curricular subjects must be noted in particular. Other curricular areas frequently provide content for the skills taught in the language arts "period" (for example, the need to write a report in social studies). And use—along with incidental and direct instruction—can permeate other curricular areas. The teacher who limits language arts instruction totally to a "period," and who instructs each of the language arts as a separate facet, will likely achieve only teacher frustration, not pupil change and growth.

The principle of "use before practice," or "use leads to practice," inherent in the above discussion, is illustrated below.

use $\longrightarrow$ evaluate use $\longrightarrow$ practice $\longrightarrow$ refined, higher-level use

MATERIALS FOR THE CLASSROOM

Some basic materials for the language arts program include: textbooks, workbooks, files, activity and game books, and other learning materials. Each will be discussed in turn.

Textbooks

In many schools, no other single basic source of language knowledge is more conveniently available to all the pupils within the classroom than the textbook. Although it is unthinkable that the language program should consist of a series of page assignments in a single text, it is well to keep in mind that the textbook is, in all likelihood, the most important teaching aid the teacher has at his disposal. In most good schools this is recognized and the classrooms are not "textless," nor are the language texts all stored in a faraway closet to become dusty.

A good textbook series, prepared by a team of professionals, obviously has a number of strengths. The material, typically, is sequentially organized and carefully structured. A textbook provides a source of ideas for expressional skills that can be applied to current work being done in any subject in the curriculum; in addition, it offers a number of models (letters, book reports, etc.) that can be used in discussion of content and organization. It supplies supplementary and practice exercises for pupils needing reinforcement materials. The text, along with the teacher's edition, provides a ready source of evaluation materials, such as: diagnostic pretests, inventory tests, self-checking devices, spot reviews, chapter reviews and tests, cumulative reviews, and similar features that can help the pupil develop self-direction and independence and help the teacher individualize language instruction. Many texts carry enrichment and remedial suggestions (optional chapters, starred exercises, and the like). However, a single text or manual simply cannot provide materials for every pupil from every cultural or socioeconomic background. Even the use of more than one textbook in a class can scarcely meet this need. But the texts can provide the teacher with some ideas. In addition, the teacher's edition serves as a reservoir of suggestions on methods of instruction. Teachers who do not use guidebooks or manuals are making a costly blunder.

The most effective use should be made of language textbooks and related materials. In introducing a lesson or topic, the teacher is encouraged to build interest and motivation first by asking pupils to reveal what they already know about the topic under consideration — instead of beginning with "Open your textbooks to page 63 for the lesson on paragraph writing."

Many language concepts are best taught and learned if the textbook is used as a reference source, rather than proceeding through it page by page. This occurs when a real need arises, such as writing a business letter, searching for information in the library in preparation for an oral or written report, or checking a grammar point.

In every case, modification is needed according to variation in ability and achievement within the class without overlooking the importance of a year-by-year developmental program. To assist in this task, textbooks for the various age levels—and from a variety of publishers—can offer valuable corrective and remedial materials as well as vertical enrichment ideas. In particular, the superior teacher has a total picture of the developmental sequence of the skills areas of the language arts and the instructional approaches for attaining them. A teacher who knows in general what is involved in sentence making, paragraph composing, story writing, reporting, etc., and who can diagnose what has been learned previously and what still needs attention, is better able to provide the level and amount of instruction needed to care for the varied achievement differences found among pupils.

Workbooks

There are arguments for and against supplementary materials such as workbooks. These sources do provide a ready supply of additional instructional materials, drills, and practice materials similar to those found in the textbook; and the best ones have inventory tests, self-checking devices, and other features which, if properly used, can help the teacher individualize language instruction.

The "good" or "bad" of a workbook probably lies in its use rather than in the material itself. Below are some suggestions for using language workbooks and other practice materials.

1. The teacher should determine just what he wants to accomplish through the use of any material.
2. Inventory tests over the items taught should help in identifying the needs of individual pupils for further practice as well as the skill areas in which practice is required.
3. Each exercise should be checked and results reported to children as soon as possible.
4. A record should be maintained by the pupil of his progress through the use of practice materials.
5. There is no justification for assigning the same practice or workbook lesson to the entire class unless it is actually needed by all.

Each teacher should make an analysis of practices stressed in a language arts workbook. Topics such as oral expression, written expression, usage, listening, creative writing, and literature may be checked for frequency, distribution, and recurrence of practice.

Like textbooks, workbooks may be used either as a valuable resource for learning or as a substitute for good teaching. If they are used merely to keep a child busy, their use should be discontinued. If, on the other hand, they provide a means of individualizing instruction, provide practice in needed skills, and help pupils develop self-direction and independence, their use may be encouraged. Basically, however, workbook exercises have a severely limited kind of usefulness. Experiments dating back many years have consistently shown little or no carry-over from the kinds of skills developed by these exercises to the practical application of these skills in related writing.

Files

• *Picture*   Pictures may be secured from magazines, discarded books, calendars, book jackets, posters, travel pamphlets, picture maps, and other sources. Pictures will help initiate a new topic or catch the interest of children as they look at and talk about them. They may be used by an individual child to illustrate a poem or story that he particularly likes. Questions like the following could be written on the back of the picture to guide discussion.

What person do you see in the picture?
What time is it?
How does the person feel?
Where is he?
Where is he going?
What has he been doing?
Do you like him or not?

• *Poetry*   To be ready with the right poem at the right moment often means having your own poetry collection. Five-by-eight inch index cards or looseleaf notebooks are convenient for this purpose. The poems may be filed under different classifications for varying purposes. Poems may be labeled as to suitability for dramatizing, choric reading, memorizing, or reading for enjoyment. An example is provided below:

Card: Poetry File
"Husky Hi" (Norwegian)
Ages 9–12

Husky hi, husky hi,
Here comes Keery galloping by.
She carries her husband tied in a sack,
She carries him home on her horse's back.
Husky hi, husky hi,
Here comes Keery galloping by![2]

Suitability: Choric reading (unison)

Type: Humorous

---

2. From *Picture Rhymes from Foreign Lands* by Rose Fyleman. Copyright 1935, © renewed 1963 by Rose Fyleman. Reprinted by permission of J. B. Lippincott Company.

• *Skill*   A skill file may be nothing more than pages cut from various grade level workbooks, which are then grouped according to skill and filed by levels in a file cabinet or wooden or cardboard box. Handwriting, spelling, grammar, and usage lend themselves particularly well to this type of organization. Many aspects of written composition, such as punctuation, capitalization, improving sentence construction, outlining, use of the dictionary and other references, and even proofreading and functional and creative writing, can be organized this way.

When a teacher discovers that a child needs additional practice with commas (or with run-on sentences, the cursive letters *d* and *r*, synonyms for *said*, etc.), he can find one or more worksheets at the correct level of difficulty. (See chapter 12, page 445 for a skill worksheet example.)

Commercial and teacher-made worksheets can be reuseable if they are mounted on oaktag and covered with clear contact paper or laminated with a drymount press so that pupils can write on them with grease pencils or water-soluble markers. Each sheet should be labeled or color coded with the following information: level of difficulty, skill, and worksheet number. They can be made self-checking either by pasting answers on the back or by having the answers in a separate file. If multiple copies of each worksheet are prepared, several pupils can work simultaneously.

Teachers can find learning materials other than worksheets to include in a file of this nature. Games, transparencies, filmstrips, and audio tapes can be prescribed and used individually or in small groups without direct teacher supervision.

• *Story*   A file of stories (kept on index cards or in a notebook) contains the name of the story, the author, the publisher, and the age level for which the material is most suitable. There should also be a brief summary identifying the plot and the characters. The stories may be categorized as suitable for telling, dramatizing, puppetry, making up other endings, or reading for enjoyment. An example is provided on page 13.

• *Word*   One idea for a word file would be to choose a topic such as "fabrics," list twelve to fifteen words that are related to the topic, and then paste appropriate patches on a piece of oaktag. Of value to intermediate level pupils would be a word-origin file. (See chapter 8, pages 324–325.)

Card: Story File
Peter's Chair, Ezra Jack Keats   illustrated by author
Harper & Row, 1967   (collage illustrations
Ages 5–8   are excellent)

Résumé: Peter's old cradle, high chair, and crib are all painted pink for his new baby sister. He is so unhappy that he decides to take his little blue chair and run away from home. Finally, he discovers his chair is too small for him and he gives it to Susie, his baby sister.

Suitability/Topics: Read for enjoyment; multi-ethnic; family-life story about a new baby; discover Peter's feelings with children.

Activity or game books

Activity or game books, such as the following, can be used as reference sources by both the teacher and the learner.

Bureau of Curriculum Development. *Language Arts Games.* New York: Board of Education of the City of New York, 1971.

Rockowitz, Murray. *Arrow Book of Word Games.* New York: Scholastic Book Services, Division of Scholastic Magazines, 1964.

————, and Weiss, Irwin. *Arrow Book of Crossword Puzzles.* New York: Scholastic Book Services, Division of Scholastic Magazines, 1959.

Wagner, Guy, et al. *Learning Games for Intermediate Grades.* Darien, Conn.: Teachers Publishing Corp., 1972.

Other learning materials

Language activities often seem less like assignments if made available to children on individual cards, filed according to category. Such cards are referred to as "activity cards." Samples appear throughout the book (see chapter 6, page 212, for example).

Learning and interest centers and materials for them are described in various chapters (see chapter 4, pages 115–117, for example).

Even with good texts, considerable energy and time still will be required on the part of teachers to prepare many kinds of needed language arts instructional materials that are not commonly found in textbooks. Most materials will be structured to help differentiate instruction: for example, special worksheets or exercises for the linguistically gifted; materials for the slower learner who needs considerable corrective work; and enrichment exercises that will provide an opportunity for pupils to work at tasks and at rates that are commensurate with their ability (see chapter 4, pages 110–115). Other materials would include instructional charts (see chapter 11, pages 413–414); study guide sheets (see chapter 10, page 371); bulletin board materials (see chapter 2, page 53); and the like. Finally, there is a place in the program for specialized resources, such as writing laboratories and other commercially available materials.

APPROACHES TO LANGUAGE ARTS INSTRUCTION

With such a wide variety of materials available, the teacher will have options for various instructional strategies that best fit his needs, those of the child, and the topic under consideration. Two major approaches to language arts instruction may be termed *exploratory* and *systematic*.

Exploratory

As a basic instructional procedure, the guided discovery pattern appears promising. Basic to this approach are a problem situation, conclusions from pupils, and mastery of skills through the use of multiple methods. Such a "find-out-for-yourself" approach permits teachers to make use of the tremendous background in language that the child brings with him to school. This approach does not assume that children are learning everything about language for the first time. Pupils who participate in a rich environment of language activities in the classroom should learn the skills of language through the process of self-discovery as they observe how they and the people around them use language. With this approach, children are challenged to think for themselves. Teachers take seriously the old saying: "If he is indeed wise, he does not bid you enter the house of his wisdom, but rather leads you to the threshold of your own mind."

Following is an example that illustrates some of the characteristics of the "find-out-for-yourself" approach. After the children have written several stories during the school year, the teacher may detect a common need for improving opening sentences.

LESSON PLAN: Improving Opening Sentences

TEACHING STRATEGY

Problem: On the chalkboard, the teacher writes a set of four sentences and asks which one is the best:
1. On our vacation, we went to Yellowstone.
2. Slowly the door inched open.
3. Bob could never seem to avoid getting into trouble.
4. There was a fire at our neighbor's house last week.

Speculation: Pupils respond with choices and provide reasons for their selection. From this discussion, they suggest some "do's and don't's" for opening sentences.

Verification: To check their thinking and to provide for any additional ideas or revision of ideas, the children examine several language textbooks concerning this point.

Expansion: After studying the text material, a summary of ideas for a good opening sentence is drawn up.

> *A Good Opening Sentence*
> 1. is an important part of the story.
> 2. makes you want to know more.
> 3. does *not* let the reader know what happened.

Practice and use: A worksheet with sets of opening sentences on it is provided for pupils to choose the best one from each set and give an explanation for their choices. Then a story recently written by each child is examined with the direction, "Write the best possible opening sentence for your story."

The emphasis upon activity—rather than passive listening—leading to the development of new facts, concepts, or generalizations is in agreement with the best principles of learning.

Here is another example of the exploratory approach.

Here are three sets of sentences. Notice that each set uses a different spelling — *to, two, too.* You are to figure out what differences among the three sets account for the differences in the spelling of these words. You can ask me questions to help you gather the facts you need to construct your ideas or reasons.

Set A —*to*
1. Bill went *to* the movie.
2. . . . .
3. . . . .

Set B —*two*
1. Alice ate *two* cookies.
2. . . . .
3. . . . .

Set C —*too*
1. Jill ate *too* much.
2. . . . .
3. . . . .

A problem situation now presents itself. Children are encouraged to see a pattern for themselves and then to come to an acceptable conclusion about the three different spellings. This generalization could then be tested by referring to printed material, including the language textbook. Practice would come after attempts to develop understanding and would be individualized according to need.

The advantages of this exploratory approach are obvious. The importance of clear-cut pupil purposes in learning can scarcely be overemphasized; they provide direction for individual efforts and are also a powerful motivating factor. The emphasis upon activity—rather than passive listening—leading to the development of new facts, concepts, or generalizations is in agreement with the best principles of learning. Such an approach leads to a spirit of inquiry and a feeling of enthusiasm. It helps pupils to develop and exercise initiative. Perhaps of greatest importance, if certain patterns of the language are forgotten, is that rediscovery is facilitated through this teaching strategy. In the following chapters, illustrations for its use are provided for the various topics under consideration.

Systematic

For follow-up work with an individual or a small group of children who reveal a common weakness in a language ability or skill, a direct, or systematic, approach may be utilized, provided that the teacher has defined the instructional program in terms of specific skills and determined the child's level of performance in the skill (and subskills). An example is shown on page 17.

LESSON PLAN: Oral Announcement (School Program)

Performance Objective:
> Given a set of data, the learner makes an oral announcement about a school program, including five basic facts of information.

Pretest:
> Select an announcement appropriate to the learner and the situation and read it to the class. For example: "Miss Brown's class invites you to our program about tools on Wednesday, November 23, at 2:00 P.M., in our classroom, room 112. We hope you will be able to come." Then ask the learner for the number of basic facts supplied. These facts should be of the *who, what, when, where,* and *why* nature. Included would be a description of the event, who is invited, the date, the time, the place, and the price of admission if required. Criterion for mastery is 80 percent of the five or six items. The purpose of this exercise is to be certain that the learner attends to the basic facts needed in an oral announcement about a school program.

Teaching Suggestions:
1. Before reading another announcement, write the following purpose-setting formula on the chalkboard: Who? What? When? Where? Why?
2. Ask the learner to use this formula as a guide and to write an announcement about a pet show to be held by his class.

Mastery or Posttest Suggestions:
1. Assign a forthcoming event as a topic for an oral announcement. Prior to giving his announcement, direct the learner to list the five facts contained in his statement.
2. The suggestions provided in the pretest may be adopted and used in the posttest.

Reteaching Suggestions:
1. Select a well-written announcement to read aloud to the learner. Direct him to find the five Ws.
2. Ask the learner to list the key words that answer the five formula questions in his own announcement.

A few words of explanation about the systematic approach: first, a specific skill must be identified and stated in performance terms — in terms of what a learner can do when he possesses the skill. The pretest helps to determine if the learner needs practice in the skill. Direct instruction is then designed to develop the skill under consideration. The posttest is used to determine whether the instruction has been successful. The reteaching suggestions are provided for children who need further practice to reach the mastery criterion.

Whatever decisions are made by the teacher as to the basic or supplementary instructional strategy, the teacher needs to (1) be aware of specific experiences and skills of the language arts; (2) know and be able to use specific procedures for effectively teaching these experiences and skills; and (3) be able to develop a blending or variety of situations that provide each child with optimal language learnings. Examples of both exploratory and systematic instruction are provided for the various topics treated in this book.

LANGUAGE ARTS AND THE AFFECTIVE DOMAIN

Perhaps one of the most neglected aspects of the teaching of elementary school language arts is the affective domain; but this aspect is beginning to receive considerable attention as increased emphasis is being placed on the "humanistic" curriculum. Not much research has been conducted in the area of children's attitudes, but preferences of middle-graders have consistently shown that children "like" spelling and "dislike" handwriting and English.[3] If this is so, the evidence suggests that there is a motivation problem with regard to the general area called English and the specific skill of handwriting. Classroom teachers should be as sensitive as possible to the probable causes of these likes and dislikes.

Hierarchy of affective objectives

Krathwohl, Bloom, and Masia have classified the affective domain into five main levels, as follows.[4]

1. Receiving (attending): The student is at least willing to hear or study the information.
   Is the student able to perceive the language concepts?
   Does he wish to identify what he does not understand in language arts?

---

3. W. Linwood Chase, "Subject Preferences of Fifth-grade Children," *Elementary School Journal* 50 (December 1949): 204–211; Robert L. Curry, "Subject Preferences of Fifth-grade Children," *Peabody Journal of Education* 41 (July 1963): 23–27; E. L. Greenblatt, "An Analysis of School Subject Preferences of School Children of the Middle Grades," *Journal of Educational Research* 55 (August 1962): 554–560; Wayne L. Herman, "How Intermediate Children Rank the Subjects," *Journal of Educational Research* 56 (April 1963): 435–436; James Inskeep and Monroe Rowland, "An Analysis of School Subject Preferences of Elementary School Children of the Middle Grades: Another Look," *Journal of Educational Research* 58 (January 1965): 225–228; Harold V. Siegrist, "The Degree of Preference for Elementary School Subjects," *Reading Quarterly* 4 (February 1971): 15–20.

4. David Krathwohl, B. Bloom, and B. Masia, *Taxonomy of Educational Objectives: The Classification of Educational Goals, Handbook 2: The Affective Domain* (New York: McKay, 1964), Appendix A, pp. 176–185.

Does he listen carefully?

Does he pay attention when the teacher reviews his weak areas?

2. Responding: The student will respond about the material being studied.

Is the student doing something with language?

Does he complete his language arts homework?

Does he voluntarily read about word origins?

Does he derive pleasure from solving a word puzzle?

3. Valuing: The student has a commitment to what is being learned and believes it has worth.

Does the student perceive his language arts endeavors as having worth?

Does he converse about language with friends?

Does he actively participate in a book fair?

4. Organization: The study has a hierarchy of values—a value system.

Does the student examine the relationships among his values, with some emerging as being more important than others?

Does he eagerly await certain language arts activities?

Does he regulate "language arts time" with "playtime"?

5. Characterization by a value or value complex: The student has an internalized value complex directing his total behavior. He has integrated his beliefs, ideas, and attitudes into a philosophy of life.

Does the student demonstrate consistently high achievement behavior in the language arts?

This taxonomy can help structure the teacher's thinking in diagnosing appreciations, feelings, values, and attitudes of students with regard to the elementary school language arts.

Measurement of the affective domain

There are several ways to measure the affective domain. This section discusses three possibilities: (1) nonverbal behavior, (2) self-evaluation inventory, and (3) others.

• *Nonverbal behavior*   Nonverbal behavior can be measured by observational rating scales scored by the teacher. Chart 1.1 on page 20 is a sample rating scale.

CHART 1.1: Nonverbal Rating Scale

*____ 1. He listens attentively throughout the language arts class.
____ 2. He participates enthusiastically in language arts activities.
____ 3. He purchases trade books dealing with language concepts.
____ 4. He selects and reads library trade books that present language
           arts concepts.
____ 5. He visits the language arts table regularly.
____ 6. He assists peers with language arts activities and shares his
           activities with them.
____ 7. He constructs language games.
____ 8. He works actively and aggressively on his language arts as-
           signments.
____ 9. He prefers language arts activities during his "free time."
____ 10. He volunteers to do additional language arts work.

*The letter for the most appropriate statement would be written by each
item—(a) *always occurs,* (b) *often occurs,* (c) *occasionally occurs,* (d) *seldom occurs,* and (e) *never occurs.*

• *Self-evaluation inventory*   It is difficult to construct items for
a self-evaluation inventory that are comprehensive and yet not transparent to children. Essay questions are simple to construct and can
elicit a wide range of interesting responses, but they are difficult to
quantify. Most multiple-choice and standard scaling-type items are
usually transparent, or at least it is difficult to construct the items so
they will not be.

A sample of a self-evaluation inventory, adapted from Stright, is
presented in chart 1.2.

CHART 1.2: Self-Evaluation Inventory

*____ 1. If I had my way, everybody would study English.
____ 2. English is one of the most useful subjects I know.
____ 3. All people should know English.
____ 4. English will help us in our daily lives.
____ 5. English has its faults, but I still like it.
____ 6. English is very uninteresting.
____ 7. Nobody in our room likes English.
____ 8. English might be worthwhile if it were taught correctly.
____ 9. English is dull and boring.

_____ 10. I wouldn't take English if I didn't have to.
_____ 11. I don't even try to do my best in English.
_____ 12. I can't see how English will help me.
_____ 13. I really enjoy English.
_____ 14. I wish we'd miss English more often.
_____ 15. I like to work hard in English.
_____ 16. I've found English is useful at home.
_____ 17. I sometimes do extra work in English just for fun.
_____ 18. English is just too hard for me to understand.
_____ 19. We get too much English.
_____ 20. I can't see how English will be very useful to me out of school.
_____ 21. English teaches me to be accurate.
_____ 22. English is a waste of time.
_____ 23. English is the best subject in school.
_____ 24. English is OK.
_____ 25. I wish we had English more often.

*Key: A — Strongly agree   C—Disagree
       B — Agree   D— Strongly disagree

To secure a numerical score from the scale, the following values may be assigned for each item; the more positive attitudes are reflected by the higher numerical scores (100 possible points).

	A	B	C	D
Items (positive) 1, 2, 3, 4, 5, 13, 15, 16, 17, 21, 23, 24, 25	4	3	2	1
Items (negative) 6, 7, 8, 9, 10, 11, 12, 14, 18, 19, 20, 22	1	2	3	4

SOURCE: Virginia M. Stright, "A Study of the Attitudes Toward Arithmetic of Students and Teachers in the Third, Fourth, and Sixth Grades," *The Arithmetic Teacher* 7 (October 1960): 280–286.

• *Others*   Determining attitudes is difficult and there is no one best approach to the task. Some other approaches and sample items follow.

1. Multiple choice questionnaire
   For example: I find the subject of language arts
   a. exciting.
   b. interesting.
   c. uninteresting.
   d. dull.
2. Completion test
   For example: I find language arts _____ because
   _____.
3. Adjective checklist
   For example: Circle each of the words that tells your opinion
   of language arts.
   fun   hard   easy   boring   worthless
4. Write a paragraph about how you feel about language arts.

While the authors of this book recognize the possible limitations of the cited examplars of attitude probes (feeling of irrelevance of the probe by the child, resulting in nonserious responses; inappropriate format or vocabulary for the respondent), it seems necessary for the teacher to seek an awareness of the attitudes of pupils toward the topics, the materials, the learning activities, and the teaching strategies involved in the study of language arts.

There are various uses that may be made of the results of informal probes: (1) identification of major topics and procedures of interest to children, (2) utilization of highly stimulating learning experiences and teaching strategies with areas of study where negative feelings are evident, and (3) determination of topics or teaching and learning procedures where attitudes and interests may need expansion.

Some questions and answers

1. *When are pupils' attitudes toward language arts developed?* Attitudes for or against language arts have been developed as early as the third grade, but grades four through eight appear to be the most crucial years in developing attitudes towards language arts. Girls seem to prefer language arts slightly more than do boys.

2. *What is the teacher's role in the development of attitudes?* The teacher has the responsibility of seeing that each child builds a positive attitude toward language arts. This may result from several things, such as the teacher's own attitude, deliberate attempts to develop attitudes, and the methods of instruction used. Often what the teacher does speaks louder than what he says.

3. *What effect do methods of instruction have upon attitudes?* Attitudes toward elementary school language arts are formed by many forces: parents, classmates, and teachers. The way in which the teacher provides instruction is of importance. The methods and materials he uses, as well as his manner, probably affect pupil attitudes.

4. *Are attitudes and achievement related?* The cognitive and affective domains cannot and should not be separated. Generally speaking, there seems to be a positive correlation between the intensity of these domains. The more a student knows about language arts, the higher he tends to value them. Conversely, a student who values the language arts may attempt to become more cognizant in this area.

5. *What are the effects of homework?* Generally, it has been found that homework has no significant effect on the measured attitudes of pupils. Many authorities feel that teachers might well be sensitive to pupils' ideas and feelings about homework and actively solicit pupils' comments about assignments. Moreover, planned parental involvement should be considered in designing a homework program.[5]

6. *What relationship is there between self-concept and language arts?* Language is more than a way of expressing ideas to others; it is a mirror with which each person can view himself, and it is a device that can either enhance or diminish him as a person. The teacher's role is to guide development of the child's language growth, closely interrelating it to the child's image of his humanness. Oral language is the base for other language expansion; the young child first needs to build confidence that his oral language, one of his most intimate and personal possessions, is worthwhile. For the teacher, this means respecting and valuing the child's language — developing a wholesome attitude toward different patterns of speech. It further suggests "celebration" of the learner's unique creations in speech and writing; he needs to feel secure in his self-expression. In short, the teacher should instill acceptance of each person as an individual, with his own cultural heritage and a place in that culture. Because of its creative and personal nature, perhaps the elementary school "subject" closest to the child's self-concept may be the language arts — and nothing can build security better than his feeling that the teacher has an abiding regard for him. True respect makes a climate favorable to response, and acceptance by the teacher gives

---

5. John A. Mengel et al., "Attitudes toward Homework," *Elementary School Journal* 66 (October 1966): 41–44.

the pupil the courage to be himself. To have access to his creative sources, the child needs to believe in himself; and he needs to feel adequate before he dares exhibit in the open his thoughts and feelings. An individual who believes in himself and possesses self-confidence and self-respect has a built-in facilitator for learning. (The close relationship of development of self-concept and language is suggested throughout this book. See, for example, the following sections: "The Different Child" in chapter 2; "Usage" in chapter 5; question 4, pages 220–221, in chapter 6; "Evaluation of Written Expression" in chapter 7; and "Special Children" in chapter 12.)

SELECTED REFERENCES

The reader is encouraged to compare critically the suggestions made in this and the following chapters with those in other professional references, thus providing a more intensive study of the subject. The following general bibliography provides a beginning place for such study.

Anderson, Paul S. *Language Skills in Elementary Education.* 2d ed. New York: Macmillan, 1972.

Ashley, Rosalind. *Successful Techniques for Teaching Elementary Language Arts.* West Nyack, N.Y.: Parker Publishing, 1970.

Boyd, Gertrude A. *Teaching Communications Skills in the Elementary School.* New York: Van Nostrand Reinhold, 1970.

Brooks, Charlotte. *They Can Learn English.* Belmont, Calif.: Wadsworth Publishing, 1972.

Burns, Paul C., and Schell, Leo M., eds. *Elementary School Language Arts: Selected Readings.* 2d ed. Chicago: Rand McNally, 1973.

Burrows, Alvina T.; Monson, Dianne L.; and Stauffer, Russell G. *New Horizons in the Language Arts.* New York: Harper & Row, 1972.

Corcoran, Gertrude B. *Language Arts in the Elementary School: A Modern Linguistic Approach.* New York: Ronald, 1970.

Dallmann, Martha. *Teaching the Language Arts in the Elementary School.* 2d ed. Dubuque, Iowa: William C. Brown, 1971.

Frazier, Alexander, ed. *New Directions in Elementary English.* Urbana, Ill.: National Council of Teachers of English, 1967.

Funk, Hal D., and Triplett, DeWayne, eds. *Language Arts in Elementary School: Readings.* Philadelphia: Lippincott, 1972.

Greene, Harry A., and Petty, Walter T. *Developing Language Skills in the Elementary Schools.* 4th ed. Boston: Allyn and Bacon, 1971.

King, Martha; Emans, Robert; and Cianciola, Patricia J. *The Language Arts in the Elementary School: A Form for Focus.* Urbana, Ill.: National Council of Teachers of English, 1973.

Lamb, Pose, ed. *Guiding Children's Language Learning.* 2d ed. Dubuque, Iowa: William C. Brown, 1971.

Logan, Lillian M., and Logan, Virgil G. *Creative Communication: Teaching the Language Arts.* New York: McGraw-Hill, 1972.

May, Frank B. *Teaching Language as Communication to Children.* Columbus, Ohio: Merrill, 1967.

Moffett, James A. *A Student-Centered Language Arts Curriculum, Grades K–6: A Handbook for Teachers.* Boston: Houghton Mifflin, 1968.

Newman, Harold. *Effective Language Arts Practices in the Elementary Schools.* New York: Wiley, 1972.

Petty, Walter T.; Petty, Dorothy C.; and Becking, Marjorie F. *Experiences in Language: Tools and Techniques for Language Arts Methods.* Boston: Allyn and Bacon, 1973.

Ruddell, Robert. *Reading-Language Instruction: Innovative Practices.* Englewood Cliffs, N.J.: Prentice-Hall, 1974.

Shane, Harold G.; Walden, James; and Green, Ronald. *Interpreting Language Arts Research for the Teacher.* Washington, D.C.: NEA, Association for Supervision and Curriculum Development, 1971.

Smith, E. Brooks, et al. *Language and Thinking in the Elementary School: Curriculum and Teaching to Develop Children's Symbolic Processes.* New York: Holt, Rinehart and Winston, 1970.

Smith, James A. *Adventures in Communication.* Boston: Allyn and Bacon, 1972.

Stewig, John W. *Exploring Language With Children.* Columbus, Ohio: Merrill, 1974.

Strickland, Ruth. *The Language Arts in Elementary School.* 3rd ed. Lexington, Mass.: D. C. Heath, 1969.

Tidyman, Willard; Smith, Charlene W.; and Butterfield, Claire. *Teaching the Language Arts.* 3rd ed. New York: McGraw-Hill, 1969.

Tiedt, Iris, and Tiedt, Sidney W. *Contemporary English in the Elementary School.* Englewood Cliffs, N.J.: Prentice-Hall, 1967.

Wolfe, Don. *Language Arts and Life Patterns.* 2d ed. Indianapolis: Odyssey Press, 1972.

Another suggestion to students for facilitating the further study of elementary school language arts is to participate in the activities of such organizations as the National Council of Teachers of English. The meetings, the publications (particularly *Elementary English*), and the projects sponsored by the organization are some of the best ways to keep informed about new ideas for teaching the subject.

Children's Language and
Language Study

CHILDREN'S LANGUAGE AND
LANGUAGE STUDY

OBJECTIVES	PERFORMANCE RESPONSES
1. **To identify and explain several functions of language**	1. Interview a child and an adult on the topic "How do you use language?" Compare responses.
2. **To explain typical language acquisition and development of young children in terms of four features—phonology, morphology, syntax, and semantics**	2. Record on tape the speech of a one-and-one-half to three-year-old "average" child. What statements, in terms of the four language features, can be made about the sample speech?
3. **To compare and contrast language development of atypical children**	3. Repeat Performance Response 2 with an atypical child.
4. **To illustrate five major characteristics of language—relatedness, arbitrariness, system, change, and variety**	4. Develop a teaching idea to impress upon a child or group of children the idea that language changes.
5. **To plan an activity that highlights a language concept**	5. Prepare an introduction to a lesson tracing the development of the English language.
6. **To identify trade books that delineate aspects of language**	6. Select a trade book that will help children learn more about language. Plan a presentation using the book. Evaluate your performance.

THE FUNCTIONS OF LANGUAGE

The marvel of language acquisition as a natural, normal occurrence is a fascinating phenomenon. Children acquire and develop language within their immediate environment from family members and other individuals who are involved with their daily life.

To the youngster, the most obvious characteristic of his language is that he learns words and sentences that fulfill most of his needs. Learning the names of those things in his immediate environment, the child continues to be involved in feelings, actions, and ideas.

At an early age, language becomes the "cement" of the personal reactions of the individual and the verbal symbols of communication with others. Language is now a social function and the child has become an interacting member of society.

The following eight basic functions of language have been suggested.

1. Language identifies wants and needs.
2. Language facilitates the acquisition and exchange of information and ideas.
3. Language is a means of expressing feelings and emotions.
4. Language is a means of self-identification.
5. Language is a means of social interaction.
6. Language is a basis for reflective thinking.
7. Language is a basis for extended (creative) thinking.
8. Language is adaptable to alternate forms of communication (oral, gesture, and graphic).[1]

A child's language is not only of great importance to him, but the quality of it may have a major impact on the kinds of teaching and learning experiences that are available to him at the most crucial time of his instructional life—the elementary school years.

TYPICAL LANGUAGE ACQUISITION AND DEVELOPMENT OF YOUNG CHILDREN

Chart 2.1 is based on the findings of several language authorities and presents facts about a young child's language growth. Such knowledge is useful to the prospective or practicing teacher so that

To the youngster, the most obvious characteristic of his language is that he learns words and sentences that fulfill most of his needs.

HELP!

---

1. John W. Stewig, *Exploring Language with Children* (Columbus, Ohio: Merrill, 1974), chapter 3 by Harlan S. and Ruth M. Hansen, pp. 58–60.

Observation and interpretation of pictures are important factors in the process of language and literacy development.

he may anticipate language problems met by children at differing stages and develop an appropriate language program for each child. The following language features will be presented after the chart.

Phonology: A phoneme is the smallest distinctive unit of sound in a language. For example, the word *fat* is composed of three phonemes. There are about forty significant units of speech sounds, or phonemes, in the English language.

Morphology: A morpheme is the smallest unit of meaning in a language. For example, *sing* is a word as well as a morpheme, but morpheme is a more specific term. *Sing* is one word and one morpheme, but *singer* is one word and two morphemes—*sing* and *er*. *Sing*, which can stand by itself, is called a free form morpheme, but a bound morpheme, such as *er*, must always be joined to another morpheme. Intonation (stress, pitch, and juncture) is also a part of morphology.

Syntax: Morphemes are put together in larger patterns that transmit ideas, the structure of which is called syntax. Syntax involves word-order patterns, the functioning of the various parts of speech, the uses English makes of function words, the connecting signals between parts of speech in English utterances, and the devices for compounding and modifying the patterns of English.

Semantics: Semantics is the study of meaning in language forms.[2]

CHART 2.1: Summary of Language Development to Sixty Months

Age in Months	Listening	Speaking
1	Activity decreased by sound, calmed by voice	Vocalizes when crying, throaty noises
2	Listens to human voice	Cooing and babbling, crying for hunger and pain is different
3	Looks to source of sound, eyes follow ringing bell	Chuckles when pleased, vocalizes when talked to
4	Moves head toward sound, searches for voice	Babbles syllables "ba-ba-ba," loud laughter
5	Distinguishes between friendly and angry voices	Babbles to people, vocalizes displeasure
6	Turns head to bell twelve inches from either ear	Vocalizes well-defined syllables

2. For a summary of the nature of language, its functions, language development, and theories of language learning, see Walter M. McGinitie, "Language Development," *Encyclopedia of Educational Research*, 4th ed. (New York: Macmillan, 1969), pp. 686–699.

7	Responds when called	Combines vowel sounds
8	Looks at persons or objects named	Repeats "mama" or "dada," but not consistently
9	Activity stops on "no-no" or his name	Imitates sounds as tongue click, says "mama" or "dada" consistently
10	Waves "bye-bye" on request	Shakes head for "no," imitates syllables
11	Enjoys listening to voice and music	Uses consonants h, d, b, ng, z, g
12	Responds to request "give me toy"	Says one or two words besides "mama" and "dada"
13	Gives toys on request	Fluency practice, points while babbling
15	Points to picture named	Imitates adult demonstrations, acquires four or five new words, says equivalent of "thank you"
18	Follows two directions with ball	Asks for milk, cookie—by name, has ten-word vocabulary
21	Points to parts of doll named	Twenty-word vocabulary, begins two-word sentences
24	Carries out four directions with ball	Jargon begins to fade
30	Identifies body parts, discriminates prepositions, points to named objects, identifies objects by use	Says name, uses pronoun *me*, repeats two digits, names objects
36	Obeys simple commands, understands taking turns, carries out two commands, discriminates size	Tells male-female names, drawings, repeats three digits, repeats seven-syllable sentence, uses plurals

48	Understands concepts—sleepy, cold; remembers four commands; understands similarities and differences; understands prepositions	Repeats twelve-syllable sentence, can tell opposites, defines words, counts three objects in sequence, uses conjunctions
60	Identifies coins, identifies four colors, carries out three-part command	Names and points to ten objects, describes objects, tells part of day

Source: *How Children Learn to Speak* (Los Angeles: Western Psychological Services, 1969), pp. 13–14. Copyright © 1969 by Western Psychological Services. Reprinted by permission.

Phonology

The onset of speech is an extremely regular phenomenon and follows a fixed sequence of events. Speech sounds are started in the first months of life, the sounds becoming distinguishable words at about nine to twelve months. Vowel (front and middle) phonemes are uttered prior to consonant phonemes; consonant phonemes become interspersed around the age of five months. Some children in the beginning school years are unable to articulate clearly certain sounds—but the data below indicate the latest ages considered "usual" for the development of facility in the use of sounds represented by these letters:

3 years	*m, n, ng, p, f, h, w*
3½ years	*y*
4 years	*k, b, d, g, r*
4½ years	*s, sh, ch*
6 years	*t, th, v, l*
7 years	*th* (voiced), *z, zh, j*[3]

(See pages 452–456 for a brief overview of the elementary school speech program.)

Morphology

The one-word utterances (six to twelve months) are usually nouns —names for common objects. Verbs follow shortly thereafter. Single-

---

3. Mildred A. Templin, *Certain Language Skills in Children: Their Development and Interrelationships* (Minneapolis: University of Minnesota Press, 1957), p. 53.

word utterances expressing a complex of ideas *(holophrases)* are prevalent from age one year to one-and-one-half years. Chart 2.1 indicates that once the child has developed some capacity with morphemes, growth is rapid from eighteen to thirty-six months. Three processes may be noted as operating in this period:

Reduction: In his early speech, the child often imitates adult speech (e.g., "Little baby will go to sleep."), but omits the function words—articles, prepositions, auxiliary verbs (e.g., "Baby sleep."). This is often referred to as telegraphic speech.

Expansion: Parents and others often imitate the child's speech with expansion (e.g., "Yes, baby will go to sleep now."). How important are these expansions upon the child's telegraphic speech? There is not enough research on this question for a firm answer at present, but it likely does have an effect upon the language *performance* by the child.

Latent structure: While some authorities feel that language development is no different from other learned behaviors in any fundamental ways,[4] there are others who feel that the human infant is endowed with a learning mechanism (biological propensity) suited for learning language.[5] It seems clear that language is a part of the structure of the human organism, a part of his external environment and the interrelationship between the two. The interrelationship between them is unknown, and there are different schools of thought about which is dominant.

Between ages one-and-one-half to three, the child makes every effort to assimilate the basic elements of his linguistic culture. In his efforts, he often overgeneralizes—uttering such terms as *foots* or *digged*—before becoming familiar with the "exceptions." Such "errors" (analogical substitutions) suggest that the child possesses construction rules—he does not just imitate language patterns. (See chapter 8, pages 305–311, for the instructional program for morphology at the elementary school level.)

Syntax

As chart 2.1 suggests, the child begins combining words around eighteen to twenty-four months. His first sentences are often telegraphic—two words. The structure of the two-word sentences has been referred to as "pivot-open class" construction:

4. B. F. Skinner, *Verbal Behavior* (New York: Appleton-Century-Crofts, 1957).

5. Noam Chomsky, *Synatctic Structures* (New York: Humanities, 1957); Eric H. Lenneberg, *Biological Foundations of Language* (New York: Wiley, 1967).

Front position pivot: *more cake, more milk, more soup*

Second position pivot: *shoe off, light off, dress off*

The negative and the question transformations appear:

Negative: *I can go.* $\longrightarrow$ *I cannot go.*

Question: *Bill is playing.* $\longrightarrow$ *Is Bill playing?* (yes-no question)

Passive transformations appear a bit more difficult for the young child:

Mary hit the ball. $\longrightarrow$ The ball was hit by Mary.

By five years of age, the S-V-O sentence order (subject-verb-object) is strongly grounded, although the child may have produced every conceivable sentence type. By the time the child is three-and-one-half or four years of age, he has likely used every part of speech and every sentence form; in brief, when judged on the basis of sentence structure, the child's spoken language has reached 90 percent of its mature level.[6] As he matures, vocabulary will increase; a few more patterns will be absorbed (e.g., pluralization rules for /-s/, /-z/, /-əz/—*bets, beds, matches*); and some additional skills in the use of sentences will appear but the essentials of oral language are present. (See chapter 9 for the elementary school grammar program.)

Semantics

The factor of semantics is the most difficult to pinpoint. Children begin to differentiate among antonyms—making more discriminating responses as they grow older. Children make overgeneralizations in semantics as they do in morphology. For example, once the child has learned the word *car*, he may apply it to any motor vehicle, making no differentiation for trucks or other types of vehicles. Semantic development takes place at a slower rate and over a much longer period of time than any of the preceding language factors; the other three features (phonology, morphology, syntax) are quite well along by the age of five. (See chapter 8, pages 312–316, for semantic study at the elementary school level.)

Summary comments

There are a number of influences on language development. Biological differences would account for variations among individual growth patterns. Environmental features must also be considered.

---

6. John E. Anderson, "Principles of Growth and Maturity in Language," *Elementary English Review* 18 (November 1949): 250–254. *See also* Susan M. Ervin and Wick R. Miller, *Language Development,* 62d Yearbook of the National Society for the Study of Education, vol. 62, pt. 1, 1963 (Chicago: University of Chicago Press), pp. 108–143.

For example, geography and social class are major influences since the child acquires not only the language but also the dialect furnished by his environment. Handicaps, such as deafness, are another pertinent variable related to language development. Between ages three and eight, differences between the sexes favor girls to some extent. Twins are sometimes slow in language development during the preschool years. The only child is often accelerated in all phases of language growth.[7]

The teacher, however, is probably more interested in using and applying facts about language acquisition and development than in merely knowing them. Perhaps the major implication is for the reader to reflect upon the circumstances under which much language learning occurs and to try to approximate, to some extent at least, these circumstances within the classroom. The teacher's main objective should be to help children use language as a means of expression and communication. The means: provide a rich physical environment and an interesting assortment and sequence of experiences that provoke natural, normal, and meaningful speaking and listening situations. Encourage a free flow of verbal communication; lead gradually into the context of reading and writing, always in ways that are meaningful and useful to the child; and provide the necessary help along the way with skills associated with language instruction. Begin with meaning and usage, so that the child understands the reasons for skills instruction.

THE DIFFERENT CHILD

Three distinct types of the "different" child deserve mention in addition to the "typical" language development description provided in the preceding section. The gifted, the socially disadvantaged, and non-native speaker of English will be discussed in turn. (Chapter 12 suggests a differentiated instructional program for these and other "special" children.)

The gifted

One of the ways in which brightness first becomes evident is

---

7. Dorothea McCarty, "Some Possible Explanations of Sex Differences in Language Development and Disorders," *Journal of Psychology* 35 (January 1953): 155–160; Edith A. Davis, *The Development of Linguistic Skill in Twins, Singletons with Siblings and Only Children from Ages Five to Ten Years,* Institute of Child Welfare, Monograph Series No. 14 (Minneapolis: University of Minnesota Press, 1937).

The linguistically advanced child needs a different kind of guidance than that required by the average or slow learner.

through precociously early reading. Frequently, extremely bright children teach themselves to read without any formal instruction and often are able to read easily and independently those materials designed for beginning reading before they enter school. Studies show that approximately half of the children classified as gifted by intelligence tests could read at the kindergarten level, and nearly all of them at the beginning of first grade.

The gifted child usually is advanced in linguistic development. He is accelerated in use of and understanding of vocabulary, in maturity of sentence structure, and in originality of expression. Two studies have confirmed the fact that bright children tend to be ahead of others in the use of oral language.[8] In Loban's analysis of all forms of language used by a wide cross section of elementary school children, the highest correlation was between results of the Kuhlmann-Anderson intelligence test and an oral vocabulary test. Bright children, according to Strickland, use longer, more complex sentences and more mature expressions than do other children their age. Although all normal, young children learn the language of their environment without formal instruction, the bright child learns the language faster.

The socially disadvantaged

The terms *culturally different, culturally deprived, educationally deprived, deprived, underprivileged, disadvantaged, lower class,* and *lower socioeconomic group* are used in current literature to describe this child. Thousands of such individuals can be found in large American cities and isolated rural areas—and many become a part of the school dropout statistics.

During his early years, the disadvantaged child may have had a lack of vocal stimulation, a paucity of experiences in conversation with verbally mature adults, and limited opportunities for broad experiential contacts. Thus, he has limited opportunities for conceptualizing and for utilizing the labels (words) conventionally used in a society for its objects, actions, and ideas. His verbal environment is likely permeated with (1) models of different—not necessarily deficient—vocabulary and sentence structure; (2) simple, monosyllabic words; (3) infrequent use of descriptive or qualifying terms; (4) the simple sentence; and (5) profuse use of regionalisms, slang, and cant.[9] He may deviate from standard English by speaking with nonagreement of subject and verb, sentence fragments, omission of some auxiliaries, and poor articulation of sounds.

This child should not be labeled as "nonverbal," or verbally destitute, unless he truly has less language ability than other children. The socially disadvantaged child often has a fully developed but "nonstandard English": that is, he can be understood by his family and friends but does not speak the "language of the school." Sometimes the socially disadvantaged child has an underdeveloped

---

8. Walter D. Loban, *Language of Elementary School Children* (Urbana, Ill.: National Council of Teachers of English, 1963), p. 79; Ruth G. Strickland, "The Language of Elementary School Children," *Bulletin of the School of Education* No. 38 (Bloomington: Indiana University Press, 1960), p. 4.

9. Eunice S. Newton, "The Culturally Deprived Child in Our Verbal Schools," *Journal of Negro Education* 31 (Spring 1962): 185.

language ability because he does not have a fund of conceptualized experiences with which he can verbalize certain meanings valued by schools. He usually expresses himself well in unstructured, spontaneous situations and verbalizes freely around actions and things he can taste, touch, smell, manipulate, see, and feel. (This is the way all children learn—by active encounter with things that make a difference to them.)

Some effort should be made to detect the exact nature of the language of the child so that instruction can be tailor-made to his needs. Just how does language acquisition of the socially disadvantaged child deviate from that of the middle-class child and how do language and speech characteristics vary according to social class? Irwin found that in homes of lower occupational status, the basic phoneme production and frequency of vocalization of infants between thirteen and thirty months were inferior to children from the upper socioeconomic levels.[10] Davis found that the percentage of children with good articulation was higher among upper occupational groups than among lower.[11] Templin demonstrated a significant difference, in favor of the upper group, between children of upper and lower socioeconomic groups on both screening and diagnostic tests of articulation.[12] She stated that according to her extensive data, children of the lower socioeconomic group take about a year longer than do those of the upper group to reach essentially mature articulation. Pavenstedt said that three- and four-year-old children from very low socioeconomic families form their words so poorly that it is almost impossible to understand them.[13]

Using a structured, oral interview, Thomas studied sentence development and vocabulary usage in the spoken language of white and black kindergarten children from low socioeconomic circumstances in a midwestern urban setting.[14] The traditional measures of length of verbal responses, complexity of sentence structure, proportion of parts of speech, and frequency of grammatical errors yielded a great number of comparisons. Notable among these was the finding that his subjects used significantly fewer words per remark than

10. Orvis C. Irwin, "Infant Speech: The Effect of Systematic Reading of Stories," *Journal of Speech and Hearing Research* 3 (June 1960): 187–190.

11. Davis, *The Development of Linguistic Skill.*

12. Templin, "Norms on Screening Test of Articulation for Ages Three Through Eight," *Journal of Speech and Hearing Disorders* 18 (December 1953): 323–331.

13. Eleanor Pavenstedt, "A Comparison of the Child-Rearing Environment of Upper, Lower and Very Low Lower Class Families," *American Journal of Orthopsychiatry* 35 (January 1965): 89–98.

14. Dominic Richard Thomas, "Oral Language, Sentence Structure and Vocabulary of Kindergarten Children Living in Low Socio-Economic Urban Areas" (Ph.D. diss., Wayne State University, Detroit Mich., 1962).

did Templin's subjects drawn from a middle-class socioeconomic group.[15]

Bernstein's research with British youth delineates middle- and lower-class language differences.[16] The speech patterns of the middle-class children were clearer because of use of greater variety of sentence patterns. This presents a marked contrast with the working-class children, who were found to have a comparatively rigid and limited use of the organizational possibilities of sentence construction. Loban has found that southern black children have about twelve times as much trouble with the form of the verb *to be* as do northern white subjects.[17] Other difficulties found by Loban include confusion of present with past tense, lack of agreement between subject and predicate, and use of sentence fragments.

The non-native speaker of English

In the United States, bilingualism is prevalent in the large metropolitan areas, in the rural areas of the Middle West, in the five southwestern states, and in Hawaii. It has been estimated that about one-fourth of the school population in the United States is bilingual. The five southwestern states of Texas, New Mexico, Arizona, Colorado, and California are reported to have about three million Spanish-speaking people. Large numbers of Spanish-speaking children in these five states enter school with little or no knowledge of English.

Is this need for learning English as a second language a curse or a blessing? Often a child who is not a native speaker of English has some special problems. For example, a Spanish-speaking youngster may add a vowel before some initial consonant blends and may omit final consonants in English, for many of his Spanish words end in vowels. The fact that the Spanish-speaking child pronounces every vowel in his native language makes it difficult for him to pronounce English words containing "silent" vowels. American Indian children are also handicapped when the language spoken at home is not English. Moreover, the accent or stress on syllables and words varies from one language to another, as do rhythm and intonation patterns.

Generalizing about bilingualism from research findings is difficult because of several factors: varying definitions of bilingualism,

---

15. Templin, *Certain Language Skills in Children.*

16. Basil Bernstein, "Language and Social Class," *British Journal of Sociology* 11 (1960): 271–276.

17. Loban, "Language Ability in the Elementary School," *Improving English Skills of Culturally Different Youth,* ed. by Arno Jewett et al. (Washington, D.C.: United States Government Printing Office, 1964), p. 62.

The effectiveness of a language arts program for the non-native speaker of English depends greatly upon how he perceives himself in relation to the school, the teacher, and others.

studies that are too limited and not necessarily representative, and diverse procedures employed in the studies. Many of the older studies concluded that bilinguals were handicapped in speech development (faulty articulation and inappropriate pronunciation), disadvantaged in language development (since some interference is bound to occur in learning two or more languages), slowed down in intellectual and educational progress, and emotionally unstable. More recent studies, however, have generally arrived at more positive features of bilingualism. These studies have emphasized that desirable attitudes and procedures for the bilingual child include: a healthy home for language learning, good speech models at home and at school, and, most importantly, increased teacher knowledge about the bilingual child with resultant increased understanding of his needs.

In the primary years, English as a second language should be taught orally, informally, and in an atmosphere of "play." The child should learn the language through specific techniques like telling stories; playing games; using picture books, puppets, and toys; singing songs and rhymes; and conversing about classroom activities, news of the day, personal experiences, and plans. In brief, procedures for presenting language to the child should be through situations that approximate life experiences.

Some authorities believe that the school child learning English for the first time should be in the "exceptional child" category and thus receive special attention. They suggest that special classes in the study of English be provided and that these classes stress phonetics and phonemics, English structure, ear training, articulation, vocabulary enlargement, and many other aural-oral experiences. All of these should be introduced prior to the child's reading and writing of English.

Other educators concerned with childhood bilingualism stress that the greatest need is for better qualified teachers. Not enough teachers have the linguistic training required to teach English as a second language. They feel there is a need for teacher-preparation institutions to establish special courses in methods of teaching English as a second language. All teachers, even without specialized training, ought to exhibit a good model in their own speech, encourage free expression, and demonstrate a positive appreciation of good results. They must also develop an appreciation of diverse cultural backgrounds and should patiently endeavor to understand and reduce the child's difficulties.

Ideally, the teacher should know the native language of the children of the class so that he can recognize possible trouble spots, or at least be familiar with the structural and pronunciation patterns of the foreign language. Finally, he must remember that his purpose is to introduce the child to a new language and culture, not to erase the old.

Some methodology and primary-school-level materials are suggested below.

Allen, Harold B. *Teaching English as a Second Language: A Book of Readings.* New York: McGraw-Hill, 1965.

Bumpass, Faye L. *Teaching Young Students English as a Foreign Language*. New York: American Book, 1963. (Pupil materials by Bumpass include: *Let's Read Stories*, 5 vols.; *We Learn English*, 6 vols.; and *We Speak English*, 2 vols.)

Finocchiaro, Mary. *English as a Second Language: From Theory to Practice*. New York: Regents Publishing, 1964. (Pupil materials by Finocchiaro include: *Learning to Use English*, 2 vols.)

Lancaster, Louise. *Introducing English*. Boston: Houghton Mifflin, 1966.

Puerto Rico, Department of Education. *American English Series*, 4 vols. Boston: D. C. Heath, 1965–67.

Wheeler, D. G. *Let's Speak English*, 6 vols. New York: McGraw-Hill, 1967.

THE NATURE OF LANGUAGE

The subject matter taught by language arts teachers is such an integral part of everyday life that it is easy to take it for granted, failing to recognize language as the miracle it really is. For teachers to be unmindful of its infinite potentialities is dangerous indeed; as great an understanding of this field as can possibly be acquired is needed.

Several theories about the origin of formal language are listed on the next page.

Imaginative teachers can devise learning activities that give children an opportunity to examine and become interested in the heritage of their language.

1. The "ding-dong" theory suggests that characteristic sounds evoked from man came to be associated with the particular object that elicited them.
2. The "bow-wow" theory assumes that primitive man learned to use the sounds made by certain animals; this mimicry of animals was generalized to other objects and events, such as the "rumbling" of thunder or the "gurgling" of water.
3. The "pooh-pooh" theory holds that man's interjections in times of pain, surprise, or anger formed the basis for primitive man's earliest means of oral expression.
4. The "yum-yum" or "tongue-tied" theory assumes that the tongue is coordinated with the body and that gestures of the hands, arms, and legs are synchronized with the organs of speech.
5. The "babble-luck" theory assumes that primitive man likely prattled while he worked, much as a child of one or two years of age prattles as he plays. Through chance, a particular babble came to be associated with a particular object, event, or activity. This association was perpetuated by habit and a private language was born. Through joint endeavor with associates, some of these private words were adopted by others, and a social language was born.

All of these theories are highly speculative and none seem very satisfactory. Nor do we know exactly when language began, although writing has been a part of human culture for about 5,000 years.

However primitive man received or developed a language, from this uncertain beginning there have developed some 5,000 different languages or 200 language families, not including the various dialects. The major families are shown in figure 2.1.

Indo-European is the most important language family to us and is spoken by people living in the area from northern India across the continent of Europe and in parts of Asia. There are many branches of this family. English belongs to the Germanic branch, as shown in figure 2.2.

Language characteristics

• *Relatedness*   A linguistic point of view emphasizes the primacy of speech over writing —and for some obviously valid reasons. First, from a historical point of view, speaking preceded writing by

FIGURE 2.1: Chief Language Families

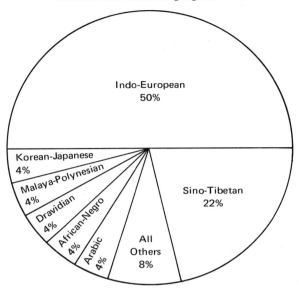

SOURCE: Paul Hanna et al., *Spelling: Structure and Strategies* (Boston: Houghton Mifflin, 1971), p. 32. Reprinted by permission of Houghton Mifflin Company.

FIGURE 2.2: Major Branches of the Indo-European Family

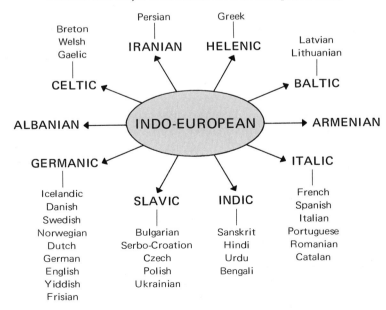

hundreds of thousands of years. Spoken language is considered by linguists to be the "real" language and reading and writing to be but pale imitations. Second, an individual speaks far more than he writes. Third, speaking precedes writing in an individual's development of language: that is, he is able to speak four or five years before he is able to read and write. Finally, oral language development is the basis for achievement in other areas of learning, such as listening, reading, and writing.[18] There are many differences and similarities between oral and written expression. For example, pitch, stress, and juncture in oral expression are roughly equivalent to punctuation in written expression.

• *Arbitrariness*   The elementary school child needs to understand that language is a system of sounds, and the connection between the sounds and the objects and ideas they represent is purely arbitrary. Counting to ten in more than one language could be put to use at this point, calling attention to the fact that a sound occurring in a foreign language may not exist in English, as is true of the sound of the German letter ü. In elementary schools offering a foreign language, understanding of the idea that the patterns of sounds convey a meaning only to those who know the language should be clarified. Where a foreign language is not offered, children can build a glossary of words as they study the various countries in their social studies course or perhaps learn some of the songs of different countries.

• *System*   Children also need to learn that language is systematic: that is, sounds are put together in recurrent designs. The child learning to speak and to be understood has had to detect and use some of the structures of language. He has recognized that sounds convey meaning only when put together in patterns of words and sentences. The studies of Loban, Noell, Strickland, and others confirm the fact that children's language patterns are largely set by the time they reach school age and that they have already learned to use whatever sound system, grammar, and vocabulary are characteristic of their home and neighborhood.[19] These reports indicate that

18.   Helen K. Mackintosh, ed., *Children and Oral Language* (Urbana, Ill.: National Council of Teachers of English, 1964), pp. 15–17.

19.   Loban, *Language of Elementary School Children*; Doris L. Noell, "A Comparative Study of the Relationship Between the Quality of the Child's Language Usage and the Quality and Types of Language Used in the Home," *Journal of Educational Research* 47 (November 1953); 161–167; Strickland, *Language of Elementary School Children*.

children employ all the common sentence patterns identified as basic to the English language. While Loban's study showed that elementary school boys of low, socioeconomic status are typically less proficient in oral language than girls of the same group, the implication of his study is that most preschool children are linguistically sophisticated.[20] Furthermore, this same research indicates that those children with the greatest proficiency use the same basic sentence patterns as those who lack proficiency. The difference lies more in the preciseness and complexity of thinking.

• *Change*   The English of today is not the same as the English language at its origin. Language is constantly changing. The Bible offers a wealth of parallels to illustrate language change. See one such illustration below—Matthew 8:27—translated at various times into the English language.

1. Before the year 1000 (Old English):

    Gewisslíce ðā men wundroden, and ðus cwǣdon, Hwæt is ðēs, ðæt windas and sǣ him hyrsumiap?

2. About 1385 (Middle English):

    Forsothe the men wondreden, sayinge, What manere man is he, for the wydis and the see obeishen to hym?

3. About 1525 (Modern English):

    And men amarveyled, and said, What man is this, that bothe wydes and see obey him?

4. In 1611 (The King James Version):

    But the men marveiled, saying, What manner of man is this, that even the winds and sea obey him?

5. In 1946 (The Revised Standard Version):

    And the men marvelled, saying, What sort of man is this, that even winds and sea obey him?

Children need to see that language changes—old words may be given new meanings or new uses and new words may be coined

---

20. Loban, *Language of Elementary School Children*, pp. 84, 86.

from parts of old words to represent new meanings or modifications of old ones. Even in the beginning language arts program, pupils will encounter words in the Mother Goose rhymes that are old words, rarely if ever used by most people today, such as *fetch* or *tuffet*. Folk stories also exhibit old words that are no longer commonly used. Most words added to the language to meet new needs are made from parts of old words. The words *television* and *supersonic* are clearly in that category.

As has been said, "Change is an aspect of human language as regular and relentless as the birth and death of man. It asks no man's permission and waits on no man's approval."[21] Change occurs in various ways.

1. Our language contains many words that have several different meanings. Some examples are *run*, *box*, and *ring*.

2. The meanings of words sometimes change. For example, *nice* comes from a Latin-French word meaning "foolish." When medieval philosophers wrangled, they often made nice—hairsplitting or foolish—distinctions. These "nice" distinctions came to be admired for their subtlety, so *nice* came to mean "pleasing." Thus we can say that the meaning of *nice* has been elevated. What it meant earlier is no guide to what it should mean now. The only guide to what a word should mean is what it actually does mean in the mouths of the people who use it. Some words have been degraded. For example, *villain* was originally a farm laborer, but today is a scheming evildoer.

3. Usage has narrowed the meaning of some words. For example, *garage*, which earlier meant "to make safe or secure," is now restricted to mean "a building for housing automotive vehicles or a repair shop for such vehicles." The meaning of other words has expanded. *Barn*, originally restricted to mean "a place for storing barley," now refers to a covered building for keeping livestock or storing grain and hay.

4. Changes often occur in the makeup of words. Sometimes words are made into compounds *(beforehand)*; neologisms develop *(edit* from *editor)*; portmanteau words are devised

---

21. Donald Lloyd and Henry Warfel, *American English in Its Cultural Setting* (New York: Knopf, 1956), p. 7.

(*smog* is made out of *smoke* and *fog*); derivatives are formed (*deplane, eightish*); acronyms are made (*LP* for *long playing*); parts of speech shift (*premiere – premiered*); coinages (*kodak, dacron*) and shortenings occur (*phone, bus, copter, props, pub, flu*); reduplication (*hush-hush, shilly-shally, roly-poly*); echoisms (*ack-ack, bebop*); and back formations (*babysit, fact-find*) occur.

• *Variety*   The term most often applied to linguistic variations is *dialect*. Dialect may be defined as a variation of a language sufficiently different to be considered a separate entity, but not different enough to be classed as a separate language. (In truth, we all speak a regional dialect of some sort and differences exist socially within the regional pattern. *Idiolect* is the term so applied to the individual, unique style.) These differences occur in pronunciation, vocabulary, and, to a limited extent, in grammatical construction (syntax). However, there is no pejorative meaning to the term *dialect*. Since we do not have a "standard dialect," there is no such thing as a "substandard dialect." There are, of course, dialect differences; but differences and deficiencies are not the same thing. In terms of the teacher, the major responsibility is for adjustment to the humanitarian requirement of respect for idiolects and dialects as well as to the linguistic facts of life. And this responsibility is the teacher's, not the child's.

Some examples of variations in pronunciation may be helpful at this point. On all social levels in most of the South, the diphthongal vowel in *down, cow,* and *crowd* begins like the vowel sound of *man*; whereas in New England and elsewhere, this pronunciation is confined to folk speech. Eastern New England and western Pennsylvania have the same vowel sound in *law, caught,* and *salt* as in *lot, cot,* and *rod*; all other sections of the eastern states have contrasting vowels in these two sets. In eastern New England, the /r/ in *park* or *father* is lost, and the linking or intrusive /r/ is common, as in *idea(r)*. In the midland, /r/ frequently intrudes, as in *wa(r)sh*. On the Atlantic seaboard, there are no social implications in the fact that the vowel sound in *care, chair,* and *stairs* ranges regionally all the way from the /æ/ of *cat* to the /ɛ/ of *get* and the /e/ of *gate*. *Hoarse* and *horse, mourning* and *morning* are homophonous in some, but not all, parts of the eastern states. In eastern New England, middle New York, Virginia, and South Carolina, the postvocalic /r/ as in *ear, care, four,* and *poor* is not pronounced as such by a considerable majority; this /r/ is kept by midland speakers, however. In eastern Virginia, South Carolina, and the Georgia low country, the words *log*, *hog*, *frog*, and *fog* rhyme, but not *dog*. Many southerners do not distinguish /I/ and /ɛ/ before nasals, so that *pin* and *pen* are pronounced alike.

Some examples of variations in vocabulary may also be helpful. In the North (eastern New England, Inland Northern, and New York City) the *earthworm* is known as an *angleworm*. Speakers in other areas refer to the same object as *fishworm* or *mudworm*. *Cottage cheese* is *dutch cheese* in the Inland North, *pot cheese* in the Hudson Valley, *smearcase* in Pennsylvania, and *clabber cheese* in the South. Other terms that have regional associations include *bucket*, *pail*, *clapboards*, *cherry pit*, *blinds*, *window shades*, *pavement*, *skillet*, *frying pan*, *clabber milk*, *snap beans*, *string beans*, *mouthharp*, *fritters*, *batter bread*, *light bread*, and *pully bone*.

With regard to grammar variations, when a pupil says, "He dove in," "quarter till eleven," "hadn't ought," or "I might could," should the teacher correct him or merely point out that others say, "dived in," "quarter to eleven," "oughtn't," "I could," or "I might"?[22]

Additional dialect information can be obtained from sources given in the footnote.[23] Further information may be gathered from the American Dialect Society and the Center for Applied Linguistics.[24] Dialect is a frequent topic in professional journals.[25] And one potential source of information (now in progress) is *Dictionary of American Regional English* or *DARE*, which hopefully will be ready for publication around 1978.

Information gleaned from such sources should prove beneficial to classroom teachers in forming desirable attitudes toward language. By knowing the marvelous diversity of current American English, teachers can observe and discuss language behavior in an objective manner. The concept of individual differences will be easier to accept if teachers will expect individual differences in language, and will realize that their function is not to tell the child his idiolect is wrong but to add to it in order to increase his social and intellectual mobility. (See chapter 5, pages 169–177, for an instructional program on dialect differences.)

---

22. Examples drawn in large part from: Hans Kurath, "Area Linguistics and the Teacher of English," *Language Learning* 2 (March 1961): 9–14.

23. Hans Kurath et al., eds., *Linguistic Atlas of New England*, reprint of 1939 edition (New York: AMS Press); Harold B. Allen, *Linguistic Atlas of the Upper Middle West*, vol. 1 (Minneapolis: University of Minnesota Press, 1973).

24. American Dialect Society, Box 1494, Tuscaloosa, University of Alabama; Center for Applied Linguistics, 1755 Massachusetts Ave., N.W., Washington, D.C. 20036.

25. For example, *Elementary English* 45 (May 1968): 558–599, 608.

CHILDREN'S STUDY OF LANGUAGE

Of what use is the preceding information to the prospective or practicing teacher? Consistent with earlier comments, the authors of this book believe that formal study of language is more of a "discipline" for adults than for children. Nonetheless, certain aspects of language can legitimately be isolated for attention as children mature and become interested. At appropriate times, teachers can and should provide accurate information about language so that children will see that there is interesting and pertinent content in English and that it is worthy of study. In this way, they will come to a conscious understanding of its system and the way it operates.

The following list of topics might be included in children's study of language at the primary level.

language as symbols
word order in sentences and questions
pitch, stress, and juncture in speech
word changes in meaning and spelling
development of the alphabet
origins of words

Topics appropriate for the intermediate years:

Celtic, Latin, and Anglo-Saxon words in English
the dictionary as a source of language history
euphemisms
comparison of British and American English
English loanwords
development of a written language
changes in language
language usage
idioms
dialect differences
the development of American dictionaries

More specific examples and illustrations for various language concepts have been assigned categories and are presented below.

1. Nonverbal language: Pictures and photographs can be examined for facial (nonverbal) expressions of emotion; anger, grief, delight, etc. Signs can be interpreted: for example, a fence with barbed wire (stay out) or a rural mailbox with the flag up (collect

mail). Pantomiming a situation can be done to show that a message can be sent without language. For example, an individual or small group could mime the following incident:

Mime Task Card

Our scout cabin is on fire. It started in the kitchen. Some people may be trapped in the flames and cannot escape. There is no water nearby to put out the fire. The cabin is located just a short distance from here. We must hurry. Gather together and let us go at once.

Such activities can be effective in pointing out various ways of communicating and the role of language as an effective means of communication.

2. Language characteristics: A bulletin board (with the title, "What Are the Names of These Objects?") can highlight the idea of the arbitrary nature of sounds and objects. That is, an object is usually named by a different pattern of sounds (word) in different parts of the world as suggested below.

truck ⟶ *camion* (French) ⟶ *Lastwagen* (German)
cat ⟶ *chat* (French) ⟶ *Katze* (German)

To sense the system of language, the following words could be placed on individual cards and distributed to seven members of the class.

his   he   a   yesterday   bought   tie   father

The pupils would be instructed to make a sentence out of the words by standing in position. The sentence could read, "He bought his father a tie yesterday," or "Yesterday he bought his father a tie." If the sequence were "His father yesterday he a tie bought," pupils would instantly recognize it as an atypical sentence pattern. "Movables" such as *yesterday* would be recognized.

Change in language can often be detected in reading rhymes or stories that tell of older days. For example, the knight's question, "Prithee, sir, whither goest thou?" can be compared with today's, "Hey, you, where're you going?"

Often an activity card or bulletin board display can be used to present an idea.

Question of the Day

These words and definitions appeared in Samuel Johnson's *Dictionary of the English Language*, 1755. Can you write pairs of sentences using each word to show its meaning over 200 years ago and its meaning today?

Whitewash—A wash to make the skin seem fair.
Tremendous—Dreadful; horrible.
Toot—To pry; to peep.
Overnight—Night before bedtime.
Catsup—A kind of pickle, made from mushrooms.
Penthouse—A shed hanging out aslope from the main wall.
Sherbet—The juice of a lemon or orange mixed with water and sugar.
Uncouth—Odd; strange; unusual.

Distinctions between "American English" and "English English" can be used effectively: *petrol – gasoline; bonnet – hood; roundabout – traffic circle; biscuits – cookies; porridge – oatmeal; sweets – candy; mackintosh – raincoat; flat – apartment; lift – elevator; wireless – radio; chemist's shop – drugstore.*

Variety in pronunciation can be highlighted through listening to a recording of voices representing various geographic regions of the United States.[26] Vocabulary differences can be noted on a worksheet exercise.

Worksheet: Vocabulary Differences

1. In what way are all the answers alike?
2. Do you know another way to state the same time?
3. Which of these terms do you use? Circle them.
    hot cakes   flapjacks   pancakes   griddlecakes
4. What terms have you heard or read to refer to a device over a sink for drawing water? (Example: *spigot*)
5. Here are some other terms. Circle any used in your area. Add other terms you have heard or read for the same thing.

bedspread	couch	brook
coverlet	davenport	bayou
roasting ears	earthworm	doughnuts
table corn	angleworm	sinkers

6. What other words do you know for *bag, pail, salt pork, snap beans, peanut?*

---

26. One such record is *Americans Speaking* prepared by Raven McDavid, Jr. et al. and available from the National Council of Teachers of English, 111 Kenyon Road, Urbana, Ill. 61801.

3. Language structure: The idea of symbols representing different sounds in other languages can be detected through such Spanish words as *tortilla* or *mesa*. Forms of words can be analyzed through their roots, such as *port: porter, import, export, deport, report, transport, portable.* Systematic instruction on related words might follow this format:

LESSON PLAN: Related Words
_____

Performance Objective:
Given a base for a "word family," the learner writes other related words.

Pretest:
Write the word *head* on the chalkboard. Then ask, "What six words do you know that are related to this one?" An example is *headache.* (Six is an arbitrary number to emphasize the concept that words exist in families, as the child does.)

Teaching Suggestion:
Write another word on the chalkboard, such as *heart.* Develop with the learner a list of related words. (Related words are *heartless, heartful, heartstring, heartland, heartily, heartrending, heartsick, hearty.*)

Mastery or Posttest Suggestions:
1. Ask the learner to select a word and write six related words.
2. The suggestions provided for the pretest may be adapted (using a different base word) to the posttest.

Reteaching Suggestions:
1. Write other words on the chalkboard, such as *light* or *love.* Ask, "What are some other related words?" Prepare an appropriate list for each word.
2. Prepare a paragraph that contains a number of related words. The learner is to find the related words.
3. Ask the learner to find related words in a reading selection.

_____

Likewise, the study of synonyms (*remove – erase, proud – vain, cheap – economical, dominate – lead, bias – conviction*) helps children to see the necessity for using the exact word; and they find the study of "new words" suggests the process of word building.

Aspects of intonation become more obvious as differing stresses are given to this question:

Where is he going? (casual)
Where is he going?

Where *is* he going?
Where is *he* going?
Where is he *going*?

The difference between the denotative meaning of a word (for example, *rat* meaning a "rodent") and its connotative meaning can be found in such a sentence as, "The dirty rat squealed on me."

Slang and euphemisms are also interesting aspects of semantics that appeal to children.

4. Language history: Children can write a rebus story, relating the concept of hieroglyphics to the alphabet. They may search for stories to tell about place names and other word origins, such as the Dewey Decimal System.[27] Another example (activity card) for a word history is presented in chapter 12, page 441.

LANGUAGE BOOKS FOR THE LIBRARY

There are a number of trade or library books that fit into the category of "books to read to learn more about language." Such books may be used by individuals or by an entire class for a free-reading experience. Several listings of such books are available.[28] Following is a sample list.

History of the English language: Ernst, Margaret. *Words: English Roots and How They Grow*. New York: Knopf, 1959.
Printing: Epstein, Sam, and Epstein, Beryl. *The First Book of Printing*. New York: Watts, 1973.
Early developments of writing: Irwin, Keith G. *The Romance of Writing*. New York: Viking Press, 1957.
Alphabet: Russell, Solveig P. *A is for Apple and Why: The Story of Our Alphabet*. Nashville, Tenn.: Abingdon, 1959.
History of books: Bartlett, Susan. *Libraries: A Book to Begin On*. New York: Holt, Rinehart and Winston, 1964.
Word origins: Ernst, Margaret. *Words: English Roots and How They Grow*. New York: Knopf, 1959.

27. For other ideas, see Bonnidell Clouse, "Help Children Appreciate Their Language," *The Instructor* 81 (December 1971): 38–39; Joan Stipetic, "Teaching Communicating as a Part of the Intermediate Grade Curriculum," *Elementary English* 49 (March 1972): 457–459.

28. Paul C. Burns, "Elementary School Language Arts Library—A Selected Bibliography," *Elementary English* 41 (December 1964): 879–884; Maxine Delmare, "Language Books for the Library," *Elementary English* 45 (January 1968): 55–66; Iris M. and Sidney W. Tiedt, "A Linguistic Library for Students," *Contemporary English in the Elementary School* (Englewood Cliffs, N.J.: Prentice-Hall, 1967), pp. 38–40.

Dictionary: Fadiman, Clifton. *Wally the Wordworm*. New York: Mac-Millan, 1964.

Letter writing: Joslin, Sesyle, and Haas, Irene. *Dear Dragon: And Other Useful Letter Forms for Young Ladies and Gentlemen Engaged in Everyday Correspondence*. New York: Harcourt, Brace and World, 1962.

Handwriting: McCain, Murray. *Writing*. New York: Farrar, Straus, & Giroux, 1964.

Clichés and idioms: Funk, Charles E. *Thereby Hangs a Tale: Stories of Curious Word Origins*. New York: Harper & Row, 1950.

Homophones: Van Gelder, Rosalind. *Monkeys Have Tails*. New York: McKay, 1966.

Homonyms: White, Mary S. *Word Twins*. Nashville, Tenn.: Abingdon, 1961.

Word play: Hymes, James L., and Hymes, Lucia. *Oodles of Noodles*. Reading, Mass.: Addison-Wesley, 1964.

SELECTED REFERENCES

General Professional

Corcoran, Gertrude B. *Language Arts in Elementary School: A Modern Linguistic Approach*. New York: Ronald, 1970, chapters 1, 2.

Dallmann, Martha. *Teaching the Language Arts in the Elementary School*. 2d ed. Dubuque, Iowa: William C. Brown, 1971, chapters 1, 2.

Greene, Harry A., and Petty, Walter T. *Developing Language Skills in the Elementary Schools*. 4th ed. Boston: Allyn and Bacon, 1971, chapter 3.

Lamb, Pose, ed. *Guiding Children's Language Learning*. 2d ed. Dubuque, Iowa: William C. Brown, 1971, chapter 1.

Smith, James A. *Adventures in Communication: Language Arts Methods*. Boston: Allyn and Bacon, 1972, chapter 2.

Strickland, Ruth G. *Language Arts in Elementary School*. 3rd ed. Lexington, Mass.: D. C. Heath, 1969, chapter 1.

Specialized

Allen, Harold B., and Underwood, Gary N. *Readings in American Dialectology*. 2d ed. New York: Appleton-Century-Crofts, 1969.

——. *Readings in Applied English Linguistics*. New York: Appleton-Century-Crofts, 1964.

Anderson, Wallace L., and Stageberg, Norman, eds. *Introductory Readings on Language*. 3rd ed. New York: Holt, Rinehart and Winston, 1970.

Baugh, Albert C. *History of the English Language*. 2d ed. New York: Appleton-Century-Crofts, 1957.

Bloomfield, Morton W., and Newmark, Leonard D. *A Linguistic Introduction to the History of English*. New York: Knopf, 1963.

Bolinger, Dwight L. *Aspects of Language*. New York: Harcourt, Brace and World, 1968.

Boyd, Gertrude. *Linguistics: Grammar, Usage, and Semantics*. Itasca, Ill.: Peacock Publishers, 1975.

Brengelman, Frederick H. *The English Language: An Introduction for Teachers*. Englewood Cliffs, N.J.: Prentice-Hall, 1970.

Brown, Roger. *Words and Things*. Glencoe, Ill.: The Free Press, 1958.

Carroll, John B. *Study of Language: A Survey of Linguistics and Related Disciplines in America*. Cambridge, Mass.: Harvard University Press, 1955.

Curriculum for English. *Language Explorations for the Elementary Grades*. Lincoln: University of Nebtaska Press, 1966.

DeStefano, Johanna S., and Fox, Sharon. *Language and the Language Arts*. Boston: Little, 1974.

Evertts, Eldonna L., ed. *Dimensions of Dialect*. Urbana, Ill.: National Council of Teachers of English, 1967.

Francis, W. Nelson. *Structure of American English*. New York: Ronald, 1958.

Gleason, H. A., Jr. *An Introduction to Descriptive Linguistics*. New York: Holt, Rinehart and Winston, 1961.

Hall, Robert A. *Introductory Linguistics*. Philadelphia: Chilton, 1965.

Hall, Robert A., Jr. *Linguistics and Your Language*. New York: Doubleday, 1960.

Hockett, Charles F. *Course in Modern Linguistics*. New York: Macmillan, 1958.

Jesperson, Otto. *Growth and Structure of the English Language*. 9th ed. New York: Free Press, 1968.

Kerr, Elizabeth M., and Alderman, Ralph M. *Aspects of American English*. 2d ed. New York: Harcourt Brace Jovanovich, 1971.

Laird, Charlton. *Miracle of Language*. New York: Fawcett, 1972.

Lamb, Pose. *Linguistics in Proper Perspective*. Columbus, Ohio: Merrill, 1967.

Langacker, Ronald W. *Language and Its Structure: Some Fundamental Linguistic Concepts*. 2d ed. New York: Harcourt Brace Jovanovich, 1973.

Lee, Donald W. *English Language Reader: Introductory Essays and Exercises*. New York: Dodd, 1963.

Lefevre, Carl A. *Linguistics, English, and Language Arts*. Boston: Allyn and Bacon, 1969.

Lenneberg, Eric H., ed. *New Directions in the Study of Language*. Cambridge: Massachusetts Institute of Technology Press, 1964.

Lloyd, Donald J., and Warfel, Henry R. *American English in its Cultural Setting*. New York: Knopf, 1956.

Lyons, John. *Introduction to Theoretical Linguistics*. New York: Cambridge University Press, 1968.

Malmstrom, Jean. *Language in Society*. New York: Hayden, 1965.

———, and Ashley, Annabell. *Dialects U.S.A.* Urbana, Ill.: National Council of Teachers of English, 1963.

Marckwardt, Albert H. *Linguistics and the Teaching of English*. Bloomington: Indiana University Press, 1966.

————, ed. *Linguistics in School Programs*. National Society for the Study of Education, 69th Yearbook, pt. 2. Chicago: University of Chicago Press, 1970.

Mencken, H. L. *American Language*. 4th ed. New York: Knopf, 1955.

Ornstein, Jacob, and Gage, William A. *The ABC's of Languages and Linguistics*. Philadelphia: Chilton, 1965.

Pei, Mario. *Language for Everybody*. New York: Pocket Books, 1959.

Piaget, Jean. *Language and Thought of the Child*. 3rd ed. New York: Humanities, 1962.

Pyles, Thomas. *Origins and Development of the English Language*. 2d ed. New York: Harcourt Brace Jovanovich, 1971.

Reed, Carrol E. *Dialects of American English*. Amherst: University of Massachusetts Press, 1973.

Robertson, Stuart, and Cassidy, F. G. *Development of Modern English*. 2d ed. New York: Prentice-Hall, 1953.

Robins, Robert H., ed. *General Linguistics: An Introductory Survey*. Bloomington: Indiana University Press, 1965.

Savage, John F., ed. *Linguistics for Teachers: Selected Readings*. Chicago: Science Research Associates, 1973.

Schlauch, Margaret. *Gift of Language*. New York: Dover, 1955.

Shane, Harold G. *Linguistics and the Classroom Teacher: Some Implications for Instruction in the Mother Tongue*. Washington, D.C.: Association for Supervision and Curriculum Development, 1967.

Shores, David L., ed. *Contemporary English: Change and Variation*. Philadelphia: Lippincott, 1972.

Shuy, Roger, ed. *Social Dialects and Language Learning*. Urbana, Ill.: National Council of Teachers of English, 1965.

Smith, Frank, and Miller, George, eds. *Genesis of Language: A Psycholinguistic Approach*. Cambridge: Massachusetts Institute of Technology Press, 1968.

Vygotsky, Lev S. *Thought and Language*. Translated by Eugenia Hanfmann and Gertrude Vakar. Cambridge: Massachusetts Institute of Technology Press, 1962.

**LANGUAGE ARTS EXPERIENCES
FOR CHILDREN FIVE AND UNDER**

OBJECTIVES	PERFORMANCE RESPONSES
1. **To identify basic approaches for teaching the language arts to young children**	1. Prepare a list of activities for one of the three basic approaches for teaching the language arts.
2. **To examine the objectives and purposes of teaching the language arts to young children**	2. Discuss the objectives and purposes and write three paragraphs describing them for a prospective teacher to consider.
3. **To identify activities that heighten sensory perceptions**	3. Sketch a bulletin board display designed to motivate interest in the five senses.
4. **To explain items to consider in reading and telling stories to young children**	4. Evaluate a story on the basis of the eight criteria on page 73.
5. **To select opportunities for oral expression and listening for the young child**	5. List five language activities that would occur every week in a program for three-, four-, or five-year-olds.
6. **To identify activities and materials for learning centers**	6. Set up one type of center and teach an introductory skill to three children.
7. **To describe the role of the teacher in planning and analyzing the language arts for the early years**	7. Observe a classroom of three-, four-, or five-year-old children. Write a report, using the ones on pages 85–87 as a guide.

How can we know if a child is well taught?

We may know a child is well taught when he is taking delight in learning new things.

A child is well taught when his curiosity about the world is steadily increasing because curiosity is the basis of all science and social studies learnings so important in his complex world.

A child is well taught if every day sees him broadening his knowledge of the stories, the poems, the songs, the music, the pictures that are a part of his cultural heritage.

A child is well taught if he is growing in ability to control his body and to take joy in a growing strength, rhythm, and grace.

A child is well taught when he is responding to opportunities to express himself through every objective means at hand—construction, painting, modeling, rhythmical activities, dramatic play—because these are the ways by which he achieves his uniqueness as a person.

A child is well taught if he comes willingly to school in the certain knowledge that he can cope with all the learning problems with which a sympathetic, understanding teacher challenges him in an environment planned to meet his developmental needs.[1]

After several years of extreme diversity in the use of methods and materials with children ages three, four, and five, programs for the very young have now become more stable and are generally based on research results, basic learning principles, and materials that have proven to be helpful in teaching children appropriate skills and content for their chronological age and innate mental ability.

Head Start; the renewed interest in Montessori methods and materials; the Bereiter and Becker intensive drill program for the disadvantaged child; the Gray-Klaus M and M reward and delayed gratification research; the culture and second language studies; the abundance of materials, equipment, aides, and consultants; and the availability of university training for teachers of the very young have all been dominant factors in determining present early childhood programs.

---

1. Helen Heffernan, speech presented at Ridgecrest, N.C., October 10, 1969, pp. 13–14.

**Curiosity and delight
are important factors in
the learning process.**

CURRENT TRENDS

Currently, there are three basic approaches to teaching the language arts to the child under six. The *developmental approach*, described below by James L. Hymes, is a program of enrichment in music, art, free and directed play, talking, listening, and the acting out of many experiences.

> They are ready for experiences in more independence. They are eager for companionship, for seeing and talking with and working side-by-side with their own age. They are pop-

ping to use their bodies, to test their strength, to climb new heights, to achieve a tingly fitness. They are thirsty for new ideas, and for new words and new sights, for new skills and accomplishments and achievements. And they are full of ideas of their own. Ideas to say, if someone will listen. Ideas to paint out and act out. Ideas to build with, if they have the tools, materials, time and space.[2]

The second approach, *compensatory education*, concerned with the economically disadvantaged or the non-native speaker of English, is designed to provide experiences that most English-speaking, middle-class children receive from their total environment. Programs of compensation duplicate and implement activities, instruction, and enrichment that middle-class children usually absorb from out-of-school experiences.

The *structure approach*, in contrast to the previous two, emphasizes a more conscious effort on the teacher's part to plan each and every activity in a sequential order of events. It is based on Piaget's research and stages of learning theory and on Skinner's manipulated environment theory to control behavior and thus control learning. The theories of the two men are presently used with slow learners, disadvantaged children, average middle-class children, and mentally superior or extremely gifted children.

The authors believe that the language arts program of the early years should be environment-oriented and developed according to each child's needs, ability, and the social setting in which he lives. This program would be based on research valuing the humanistic needs of individuals. Because the child under six is a curious and active individual, the program should provide abundant firsthand experiences.

LANGUAGE ARTS OBJECTIVES

Of necessity, any language arts program for young children must be almost totally oral, but the teacher should consciously include listening also. The limiting of the program mainly to oral language and

---

2. James L. Hymes, "The Importance of Pre-Primary Education," *Childhood Education* 39 (December 1962): 6. Reprinted by permission of James L. Hymes and the Association for Childhood Education International, 3615 Wisconsin Avenue, N.W., Washington, D.C. Copyright © 1962 by the Association.

listening does not suggest that the program be narrow in either purpose or activities. On the contrary, a well-planned and executed program can incorporate a much wider range of oral language activities and experiences than is open to a teacher at higher grade levels.

Because young children spend a large portion of their school day in speaking and listening, a teacher should not assume that the objectives of the language arts program will be automatically fulfilled. Unless the teacher organizes to gain unity and continuity, speaking and listening can become merely incidental events that happen spontaneously. Such incidental events will not provide a child with necessary understandings and learnings. For this reason, some ideas are needed for a structured program so that planned activities and opportunities will adequately incorporate the appropriate objectives.

Nature of objectives

What: The objectives of a program are the foundation on which the teacher plans activities, creates units of study, identifies the skills and content to be taught, analyzes materials and equipment to be purchased and used, and develops evaluative techniques to diagnose needs and assess growth.

Why: Program foundation objectives for three-, four-, and five-year-old children are necessary for sequential, spiral development of the skills and content in listening, speaking, literature, written expression, handwriting, and spelling.

When: Objectives are also necessary for a total integration of the other subject areas (social studies, mathematics, science, art, music, physical education, and health) with the specific skills and content of the language arts. Even though a teacher must plan and provide opportunities for direct instruction in the language arts, instruction must never be divorced from the normal and natural uses of language in the entire school program.

Where: Objectives are achieved through activities in centers or areas within a regular classroom for young children [art center, listening center, library center, family center, block and large truck center, drama or role-playing center, science center, math center, manipulative center, or a special center (see page 82)]. Some of these centers are set up for a day or two at a time, and all of them are natural situations for teaching the language arts. Some of the centers are for individual learning, some are for small group learning, and a few are for the class as a whole.

General objectives

Objectives of a typical early childhood language arts program are unique in many respects; but because the purpose of the beginning program is to be a foundation for further instruction, it has many elements in common with an overall elementary school language arts program. A representative set of objectives for the early years is stated by King and Kerber.

1. Speaking
    a. Help develop a good speaking voice that is easy to hear and understand.
    b. Encourage children to use simple and some complex sentences in talking with others and before groups.
    c. Introduce new words to help build a foundational vocabulary.
    d. Promote the relating of experiences in proper order.
2. Listening
    a. Increase attention span.
    b. Develop the ability to listen without interrupting.
    c. Encourage discrimination between sounds.
    d. Develop skill in following specific instructions.
    e. Promote the sharing, in a vicarious fashion, of the experiences of others.
3. Writing
    a. Encourage the desire to write.
    b. Provide activities to develop muscular coordination in preparation for writing.
    c. Introduce and encourage recognition of manuscript letters in each child's name.
    d. Help develop left-to-right direction for writing.[3]

CLASSROOM ACTIVITIES

Since young children are extremely active physically and because they are also very curious, teachers must plan, develop, and present activities that build on these natural and normal traits. Selecting activities that provide opportunities for individuals to perform at their own ability and experience levels must be the primary goal of the teacher.

Selecting activities that provide opportunities for young children to perform at their own ability and experience levels must be the primary goal of the teacher.

---

3. From *The Sociology of Early Childhood Education* by Edith W. King and August Kerber, pp. 91–92, copyright © 1968 by American Book Co., division of Litton Educational Publishing, Inc. Reprinted by permission of American Book Company.

Children increase verbal ability through first-hand experience, particularly those involving their senses, such as tasting.

Sensory experiences

The young child is eager to engage in activities designed to involve the five senses—sight, sound, touch, taste, and smell—as a means of perceiving his surroundings. In doing so, he enlarges his speaking and listening vocabulary, particularly when objects are classified.

Some suggested activities, along with books and poems, follow.

Seeing

1. Solve puzzles.
2. Match shapes, colors, sizes, etc.
3. Take "sight walks."
4. Finish a drawing by completing the missing parts.
5. Play games, such as "Eye Spy."
6. Describe a flower, a rock, etc.

The Color Kittens by Brown
Mirror on the Wall: How it Works by Carona
Did You Ever See? by Einsel
Inch by Inch by Lionni
Look at Your Eyes by Showers
And to Think That I Saw it on Mulberry Street by Seuss
"Horses" by Fisher
"The Magic Window" by Hammond

Hearing

1. Make "sound" mobiles (pieces of wood, bells, buttons, tin cans, aluminum foil, etc.).
2. Pass along a whispered message around a circle of five or six children.
3. Move to differing musical tempos (or a set of oral directions).
4. Record stories on tape and let children look at the book as they listen.
5. Prepare a bulletin board of things that make sounds (drum, spigot, airplane, etc.) and sound words that go with the object.
6. Classify sounds (animal, people, inside, outside, city, country, pleasant, unpleasant, etc.).

Where the Wild Things Are by Sendak
Listening Walk by Showers
"The Witch on a Windy Night" by Carlson
"Little Sounds" by De Regniers
"Our Washing Machine" by Hubbell
"Song of the Train" by McCord
"Sound of Water" by O'Neill

Feeling

1. Use a "feel box" or "feel bag" for guessing objects by touch.
2. Make a "touch" mobile and discuss how the objects feel.
3. Make mosaics of pebbles, seeds, buttons, etc.
4. Take "texture walks" in the school environment and talk about feel (furniture, play equipment, books, bricks, glass, wood, crayons, clothing, paper, grass, soil, bark, wire, etc.).

Inch by Inch by Lionni
The Mouse Book by Piers
Find Out by Touching by Showers
"Feet" by Aldis
"If I Were Wood" by Lee
"Furry Bear" by Milne

Tasting

1. Prepare fresh vegetable soup and serve it.
2. Hold a "tasting party" (salt, sugar, vinegar, etc.).
3. Sample "look alikes" that taste different (potato, coconut; radish, turnip; apple, pear; etc.).

Bread and Jam for Frances by Hoban
Lick a Pickle by Stratford
"About Candy" by Aldis
"Tastes I Like" by Allen
"Taste of Purple" by Jacobs

Smelling

1. Prepare "smell and match bottles."
2. Pantomime reactions to smells (smoke, perfume, peanut butter sandwich, peeling a banana, etc.).
3. Play a "smelling game"; identify aromatic objects tied in a small thin cloth bag, (piece of banana, fresh orange peel, onion, apple, etc.).

What is Your Favorite Smell, My Dear? by Gibson
Follow Your Nose by Showers
"Smells" by Morley
"Smells" by Worth

Source: Kansas Association for the Education of Young Children, comp., *Resources for Creative Preschool Teaching* (Kansas City: Kansas Association for the Education of Young Children, 1973).

Opportunities for oral expression

Oral expression is a constant activity in any classroom of three-, four-, or five-year-old children. Often teachers spend many hours of their time encouraging the children to stop talking. The object of teaching young children is not to stop talking but to direct the talking to constructive ideas and content so that speaking skills can be developed and so that teachers have an opportunity to observe and record needs and growth of individual children.

• **Conversing**   Young children learn the techniques of conversing from other children and from adults. Often their communication with each other is jumbled, sporadic, and quite brief. Since they are eager to communicate, they are often poor listeners and do not wait for someone else to finish before they interject their own comments. However, since conversation is important in all social situations, teachers must find time when they can converse individually or with small groups of children. A casual or informal setting for conversation is necessary and is not an appropriate time for the teacher to correct usage or sentence structure. In all likelihood, the direction of the conversation will be beyond the teacher's control or direction. And rightly so, since conversation is highly personal and informal and does not thrive on control. Two types of conversation are explained in the following paragraphs.

Spontaneous: Children use casual conversation throughout the day, whether they are painting in the art center, playing house in the housekeeping center, building with blocks in the block corner, or driving trucks on a make-believe road. Other opportunities for informal conversation occur as they enter or leave school, as they play outdoors, or as unexpected events happen during the day.

Facilitated: Organized conversation is helpful to both the teacher and the children. The teacher is afforded an opportunity to observe oral skills and also to gain insight into what the children actually know. Children have an opportunity to express their own ideas, to think about ideas of others, and to plan and evaluate critically. Opportunities to stimulate conversation occur when children are: planning activities, rules, trips, and daily experiences; evaluating previous events or ideas; discussing classroom problems; or discussing how to care for materials and equipment.

• **Sharing**   Basically, there are two kinds of sharing activities: one is represented by the child telling about something made or done during class; the other is sharing his out-of-school experiences or realia brought from home. Different art activities—drawing, painting, clay modeling—provide opportunities of the first kind, while trips, pets, and toys are examples of personal experiences and realia that can be shared. One important achievement realized by providing sharing opportunities is that even shy children can usually be encouraged to say a few words about something they have made, an enjoyable experience, or a prized toy. At times, particularly in the

When a child tells
another about his art
project, he has some-
thing to talk about—
and an interested
listener.

early stages of sharing time, some children may need questions from the teacher to help them talk.

Sharing time is held daily in most programs for young children, although some teachers prefer to hold it twice a week, or only occasionally. In some programs, there is no set sharing period because the children understand that they may share whatever they have at any time. A sharing period should be limited to a short span of time to reduce inattention.

Recently, efforts have been made to broaden the situations in which sharing (often referred to as "Show and Tell") is involved. At times, a child may want to share his talents by telling a story, singing a song, or reciting a poem. It may be that he has a new book or has heard a new record that he wishes to share with the group. He may wish to explain a newly learned game or some simple equipment that he has brought to class to be used in science study. Sharing in these ways advances ideas and provides opportunities for exploring concomitant experiences. Opportunity should be taken to encourage intellectual growth through asking questions and emphasizing sequence, recall, and generalization.

• *Storytelling and reading aloud*   Young children enjoy listening to a story if it stimulates their imagination and depicts experiences they can understand. It also helps if the children are seated comfortably and if they are listening to a good storyteller or reader.

The following criteria, developed by Leeper, Dales, Skipper, and Witherspoon, provide an excellent checklist for selecting a story that will appeal to young children.

1. A simple, well-developed plot, centered in one main sequence of events, structured so that a child can anticipate to some degree the outcome of events, with action predominant. A slight surprise element which makes the children wonder what will happen next can add much to the story.
2. A large amount of direct conversation.
3. Use of repetition, rhyme, and catch phrases that the child memorizes quickly and easily.
4. Use of carefully chosen, colorful language.
5. Situations involving familiar happenings. The new, unusual, and different may be included, but there must be enough of the familiar with which the child can identify. The "familiar happenings" will not be the same for all children. Children from less-privileged homes have often had different experiences. In selecting stories for them, their experiential background should be considered.
6. Simple and satisfying climax.
7. One main character with whom the child can easily identify. Too many characters can be confusing.
8. A variety of ethnic, cultural, and racial backgrounds. Such stories should present realistic pictures, not ridiculous stereotypes of racial or ethnic groups.[4]

---

4. Sarah Hammond Leeper et al., *Good Schools for Young Children*, 3rd ed., pp. 214–215. Copyright © 1974 by Macmillan Publishing Co., Inc.

Following are some books for telling or reading aloud.

Bennett, Rainey. *Secret Hiding Place*. Cleveland, Ohio: World Publishing, 1960.

Brown, Marcia. *How, Hippo!* New York: Scribner, 1972.

Chwast, Seymour, and Moskoff, Martin. *Still Another Number Book*. New York: McGraw-Hill, 1971.

Eastman, Philip D. *Are You My Mother?* New York: Beginner Books, Div. of Random, 1960.

Gramatky, Hardie. *Little Toot on the Thames*. New York: Putnam, 1964.

Mendoza, George. *Marcel Marceau Alphabet Book*. New York: Doubleday, 1970.

Piatti, Celestino. *The Happy Owls*. New York: Atheneum, 1964.

Scheer, Julian. *Rain Makes Applesauce*. New York: Holiday, 1964.

Schweitzer, Byrd B. *Amigo*. New York: Macmillan, 1963.

Steig, William. *Sylvester and the Magic Pebble*. New York: Simon and Schuster, 1969.

Taylor, Talus, and Tison, Annette. *The Adventures of Three Colors*. Cleveland, Ohio: World Publishing, 1971.

Wright, Blanche F. *The Real Mother Goose*. Chicago: Rand McNally, 1964.

Children can analyze and interpret illustrations in the books. Teachers can lead children to discover significant characters, main ideas (or actions), details, mood, and anticipated action. Gradually, finer discriminations may be made for shape, size, place relations, and arrangement of visual details.

Levels of picture interpretation by children can be recognized:

Level 1—enumerating items in a picture
Level 2—interpreting events shown
Level 3—creating a story suggested by the picture

Such "picture reading" by children is a strong foundation for development of visual literacy. (For further discussion of this concept, see the section on "Introducing Literature Through Film" in chapter 6; and reread the section on "Picture File" in chapter 1.) Two excellent references on picture books are:

Cianciolo, Patricia J. *Literature for Children: Illustrations in Children's Books*. Pose Lamb, ed. Dubuque, Iowa: William C. Brown, 1970.

MacCann, Donnarae, and Richard, Olga. *The Child's First Books.* Bronx, N.Y.: Wilson, 1973.

Dramatic play, puppetry, and picture stories are additional techniques of presenting literature. Each provides an informal and simple form that produces individual and creative responses.

Children love to dramatize and often become quite adept at playing roles and making up dialogue as they act out a familiar story. There should be no rehearsing. Children should take turns portraying different characters, and both their actions and speech should be spontaneous. At times, they may pantomime the story as it is told by the teacher.

Puppetry provides an excellent opportunity for the shy child to act out stories. Hidden behind the backdrop, the shy child can play many different roles without appearing before the group.

Picture stories, simply and colorfully painted or drawn, stimulate originality in the presentation of a story. Five-year-olds will often paint or draw several small pictures on one sheet of paper, portraying different events in the story and presenting the ideas of the story in sequence.

• *Explaining, directing, comparing, and evaluating*   Since oral expression is an integrating activity, explaining, directing, comparing, and evaluating skills are easily integrated into science, social studies, mathematics, art, and other content areas.

Explaining: Examples of explaining at the nursery school or kindergarten level are having the children describe why some objects float and some sink, why a plant in the room died, what a turtle eats, or what causes an airplane to fly. Any explanations similar to these require specific language. Teachers should provide time for pupils to ask questions that require simple explanations by the teacher so that they will have an adult model.

Directing: Giving directions should not be confused with explaining. For example, giving directions does not mean telling how to mail a letter. An example of directing in nursery school and kindergarten is having the children go from one place to another by listening to the teacher (and then a child) give a sequence of steps. Short trips taken by the children, inside or outside of the building, is another example of directing: the teacher could have the children repeat the route verbally. (The principal's office, the lunchroom, or the nearest store are possible destinations for oral directions.) Directions are also given in detail when the child follows a step-by-step procedure for cutting a valentine heart or preparing cookies for a party.

Comparing: An essential process in thinking is the ability to note similarities and differences, allowing for the development of accurate concepts. The everyday environment of the classroom provides a multitude of situations for comparing. Different kinds of blocks can be compared by noting their characteristics—size, weight, color. Several kinds of animals can be observed, and similarities and differences in their skin and size considered. A variety of fabrics can be compared for texture, weight, and purpose.

Evaluating: The teacher should help the children evaluate activities they have experienced by asking questions such as "How do you think Jimmy felt when he fell in the mud? Why?" or "Do you like this music? Why?" Questions similar to these will lead to others, such as "How could we have painted the chair another way?" or "What else should we do to the chair?" or "Why should we paint it this way?" The children not only attempt to evaluate experiences, they also try to solve problems. The teacher is responsible for encouraging and guiding suggestions and answers and at the same time he is responsible for helping the children evaluate their actions and thoughts. This type of evaluative responding and thinking is intended to preclude children's unthinking repetition of memorized clichés, such as: Question: "Why should we look both ways before crossing the street?" Answer: "So we won't get hit by a car."

• *Problem solving*   Numerous occasions requiring problem solving occur daily. Often this is in connection with a unit or a project where a question such as "What shall we look for at the service station?" must be answered. Other times it will concern events in the classroom. It could simply be "How shall we distribute the drawing paper?" It could be a problem, such as "What should we do with our paint brushes when we are through using them?" Whatever the occasion, suggestions should be solicited from the children and then discussed to see how workable they are. Obviously, many of these situations will present themselves on the spur of the moment; they cannot all be planned. Because of this, the teacher must allow both opportunity and thought to take place to insure the success of these problem-solving activities.

• *Units and projects*   The children's interests and questions are a guide for the teacher in selecting and developing short- or long-term units and projects. Units and projects are evolved around a central theme, such as "Different Kinds of Weather." An abundance of real and vicarious experiences resulting from units and projects furnish ideas and facts to talk about. Examples of activities that could be incorporated into a study of weather are: listening to poems about weather and composing poems about wind, rain, sun, and clouds; planning a trip to the weather station and deciding upon questions to ask the weatherman; dictating a thank-you note to the weatherman; dictating a class story about weather or the trip; drawing or painting pictures about the trip and showing and explaining them to the class.

The experiences furnished by such a group study provide a wealth of opportunities, not only for oral expression, but also for reading and writing readiness, artistic expression, and social amenities.

Opportunities for listening

The child under six needs to listen to be able to follow directions, to gain information, to enjoy stories, to share experiences with others, and to participate in all of the activities during the school day. Listening is also necessary for group living. Because young children are curious, active, and very talkative, they are considered to be poor listeners. Therefore, listening activities must be simple and short. Children need opportunities to listen to records, tapes, musical instruments, the radio, television, other children, and adults.

The role of the teacher is a very important factor in whether or not a child becomes a good listener. The teacher must plan and provide activities that require a variety of listening skills, and at the same time he must be an observer and evaluator of the child's listening ability. Many times both the teacher and aide will be listeners and through their modeling of being a listener they will teach children how to listen.

Through participation in listening activities, the child will be more willing to let others talk, interrupt less frequently, learn to listen for longer periods of time, and improve his own oral sentence patterns. The following activities will reinforce listening skills necessary for participation in all of the curriculum activities.

• *Following directions*   Because young children are active and like to be physically involved in activities, finger plays are an ideal means for individual or group participation. Oral language and "acting out" are involved in finger plays, as well as listening and following directions.

Sharing a good story
extends learning,
inspires, and entertains,
as well as providing
many "by-products" for
oral expression.

THE BEEHIVE

Here is a beehive
Where are the bees? (Hold up clenched fist)
Hiding away where
  nobody sees.
Look! They are coming out! (Loosen fist slightly)
They are all alive!
One! Two! Three! Four! Five!

Of course, a body poem may involve more than the fingers:

ON MY HEAD

On my head my hands I place,
On my shoulders, on my face,
On my hips and at my side,
Then behind me they will hide.
I will hold them up so high;
Quickly make my fingers fly;
Hold them out in front of me;
Swiftly clap—one, two, three.[5]

Some favorite finger plays are "My Turtle," "Ten Fingers," "The Bus," "The Train," "Itsy, Bitsy Spider," and "Five Little Squirrels." Some sources for finger and body plays are footnoted.[6]

The use of sound stories—where children supply appropriate sounds—is another way to involve even the shyest child at a very young age. Teachers and children working together can devise all sorts of sound games and stories that involve attentive listening. A simple beginning story is suggested below, the dashes representing the places where sounds are to be supplied by the child.

Ann and Robin lived on a large ranch where they heard many animal and bird sounds ———. Early in the morning the sounds would begin very softly ——— and grow ——— and grow ———. One cold day the wind howled ———, the thunder banged ———, and the rain pattered ———. A neighbor boy dashed into their barn for shelter. His teeth chattered ———, and to warm his hands he clapped them together ———. To warm his feet he stamped them on the floor ———. Ann and Robin went to the barn to help him. As they went, they heard the wind ——— and the thunder ——— and the rain ——— and the boy's teeth ——— and his hands ———. They gave him a raincoat and took him into their house. After the storm they could again hear the animal and bird sounds ———. The sounds began very softly ———, and they grew ——— and they grew ———.

---

5. Both "The Beehive" and "On My Head" are reprinted from Handbook for *Language Arts: Pre-K, Kindergarten, Grades One and Two,* 1966, p. 33.

6. Marion Grayson, *Let's Do Fingerplays* (New York: Luce, 1965); Louise B. Scott and J. J. Thompson, *Rhymes for Fingers and Flannel-boards* (New York: McGraw-Hill, 1960); Guy Wagner et al., *Games and Activities for Early Childhood Education* (Darien, Conn.: Teachers Publishing Corp., 1967); Marianne Yamaguchi, *Fingerplays* (New York: Holt, Rinehart and Winston: 1970).

• *Answering questions*   After reading a story (or simple paragraph) to the class, the teacher can ask several questions about the main ideas or characters presented. The purpose of the questions should be to develop the thinking process and oral language skills as well as to teach the listening skills. The questions should require more than yes-no answers. Yes-no answers provide very little stimulus for thinking or speaking. An example of a paragraph and appropriate questions follow.

The boy quietly tiptoed to the door and peeked through. His mother was frosting a chocolate cake. Looking at the cake made him very hungry. He could hardly wait, for today was his birthday.

1.   What was the first thing the boy did?
2.   What does *frosting* mean?
3.   What happens when you have a birthday?

• *Retelling in sequential order*   The teacher reads a familiar short story, and as he reads he changes one of the main events, either leaving it out or putting it in some other order. An excellent story for this activity is "Goldilocks and the Three Bears." Mixing up the order of eating the porridge or sitting in the chairs creates great glee. Other appropriate stories are "The Three Little Pigs," "The Gingerbread Man," and "The Three Billy Goats Gruff."

• *Detecting irrelevant sentences*   A short paragraph containing one sentence that does not fit with the rest of the paragraph is read aloud by the teacher. After the children have listened to the entire paragraph, they identify the sentence. An example of this activity follows.

Sandy brought a kitten to school. His name is Sleepy because he sleeps so much. There is a red car in the garage. Sleepy likes to drink milk.

The length and complexity of the sentences vary according to the child's age and ability.

• *Solving riddles*   The teacher describes a prominent object in the classroom. The children listen to the description and take turns telling what they think the teacher has described. Soon, some children can describe objects, and other children can guess what they have described. Later, the teacher can select an object or a person not in the classroom for the children to guess, such as a circus animal, a policeman, a jet plane, or a busy city street.

• *Completing rhymes*   Simple rymes and jingles can be used to draw attention to similarities in sentence endings. The teacher reads all but the last word in the rhyme, and the children take turns filling in the rhyming word. Two examples of completing rhymes follow.

Jack be nimble, Jack be quick,
Jack jumped over the _____.

Mary had a little lamb,
Its fleece was white as snow;
And everywhere that Mary went
The lamb was sure to _____.

• *Detecting unrhyming words*   Saying one word that does not rhyme with four or five rhyming words provides an opportunity for children to develop another listening skill. Series of words, such as *cat, lap, nap, lip,* and *map* or *stop, shop, chop,* and *throw,* are examples for these series.

• *Distinguishing sounds*   Tape-recording familiar sounds, such as a typewriter, a telephone bell, a dismissal bell, an airplane, or running water, provides an interesting activity for distinguishing sounds. Children sometimes are told in advance what sounds are on the tape; as they listen, they identify what they are hearing. Another practice—listening for the right word—helps build readiness for reading and spelling. Simple sentences or questions, such as "Do we play ball with a *pat* or a *bat*?" or "Do we wear a *cap* or a *lap*?", are examples appropriate for the better listener.

Opportunities for writing

To encourage the desire to write, the teacher provides opportunities for children to engage in games, rhythms, finger play, and manipulating tools and materials. Children's ideas are recorded in manuscript form on the chalkboard, in charts, or on individual drawings; then (and most importantly) the teacher reads what he has written so that the children will value the ability of being able to write. (For manuscript form, see page 400.)

The development of small and large muscles and eye-hand coordination, which are necessary for writing, can be helped by activities such as jumping, climbing, hammering, sawing, finger painting, pounding, shaping clay, tying shoes, dialing a telephone, easel painting, and using pencils and crayons.

Every child is interested in his own name. Large place cards may be available for labeling a child's coat hook and his private storage place; small cards may be used for name tags for field trips.

Simple activities can help to develop left-to-right concepts. Top-to-bottom, shapes, and long-and-short concepts can be developed through the use of stories, games, blocks, comparison of objects, and dances.

Young children have experiences in written expression when they dictate stories and letters to the teacher. These stories and letters are written by the teacher just as they are dictated. Children enjoy hearing their original stories read back to them. Stories and letters can be used to teach page orientation of left to right and top to bottom, and to develop interest in reading. (See the language experience approach, chapter 7, pages 234–235. Also see the readiness section in chapter 14, pages 490–492.)

MATERIALS AND SKILLS FOR LEARNING-CENTER ACTIVITIES

Centers (areas within the classroom) provide opportunities for children to learn at their own rate and at their own level of maturity; they also allow for varying lengths of attention. Individual needs and interests are met through the great variety of materials and equipment in the centers. Since nursery school and kindergarten children learn by doing or through activity, the learning-center approach is very adaptive for planning successful language arts activities and experiences.

Following are some suggestions for materials to be used and skills to be developed in learning centers for teaching the language arts to young children.

TYPE OF CENTER	MATERIALS	SKILLS
art	easels, paint, crayons, clay, brushes, paper, scissors, paste, glue, pencils, chalk, magic markers	oral composition: vocabulary building (e.g., words for color) handwriting: large and small arm, hand, and finger muscles; eye-hand coordination creative writing: creativity, free expression, oral responses
listening	tape recorders and tapes, record player and records, television, radio, headphones and jacks, slide projectors (individual and large group), filmstrip viewers (individual and large group) and filmstrips, *Language Master* and strips,[7] *System 80* and strips,[8] and *Hoffman Readers* and records[9]	oral composition: vocabulary (word meaning and usage) listening: following directions, comprehension spelling: distinguishing sounds and correct pronunciation
library	books, magazines, filmstrip stories with records, recorded stories, taped stories	reading: picture reading; introduction to fables, fairy tales, poetry, rhymes, traditional and modern stories listening: oral comprehension oral composition: vocabulary building, sharing, modeling of pronunciation, sentence structure, sequence
family	play kitchen equipment, doll bed, dolls, doll clothes, rocker, chairs, dress-up clothes, mirror, empty cans and food packages	oral composition: role-playing, sharing, conversing, vocabulary development listening: following directions

7. Charles E. Merrill (Bell and Howell), Columbus, Ohio.
8. Borg-Warner Educational Systems, Niles, Ill.
9. Hoffman Information Systems Division, Electronic Corporation, Acadia, Calif.

block and large truck	unit blocks, cardboard blocks, cars, trucks, boards, small blocks, wheelbarrow, toy people and animals	oral composition: role-playing, discussion, sharing, vocabulary listening: following directions handwriting: large and small arm, hand, and finger muscles
drama or role-playing	old clothes, costumes, puppets, flannel board and flannel characters, false TV screen, video tapes for taping action, camera	oral composition: role-playing, directing, explaining, conversing, vocabulary (e.g., words for textures)
science	magnets, animals, magnifying glass, plants, clock, thermometer, locks and keys, charts, games, minerals	oral composition: vocabulary, (e.g., words for temperature), problem solving, explaining, classification, comparing, sharing
mathematics	geometric shapes, small blocks, colored disks, dominoes, scales, balances, beads, counting rods, games, measuring cup, yardstick, rulers, money	oral composition: vocabulary (e.g., words for shapes, forms, and numbers); problem solving; explaining; comparing; sharing handwriting: fine motor development, eye-hand coordination
manipulative	games, puzzles, sewing boards, pegs and boards, patterning cards, cut-outs, hammers, nails, boards, parquetry sets, dressing frames, buttons, snaps, and lacing materials	oral composition: sharing, explaining, discussing, problem solving, vocabulary development handwriting: large and small muscle development, eye-hand coordination, visual discrimination
special	special holiday materials, special interest materials, introductory unit or project materials, "mystery" box	oral composition: introduction of new words, sharing, comparing, explaining, directing spelling: labeling of materials, chart making handwriting: manuscript form

OBSERVING AND RATING LANGUAGE ARTS GROWTH

Diagnosing and analyzing children's needs and progress is an on-going process. Because young children are unable to read and write, their needs and progress have to be detected through oral questioning and through observation by the teacher.

Two common strategies for observing and rating follow. (These are only suggested approaches; teachers are encouraged to be creative with the examples and to design their own procedures.)

Observing

One way to analyze what children are learning is to ask three simple questions: "What did the teacher teach?" "What did the children learn?" and "How do you know?" Although these are not very learned questions, they cover the basics. Actual classroom observations of teachers and aides teaching language art skills to three-, four-, and five-year-olds follow.

THREE-YEAR-OLDS

Free Play Time (Oral Composition and Listening)
What did the teacher teach?

> The teacher taught the names of colors and animals in a puzzle to one girl.

> The aide taught two children about the care and feeding of a fish.

> The teacher talked to one girl about the use of the magnifying glass and showed her how the glass made things appear larger.

What did the children learn?

> One girl learned to name correctly the colors and animals in a puzzle.

> Two children learned how to care for and feed the fish they were going to take home.

> One child learned that a magnifying glass will make things appear to be larger than they are.

How do you know?

> The child misnamed some of the animals and colors at first, but before she was finished with the puzzle she could name them correctly.

The two children asked questions about the fish and seemed to understand the answers about how to care for and feed it.

The child looking through the magnifying glass told the teacher that her hand was bigger when she looked at it through the magnifying glass and then she showed other children the glass and told them all about it.

FOUR-YEAR-OLDS

Social Studies (Listening, Oral Composition, and Literature)
What did the teacher teach?

The teacher was extending the concepts of seeing, feeling, and listening by conducting short walks and encouraging the children to use these senses. She also encouraged the children to share storybooks.

What did the children learn?

The children, by exercising their senses, were able to tell the teacher and other classmates what they had seen, heard, and felt on the walks.

The children were eager to share a picture or book with some of their friends.

How do you know?

Using the senses emphasized on their walks, the children were able to discuss and tell the teacher they *saw* a squirrel, cats, dogs, a lizard, and a horse; *heard* a rooster crow, a puppy panting, and cars moving in the street; *felt* a shingle, beans, a rusted tin can, and a cactus.

During rest period, several children enthusiastically said, "Look at this _____!" "Do you want my book?" or "Let's trade books."

FIVE-YEAR-OLDS

Social Studies (Listening, Oral Composition, Handwriting)
What did the teacher teach?

The teacher taught one child to follow directions by asking the child to bring him a box of materials.

The teacher taught a new word, *slashes*, while cutting construction paper feathers.

The teacher taught that names have meaning as he
gave each child an Indian name and wrote it on the
headbands they were making.

What did the children learn?

One child learned to follow directions.

All the children learned to cut and make slashes.

The children learned Indian names.

How do you know?

One child brought the teacher the box and was quite
pleased with his accomplishment (shown by his expression and comments to friends).

All the children cut slashes to the best of their individual
abilities.

The children practiced saying their own Indian names
as the teacher labeled the headbands; they shared
names and name meanings with each other.

Rating

During the years of education for young children, the typical
child learns to work in a group, to express his emotions through play
and art media, to listen and share ideas, and to grow in his ability to
understand and use language through all his activities. The wise
teacher not only provides for these immediate developmental tasks,
but anticipates the language skills that the child will need in reading
and writing. To aid the teacher in this undertaking, the following
checklist for individual language readiness can be used for identifying skills already developed and skills that need to be developed
further.

Checklist for Individual Language Readiness

Hearing	Yes	No
Does he respond to his name?	_____	_____
Does he respond to simple questions?	_____	_____
Does he ask to have questions repeated?	_____	_____

Speech
  Does he speak clearly and distinctly
    enough to be heard?   _____   _____
  Does he repeat spoken words
    correctly?   _____   _____
General Skills
  Does he listen attentively?   _____   _____
  Does he follow simple oral directions?   _____   _____
  Does he listen to stories with
    understanding?   _____   _____
  Does he listen when other children
    are talking?   _____   _____
  Does he speak spontaneously in
    sharing time?   _____   _____
  Does he express himself in telling
    about his art pictures?   _____   _____
  Does he express simple ideas in
    complete sentences?   _____   _____
  Does he tell a story in sequence?   _____   _____
  Does he predict outcomes of a story?   _____   _____
  Does he ask the meanings of words
    and signs?   _____   _____
  Does he show an interest in books?   _____   _____
  Does he recognize rhyming words?   _____   _____
  Does he recognize words that begin
    with the same sound?   _____   _____
  Does he show an interest in alpha-
    bet repeating and reading
    alphabet letters?   _____   _____
  Does he write his name?   _____   _____

While vision and eye-hand coordination may not be labeled
"language skills," the teacher must consider such questions as:

Does the child appear to be able to see from any place in the
  room?
Does he hold materials at the proper distance from his eyes?
Does he look at pictures in books?
Does he turn the pages of a book with ease?
Does he hold and use crayons with ease?
Does he use scissors?
Does he stay on a line with reasonable accuracy when cutting?

SOME PERTINENT QUESTIONS FOR CONSIDERATION

1.   *How do the ideas proposed in this chapter relate to the tenets of Montessori and Piaget?* Montessori methods and materials, long neglected and often criticized by educators in the United States, are now presently used widely—either adopted in part or as an entire program. Although certain aspects of Montessori's original program for retarded children are not applicable for normal children in the 1970s, due to differences in innate ability and environmental changes, some basic ideas are viable for programs of today, such as: well-planned, organized procedures; correlation of language arts skills within all content areas; sequential development of skills; use of manipulative materials and learning centers; availability of adults as listeners; and play opportunities that are basically learning situations. The authors question a few aspects of the original Montessori system, such as: the early age for formal instruction in writing, the requirement of participation in each task each day, and repetition (drill) for early mastery in contrast to establishing a foundation of skills over a period of time.

Piaget has also greatly influenced current programs for young children. Piaget's research and theories are more of an understanding of the what, how, and why children learn than a basic program. All teachers should be aware of Piaget's stages of sequential development of language skills, his research on reasoning and understanding of concepts, and his theories of how children learn, all of which form the basis for experiences and activities that are important for effective instruction.

2.   *How do the recommendations in this chapter relate to the British Infant School program?* The British Infant School is one of the current influences upon early childhood education in the United States. Many of the elements in this program are recommended by the authors, such as a well-planned instructional format, an oral approach to early instruction, parent education and school involvement, learning centers, and the creative thrust through drama, literature, art, and music. Although the authors agree with many of the aspects of the British Infant Schools, we question the early age for formal instruction in handwriting, spelling, and reading. We also disagree with the length of school day—usually a seven-hour day versus a three-and-one-half to four-hour day in the United States.

3.   *What are some reference books for teachers of young children in the fields of art, music, and movement?*

Art Activities

Carmichael, Viela S. *Curriculum Ideas for Young Children.* Los Angeles: Southern California Association for the Education of Young Children, 1971.

Cherry, Clare. *Creative Art for the Developing Child.* Belmont, Calif.: Fearon, 1972.

Croft, Doreen J., and Hess, Robert D. *An Activities Handbook for Teachers of Young Children.* Boston: Houghton Mifflin, 1972.

Books about Art

Eisner, Elliott W., and Echer, David W., eds. *Readings in Art Education.* Waltham, Mass.: Blaisdell, 1966.

Jameson, Kenneth. *Art and the Young Child.* New York: Viking Press, 1969.

Kellogg, Rhoda, and O'Dell, Scott. *The Psychology of Children's Art.* Del Mar, Calif.: CRM Associates, 1967.

Activity Song Books

Croweninshield, Ethel. *Stories That Sing.* Boston: Boston Music Co., 1955.

Miller, Mary, and Zajan, Paula. *Finger Play.* New York: Schirner, 1955.

Winn, Marie, et al. *What Shall We Do and Allee Galloo!* New York: Harper & Row, 1970.

Song Books

McCall, Adeline. *This is Music, for Kindergarten and Nursery School.* Boston: Allyn and Bacon, 1965.

McLaughlin, Roberta, and Schliestett, Patti. *The Joy of Music: Early Childhood.* Evanston, Ill.: Summy-Birchard, 1967.

Movement Activities

Andrews, Gladys. *Creative Rhythmic Movement for Children.* Englewood Cliffs, N.J.: Prentice-Hall, 1954.

Cherry, Clare. *Creative Movement for the Developing Child.* 2d ed. Belmont, Calif.: Fearon, 1971.

Jones, Elizabeth. *What is Music for Young Children?* Washington, D.C.: National Association for the Education of Young Children, 1969.

Cratty, Bryant J. *Learning and Playing, Fifty Vigorous Activities for the Atypical Child.* Freeport, N.Y.: Educational Activities, 1968.

Books about Movement

Hackett, Layne C., and Jenson, Robert G. *A Guide to Movement Exploration*. Palo Alto, Calif.: Peek Publications, 1967.

Porter, Lorena. *Movement Education for Children*. Washington, D.C.: American Association of Elementary-Kindergarten-Nursery Educators, 1969.

Two other questions worthy of serious consideration are:

4. *What are the newer trends toward home programs for young children?*

5. *What guidelines are helpful in the use of commercial materials available for early childhood education programs?*

Adventures in Discovery. New York: Western Publishing.

Children's World. New York: Holt, Rinehart and Winston.

Distar Language. Chicago, Ill.: Science Research Associates.

Early Childhood Curriculum: A Piaget Program. Boston, Mass: American Science and Engineering.

Early Childhood Discovery Materials. New York: Macmillan.

Experiences for Young Children. New York: Noble and Noble.

Language Experiences in Early Childhood (LEEC). Chicago, Ill.: Encyclopaedia Britannica Educational Corp.

Peabody Language Development Kits. Circle Pines, Minn.: American Guidance Service.

Playway: An Interest Center Approach to Initial Education. New York: Winston Press.

The Sounds and Patterns of Language. New York: Holt, Rinehart and Winston.

Learning Language Skills. Manchester, Mo.: Webster/McGraw-Hill.

An excellent guide, "How to Select and Evaluate Materials," *Early Childhood Education*, No. 42, is available from Educational Products Information Exchange Institute (EPIE), New York, 1972.

(Write for catalogs or descriptive literature about early childhood education language arts materials from major publishers as listed at the conclusion of this chapter.)

SELECTED REFERENCES

General Professional

Strickland, Ruth. *Language Arts in the Elementary School*. 3rd ed. Lexington, Mass.: D. C. Heath, 1969, chapter 5.

Specialized

Bereiter, Carl, and Engelmann, Seigfried. *Teaching Disadvantaged Children in the Preschool*. Englewood Cliffs, N.J.: Prentice-Hall, 1966.

Cazden, Courtney B. *Child Language and Education*. New York: Holt, Rinehart and Winston, 1972.

Chukovsky, Kornei. *From Two to Five*. Berkeley: University of California Press, 1963.

Council for Exceptional Children. *Helping Young Children Develop Language Skills: A Book of Activities*. Arlington, Va.: Council for Exceptional Children, 1968.

Evans, Ellis D. *Contemporary Influences in Early Childhood Education*. New York: Holt, Rinehart and Winston, 1971.

Frost, Joe L. *Revisiting Early Childhood Education: Readings*. New York: Holt, Rinehart and Winston, 1973.

Furth, Hans G. *Piaget for Teachers*. Englewood Cliffs, N.J.: Prentice-Hall, 1970.

Gesell, Arnold, and Ilg, Frances L. *Child from Five to Ten*. New York: Harper & Row, 1946.

Hess, Robert D., and Croft, Doreen J. *Teachers of Young Children*. Boston: Houghton Mifflin, 1972.

Hildebrand, Verna. *Introduction to Early Childhood Education*. New York: Macmillan, 1971.

Hymes, James L. *Teaching the Child Under Six*. 2d ed. Columbus, Ohio: Merrill, 1974.

King, Edith W., and Kerber, August. *Sociology of Early Childhood Education*. New York: Van Nostrand Reinhold, 1968.

Lavatelli, C. B. *Preschool Language Training*. Urbana: University of Illinois Press, 1970.

Leeper, Sarah H., et al. *Good Schools for Young Children*. 2d ed. New York: Macmillan, 1968.

Lillard, Paula Polk. *Montessori: A Modern Approach*. New York: Schocken, 1972.

Moffett, James. *Student-Centered Language Arts Curriculum, Grades K–13*. New York: Houghton Mifflin, 1973.

Parker, Ronald K., ed. *The Preschool in Action: Exploring Early Childhood Programs*. Boston: Allyn and Bacon, 1972.

Read, Katherine H. *Nursery School: A Human Relationships Laboratory*. 5th ed. Philadelphia: Saunders, 1971.

Spodek, Bernard. *Teaching in the Early Years*. Englewood Cliffs, N.J.: Prentice-Hall, 1972.

Stanley, Julian C. *Preschool Programs for the Disadvantaged: Five Experimental Approaches to Early Childhood Education*. Baltimore: Johns Hopkins University Press, 1972.

Todd, Vivian E., and Heffernan, Helen. *Years Before School: Guiding Preschool Children*. 2d ed. New York: Macmillan, 1970.

Weber, Evelyn. *Early Childhood Education: Perspectives on Change*. Worthington, Ohio: Charles A. Jones, 1970.

Organizations and journals associated with early childhood education

Allen Raymond, Inc., 1 Hale Lane, Darien, Conn. 06820: *Early Years.*

Association for Childhood Education International, 3615 Wisconsin Ave., N.W., Washington, D.C.: *Childhood Education.*

Merrill-Palmer Institute, 71 E. Ferry Ave., Detroit, Mich.: *Merrill Palmer Quarterly.*

National Association for the Education of Young Children, 1834 Connecticut Ave., Washington D.C.: *Young Children.*

National Congress of Parents and Teachers, 700 N. Rush St., Chicago, Ill.: *The National PTA Bulletin.*

National Educational Association, 1201 16th St., N.W., Washington, D.C., Department of Elementary-Kindergarten-Nursery Education: *Early Education.*

Society for Research in Child Development, Inc., University of Chicago Press, 5801 Ellis Ave., Chicago, Ill.: *Child Development; Child Development Abstracts; and Monographs of the Society for Research in Child Development.*

U. S. Department of Health, Education, and Welfare, 330 Independence Ave., S.W., Washington, D.C.: *Children.*

Publishers of early childhood learning materials

Allyn and Bacon, Inc., 470 Atlantic Ave., Boston, Mass. 02210.

American Guidance Service, Inc., Publishers' Building, Circle Pines, Minn. 55014.

American Science and Engineering, 20 Overland St., Boston, Mass. 02215.

Creative Playthings, Department Number 103, Princeton, N.J. 08540.

Encyclopaedia Britannica, 425 N. Michigan Ave., Chicago, Ill. 60611.

General Learning Corporation, Early Learning Division, 250 James St., Morristown, N.J. 07960.

Houghton Mifflin, 1 Beacon St., Boston, Mass. 02108.

J. B. Lippincott Co., E. Washington Square, Philadelphia, Pa. 01905.

Little Tikes, Rotadyne, Inc., Solon, Ohio 44139.

Lyndon Craft, P. O. Box 12 B, Rosemead, Calif. 91770.

Mead Educational Services, 245 N. Highland Ave., Atlanta, Ga. 30307.

Milton Bradley Co., 1500 Main St., Springfield, Mass. 01101.

McGraw-Hill Book Co., 1221 Avenue of the Americas, New York, N.Y. 10020.

Noble and Noble, Publishers, 1 Dag Hammarskjöld Plaza, New York, N.Y. 10017.

Random House/Singer School Division, 201 E. 50 St., New York, N.Y. 10022.

Science Research Associates, Inc., 259 E. Erie St., Chicago, Ill. 61611.

The Child's World, P. O. Box 681, Elgin, Ill. 60120.

Western Publishing Co., Inc., Education Division, 850 Third Ave., New York, N.Y. 10022.

Books for parents of young children

General

Arnold, Arnold. *Teaching Your Child to Learn from Birth to School Age.* Englewood Cliffs, N.J.: Prentice-Hall, 1971.

Cohen, Dorothy H. *The Learning Child.* New York: Random, 1973.

Gore, Lillian L. *Educating Children in Nursery Schools and Kindergartens.* Washington, D.C.: U.S. Government Printing Office, 1964.

Gudrige, Beatrice M. *How to Help Your Child Learn: A Handbook for Parents of Children in Kindergarten through Grade 6.* Washington, D.C.: National Education Association, 1960.

Hymes, James L. *Teaching the Children Under Six.* 2d ed. Columbus, Ohio: Merrill, 1974.

Newman, Sylvia. *Guidelines to Parent-Teacher Cooperation in Early Childhood Education.* Brooklyn, N.Y.: Book-Lab, 1972.

Special Needs

Berman, Alicerose, and Cohen, Lisa. *Help for Your Troubled Child, Public Affairs Pamphlet No. 454.* New York: Public Affairs Committee, 1970.

Clinebell, Charlotte, and Clinebell, Howard, J. *Crisis and Growth: Helping Your Troubled Child.* Philadelphia: Fortress, 1971.

Isaacs, Susan. *Troubles of Children and Parents.* New York: Schocken, 1973.

Play: The Child Strives Toward Self-Realization. Washington, D.C.: National Association for the Education of Young Children, 1971.

Raths, Louis E. *Meeting the Needs of Children: Creating Trust and Security.* Columbus, Ohio: Merrill, 1972.

Significance of the Young Child's Motor Development. Washington, D.C.: National Association for the Education of Young Children, 1971.

Van Riper, Charles. *Teaching Your Child to Talk.* New York: Harper & Row, 1950.

The following pamphlets may be purchased for a minimal fee from the Superintendent of Documents, U.S. Government Printing Office, Washington, D.C. 20402:

Your Child from 1 to 3—Children's Bureau Pub. #413
Your Child from 3 to 4—Children's Bureau Pub. #446
Your Child from 1 to 6—Children's Bureau Pub. #30
Home Play and Play Equipment—Children's Bureau Pub. #238
The Child with a Speech Problem—Children's Bureau Pub. #43

LISTENING

Listening

OBJECTIVES	PERFORMANCE RESPONSES
1. To differentiate hearing skills from listening skills	1. Prepare a list of sounds and write a paragraph on three of the sounds, describing how hearing the sounds becomes a listening experience.
2. To describe the "why" and "what" of listening	2. a. Visit a classroom. Make a record of activities. Put the needed listening skills under appropriate categories. b. Make a poster, stressing the characteristics of a good appreciational or critical listener.
3. To relate listening skills to other instructional areas	3. Write a short paragraph relating listening and reading.
4. To identify some causes of nonlistening	4. Visit a classroom and observe a poor listener. Try to determine probable causes for his nonlistening.
5. To differentiate between listening attitude and listening skill	5. Suggest an activity for one grade level that focuses upon attitude (importance of listening, responsibility of the listener, factors that affect listening, etc.) more than upon a specific listening skill.
6. To contrast major approaches to listening instruction	6. a. List the strengths and limitations of each of the major approaches. b. Prepare a systematic lesson plan for one listening skill (see page 99 for some skills). c. Utilize the learning-center concept for one listening skill, suggesting any subskills, tasks, and needed materials.
7. To become acquainted with instructional listening materials and activities	7. Select one instructional listening aid or activity and report on its possible uses.
8. To examine techniques for evaluating listening performance	8. Make a checklist for evaluating one listening skill.

Twenty-five pairs of ears, twenty-five levels of listening! The frustration caused by the divergence of listening skills in the average classroom often tends to make teachers caustic and defensive about the progress or nonprogress of their pupils. Listening or nonlistening is hard to detect. For example, just as soon as a teacher is confident that he can detect whether or not a child is listening, he is amazed to discover that the child who focused on his every movement, did not talk, and seemed to be concentrating, cannot answer an oral question, failed a written test, did not do his homework, or could not re-

Learning to participate in the process of listening demands that the child possess the needed skills for dealing with his aural environment.

member in a 10:00 A.M. spelling class certain skills that had been presented an hour earlier in a reading class.

Hearing and listening are often confused and thought of as the same skill. According to Neville:

> More failure in academic and social growth can be traced to inability to listen than to any other single aspect of the language arts . . . . We must not take for granted that a person can listen because he can hear.[1]

Of course, hearing is the basis for listening. Hearing depends on the proper functioning of the ears, nervous system, and the brain, but listening extends hearing to reaction, identification, and thought. For example, a car horn breaks the silence. A car horn is heard by one person (hearing). Another person looks to see where the sound is coming from, identifies the horn as a familiar or unfamiliar sound, and wonders why it was blown (listening). (Refer to chart 2.1, chapter 2, pages 31–33, for listening development in the early years.)

Today, as never before, people are being bombarded by information and misinformation: by propaganda, drama, lectures, panel discussions, news reports, and advertising campaigns. The ability to listen intelligently is important. Research has not shown that such increased use of the ears has necessarily brought about greater ability to listen efficiently. Research has suggested that the average person will retain only 50 percent of what he hears, no matter how hard he concentrates, and that two months later he can be expected to remember only 25 percent of what was said.[2] The ears need "educating" if the ability to listen better and more discriminately is to be achieved.

THE "WHY" AND "WHAT" ASPECTS OF LISTENING

There are several types of listening. Subskills may be noted for each type. Characteristics may then evolve that will describe the good listener.

---

1. Mark A. Neville, "Listening is an Art; Practice It," *Elementary English* 36 (April 1959): 226.

2. Stanford E. Taylor, "Listening," *What Research Says to the Teacher*, No. 29 (Washington, D.C.: National Education Association, 1964), p. 4.

Why do children listen?

When planning activities, teachers need to keep in mind the various reasons why children listen. Activities can become boring and counteract the main thrust of the activity. Purposes for listening (which are categorized below as types and skills) provide ideas for planning an appropriate listening program.

CHART 4.1: Purposes for Listening

TYPE I: INFORMATIONAL		TYPE II: APPRECIATIVE	
Skills:	to note main ideas to remember details to detect sequence to follow directions to distinguish relevant/ irrelevant materials to anticipate conclu- sions/inferences	*Skills:*	to enjoy prose to note pleasing rhyme/ rhythm to sense images to sense moods
		TYPE III: CRITICAL (ANALYTICAL)	
		Skills:	to sense bias/prejudice to judge validity of information to distinguish fact from opinion

What does a good listener do?

One way to evaluate whether or not a child is a good listener is to know and understand the characteristics of a good listener. Teachers may wish to develop a checklist using the following criteria as a guide for good informational listening.

A good listener is an individual who

1. concentrates alertly and consciously.
2. identifies the central idea of the speaker.
3. identifies and relates the supporting ideas or details of the speaker.
4. retains the logical sequence of the topic, mentally maintaining a running summary of the speaker's points.
5. asks mental questions and listens for their answers as the topic is discussed.

Good listening is an active, not a passive, skill.

6. critically identifies emotional tones or catch phrases.
7. relates other knowledge to the topic as it is being presented, making justifiable inferences.
8. makes mental notes of agreement and disagreement and later asks questions for clarification.

Listening involves grasping immediately what is being said, because in most verbal relating the statement is spoken but once. Only in the case of the tape recorder, records, and face-to-face encounter can the listener "hear again" the material that he has missed. Today's world of television, radio, large group instruction, and listening stations for children make accurate, first-time listening a must.

Good listening is an active, not a passive, skill. A child must give active attention to the words, phrases, and intonation of a speaker and must comprehend the ideas presented through relating them to his own past experiences. As the child listens, he is forming his own image of what is being said. All oral communication requires an active listener.

Listening is not only active, but it is also a thinking-related skill. The term *critical listening* means a questioning attitude, analysis, and judgment of spoken material; it is equivalent to *critical reading* of written material. Such a view supports the necessity of relating thinking skills to listening, such as detection of the speaker's purpose, propaganda, and argument techniques.[3] Thinking is an integral part of good listening.

LISTENING AND THE OTHER INSTRUCTIONAL AREAS

All of the language arts require skilled listening ability. Listening provides the vocabulary, the sentence patterns, and the auditory discrimination that build a foundation for children to speak, read, spell, and compose.

Even before the advent of the newer media of communication, an early researcher had written that "listening is the most frequently used language activity, the average adult spending approximately three times as much time listening as reading."[4] He found that his

3. Sara W. Lundsteen, "Teaching and Testing Critical Listening in the Fifth and Sixth Grades," *Elementary English* 41 (November 1964): 743–747, 752.

4. Paul T. Rankin, "Listening Ability," Proceedings of the Ohio State Education Conference, 1929, Ohio State University, pp. 172–183.

subjects, who spent about 70 percent of the waking day in verbal communication, were spending 11 percent of the day in writing, 15 percent in reading, 32 percent in talking, and 42 percent in listening. (See Figure 4.1 below.)

FIGURE 4.1: Comparative Percentage of Time Spent on Language Activities by the Typical Adult

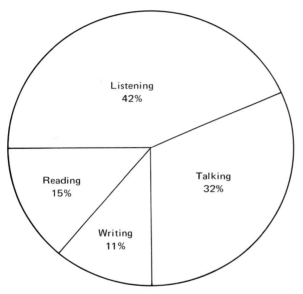

Wilt made a study to determine what percentage of the school day elementary school pupils are expected to listen. She also wanted to discover whether teachers are aware of the amount of time they expect children to listen.[5] Teachers estimated that children learned by listening on the average of 74.3 minutes per day, but observations in classrooms showed they listened 158 minutes—more than half the time they were in the classroom. More time was spent in listening than in any other single classroom activity. The largest percentage of the time the children were "supposed to listen" was the time spent listening to the teacher talk, followed by the time in which they lis-

---

5. Miriam E. Wilt, "A Study of Teacher Awareness of Listening as a Factor in Elementary Education," *Journal of Educational Research* 43 (April 1950): 626–636.

tened to questions asked by the teacher and answered by one child. Children were expected to listen less to each other than to the teacher. Obviously, many teachers are unaware of the amount of time they expect pupils to listen, suggesting that teachers need to become more sensitive to the importance of skillful listening as a factor in communication and as a learning experience.

In a 1967 study, Herman revealed that children spent 75 percent of the time during their social studies classes in listening activities. Over 42 percent of this time occurred during verbal interactions between the children and the teacher.[6]

In another study, Ross found that a poor listener is usually below average in reading, arithmetic, intelligence, and general school achievement. He suggests that "It may be more logical to group pupils in our schools on the basis of listening scores rather than reading scores."[7]

A "special relationship" exists between listening and reading. Listening and reading are *receptive* phases of language, as opposed to speaking and writing, which are *expressive* phases. Listening skills are important in learning to read, for direct association of sound, meaning, and word form must be established from the start. The ability to identify sounds heard at the beginning, middle, or end of a word and to discriminate among sounds is essential to success in analyzing words phonetically. From the standpoint of interpreting what is read, skillful listening is indispensable. The listening comprehension of elementary-school children is generally superior to their reading comprehension, particularly with easy materials.[8] Listening and reading reach equivalence in both word-recognition rate and word-per-minute rate late in the elementary-school years. Not until the latter part of the sixth or seventh grade does reading appear to gain sufficient efficiency to cause it to be preferred over the usual act of listening in many learning situations. This implies that it is profitable to present instruction orally in the elementary school. Generally, more advanced pupils prefer learning through reading; slower ones prefer learning through listening, particularly when the content is easy. When, however, the content taxes their listening skill, the slower pupils will likely prefer reading. While reading and listening are not identical (each has its own advantages), the important fact is that

6. Wayne L. Herman, "The Use of Language Arts in Social Studies Lessons," *American Education Review Journal* 4 (March 1967): 117–124.

7. Ramon Ross, "A Look at Listeners," *Elementary School Journal* 64 (April 1964): 369–372.

8. Richard S. Hampleman, "Comparison of Listening and Reading Comprehension Ability of Fourth and Sixth Grade Pupils," *Elementary English* 35 (January 1958): 49–53.

there are many aspects in which reading and listening are alike and teachers must be aware of these similarities for economy and efficiency of instruction.

Practically all of the other content areas—mathematics, science, social studies, health, etc.—require reading, writing, spelling, speaking, and listening skills. Often the ability to follow oral directions in these subjects becomes the key to success in completing an assignment.

Nonlistening in a school setting

Although there are many reasons why children do not listen, teachers often consider a short attention span to be the main problem in teaching any subject. A short attention span implies that the individual child does not have the ability to listen long enough to comprehend what he is supposed to do, what he is supposed to know.

In 1970, Broman studied seven youngsters who had been identified by teachers, principals, parents, and aides as children who did not and who would not listen.[9] These children were observed on several occasions for three to six hours at a time. The following reports illustrate the short attention span and the nonlistening activities of three of these youngsters.

OBSERVATION, THIRD GRADE

A third-grade boy started the day by not hanging up his sweater after being told twice to do so, got out his social studies book instead of his reading book, and had to be told he had the wrong book. He stared at the floor while others participated in a class discussion on the main character of the story, and he rested his head on his hand while he slowly worked three addition problems in five minutes. Later, during recess, he organized three boys in getting bats, balls, mitts and bases, sent one boy out to "claim the diamond," divided the boys of the class into two teams, and had a ball game underway in six minutes.

Child's response to questioning: "School work is too hard. I don't understand it."

9. Betty L. Broman, "The Short Attention Span: Fact and Myth," *Childhood Education* 47 (December 1970): 156–158.

Probable cause: Records show low mental ability (83 IQ average on four individual tests), an average achievement level of beginning second-grade material, and advanced physical development for chronological age. The child was studying from material approximately a year too advanced for his ability in reading, spelling, arithmetic and other whole-group activities. Teacher comments: "A leader, dependable, does well in art."

OBSERVATION, FOURTH GRADE

After a discussion on what each student needed to finish, a fourth-grade girl (who had replied that she had an art project to finish) combed her hair, tied her belt, pulled up her socks, patted her hair, and asked the teacher if she could go to the library. Upon being asked whether she had finished her art project, the child looked bewildered for a moment and then blushed and said she had forgotten it. She then returned to her table and finished her project without interruption.

Child's response to questioning: "When I grow up I am going to be a librarian because they are so nice."

Probable cause: The observer spent a half-hour in the library and discovered that the librarian complimented the children, inquired about each of their needs, asked their help in running the library, permitted the children to talk, thanked them for coming, and when they left said, "I'll see you tomorrow." The library was a pleasant place and the librarian a person to be admired. The child wanted to be like her.

OBSERVATION, FIFTH GRADE

A fifth-grade boy selected famous stock car racers as a topic for an oral report. After returning from the library with four books, the child sat engrossed in the books for forty minutes. That same afternoon, during an art class, the student wandered around the room, gazed out the window, "stole" a girl's pencil, was reminded three times that his clay monster had to be glazed, watched another boy whittle a piece of pine, asked what the class would do tomorrow, and ended the period with a still unglazed monster.

Child's response to questioning: "Art is sissy stuff."

Probable cause: When the student records were checked, all evidence indicated small muscles were not developed. Poor writer. Jerky movements in anything that took small-muscle control, such as painting, cutting, drawing. All teachers indicated that paper work was messy and poorly done. An A and B student in reading, science, math, social studies, and language.

Oral communication can never be a one-way process. It must always involve both transmission and reception. In all areas of instruction, oral communication is a widely used technique of teaching, and because of this the listener is as vital as the speaker.

TEACHING LISTENING

Some teachers believe that listening develops naturally and that it requires no instruction. They believe that if experiences and situations conducive to listening are provided during the regular instructional program that the child will automatically learn how to listen. Listening has been neglected for various reasons, but one reason is the lack of lessons on listening in children's instructional materials. Two studies by Brown,[10] who examined texts for children in grades 3 through 6, showed that few lessons or materials are devoted to the teaching of listening. Teachers must therefore rely on supplementary activities, ideas, and materials to teach listening adequately.

In order to teach listening, teachers must provide conditions that are conducive to attentive listening. The following suggestions by Smith can aid in developing a positive attitude toward listening.

A teacher should

1. provide proper physical conditions for optimum listening.
2. speak in an animated and interested manner and pace his speaking speed to the children's listening speed.
3. help children develop rules for good listening habits.
4. check comprehension of the children's listening ability in

---

10. Kenneth L. Brown, "Speech and Listening in Language Arts Textbooks: Part 1." *Elementary English* 4 (April 1967): 336–341; idem, "Speech and Listening in Language Arts Textbooks: Part 2," *Elementary English* 5 (May 1967): 461–465.

the same way as he checks comprehension in a reading class.
5. praise the children for good listening.
6. be a good listener himself.
7. avoid needless repetition in his teaching.
8. avoid needless demands of children's attention.
9. allow the children to talk.
10. provide listening opportunities that are purposeful, accurate, critical, responsive, or appreciative.
11. help children eliminate poor listening habits.
12. avoid overuse of listening for reproducing and encourage children to think about what they hear.
13. help children realize that varying degrees of attention are required for different kinds of listening.[11]

Once the proper atmosphere for listening is provided, the teacher can profitably plan definite lessons on how to listen. Emphasis upon listening skills can be instrumental in raising the general level of listening ability, provided attention is given to all skills associated with the process rather than just to superficial aspects of listening. Experimental studies support the preceding statement as well as the statement that such a planned program of instruction benefits children with low, average, and high intelligence.[12]

Activities to enhance listening attitude

Listening is inherent in many regular classroom activities, thus providing a natural setting for development of positive listening attitudes. Children listen to the development of a story, to the answer to a specific question, and to discriminate between fact and opinion. They listen to tape recordings of reports, to films on socially significant topics, and to directions for making things.

---

11. Adapted from James A. Smith, *Creative Teaching of the Language Arts in the Elementary School*, 2d ed. (Boston: Allyn and Bacon, 1973), pp. 101–103.

12. For example, see Albert M. Desousa and Milly Cowles, "An Experimental Study To Determine the Efficacy of Specific Training in Listening," *Elementary English* 46 (April 1969): 512; Annabel E. Fawcett, "Training in Listening," *Elementary English* 43 (May 1966): 4373–4376; Robert E. Kraner, "A Comparison of Two Methods of Listening Instruction," *Elementary English* 46 (April 1969): 515–516; Sara W. Lundsteen, "Critical Listening: An Experiment," *Elementary School Journal* 66 (March 1966): 311–315; idem., "Listening, Reading, and Qualitative Levels of Thinking in Problem Solving," *California Journal of Educational Research* 18 (November 1967): 230–237; idem., "Teaching and testing Critical Listening in the Fifth and Sixth Grades," *Elementary English* 41 (November 1964): 743–747; Edward Pratt, "Experimental Evaluation of a Program for the Improvement of Listening," *Elementary School Journal* 56 (March 1965): 315–320; Elaine Prescott, Robert E. Potter, and Richard J. Franks, "Are You Teaching Auding?" *Peabody Journal of Education* 46 (November 1968): 150–154; John Van Valkenburg, "Learning Through Listening: Implications for Reading," Ph.D. diss. (Rochester, N.Y.: University of Rochester, 1968), *Dissertation Abstracts* 29(6) December 1968: 1692A.

In the intermediate grades, the listening act becomes an even stronger force in influencing attitudes, in furnishing information, and in forming opinions. With panel discussions, guest speakers, news reports and analyses, political campaigns, advertising, and entertainment to be intelligently attended to and evaluated for pleasure or information, the variety of listening experiences is wide and the need for listening is great.

Real purposes and evaluation make listening more directed. The pupil listens more effectively if he has certain things to listen for. For example, before a pupil gives an oral report, he can state a few questions that his report will cover. The teacher could also prepare questions as a "check-up" to be given before and after the report. This procedure will not only be a good follow-up, but will also stress speaking along with listening.

Discussions may be held concerning practices that could encourage better listening. Discussions centering around such questions as the following have been found helpful by some teachers.

What is the importance of listening?
How does one increase auditory acuity?
How does one add to his information and understanding through better listening?
How may a person help others to be good listeners?
How does a person use information he has gained through listening?

To help stress the importance of careful listening, pupils may be asked to rephrase an answer to a question or to restate an assignment given orally only once by the teacher. (They will make considerable progress in hearing the instructions the first time if a businesslike, efficient atmosphere is established by the teacher. Asking an individual in the class to repeat his idea of the assignment not only tests how well he listened but also checks the effectiveness with which the teacher communicated with him.) The teacher may use test items based on reports given orally by others, reject "repeat" comments by members of a class, and occasionally administer oral tests. Oral testing may be time-consuming, but it does provide a crucial listening situation; and the practice that oral testing gives in following directions is important enough to justify its occasional use.

Furthermore, teachers need to be aware of the possible effects of their questions on pupil listening and the subsequent thinking. For example, note the difference between the following two questions asked after an oral reading selection: "How many tickets were sold?" and "When did you get the first hint that the ticket sale was going to be a success?" (For discussion of questioning strategies, see chapter 14, pages 520–521.)

Other ideas for bringing listening forcefully to the attention of pupils include: keeping a record of all listening activities for one day, evaluating class conversation, dramatizing selections presented as listening activities, telling "chain stories," and cooperatively devising rating sheets for listening to the radio and television. Some teachers have found the tape recorder to be effective for developing habits of concentrated attention when presenting certain types of materials (for example, questions of number facts or lists of spelling words). In such motivating situations, individuals are encouraged to practice active listening.

Major instructional approaches

• *Correlated*   Teachers can design a listening curriculum that provides sequential experiences that are integrated within the entire instructional program (social studies, mathematics, science, art, music, physical education, health, and the language arts). The following activities for children are merely suggestions; they can be varied to fit the needs of many ages, the content of the material, and other activities that are a part of the modern curriculum.

Social studies activities:
1. List the conversations heard in the lunchroom that show how people work together.
2. Listen for unknown terms used in a report on pioneer candle-making.

Mathematics activities:
1. Write a paragraph on how numbers are used in the radio and television commercials.
2. Listen for mathematical terms used by persons in everyday conversations.

Science activities:
1. Listen to directions for making a paper pinwheel to be used for testing the wind direction.
2. Make a daily chart of conversations or sounds heard during the day.

Art and music activities:
1. Use pastels for drawing scenes of listening at home.
2. Match the sound with its musical instrument (from the recording *Instruments of the Orchestra*).

Physical education activities:
1. Listen to recorded directions for performing a folk dance.

2. Take turns giving and listening to directions for playing new games.

Health activities:

1. Listen to oral reports on the care of the body.
2. Listen to a film on a child's daily diet and then write a short paragraph on it.

Language arts activities:

Speaking:

1. Listen to poems and repeat them.
2. Listen to tapes that have good, average, and poor speaking skills recorded on them.
3. Tape oral reports and then listen for ideas for improvement.

Reading:

1. Listen to another child read a short tall tale.
2. Listen to recordings of several children's stories.
3. Listen to good oral reading and poor oral reading techniques and then analyze the differences.

Writing:

1. Listen and record a dictated paragraph.
2. Listen and write the sounds heard.
3. Write a paragraph describing a musical selection.

Spelling:

1. Listen to spelling tapes and write each word.
2. Listen to spelling "rules" and write an example for each "rule."
3. Pair off and listen to each other spell words orally.

Composing:

1. Listen to part of a story and then compose a new ending.
2. Listen to a record of sounds of the city and then compose a short story.
3. Listen to a conversation at the dinner table and then compose a paragraph on "Dinner at Home."

• *Interrelated*   The teaching of listening is often interwoven with the teaching of other language arts skills. Teachers must look for and take advantage of these teaching opportunities that are incorporated into the teaching suggestions found in many textbooks. The following example illustrates the teaching of listening, choral reading, choral speaking, language analysis, and personal writing.[13]

---

13. Adapted from Leland B. Jacobs, "Good Night, Mr. Beetle," *Sounds of Home*, Bill Martin, Jr. (New York: Holt, Rinehart and Winston, 1966), pp. 48–61, copyright 1966. Reprinted by permission of Holt, Rinehart and Winston, Inc.

GOOD NIGHT, MR. BEETLE
by Leland B. Jacobs

Good night, Mr. Beetle,
Good night, Mr. Fly,
Good night, Mrs. Ladybug,
The moon's in the sky.

Good night, Mr. Rooster,
Good night, Mrs. Sheep,
Good night, Mr. Horse,
We must all go to sleep.

Good night, Miss Kitten,
Good night, Mr. Pup,
I'll see you in the morning
When the sun comes up.

The learning sequence for this poem is accomplished through:

1. Exploring meanings (noting rhyming words)
2. Transforming sentences (for example, changing the fourth line of the first quatrain to "I'll see you by and by")
3. Analyzing language (using word-unlocking skills in restudy of the individual words and lines)
4. Responding with writing (writing their own poem by using the structure of the poem as a model)

Listening is involved as the poem is read by the teacher. Later, after being able to read the poem on their own with ease and fluency, the pupils may read the poem in choral fashion.

• **Separated**   A formal listening lesson might consist of material to be read to a small group, followed by a set of written questions. The material could be from some other content area—science or social studies, for example. It should be material at a higher level than the group normally reads since there is generally a discrepancy in favor of listening over reading. For most effective listening instruction, the teacher should consider forming homogeneous groups on the basis of listening ability and presenting appropriate level lessons to the different groups. (See the section on "Evaluation of Listening

Performance" for tests available to determine listening levels, page 124.)

At the present time, there is a shortage of instructional materials for use with differing listening achievement levels within a class, yet it is obvious that the child with superior listening achievement is especially in need of challenging material. There is also a need for interesting material that fits the needs of the child with lower listening achievement. If homogeneous grouping is to be of value, materials designed to take advantage of the potential of such groups are very much needed. The following is an example of this kind of material.

Worksheet: Choose Your Work for Today (Part A or Part B)

Listening: Look for main ideas and supporting ideas. Helpful techniques: note-taking during listening and outlining after listening.

Part A: Materials: Short, prerecorded, informative selection from social studies, science, or other content subject.
Directions: Listen for the main idea and important details; then answer the questions that follow.

1. What would be a good title for the selection?
2. What are two supporting ideas given for the main topic of the selection?
3. What would be a good, one-sentence summary of the selection? Listen again to the selection. Make notes only on ideas that tell about the subject. Number your notes 1, 2, 3, etc.
4. Which of your notes help you check your answers to questions 1, 2, 3, etc.?
5. What would you write for this outline form?
    Title of the selection
        Topic sentence
            A supporting idea
            Another supporting idea
6. Which, if any, of your notes stated the main topic of the selection and some supporting ideas?
7. What should you remember to do in writing a topic sentence in an outline? The supporting ideas?
8. Use your notes and outline to write a paragraph about the selection.

Part B: Materials: Longer, informative selection from social studies, science, or other content subject (read by the teacher or an aide).

Directions: Listen to the entire selection. Make notes as you listen that answer the following questions: "Who?" "What?" "When?" "Where?" "Why?" "How?" "For what reason?" or "In what way?" Then do the exercises below.

1. How can note-taking help you to be a better listener?
2. Complete this outline; repeat the pattern as often as necessary.

> Title of the selection
> I. First main topic
>   A. First subtopic
>   1. First detail
>   2. Second detail

3. How can making an outline help you to listen to a selection?
4. What part do main topics play in a selection? Subtopics? Details?
5. What are some things you can do to find out what the main topics in a selection are? How can you find out whether your choices of ideas for the main topics are correct?
6. What are some things you can do to find out what the subtopics in a selection are? How can you find out whether your choices of ideas for the subtopics are correct?
7. Be prepared to give an oral report from your outline about the selection to which you listened.

Part A materials are devoted to exercises for practice in detecting main and subordinate ideas in a listening situation. Part B materials are concerned with exercises for expanding note-taking and outlining techniques as a way of indexing an oral message. Some teachers may wish to utilize A and B as a single teaching unit; others may want to adjust their uses to the needs of the particular class.

One intermediate-level teacher began the lesson of the preceding materials with the following remarks: "Your experiences with the informal test on listening last week and the listening lessons this week indicate that some of you would enjoy working with more difficult material. All of you look at part B and see whether you want to try these exercises."

(Often a weakness of grouping is the undesirable attitude created by the teacher's selection of a group. In an effort to overcome or to minimize the undesirable attitude that may result from such selections, some teachers permit pupils to choose the group in which they want to participate. This works well when the difficulty of materials between part A and part B is readily apparent. One way to convince a pupil that he should work with the less difficult material is to have him check his ability by explaining one of the more difficult exercises to his classmates. Of course, the teacher will attempt to guide the choice of appropriate material through conferences and explanations during discussion periods. The authors consider it important that an individual select his own set of exercises. A great part of the value of such materials rests on the teacher's willingness to permit pupils to make their own choices when such study is undertaken.)

"I am going to work particularly closely with those interested in the materials presented in part A. If you had some difficulty as we worked with our listening materials this past couple of weeks, you will probably want to do the exercises in part A. Part A will help you become more sure of your grasp of the main ideas and important details in a selection. Those of you who wish to do the work in part A may begin your work now in the front of the room with the tape recorder. Work individually at first, but after completing three or four exercises, you may want to compare your answers with others or check with me.

"If you choose to work with the exercises in part B, you will find the answers to the exercises posted on the bulletin board. You may consult them when you finish. If you find that some of your answers do not agree with the posted answer, try to check yourself and then confer with others who have tried it."

As the pupils began to do the exercises after listening to the selections, the teacher went about the room offering encouragement and assistance to those working on part A. The others worked independently during the class period. The entire class engaged in a brief discussion during the concluding part of the period, when a few specific exercises from parts A and B were discussed.

Planned lessons of a similar nature, utilizing oral presentation of material, should center upon specific skills of listening. They should include the use of various media: films, recordings, radio, tapes, television, etc. They should also include various types of listening activities: listening to a speaker; listening to a conversation; listening to several speakers in a discussion session or a panel presentation; listening to groups involved in reporting, storytelling, creative drama, and choral reading or speaking. Note-taking during appropriate

LESSON PLAN: Listening (Main Ideas)

Performance Objective:

Read a short, informational paragraph; then have the learner state the main idea.

Pretest:

Select a short, informational paragraph appropriate to the listening level of the learner. Read it aloud carefully to the learner. Then ask, "Can you tell me what this paragraph is about *in one word?*" This sets the task for the learner. Next say, "Can you tell me what this paragraph is about using *less than six words?*" (Six is an arbitrary number to limit the learner to the main idea.) Criterion for mastery is your judgment regarding how well he has grasped the main idea.

Teaching Suggestion:

Select a well-written, informational paragraph. In such a paragraph, the first sentence is often the topic sentence. Number all the details and write them in short phrases on the chalkboard; then direct the learner to study each phrase and make his own sentence that expresses the main idea of the details.

Mastery or Posttest Suggestions:

1. Ask the pupils to listen to a paragraph for the main idea and, if desired, the supporting details. A form such as this one could be provided for the learner's response.

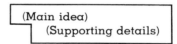

(Main idea)
(Supporting details)

2. The suggestions provided for the pretest may be adapted to the posttest.

Reteaching Suggestions:

1. The main idea can be taught in narration or story writing. Here you have the learner listen to a story and create a good title. If carefully thought out, this title will be the main idea or point of the story.

2. Outlining is an aid to teaching the main idea of an informational selection. Even as early as second grade, your learners can be told, "There are three important ideas in this listening lesson. See if you can hear them as I read the selection to you." Later, you can put them on the chalkboard and discuss how each learner determined what an important idea was.

listening situations as well as outlining afterwards may receive instructional attention.

Systematic lesson plans may be required for some children or for an individual learner, as suggested on page 114.

• *Listening learning center*   The learning center approach is an excellent way to individualize part of the listening program, particularly the skills aspects, through providing for differences in ability, learning rate, mode of learning, and interest.

The teacher goes through certain steps when planning to use a learning center. He must:

1. identify the content area.
2. pretest to diagnose strengths and weaknesses of pupils in the area.
3. determine the skills or learnings to be treated at the center.
4. establish the sequence of tasks from easiest to most difficult.
5. identify different kinds of instructional materials to use and devise varied ways to present these in tasks of graduated difficulty.
6. posttest to evaluate each major segment of the center.

Three kinds of listening could be a part of the center—informational, appreciative, and critical. The teacher will evaluate the children's listening through such devices as standardized tests, informal checklists, or recorded tapes that are representative samples of skills to be presented through the listening center. Use could be made of commercially available material where appropriate, teacher-developed materials, radios, tape recorders (with jacks and headsets) and tapes, record players (also with jacks and headsets) and records, or perhaps closed-circuit TV with earphones. Many other kinds of materials could be a part of the learning center. (See the section later in this chapter, pages 119–121, on special instructional aids and materials for teaching listening.) Some activities would be for individuals, others for pairs or a group of peers.

Following are examples of tasks and materials that might be a part of a primary-level listening center focusing upon listening awareness. Each task needs to be preceded and followed by many other similar tasks in order to assure mastery. And, of course, the teacher evaluates and revises the center tasks as they are used by the children.

SKILL: LISTENING AWARENESS	TASKS	MATERIALS NEEDED
sounds heard in nature	Record sounds in immediate environment.	a quiet place outside, paper and pencil
	Identify sounds made by common farm and other animals.	commercial record, check-list, book: *Gobble, Growl, Grunt* by Spier, paper and pencil
	Make animal sounds for a partner to guess.	quiet area, set of animal pictures for response by partner
	Recognize bird calls.	record of bird calls, time outdoors where birds might be observed and heard, a short list of local birds to check
sounds made by machines	Detect danger signals.	tape of fire siren, screeching car brakes, police whistle, etc.; checklist
	Identify sounds of common machines.	tape of car motor, tractor, telephone ring, etc.; list of machines to number order of sounds on the tape (Or use paper and pencil to record sounds of machines heard on a television or radio program.)
	Describe sounds made by machines.	tape of machine sounds and list of words to choose from for each sound
sounds made by humans	Recognize voices of class-mates.	blank tapes to record class members, time to present tape to a small group
	Differentiate ages of speakers.	tapes of speakers of different ages, pictures to paste by each number after listening
	Identify emotional state of the speaker.	tapes of people to illustrate sorrow, joy, fear, etc.

Some examples of tasks and materials to be used in a listening center focusing upon informational, appreciative, and critical listening skills are listed below; these tasks and materials are appropriate for the middle-school level.

SKILLS	TASKS	MATERIALS NEEDED
detail	Find answers to specific questions.	tapes of graded difficulty, questions to answer
sequence	Establish sequence.	set of sequential pictures to arrange according to a taped story
directions	Construct according to directions.	arts and crafts materials, set of directions to be read aloud by a peer
rhyme and rhythm	Mark stress in a sonnet.	poetry record, copy of poem to mark stressed and unstressed syllables
images	Illustrate or describe the "picture" communicated.	lyric poem read aloud by a peer
moods	Contrast poems written with differing moods.	poetry tape, crayons, finger paint, paper
bias/prejudice	Compare reports of same incident.	teacher-made tape from two newspaper accounts
validity of information	Analyze advertisements on television.	television, list of "band-wagon" techniques
fact/opinion	Detect clues for opinions.	television documentary, identify clues to "opinions"

LISTENING AND VIEWING

Mass media may be defined as those instruments of communication that can convey identical messages to large numbers of persons who are often physically separated. Two such media, television and motion pictures, involve both listening and viewing (radio involves

Viewing and listening
to television have possi-
bilities for enriching
concepts and vocabulary
—if supported by
appropriate teaching-
learning activities.

only listening) and introduce children to many experiences, ideas, and concepts. Evidence shows that by age twelve the average child watches television twenty-five hours a week.[14] Research data also confirm the theory that television can be used effectively to develop listening skills.[15]

The teacher should keep himself informed about the content and nature of films and of television and radio programs that many children hear and see. The teacher can help gain the confidence of pupils when he is able to discuss films and programs with them. Occasional sharing and discussion of favorites may help to improve children's tastes and stimulate them to view and listen to some of the more constructive fare for their age group. A positive approach to

---

14. "Video Boy," *Time* 91 (January 26, 1968): 54–55.

15. Lois Virginia Edinger, "The Effectiveness of Television Teaching in Developing Pupil Skills of Listening, Comprehension, and Critical Thinking," Ph.D. diss. (University of North Carolina at Chapel Hill, 1964), 157 pp., *Dissertation Abstracts* 26(3) (September 1965): 1509; C. O. Neidt, "Use of Videotaped Instructional Television for Teaching Study Skills in a University Setting," *Audio-Visual Communication Review* 15 (Fall 1967): 269–284; Boyd Andra Purdom, "An Analysis of Listening Skill Development Using the Midwest Program on Airborne Television Instruction," Ph.D. diss. (Nashville, Tenn.: George Peabody College for Teachers, 1968), 148 pp., *Dissertation Abstracts* 29 (March 1969): 3046A–3047A.

encourage independent and critical judgment may be made through such cooperative teacher-pupil activities as:

1. Calling attention to programs of quality
2. Formulating standards of selection dealing with purpose, consistency, presentation, and effects of particular productions
3. Discussing, evaluating, and analyzing programs
4. Analyzing radio, television, and film advertising—its description, appeal, truth, and slogans
5. Reading and writing reviews of radio and television programs and motion pictures
6. Comparing film and television productions with the books on which they are based
7. Displaying books related to film and radio and television programs
8. Preparing an advance list for parents of good children's programs

SPECIAL INSTRUCTIONAL MATERIALS AND ACTIVITIES FOR TEACHING LISTENING

As previously suggested, a listening center provides many opportunities for listening instruction. A listening center can combine listening with reading when children use earphones to hear a story while they follow the words in a book. An example of this would be the materials by Anderson and others, which present recordings of poetry, short stories, dramatizations, and choral reading for use in developing appreciation and better listening skills.[16] Commercial radio and television provide educational fare, and many stations print schedules far enough in advance so that those programs of educational value can be announced by the teacher. Educational television is available for school and home viewing. Other varieties of listening activities may be found in the teacher's manual of several modern basal readers.[17] The Science Research Associates' *Reading Laboratory* includes a number of listening-skill exercises: material is provided for reading aloud by the teacher, followed by discussion questions and comprehension checks.[18] Of course, some

---

16. Lorena Anderson et al., *Listening and Reading Tapes* (Huntington, N.Y.: Educational Developmental Laboratories, 1963).

17. For example, Paul McKee, *Reading for Meaning* (Boston: Houghton Mifflin, 1962).

18. *Reading Laboratory* (Chicago: Science Research Associates, 1959).

A listening learning
center provides an
opportunity for children
to learn at their own
rate and level of
maturity.

language textbooks for children include specific lessons for the development of listening. Examination of these or similar sources will provide numerous examples and suggestions for the reader.

Filmstrips
How to Listen. Chicago: Society for Visual Education.
Listen Well, Learn Well. Chicago: Coronet Films.

Literature Records
Hans Christian Anderson Fairy Tales, Just So Stories, Old Possum's Book of Practical Cats, You Know Who. Chicago: Encyclopaedia Britannica.

Multi-level Programs
Listen-Think Tapes. Huntington, N.Y.: Educational Development Laboratories, 1969.
Listen and Do. Boston: Houghton Mifflin, 1963.
Listening and Learning. Boston: Houghton Mifflin, 1969.
Listening Skills Program. Chicago: Science Research Associates, 1969.

Records
The Downtown Story, The Sounds of Camp, Sounds of My City, Sounds of Animals, Sounds of Insects, and *Sounds of the Satellites.* New York: Folkways/Scholastic Records.

Literature Tapes
Stories are Fun, Open the Door, Land of Make Believe. Washington, D.C.: National Tape Recording Repository.

Films
The Loon's Necklace; The Bear and the Hunter; Adventures of a Baby Fox; Morning Star; Gray Gull, the Hunter; Korochan, the Little Bear. Chicago: Encyclopaedia Britannica.

Trade Books
Borton, Helen. *Do You Hear What I Hear?* New York: Abelard, 1963.
Brown, Margaret W. *The Noisy Book—City.* New York: Harper & Brothers, 1939.
Carlson, Bernice W. *Listen! And Help The Story.* Nashville, Tenn.: Abingdon, 1965.
Reid, Alastair. *Ounce, Dice, Trice.* Boston: Little, 1958.
Showers, Paul. *Listening Walk.* New York: Thomas Y. Crowell, 1961.

Teacher References
Russell, David, and Russell, Elizabeth. *Listening Aids Through the Grades.* New York: Teachers College Press, Columbia University, 1959.
Wagner, Guy. *Listening Games.* Darien, Conn.: Teachers Publishing Corp., 1962.

From such resources, the interested teacher will find many valuable suggestions for listening activities. Other general suggestions for the primary- and middle-school levels are provided below.

Primary

1. Sound stories: Here the pupil listens to the story in order to make a sound on cue and to produce the desired effect (example story: *Gerald McBoingboing*).
2. Sound box: Listening activities are conducted utilizing the objects in the box (e.g., glass, cellophane, coins, etc.).

3. Sequence stories: Each child is given a picture and retells his portion of the story in proper sequence.
4. Picture books: Children can prepare their own books—one page for sounds at home (pictured or illustrated), another for sounds at school, etc.
5. Records: Listen to records (e.g., *I Went For a Walk in the Forest*, Young People's Record), which can be dramatized through close listening.
6. Oral arithmetic: For example, "Take ten, add seven, subtract three, divide by two. Where are you?"
7. Games: For example, "Simon Says," "Do as I Say" (directions to be followed), or "Airplane Fly"
8. Paper and pencil exercises: Use graph paper and follow a series of oral directions; the results are a design or a picture.

Intermediate

1. Road maps: Children follow oral directions. For example, "From Fernville, travel south on Route 77 to U.S. 12, then east to the intersection with State Route 133. What town is located there?"
2. Role Play: This might be a telephone message for an intended receiver. Ask the children to write down the message they would leave for the person.
3. Phrases: Prepare sheets of papers with such headings as: *Who*, *What*, *When*, *Where*, *Why*, and *How*. Read a selection that lends itself to this sort of categorizing. Pupils write phrases under the appropriate headings.
4. Sound words: Pupils collect onomatopoeic words (e.g., *hum*, *whistle*, *chirp*, *groan*, *honk*, *tinkle*, *bark*, *buzz*, etc.).
5. Directions and numbers: A wide variety of exercises are possible in this activity—from simple to complex. For example, "Listen to this series of numbers and write the third one: 5, 9, 4, 2, 7." Variation: use letters, as *q, w, t, e, h.*
6. Spell-a-Word: Children listen for the first letter of each word in a sentence and then combine the letters to spell a word. For example, Cindy lost a small shoe: *class.* A variation would be to use the last letter of a set of words to spell a word. For example, Hit a small tack: *talk.*

7. Reverse order: Read groups of letters and ask pupils to write them in reverse order. For example, *mlif* $\longrightarrow$ *film*. Variation: use numerals, as *51092* $\longrightarrow$ *29015*.

8. Noun game: A child begins with a noun, such as *rug*. The next child must say a noun beginning with the last letter of the previous word, such as *goat*. The next child says *toad*, and so on.

Some words are related to sound—and sensory words provide an excellent starting point in the word-building program.

EVALUATION OF LISTENING PERFORMANCE

Evaluating listening skills should be done by both teachers and children. First, a teacher must be a good listener himself and therefore provide a good model for the children. Secondly, children must be consciously aware of what makes a good listener and therefore be able to evaluate their own listening ability.

The teacher wears two hats—one as an evaluator of his own methods of teaching listening and one as an evaluator of children's listening skills.

The teacher

• *Self-evaluator*   Experienced elementary school teachers have been teaching listening for a long time, whether it was called that specifically or not. They have asked themselves:

> Do I provide an emotional and physical classroom environment that encourages good listening?
> Am I a good listener and do I listen to my students?
> Do I use proper tone, pitch, volume, and speed in presenting my own experiences (films, discussions, debates, reports), which are of interest to the children?
> Am I aware of opportunities for teaching listening throughout the day?
> Do I establish the purpose for which the children should listen in each activity?
> Do I help them realize the importance and value of being good listeners?
> Do I build a program in which listening skills are consistently taught and practiced?

• *Evaluator of children's skills*   Early in the school year, the teacher might evaluate the listening skills of the children by asking the following questions:

> How well do the children follow directions?
> How often must I repeat instructions?
> Do the children's responses reveal comprehension through listening?

Are the children accurate in giving recall information and description after a listening experience?

Is there appropriate questioning of content, new words, and concepts?

Are the children listening actively rather than passively?[19]

Good teachers, whether they are beginners or have many years of experience, realize the importance of skillful listening for more effective learning, but find it difficult to check the effectiveness of their efforts.

One method of checking the effectiveness of the teaching of listening skills is a standardized test. The *Durrell Listening-Reading Series* test attempts to answer such questions as the following:

Which children are limited in reading achievement because of lack of understanding of the spoken language?

How far above reading level is each child's listening comprehension?

Among those who are candidates for remedial instruction, which have the highest learning potential?[20]

The primary-level test (for grades 1–2) is divided into four sections: vocabulary listening, vocabulary reading, sentence listening, and sentence reading. The intermediate-level test (for grades 3–6) covers vocabulary listening, vocabulary reading, paragraph listening, and paragraph reading.

This test series, or a similar one,[21] can be helpful to teachers by providing more solid evidence than a "mere visceral feeling" about how well pupils are developing in this very significant area of the language arts. In addition, astute observation by the teacher during daily activities and occasional teacher-made listening tests is an important part of the evaluation program.

The child

Children can evaluate their own listening skills by using informal checklists such as the one that follows.

---

19. Muriel Farrell and Shirley H. Flint, "Are They Listening?" *Childhood Education* 43 (May 1967): 528–529.

20. *Durrell Listening-Reading Series* (New York: Harcourt, Brace and World, 1969).

21. Sequential Test of Educational Progress, *Listening* (Princeton, N.J.: Educational Testing Service, Cooperative Test Division, 1957). Also the *Cooperative Primary Test*, 1967, contains a listening section (same publisher). The 1973 *Stanford Achievement Tests* (New York: Harcourt Brace Jovanovich) contain a listening test for primary and intermediate levels.

Checking-up on My Listening

	Yes	No
1. Did I remember to get ready for listening?	___	___
a. Was I seated comfortably where I could see and hear?	___	___
b. Were my eyes focused on the speaker?	___	___
2. Was my mind ready to concentrate on what the speaker had to say?	___	___
a. Was I able to push other thoughts out of my mind for the time being?	___	___
b. Was I ready to think about the topic and call to mind the things I already know about it?	___	___
3. Was I ready for "takeoff"?	___	___
a. Did I discover in the first few minutes where the speaker was taking me?	___	___
b. Did I discover his central idea so that I could follow it through the speech?	___	___
4. Was I able to pick out the ideas that supported the main idea?	___	___
a. Did I take advantage of the speaker's clues (such as *first, next,* etc.) to help organize the ideas in my mind?	___	___
b. Did I use my extra "think" time to summarize and take notes, either mentally or on paper?	___	___
5. After the speaker finished and the facts were all in, did I evaluate what had been said?	___	___
a. Did this new knowledge seem to fit with the knowledge I already had?	___	___
b. Did I weigh each idea to see if I agreed with the speaker?	___	___

If you marked questions NO, decide why you could not honestly answer them YES.

Source: O. W. Kopp, "The Evaluation of Oral Language Activities: Teaching and Learning," *Elementary English* 44 (February 1967): 117. Reprinted by permission of the National Council of Teachers of English.

SELECTED REFERENCES

General Professional

Anderson, Paul S. *Language Skills in Elementary Education.* 2d ed. New York: Macmillan, 1972, chapter 2.

Boyd, Gertrude. *Teaching Communication Skills in the Elementary School.* New York: Van Nostrand Reinhold, 1970, chapter 6.

Corcoron, Gertrude B. *Language Arts in Elementary School.* New York: Ronald, 1970, chapter 5.

Greene, Harry A., and Petty, Walter T. *Developing Language Skills in Elementary Schools.* 4th ed. Boston: Allyn and Bacon, 1971, chapter 6.

Lamb, Pose. *Guiding Children's Language Learning.* 2d ed. Dubuque, Iowa: William C. Brown, 1971, chapter 5.

Smith, James A. *Adventures in Communication: Language Arts Methods.* Boston: Allyn and Bacon, 1972, chapter 5.

Strickland, Ruth. *The Language Arts in Elementary School.* 3rd ed. Lexington, Mass.: D. C. Heath, 1969, chapter 6.

Specialized

Cayer, Roger L., et al. *Listening and Speaking in English Classrooms.* New York: Macmillan, 1971.

Duker, Sam. *Teaching Listening in Elementary School.* New York: Scarecrow Press, 1971.

Harris, Mary Imogene. *A Handbook of Speaking and Listening Activities for Elementary School.* Minneapolis: T. S. Denison, 1971.

ORAL COMPOSITION

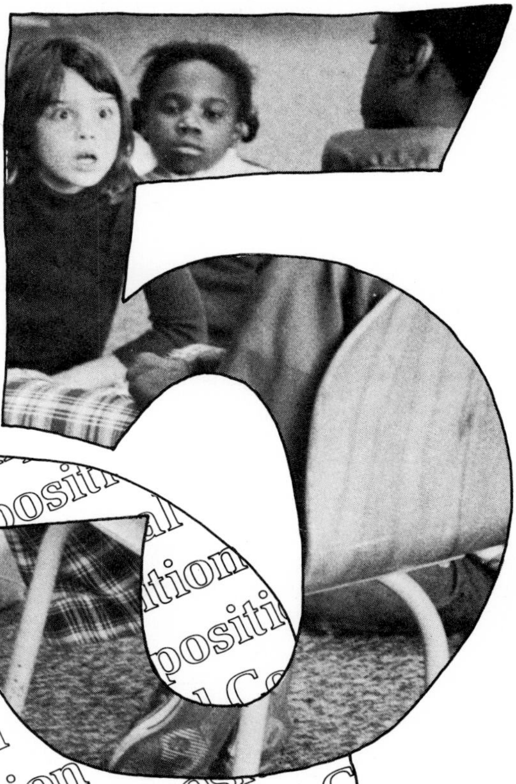

5 Oral Composition

OBJECTIVES	PERFORMANCE RESPONSES
1. **To relate oral expression with other curricular areas**	1. Write a short review of one of the research projects on oral composition and other curricular areas. (See footnote 1.)
2. **To identify several teaching strategies for conversation**	2. Cite (with reasons) what you consider the best procedures for teaching conversation, including evaluative techniques.
3. **To experiment with topics for discussion**	3. Try a few of the "What would you do if . . . ." situations with a small group of primary or intermediate level children. In doing so, use one of Possien's discussion experiences.
4. **To utilize storytelling as an oral language experience**	4. a. Use one of the techniques proposed in the chapter to tell a story to a small group of children or peers. Use a flannel board or overhead projectuals, if appropriate. b. Use a "wordless (textless) book" with a child. Tape his story and share with the class.
5. **To gain insight into the drama process**	5. Use one of the components of drama with a small group of children or peers.
6. **To apply choral reading/speaking skills**	6. Present one type of choral reading/speaking to a small group of children or peers.
7. **To illustrate instructional procedures for other oral expression experiences**	7. Prepare a systematic lesson for one of the experiences (such as a movie or television review). See an example of such a systematic lesson plan for "announcements" in chapter 1.
8. **To delineate regional and social differences in oral speech**	8. a. Give an oral report on speech characteristics of people in your area of the country. b. Visit a low-income area school and a middle- or high-income area school. Tape some classroom conversation/discussion. Compare the speech with characteristics provided in this chapter. Design a "second language" outline for one nonstandard feature.

9. **To examine methods of evaluating oral composition skills**

9. Prepare a checklist for one of the oral language experiences where guidelines are *not* provided in this chapter.

Throughout the school years, children have many opportunities for oral expression: they are asked to give clear explanations of arithmetic problems, to relate personal experiences, to explain carefully different points in social studies, to participate in planning periods, to discuss problems that arise on the playground, to report on books they have enjoyed, to play roles in class plays, to discuss and plan art work. Even so, in spite of the numerous opportunities that are available for helping children in this area, a large percentage of them, even at the end of the elementary school years, show ineptness and reluctance in participating in speaking situations. With effective instruction in such activities, however, most will develop considerable ability in oral communication—provided teachers use these valuable speaking situations to stimulate fullness of oral expression.

CORRELATING ORAL COMPOSITION WITH OTHER CURRICULAR AREAS

The teacher has the responsibility throughout the school day of helping children speak clearly, expressively, and effectively in situations where speech is required. The teacher should seize all opportunities for oral language teaching that arise. Instruction is effective only to the extent that the learnings are applied on all speaking occasions.

Teachers need to design an oral language program that provides sequential experiences correlated with the entire instructional program (social studies, mathematics, science, art, music, physical education, health, and other language arts). The following activities planned for children can be varied to meet the needs of many ages in the elementary school.

Social studies activities:
1. Tape social studies reports.
2. Give oral directions for driving to the nearest city.
Mathematics activities:
1. Create oral mathematical puzzles.

2. Work in groups of four, each taking turns asking mathematical questions.

Science activities:

1. Give oral descriptions of the natural phenomena in the school yard.
2. Present monthly, weekly, and daily weather reports.

Art activities:

1. Explain how a papier-maché animal is formed.
2. Give directions for an art activity.

Music activities:

1. Present oral reports on composers.
2. Discuss various styles of music, such as folk, classical, jazz, and popular.

Physical education activities:

1. Give directions for a new game.
2. Direct physical exercises.

Health activities:

1. Prepare and present a panel discussion on the care of the body.
2. Tape short discussions on daily diet needs, mental health, and hygiene.

Other language activities:

1. Listen to oral reports in instructional areas other than language arts.
2. Write a book report to be read orally.
3. Read a poem aloud.
4. Compose an original story and read it to the class.

Remedial oral language development with pupils has been shown to be highly successful when the substantive ideas of the communication have been chosen from direct-experience and content areas such as science, mathematics, or literature.[1]

---

1. American Institute for Research in the Behavioral Sciences, "Early Childhood Project, New York City; One of a Series of Successful Compensatory Education," *It Works, Preschool Program in Compensatory Education* (Stanford, Calif.: American Institute for Research in the Behavioral Sciences, 1969); Richard D. Arnold, *San Antonio Language Research Project, 1965–66 (Year Two) Findings* (Austin: University of Texas, Research and Development Center for Teacher Education, 1968); J. Ayers and G. Mason, "Differential Effects of Science—A Process Approach Upon Change in Metropolitan Readiness Test Scores Among Kindergarten Children," *Reading Teacher* 5 (1969): 435–439; Rose C. Engel et al., *Language Development Experiences for Young Children* (Los Angeles: University of California, 1966); Robert L. Fichtenau, *Teaching Rhetorical Concepts to Elementary Children, A Research Report* (Pontiac, Mich.: Oakland Schools, 1968); Marlene Glaus, *From Thoughts to Words* (Urbana, Ill.: National Council of Teachers of English, 1965); Mabel W. Henry, ed., *Creative Experiences in Oral Language* (Urbana, Ill.: National Council of Teachers of English, 1967); Freeman McConnell, "Research Findings From a Language and Sensory-Perceptual Training Program" (paper delivered at a meeting of the Council for Exceptional Children, Denver, April 1969).

ORAL EXPERIENCES

Major oral language experiences include conversation, discussion, reporting, storytelling, and creative drama.

Conversation

Conversation can be defined as informal talk on a topic of common interest. It is a social-promoting activity that enables everyone to develop tact, friendliness, sincerity, and interest in others.

The purpose of conversation during the school day is the communication of ideas. Children should be encouraged to talk freely to one another as they play and work together in planning, constructing, and evaluating. Teachers must provide frequent opportunities for conversation during the school day so that every child will be able to use the language skills required for developing the ability to present ideas in a logical order, to fit the conversation to the occasion, and to change the topic of conversation at the appropriate time.

• *Stimuli and procedures*   Often pupils will need help in starting a conversation. To aid children in developing a topic for conversation, suggesting the following topics may prove helpful.

Experiences: a hobby, a garden, a stamp collection, building model airplanes, caring for and raising animals, trips, vacations, field trips

Items: a story; a picture; a movie; a radio program; newspaper and magazine articles; a poem; objects (apples, skates, gloves, etc.); recordings; drawings; tapes

Situations: an assembly speech, classroom speaking, club and activity talk, a conversation between teacher and pupil or pupil and pupil

Several approaches have proved effective in teaching the skills of conversation. One approach is to divide the class into interest groups and let each group converse on topics of special interest to them. A second approach is to divide the class into groups on the basis of number alone (five or six members per group), with the conversation mainly centered on some theme or adventure that is of interest to the entire class. Another possible approach is to have a group of five or six pupils hold a conversation while others listen. All of these procedures provide a far greater opportunity for each child to talk than if the entire class listens to two speakers having a conversation. Also, dividing the class into small groups is helpful to the shy child who may not mind speaking to a few pupils but is not ready to talk in front of the entire class.

Some teachers have found a talk center to be a useful idea. This center provides an area where small groups of children can sit and converse. Here they can share realia brought from home or they may discuss objects that the teacher has placed there in the "mystery bag." Conversations about numerous items can occur: a favorite book, a radio or television program, pictures, articles from newspapers and magazines, etc.

• *Evaluation*   After conversation experiences such as the above, pupils will have a basis for developing criteria for good conversations. In addition, having the pupils develop their own criteria provides a feeling of psychological ownership to the pupils that might be missing if the criteria were made by the teacher or taken from a textbook. (Of course, a textbook may be referred to for ideas that may not have been considered by the class members.) The following list of criteria is an example that might be used for evaluation purposes by the teacher and the children.

CHART 5.1: Conversation Guide

1. Talk in a soft voice.
2. Help others take part. Do not talk all the time. One way to involve others is to ask questions. For example, "I like that television show, too, Mike. What about you, Lucy?" Another way to keep a conversation lively is with remarks such as, "Yes, I know just how you felt."
3. Say "Excuse me" or "Pardon me" when you interrupt someone else.
4. Buttress your opinions with reasons or examples.
5. Listen. Stick to the general theme. Do not introduce totally new topics that have no relevance to foregoing remarks.
6. React tactfully to an opinion with which you disagree. For example, "I hate it" is a poor way to respond to "That television show is really good."
7. When you have not heard what someone has said, say so politely at the proper time and then ask the person to repeat.

The preceding conversation skills should be taught and developed throughout the elementary years. Sensible use of these standards and suggestions will lead to continuous, spiral development of a most important skill.

Discussion

Discussion is more formal in nature than conversation. In conversation one is permitted to move rather freely from one topic or idea to another, while in discussion one must basically remain with the question at hand. Also, discussion requires a flexible daily schedule that will allow it to continue until its purposes have been met.

• *Stimuli and experiences*   Many opportunities for discussion are inherent in the classroom activities. Discussion may be needed on how to best organize the pet show, what the class should do for the book fair, or what should be done about pupils who are racing across lawns in the neighborhood. The subject matter studied in history, geography, and science provides almost endless opportunities for discussion. The suggestions found in language textbooks for selection of topics are usually "second best" as compared with actual classroom situations and should serve primarily for practice ideas when the main purpose of the lesson is to focus attention upon specific discussion skills.

Three major stimuli for discussion are (1) current events, (2) dilemmas or problems, and (3) children's literature. Newstime (discussion of current interesting, important news events; latest scientific developments; political skirmishes; weather conditions; etc.) is an excellent occasion for involving all the members of the class at all levels of the elementary school. Radio and television enable the below-average reader to contribute accurate and important information to such discussions. Pictures in magazines and newspapers also guide the poorer reader in gaining insight into background material on a topic. Usually newstime is held once a week, unless important events occur more often. Some teachers use bulletin boards for displaying materials that the children bring to class to aid them in their news discussion. A weekly newspaper for children is another basis for discussion of a topic or a few related news items. As criteria are being developed for news discussion, the class members may center attention upon how to talk about news, what is reportable news, why current affairs should be discussed, and how to organize news reporting.

Dilemmas or problems are almost sure-fire for discussion purposes and are open-ended for encouraging original thinking. Following are some examples of problem-situations that can be explored by discussion.

> What would you do *if:*
> your pet followed you to school?
> you lost your homework on the way to school?
> you were lost in a store and couldn't find your mother?
> you broke a neighbor's window during a ball game?
> you saw a little boy crying with a cut finger?
> your cat ran away from home?
> you found an injured, young bird?
> you overslept school time?
> you punctured the tire of your bicycle on the way to school?
> you lost the letter your father asked you to mail?

Literary discussions can take place through *round-table* discussions or *panel* discussions (as described below). Several books that lend themselves well to a discussion are *Up a Road Slowly* and *Across Five Aprils* by Irene Hunt, *Onion John* by Joseph Krumgold, and *I'll Get There, But It Had Better Be Worth the Trip* by John Donavan.

Possien describes five varieties of discussion experiences that are worthwhile.

1. A *round-table discussion* involves a small group of from three to eight people, including a moderator. Its purpose may be simply to share ideas or to deal with a particular problem in an informal manner. The moderator must guide the group so as to keep the discussion moving and on the topic. He also helps the group summarize and evaluate results. The moderator, the members of the discussion group, and the audience, if there is one, need to have clear ideas of their responsibilities.

    The entire class may be divided into small groups and each group may simultaneously engage in round-table discussion, or one group may participate while the rest of the class listens as an audience. This is the best procedure to use until the class is thoroughly familiar with round-table discussion.

2. The *panel discussion* is similar to the round-table discussion, but the procedure is somewhat more formal and is more audience-oriented. An audience is always

present for the panel discussion and is usually allowed to ask questions and participate when the discussion between the panel members is over. Panel members have a responsibility to be more than adequately prepared, for each is cast in the role of an authority on the subject.

3. *Buzz groups* constitute another type of discussion group and may be devised by dividing the class into a number of smaller subgroups of five and six members. A specific problem is given for consideration, and a limited amount of time is set for each group to arrive at an answer or a response.

   These groups may get out of hand and result in little more than wasted time unless clearly understood ground rules are laid in advance. The children need to keep their purpose firmly in mind and proceed in accomplishing their purpose with as little noise and confusion as possible.

4. *Brainstorming* is a way of getting a great many ideas from a group on a particular problem and is regarded as being a good means of releasing group creativity. This technique is based on four simple rules which must be followed for good results:

   a. No idea may be criticized, evaluated, or rejected during the brainstorming.
   b. All ideas are acceptable regardless of how improbable they may seem.
   c. Emphasis is placed on quantity of suggestion.
   d. Group members may add to, combine, or improve the ideas of others.

5. *Role-playing* is a form of creative dramatics which is very effective in encouraging children to think and to understand better another person's problem or point of view. Role-playing helps children to explore and develop different ways of solving problems. It is valuable in solving problems concerning human relationships and is very effective in helping children to develop a sense of involvement in problems of history.[2]

---

2. Wilma M. Possein, *They All Need to Talk: Oral Communication in the Language Arts Program* (New York: Meredith Corp., copyright © 1969), pp. 62–64. Reprinted by permission of Appleton-Century-Crofts.

• *Instructional procedures*   The key to a good discussion is the preparation of the participants. To make a worthwhile contribution, the child must have accurate information about the subject, be able to back up his statements with facts, and give sensible reasons for his opinions. Through first-hand experience, reading and listening, asking questions, and sharing with others, pupils become knowledgeable about areas that may be intelligently discussed.

Several approaches are effective in teaching discussion techniques. One procedure is to divide the class into a number of small discussion groups on the basis of topics. Another possible arrangement is to have five or six pupils in turn demonstrate the discussion of a problem or an issue before the other members of the class.

In introducing and conducting a discussion with the entire class relative to a controversial issue, Veatch makes an interesting proposal. The class should divide itself into three groups: the *yes* group, the *no* group, and the group that is *undecided* about the issue. Then three chairs are placed in the front of the room: the *yes* chair, the *no* chair, the *undecided* chair. Each pupil, in turn, sits in the appropriate chair and makes his contribution—first a *yes* pupil, then a *no* pupil, then an *undecided* pupil. He supports his statements and offers good reasons for his opinions when questioned or challenged.[3]

In some discussions, no final or formal decision need be reached —the purpose will have been achieved through the discussion. In others, it is desirable that some conclusion or conclusions be reached by the group. Whenever possible, voting on the issue should be avoided. Voting should be the "court of last resort" when discussion fails to help pupils reach a decision that is satisfactory to all or most of the group. Give-and-take is a part of arriving at decisions through discussion.

While the teacher is cautioned against monopolizing classroom discussions, he may need to assume some direct leadership, especially with primary pupils or with groups of pupils who have had little experience in discussion. He will want to see that all pupils have an opportunity to participate. The teacher's questions or comments can help each child to contribute according to his own special interests and abilities. He may need to guide the discussion to a satisfactory conclusion.

---

3. Jeannette Veatch, "Developing Skills in Various Subject Areas," *Curriculum for Today's Boys and Girls,* ed. Robert Fleming (Columbus, Ohio: Merrill, 1963), pp. 187–188.

• *Evaluation*   The following list of discussion skills can aid the teacher in helping the children develop their own criteria for evaluating a good discussion.

CHART 5.2: Discussion Guide

1. Choose a topic. Develop your own ideas about it.
2. Keep to the topic being discussed.
3. Listen closely to each speaker.
4. Participate in questions and answers during the discussion.
5. Help decide which ideas are the best.
6. Back up opinions with facts or valid reasons.
7. Ask for necessary explanations.
8. Contribute comments that will carry the thinking forward to a decision.
9. Draw reserved members into the discussion.

Sensible use of and reference to the above-mentioned criteria can be made when the teacher and pupils analyze discussion techniques. Additional practice may be afforded class members who need further opportunities to make use of the agreed-upon criteria. The use of the tape recorder—playing back a recording of a discussion or playing an earlier discussion with a more recent one—can help in dramatizing needs or noting improvements.

(Note: Questioning skills of both teacher and child are important in all aspects of oral expression. Discussion lends itself particularly well to practice and study of questioning skills. For classifications and examples of kinds of questions, see the section on "Comprehension" in chapter 14, pages 519–521.)

Oral reports

In every classroom there are many opportunities for sharing information, and quite often this sharing is done through oral reports.[4] It is not necessary for the teacher to assign reports on topics unrelated to classroom work (e.g., topics from a list in a language text) in order to give the necessary practice in reporting; he merely needs to take advantage of natural classroom situations where reporting is indicated. These situations include:

4. Lucille Millsap, "Oral Reporting," *Elementary English* 42 (February 1965): 197–200.

describing a recent event.

discussing ideas of other persons discovered in reading, listening to the radio, or watching television.

explaining procedures for constructing an object for a school or personal project.

giving directions for games or exercises.

With guidance from the teacher during these situations, pupils learn a variety of ways of reporting. The sharing of information should have a definite purpose that is clearly understood by the child who is giving the report. The purpose helps to determine the form the report will take.

A sequence of steps is involved in preparing an oral report: (1) taking notes, (2) using reference sources, (3) preparing bibliographies, (4) organizing ideas, and (5) making an outline. These skills are discussed in chapter 7, "Written Composition," under the topic of "Reports"—and the functional role of oral reporting is integrated into the discussion at that point.

Storytelling

Storytelling is an often-neglected art, but one which can be learned by persistent and patient effort. Teachers and children who master this art will find that the rewards are worth the effort required. Suggestions for effective storytelling by the teacher and the child are discussed in turn.

• *Teacher*   Storytelling by the teacher should provide the children with a good model of use of voice, pacing, choice and pronunciation of words, and ways of beginning and ending. Teacher-storytelling acquaints the children with literature and provides for good listening experiences.

One stimulating storyteller offers the following suggestions to beginning storytellers:

1. The story you tell must belong to you; you must like it. You must enjoy it. You must want to tell it.
2. You must know the story so well that it is a part of you. There can be no possibility of forgetting.
3. You will use all the heritage that is yours for the taking and all the individual, rich background you have built for yourself.
4. You will tell the story simply, directly, sincerely, with freedom and ease and good use of your body.

5. You will trust the medium you use—words.
6. You will develop the instrument you use—your voice—so that it has correct pitch, good timbre, and appropriate strength.
7. You will pace your telling skillfully, changing the tempo as needed and using pauses effectively.
8. You will have good rapport with your listeners so that you can create with them a living experience.[5]

The storyteller should select a story that really appeals to him—not just one that happens to be recommended or that is a "classic." He should not attempt to memorize every word of the story (and thus become more conscious of the words than the story), but he should be mindful of the story's original vocabulary and phraseology.

What stories will the teacher choose? Selection may be influenced by the personal preferences of the storyteller or by the purpose for which the story is intended. The purpose of a story could be: to increase knowledge; to impart ethical values; to entertain; to develop growth in understanding of the spoken word; to develop a sense of humor; to broaden reading interests; or to develop appreciation of myths, legends, fables, parables, folktales, etc. Folktales are especially good for telling, for they were told and told and told again long before they were ever captured in print. Myths, stories from the Bible, stories from such authors as Andersen and Kipling, even episodes from longer books may be adapted for telling. If the storyteller enjoys the telling, the audience will usually enjoy the listening.

As a general rule, picture stories should usually be read from the actual book since the illustrations are to be shared as well as the story; some memorization will be necessary to enable the reader to keep eye-contact with the listeners. Stories that depend upon the exact wording of the author should be read rather than told. These include stories like *Just So Stories*;[6] however, teachers who have a facility for memorizing should not hesitate to add these and similar stories to their repertoire.

After choosing a story with action, a closely knit plot, and lots of dialogue (and perhaps humor that fits the age level), attention and thought should be given to the story's characters (there should be no more than four) and ways of developing them so that they come to life. A sequence of steps is suggested by the guidelines below.

---

5. Ruth Tooze, *Storytelling* (Englewood Cliffs, N.J.: Prentice-Hall, copyright © 1959), p. 31. Reprinted by permission of Prentice-Hall, Inc.

6. Rudyard Kipling, *Just So Stories* (New York: Doubleday, 1902).

Guidelines for Preparing a Story to Tell

1. Read the story carefully.
2. Reread the story to get the incidents clearly in mind.
3. Reread to get a clear picture of the details.
4. Use the tape recorder to practice telling the story. Use cue cards—opening lines, main points of the story, climax, closing lines—if they help you.
5. Memorize essential parts that provide atmosphere or imagery (e.g., "Who's that tripping over my bridge?" roared the troll; or "In the high and far-off times, O best beloved . . . .").
6. Retape your story, concentrating upon improvement of pitch, range, and voice. Make sure you are enunciating clearly and that you are making good use of pauses.
7. Continue to practice telling the story. Use gestures sparingly; do not be overdramatic.

Anderson has suggested an effective device for storytelling in the classroom.

> When Hans Christian Andersen entertained the children of Denmark with his stories, he used to cut out silhouettes in order to make his characters more vivid. In ancient China, the storyteller would cast shadows to illustrate the characters in his tales of magic and ancient ways. The modern movie cartoon favorites, such as Mr. Magoo, use a combination of silhouette figures and movements to hold attention. In the modern classroom, the flannelgraph provides the storyteller the means to achieve the same movement, magic, and characterization.[7]

Using a flannel board is a simple and inexpensive technique that attracts the children's attention and stimulates interest. As children use it, the cutouts give concrete meaning to the oral vocabulary and provide a picture of events large enough for the whole class to see.

---

7. Paul S. Anderson, *Storytelling with the Flannel Board* (Minneapolis, Minn.: T. S. Denison, copyright © 1963), p. 7. Reprinted by permission of T. S. Denison and Company.

Suggestions for Use of the Flannel Board for Storytelling

1. Memorize the story or write a brief outline.
2. Number each cutout in order of use.
3. Make a large flannel board—eighteen-by-thirty-six inches—so that several cutouts can be placed on the board at one time.
4. After a phase of the story has been told, remove all the cutouts and start on the next phase.
5. Use variety in speed, volume, and pitch of voice.
6. Remember to make objects as well as characters.
7. If a story has only one or two scenes, the background objects can be placed on the board at the beginning of the story.
8. Store cutouts in a labeled box or file for convenient use by teacher or children.

The following references may be helpful.

Teacher References for Telling Stories

Arbuthnot, May Hill. "The Art of Storytelling." *Some Oral Aspects of the Language Arts Program*. Pittsburgh: University of Pittsburgh Press, 1957, pp. 41–50.

Martin, Sue Ann. "Techniques for the Creative Reading or Telling of Stories to Children." *Elementary English* 45 (May 1968): 611–618.

Sawyer, Ruth. "How to Tell a Story." Chicago: F. E. Compton, Division of Encyclopaedia Britannica, 1973.

Thornley, Gwendella. "Storytelling is Fairy Gold." *Elementary English* 45 (January 1968): 67–69, 88.

Children's Books for Storytelling

Bailey, Carolyn S., and Lewis, Clara M. *Favorite Stories for the Children's Hour*. New York: Platt, 1965.

Cathon, Laura E., and Schmidy, Thusnelda, eds. *Treasured Tales: Great Stories of Courage and Faith*. Nashville, Tenn.: Abingdon, 1960.

De La Mare, Walter. *Tales Told Again*. New York: Knopf, 1959.

Gruenberg, Sidonie M. *More Favorite Stories Old and New*. New York: Doubleday, 1960.

Untermeyer, Louis. *The World's Great Stories: Fifty-five Legends that Live Forever*. Philadelphia: M. Evans, 1964.

Withers, Carl. *The Man in the Moon: Sky Tales from Many Lands*. New York: Holt, Rinehart and Winston, 1969.

• *Pupil*   Storytelling is one literary activity that does not depend upon superior reading ability; thus, through this medium, every child can improve his speech patterns, his poise in speaking, and his ability to organize events in proper sequence.

Children soon learn the characteristics of a good story to tell: it will have an interesting plot; it may be episodic, particularly for young children; the characters are so real that one really cares what happens to them; the mood of the story makes it "live."

In selecting stories for telling to class members, each child should be free to tell the story he enjoys and wants to tell—not one assigned from the textbook or other sources. Preferably, in order to have the proper audience situation, it will be a story that few or no other class members know. No interruptions should be made during the telling of the story, no matter what mistakes the storyteller makes. Storytelling is primarily for enjoyment, and no other objectives of language instruction should infringe on this enjoyment.

Through storytelling, the child uses the most natural method of communication and furthers his oral language competencies.

• *Teaching strategies*   Rather than permitting the pupil to practice errors, the time for teacher help is in the preparation stage of his story. Make sure the pupil selects a good beginning, knows the sequence of details, uses words that fit the meaning, and pronounces the words correctly. This preventive procedure leaves the child with some knowledge to apply in judging other pupils' performances. In this way, specific help can be afforded both prior to the storytelling and after it.

After this initial, individual approach, the "team approach" of dividing the class into groups of four or five children each is recommended. Each child, in turn, will tell a story to his group. (At times, of course, the pupil will have an opportunity to tell a story to the entire class.) In the small groups, each child should check his progress (with the help of other members of the group) at incorporating the suggestions made by the teacher and other class members. Individual deficiencies are noted and corrective practice prescribed.

Class discussion concerning the characteristics of good storytelling will bring out helpful suggestions for improvement. Listening to good storytellers, either in person or on records, can help the child recognize the qualities that attract the listener. The tape recorder may be used to good advantage. By listening to his own performance, the child can see where he needs improvement. Specific "reminders" might include (1) the who, what, when, where, and why questions; (2) planning good beginning and closing sentences; (3) using interesting words; (4) having the characters exchange dialogue; (5) telling the events in order; and (6) keeping the outcome in doubt until the end of the story.

For the child reluctant to tell stories, "wordless (textless) books" with pictures are strongly recommended to elicit oral expression. Many children who are shy or need additional experience talking have no hesitation telling aloud the story from one of these books. For the younger children try:

Hutchins, Pat. *Changes, Changes.* New York: Macmillan, 1971.
Mayer, Mercer. *A Boy, a Dog and a Frog.* New York: Dial, 1967.
Schick, Eleanor. *Making Friends.* New York: Macmillan, 1969.

For the older children try:

Alexander, Martha. *Bobo's Dream.* New York: Dial, 1970.
Goodall, John. *The Adventures of Paddy Pork.* New York: Harcourt,
    Brace and World, 1968.

————. *Shrewbettina's Birthday*. New York: Harcourt Brace Jovanovich, 1971.

An independent worksheet for the advanced storyteller is presented in chapter 12, pages 438–439.

• *Anecdotes or personal experiences*   In addition to presenting literature stories, quite often children have amusing or interesting
experiences to recount. Some children are able to tell their experiences clearly and concisely, placing events in the proper order,
building up to the climax, and then quickly bringing the story to its
conclusion. Others clutter up the story with irrelevant details, relate
events out of sequence, and prolong the narrative unnecessarily.
The ability to tell a personal experience or a funny story in an interesting manner is a valuable asset. Children are naturally fascinated
by this kind of language activity and should be given the opportunity
to practice it and receive guidance in improving their performance.

Children need help in deciding which kinds of personal experiences are suitable for relating to the class. Good anecdotes may be
developed from sources such as these: an incident observed on the
way to school; something that happened "when I was very small";
an incident "when Mother was a little girl"; an unusual or amusing
episode from the life of a famous person; or what happened during
first attempts to do something, e.g., "The first time I tried ice skating"
or "The first pie I baked by myself."

In telling anecdotes or personal experiences, the child must first
be thoroughly familiar with all the details that are an integral part
of the event. He must be able to recall them in proper sequence so
that the listener is prepared for the climax. When the climax is
reached, he must quickly bring it to a close. The child needs to understand that unnecessary details may obscure the point and that drawing out the story makes it dull and boring. Simple, spontaneous expression should be encouraged. Gestures, tone of voice, and facial
expression may also make the event more interesting to the listener.

Drama

Creativity, action, and interpretation are all a part of drama in
the elementary school. The general values of dramatization include
(1) cooperating in a group and working together for a common purpose, (2) learning to appreciate character portrayal and action in
literature and increasing the pleasure in them by sharing them with

others, (3) encouraging leadership and organizational abilities, (4) providing an outlet for expression of emotions, (5) developing creative imagination, (6) fostering self-reliance in speaking, and (7) promoting variation in voice quality and pitch and encouraging accurate enunciation and pronunciation. Drama involves learning-by-doing:

> What children do is more significant to them than what they see or hear. Most boys and girls would rather get into the thick of a game than be spectators. They would choose to play in an orchestra instead of listening to one, or act in a dramatization instead of sitting in an audience.[8]

In order for children to express themselves at their optimum level, attention to drama cannot be on a hit-or-miss, catch-as-catch-can basis. Rather than a now-and-then thing, drama experiences must be as well organized as spelling, written composition, or any other language arts experiences.

Drama activities must be planned sequentially, designed for the appropriate level, and based on past learnings. A sequence such as the following for primary- and middle-school years may be implemented:

Primary
    responding creatively to prose and poetry
    beginning with simple pantomimes and dramatic play
    dramatizing activities, favorite nursery rhymes, poems, songs, and stories
    using stick puppets, hand puppets, and flannel-board figures
    identifying self with characters in stories
    preparing a class "radio" or "television" program

Intermediate
    sharing the feelings and experiences of characters in a story
    dramatizing stories and events
    presenting short plays or scenes from longer plays
    producing puppet shows
    presenting original skits, dialogues, or monologues

The drama process may be categorized as follows: (1) sense awareness, (2) movement, (3) characterization, (4) improvisation, and (5) dramatization. Each will be discussed briefly in turn.

---

8. Winfred Ward, *Playmaking with Children from Kindergarten through Junior High School*, 2d ed. (New York: Appleton-Century-Crofts, copyright © 1957), p. 1. Reprinted by permission of Appleton-Century-Crofts, Inc.

• *Sense awareness*   Close observation is involved in putting the senses into "high gear." For example, tell the pupils: "Let's look closely at the clouds. Are they moving? Which way are the clouds moving? Are they moving fast or slowly? What makes them move? Do they look different? I see some that look like white sheep. What do the clouds look like to you?" Likewise, sensitivity to sound, smell, taste, and touch needs sharpening: listening to everyday sounds, the smells of a lunch box, the taste of popcorn, or the feel of a small kitten.

• *Movement*   Through the ages, communication has taken place through body actions. Understanding of body actions was acquired long before words became a means of communication.

Movement poems or stories delight many children. Teachers and children, working together, can devise all sorts of movement stories. An illustrative movement story—the children responding through movement as indicated by the dashes—is suggested below.

> Jim tried to move his body in every way possible. He began with three giant steps _____. He tried walking slowly _____ and then quickly _____. "I can roll," he said _____. And Jim could crawl _____ and slide _____ and leap _____ and spin _____.

Pantomiming is another method of dramatization through movement. It can begin with simple activities, such as "washing my hands" or "being a squirrel in the fall" and then progress to pantomimes involving cooperation of several children (such as a policeman directing traffic or an old man and a little boy walking down the street). Children are encouraged to pay close attention to details. They love to "play in the rain," "go on a picnic," "cut down a tree," or "roll heavy stones up a hill." Children enjoy acting out words (e.g., *wet*) and letting classmates provide an opposite word (e.g., *dry*) or acting out a word that rhymes with another word (e.g., *shake*).

Young children usually know some nursery rhymes when they enter school. They enjoy hearing the familiar verses over and over again and responding to their rhythm and drama. Many of the rhymes lend themselves to pantomime: it's fun to be Jack and jump lightly over a candlestick, to be Little Bo Peep looking for her sheep, to be one of the sheep that come home "dragging their tails behind them," or to be the scary spider chasing Miss Muffet away from her tuffet. Since the words and the events are well known, children can quickly become involved in "being" the characters.

Pantomiming gives children a chance to be doers instead of spectators. It helps them become accustomed to transmitting actions, emotions, and ideas through body movements and facial expressions.

For the older child, pantomime may involve pretending something that he can do with a sports ball or it may involve several items (e.g., "You are watching your team play softball. You want them to win. The score is tied; the bases are loaded in the last inning. Everyone is set to run on the bases. Your team's best batter comes to bat, but he strikes out! Your team loses."). Or a series of items may be given orally to make a plot for pantomime:

1. Walk bow-legged in cowboy boots. Be sure your hands are on your belt.
2. Have a rope in your hands. Form a lasso. Try to lasso a steer.
3. Miss the steer. Draw the rope back with real disappointment.
4. Throw the rope again—and miss.
5. Draw the rope back again in disappointment.
6. Throw the rope again. Catch the steer. Express joy. Then the steer pulls you toward him!

Graubard divides pantomime experiences into different types, such as Mother Goose rhymes, current events, embarrassing occurrences, proverbs, advertising slogans, situations, and dramatic adverbs. Other types of pantomime and suggestions for implementing these activities include the following:

> *Fables:* If a group is familiar with Aesop's or La Fontaine's fables, have them act these out for the class to guess. This activity is also good for book-sharing time, particularly with the self-selective reading program.
>
> *Fairy tales:* Groups can act out familiar fairy tales like "Little Red Riding Hood," "Sleeping Beauty," "Rumpelstiltskin," etc.
>
> *Acting out:* This game is the most elastic and among the most creative and entertaining. Divide your group into teams and select a category for them to act out. For instance, take folk songs or books. The children must act out the plot of the song or the book, and the opposing team must guess the title.
>
> *Shadow skits:* The action all takes place behind a screen, which can be made by holding up a sheet or hanging it between a large doorway. A light should be placed about three to five feet behind the sheet. If costumes are desired, they should be kept simple. Popular songs, folk songs, dramatic poems, and familiar situations all can be acted out effectively this way.[9]

• *Characterization*   This involves "being" an animal or another person and is achieved through observation and discussion of physical attributes and feelings of animals or people. The questions *who*, *what*, *when*, *where*, and *why* can encourage one to feel and sound like a contented, happy kitten or a ferocious lion on the hunt for food! To interpret the giant in "Jack and the Beanstalk," here are some questions to ask: "How does he walk?" "What kind of person is he?" "How old is he?" "What would his facial expressions be like?" "What is his relationship with the other characters in the story?" Reenacting everyday events may be used to promote understanding of other people. The child may be the postman delivering the mail or the housewife receiving it, he may be a safety patrol boy helping children across the street, or he may be the carry-out boy at the supermarket. Characterization may help prepare the child for a visit to

---

9.   Paul S. Graubard, "Pantomime: Another Language," *Elementary English* 37 (May 1960): 305–306. Reprinted by permission of the National Council of Teachers of English.

the dentist or the doctor, an interview with the PTA president for the school newspaper, or some other anticipated experience.

• *Improvisation*   Acting without a script is involved in this form of drama. For example, children may use dialogue as they pretend to be (in order) the three Billy Goats Gruff crossing the bridge. It could be a short scene set in advance: "You three boys have stumbled upon a valuable treasure, but then you hear some men's voices. They are coming toward you!"

Role-playing is useful in many situations, but it is especially helpful in problem-situations. A dispute on the playground can be reenacted in the classroom with the participants playing themselves. Then the roles may be reversed so that each child may get an idea of what the others thought and felt. Other problems arising in the classroom or from outside may be dramatized as an aid in seeing another's viewpoint and finding a solution to the problem. The field of social studies is rich in opportunities for the use of improvisation: "Pretend you are an astronaut setting foot for the first time on a new planet," or "Act out your favorite part of the Lewis and Clark expedition."

• *Literary dramatization*   One of the most advanced drama experiences for children is dramatizing parts of stories, books, or poems. Most teachers find it helpful to begin with short vignettes.

Following is a list of materials that have been found useful in literary dramatization:

Primary Years
Mother Goose rhymes
"The Three Bears"
"The Three Billy Goats Gruff"
Aldis, Dorothy. "I'm Hiding"
Dalgliesh, Alice. *Bears on Hemlock Mountain*. New York: Scribner, 1952.
Zolotow, Charlotte. *Mister Rabbit and the Lovely Present*. New York: Harper & Row, 1962.

Intermediate Years
Fairy tales
Asbjornsen, P. C., and Moe, J. *East of the Sun and West of the Moon and Other Tales*. New York: Macmillan, 1963.

Irving, Washington. "Rip Van Winkle"

L'Engle, Madeleine. *Wrinkle in Time*. New York: Farrar, Straus & Giroux, 1962.

Lewis, C. S. *The Lion, the Witch, and the Wardrobe*. New York: Macmillan, 1951.

McCloskey, Robert. *Homer Price*. New York: Viking Press, 1943.

Thurber, James. *Many Moons*. New York: Harcourt, Brace and World, 1943.

Dramatization may be varied by using puppets or presenting a shadow play. The puppets may be simple hand puppets that the

---

Guide for Selecting and Adapting Stories and Poems for Dramatization

Choose a story that:
   can be understood by the group.
   contains characters with whom the children can identify.
   has an uncomplicated plot.
   has a conflict that needs to be resolved.
When telling or reading the story:
   be sure that you know the whole story in detail.
   speak and interpret the story with enthusiasm and feeling.
   select words that are meaningful to the age group.
When planning:
   make sure the plans are made by the children.
   emphasize the main points of the story: how it starts, events for scenes, the climax, how it ends.
   describe the main characters in the story.
   develop the setting of the story.
   discuss what will be needed for properties.
   encourage the children to try to understand the different characters.
When acting:
   let the children act only when the main points of the story have been agreed upon.
   allow for creative and spontaneous actions within the framework developed by the children.
When evaluating:
   note the development of the agreed-upon main points.
   discuss the portrayal of the characters in light of the description in the story.
   lead to a detailed study of the meaning of the story, if appropriate.

Puppetry provides an opportunity for oral expression in a functional and interesting setting.

children have made or more complicated marionettes. Simple puppets are preferable for most situations (the hand puppet—head moved with index finger and arms by third finger and thumb; or the rod puppet—controlled by one or more rigid rods to which the puppet is attached), but the marionette is often enjoyed by the upper-level pupils. Puppets may be constructed using a variety of materials: paper sack, styrofoam, rubber ball, papier-mâché, sock, fruit or vegetable, stick, etc. Sometimes children have trouble working their hands and speaking at the same time. Tape-recording the script as the children read it or act it out and then playing it back during the actual puppet or shadow-play performance will help the child concentrate on his hand movements until he can coordinate both speaking and manipulating the puppets.

In shadow play, the puppets or child actors stay behind a screen that is lighted so that only their silhouettes are seen. This appeals to the timid child who is reluctant to speak before others.[10]

---

10. Gwen Osten, "Structure in Creativity," *Elementary English* 46 (April 1969): 438–443; Betty Coody, *Using Literature with Young Children* (Dubuque, Iowa: William C. Brown, 1973) pp. 42–59; Carole M. Kirkton, "Classroom Dramatics: Developing Oral Language Skills," *Elementary English* 48 (February 1971): 254–261.

Evaluation: With younger children, very little evaluation of drama ability is done. The playing is kept a delightful game with encouragement for thought and imagination. With older pupils, positive suggestions may be pertinent and questions asked, such as: "What did you enjoy most about this? Why?" "Who could have made his acting clearer?" "Who has a suggestion as to how we might put more spirit into the dramatization?" For all, it is the process—not the product—that is most important. "It is the process which . . . shapes the players' sensitivities, their human understanding, their creative potential, and hence, the course of their lives."[11]

Even though a teacher plans thoroughly, some children may not wish to perform before an audience. While not all creative drama needs an audience situation, inhibited individuals may enter into the activity more wholeheartedly if there is a noncritical audience. While younger children will dramatize for their own satisfaction, older children generally need to work before others to help them drop their self-consciousness. An audience situation of other classmates is highly satisfactory. This recommendation is equivalent to the idea of ensuring a child's best effort in written composition through providing him with the knowledge that someone will read what he has written. A few may not wish to participate, and such wishes should be respected, but their reservations usually melt away as others participate. Once a child has performed successfully before the class, he will want to share his dramatizations again.

• *Other drama activities*   Choral reading/speaking is a form of drama. One of the simplest kinds of choral reading is echoic verse: the reader says a line and the audience repeats it, word for word, intonation for intonation, sometimes even action for action. Echoic activities have some advantages over other forms of choral reading since copies of the text are not necessary for members of the audience. "The Goat" is an example of a poem that can be used echoically.

Two other examples of poems that lend themselves well to echoic treatment are "The Mysterious Cat" by Vachel Lindsay and "The Night Will Never Stay" by Eleanor Farjeon.

Choral activities provide children with the opportunity to develop their imagination through the interpretation of the writings of others, to improve their speech, to expand their own creativity, and to engage in an active situation rather than a passive one. With choral reading, the value of group achievement is of prime importance.

---

11.   Richard Crosscup, *Children and Dramatics* (New York: Scribner, 1966), p. 135.

THE GOAT

There was a man,
Now please take note.
There was a man
Who had a goat.

He loved that goat,
Indeed he did.
He loved that goat,
Just like a kid.

One day the goat
Was feeling fine,
Ate three red shirts,
From off the line.

That man he grabbed
Him by the back,
And tied him to
A railroad track.

But when the train
Pulled into sight
That goat grew pale
And green with fright.

He heaved a sigh,
As if in pain,
Coughed up those shirts
And flagged the train![12]

There are various types of choral reading/speaking arrangements:

1. *Line-a-child:* Each child reads one or two lines individually. When the climax is reached, a few lines may be read in unison. An example of a poem suitable for this treatment in the primary years would be "The Goblin" by Rose Fyleman; for the intermediate years, "Pippa's Song" by Robert Browning.
2. *Refrain:* One individual reads or speaks the narrative part and the whole group joins in on the refrain. An example for the primary years is "The Wind" by Robert Lewis Stevenson; for the intermediate years, "Shoes and Stockings" by A. A. Milne.
3. *Two-part or antiphonal:* Two groups of children, one against the other, are involved, such as boys and girls, light voices and deep voices, or questions and answers. An example for the primary years is "Wishes" by Rose Fyleman; for the intermediate years, Psalm 24.
4. *Unison:* Unison speaking may be of two types: sequence and cumulative. In *sequence*, the individual or group is responsible for connecting the different phrases smoothly to make a finished whole. An example for the primary years is "Poor Old Woman"; for the intermediate years, "Roads" by Rachael Fields. *Cumulative* work involves beginning with a few voices and adding more voices as the power of the poem de-

12. From Ramon R. Ross, *Storyteller* (Columbus, Ohio: Merrill, 1972), pp. 89–90.

velops and demands it. An example for the primary years is "Trains" by James Tippett; for the intermediate years, "Jonathan Bing" by Beatrice Brown.

In working with choral reading/speaking, the teacher must be concerned with (1) rhythm/tempo, (2) color/quality of voice, and (3) arrangement. To help develop rhythm and tempo, children may clap, sway, or beat out the rhythm. The rhythm may be described as happy or sad; the concept of tempo, fast or slow, becomes a part of the rhythmic pattern. Nursery rhymes are excellent for primary children to feel rhythm and tempo; intermediate-level children will find the lilting rhythms of the words of A. A. Milne, Rachael Field, or Eleanor Farjeon very suitable for this purpose. Exciting, simple material may be used to help children become sensitive to pitch, inflection, and intensity: for example, "I Have Known Rivers" by Langston Hughes. The orchestration of the choral reading is a creative aspect of the project. Class members and the teacher should work together to find the best arrangement to convey the meaning of the poem, and various ways should be tried.

OTHER ORAL EXPRESSION EXPERIENCES

Making announcements

Examples of kinds of announcements would include announcements of school programs, class activities, Scout meetings, or other out-of-school functions. In making announcements of meetings or programs, children must be sure to include an adequate description of the event, who is invited, the date, the time, the place, and the price of admission, if required. When announcing that something has been lost, the pupil should describe the article clearly, tell when and where it might have been lost, to whom it should be returned, and mention a reward, if there is one.

Illustrations of different kinds of announcements follow.

A school program:
(See chapter 1, page 17, for a systematic lesson plan for this type of oral announcement.)
An out-of-school function:
The Girl Scouts will meet Monday, December 6, at 3:30 P.M., in the school cafeteria. Please bring fifty cents to pay for the Christmas wrappings and paint. Wear old clothes or bring

a smock as we will paint Christmas toys to be put in Junior
Red Cross boxes.

Lost articles:

Yesterday during the 2:00 P.M. recess, a yellow sweater with
white buttons and a rolled collar was left on the ground by
the swings. If you find the sweater, will you please return it
to Alice Goodner in Miss Jones's room?

Giving messages, directions, explanations

Frequently, in every classroom, there is need for giving brief
messages, directions, or explanations. To do this successfully, the
information must be organized and presented in clear and concise
terms so that others can understand and respond.

Group discussion helps in planning what information should be
included and how it should be arranged. If a child is carrying a message from one person to another, he must know who is sending the
message, who is to receive it, and he must be able to state the message accurately.

In giving directions, he must learn to include, in the proper order,
all the steps necessary for another person to follow the procedure.
Directions for getting from one place to another should be very specific as to distances and turns ("turn left" not "turn that way"). Directions for making or doing something should always include the correct names for objects or materials used (not "a little thing-a-ma-jig").

Explanations call for skills similar to those discussed above, but
in addition they often include reasons—telling why something is done
in a certain way or how something works. In order to be effective,
explanations require understanding and orderly arrangement of
details. For younger children, explanations may be mere enumera-
tions of points, but for older children, they will include cause-and-
effect relationships. Children will need guidance in selecting the
points necessary for a clear explanation and in omitting details that
are irrelevant or confusing.

Giving reviews of books, movies, and television programs

Too many teachers view book reports simply as checks on
whether to give credit for reading a book; this is obviously a perver-
sion of the real intent. Book reports serve to further enjoyment of
reading, extend interests, and provide clues toward individual and
group evaluation of literature. Reviewing a book reinforces under-

standing of the setting, characters, and sequence of events; develops skills of analysis; and promotes contrast of the literary experience with real-life experience.

When a child has especially enjoyed a book, he often wants to share it with others. Such sharing should be encouraged but never required. Huck and Kuhn give the following suggestions that the teacher may use in guiding discussion or reviewing for younger children. They are indicative of the points that may be developed in informal group discussion or in more formal reviews. (Also see the section on "Comprehension" in chapter 14, pages 519–521, for analysis of questions.)

> Show us your favorite picture.
> Tell us about the most exiciting part.
> What is the setting of this book?
> Who is your favorite character?
> Tell us about the part you thought was funniest.
> What other books has this author written?
> Do you think this story could have happened in our town today?
> Have you ever had an experience like this?[13]

To provide a specific illustration of how sharing of books may be developed in a classroom setting, one period with a class of eight-year-olds was recorded as follows:

> The teacher began the lesson by saying that the class members have been reading quite a bit and that today some of them might like to share with the others the books they have been reading. The first child called upon brought his book to the front of the room and gave his book report. After giving the author and title of the book, he showed pictures as he discussed the story, leaving an exciting episode untold for others who might want to read the book.
>
> After several children had given their reports, the teacher asked the class to list important things to include in a book report. Together the class and the teacher composed the following list of ideas and the teacher wrote them on the chalkboard.

---

13. Charlotte S. Huck and Doris Y. Kuhn, *Children's Literature in the Elementary School*, 2d ed. (New York: Holt, Rinehart and Winston, copyright © 1968), pp. 680–681. Reprinted by permission of Holt, Rinehart and Winston, Inc.

1. Tell something about the story, but keep us guessing.
2. Give the name of author. (Here the teacher paused and asked if this was very important. A number of children thought it was. He asked if they recalled the names of authors of books they had been reading. Again the pupils thought so. The teacher then presented cards with the names of several authors to the class and asked for their identification: Brink, Wilder, Anderson, Beem, McCloskey, d'Aulaire.)
3. Tell the title of the book.
4. Tell what kind of story it is.
5. Show illustrations from the book as you discuss.

Then the teacher asked the class to rearrange the list in the order that they would recommend in giving a book report. The list became:

1. Title of the book
2. Name of the author
3. Kind of story it is
4. Tell something about the story, but keep us guessing.
5. Show illustrations as you discuss.

The class also mentioned that one important suggestion was omitted: at the end of the report, the pupil should tell us where the book could be found.

The teacher said that he had a book he would like to read to the class. Before he read it, he asked the class to think how they would tell or give a report about it from the points they had developed and written on the chalkboard. The teacher read from *Amos Fortune: Free Man*. He would pause often to ask questions as to word meaning and definition. He read quietly but dramatically.

Older children will be able to make more detailed reports. There should be an indication of what the book is about, but not a complete summary of the plot, for this spoils the story for others who may wish to read it later. The report may include an exciting or funny part. A small portion of the book may be read aloud. The book may be compared with others on a similar topic or by the same author. The details included will vary according to the type of book and the individual's particular interests. If a child dislikes a book, he should not hesitate to say so, but he should give reasons. "This book is no good.

I didn't like it," is no more acceptable than "This is a good book. I like it."

Chart 5.3 suggests items for inclusion in oral or written book reports.

CHART 5.3: Book Reporting Guide

Early Primary Years (1–2)	*Advanced Primary Years (2–3)*	*Intermediate Years (4–6)*
your name	your name	your name
date	date	date
title of book	title of book	title of book
author	author	author
discussion of some of the story (or the part you liked best)	description of the main (or other) characters	publisher
		kind of story
	the most important events (or an exciting adventure)	discussion of the setting
	your opinion of the book and the reason for it	discussion of some of the characters
		discussion of some of the story
		your evaluation of the book

To allow more children to participate, several reviews may be given simultaneously. The class may be divided into groups during the book-sharing period, each group listening to a different review. Five to eight children can be sitting at desks or chairs in a circle. This provides an informal and relaxed atmosphere where they can attain the goals of sharing more easily than through a formal presentation to the entire class. Moreover, some children are more enthusiastic if they have something to show while giving a review: for example, prepared drawings, a bulletin board display, or other illustrative material. Other techniques such as sales talks or "commercials" advertising a particular book are variations that will add interest.

When the same book has been read by several class members, a small "group review" may be held. The discussion need not be concerned exclusively with details of the plot but may bring out such aspects as the way in which the characters react to the events of the story, how they grow and change as the story progresses, and how the book relates to the children's own experiences. The following questions, adapted from a list proposed by Cleary, can be used to stimulate profitable discussions and help the participants to contribute more meaningful comments than the frequently heard, "I liked the book because it was good."

Do you think this story could have happened?
Have you ever seen anything like this happen? When?
Has anything like this ever happened to you? What did you do about it?
What do you remember about the people in the story?
Do you think that people really do those things? Why?
How are you like the people in the story?
Would you like to live with that family?
Would you like _____ (book character) for a friend? Why?
Do you know anyone like _____ (book character)?
Do you want to be like _____ (book character)?
How did the story make you feel? Why?[14]

There are numerous ways for children to share books. The following approaches are suggested for consideration:

1. Prepare an oral review to present to a younger group of children.
2. Dramatize or pantomime parts of a story.
3. Have an imaginary interview with an author or book character.
4. Discuss two or more books on the same subject; point out similarities and differences.
5. Give a puppet or marionette show to illustrate a story.
6. Write a letter to a friend to recommend a book.
7. Make an original reference book of facts from a nonfiction book.
8. Create a series of original illustrations for a story.

---

14. Florence Damon Cleary, *Blueprints for Better Reading* (New York: H. W. Wilson, 1957), p. 141.

9. Make a colorful, pictorial timeline or map for a history book.
10. Write a letter to a favorite author. (If a reply is expected, be sure to include return postage.)
11. After watching a television adaptation of a favorite story, evaluate the presentation.
12. Write a sequel to a story using the same characters.
13. Read aloud several outstanding passages from a book.
14. Make a poster "advertising" a good book.
15. Tell or write a story about the author or illustrator of the book.[15]

Reviews of movies and television programs may be considered in much the same fashion as book reviews. They may be the subject of informal discussion or more formal reports. With guidance from the teacher, details of the plot can be developed. Reports and discussions of movies and television programs can help to deepen understanding of them and improve tastes.

Criteria for performance in giving a movie review include attention to such items as:

1. The title of the picture
2. The name of the theatre where it can be seen
3. The names of the main actors
4. Whether the picture is in color or black and white
5. What the movie is about
6. Whether it is true or make-believe, funny or serious
7. Not revealing any surprise for those who plan to see it later
8. Why it was enjoyable

Criteria for performance in giving a review of a television program includes attention to the following items:

1. The title
2. The name of the main actors
3. The station or channel
4. The time given
5. The length
6. The kind of program
7. Something interesting about it
8. Why it was enjoyable

---

15. Doris DeMontreville and Donna Hill, eds., *Third Book of Junior Authors* (New York: H. W. Wilson, 1972); Muriel Fuller, ed., *More Junior Authors* (New York: H. W. Wilson, 1963); Stanley J. Kunitz and Howard Haycraft, eds., *The Junior Book of Authors*, 2d ed. rev. (New York: H. W. Wilson, 1951); Bertha A. Mahony et al., *Illustrators of Children's Books, 1744–1945* (Boston: Horn Book, 1946); idem. *Illustrators of Children's Books, 1946–60* (Boston: Horn Book, 1958).

Using the telephone

Children using practice telephones in the classroom may enact the following situations that will enable the teacher to observe their telephone usage.

1. Pam wants to call her friend. She does not know her telephone number and needs to look it up in the telephone directory.
2. Jack wants to invite Edward to go to a movie with him. On his first attempt to reach Edward by phone, Jack gets a wrong number.
3. Peter wants to telephone a new friend who has just moved into his neighborhood. Since the telephone number is not in the current directory, he calls Directory Assistance. Sally is the operator.

Taking a field trip to a telephone exhibit can enhance appreciation for learning the important social skills in telephone usage.

4. Rebecca does not know the cleaner's telephone number. She finds the number in the Yellow Pages. While she is dialing this number, Edith, who shares the party line, interrupts, asking for the line due to an emergency.

One primary-level teacher began a unit of work on the telephone by preparing a bulletin board that showed the parts of a telephone and by using a teletrainer borrowed from the telephone company. (A teletrainer consists of two activated telephones and a speaker-control unit. It can simulate a dial tone, a busy signal, and a ringing signal.) A number of telephone directories were available for class use.

"Many of you know how to make a telephone call, especially to call mother or father, and this is fine," the teacher began. "But some of you have trouble finding a number in the directory and some of you get mixed up when trying to dial a number. Yes, there are several things that we need to know to use a telephone correctly."

Instructions followed on how to look for and call a particular number: "Suppose we wish to call Mrs. Mary Brown. How are the names in the telephone directory arranged? Why is the street address helpful?" These were the types of questions posed to the pupils.

After they had located the number, attention was directed to how to dial it: "Let's suggest some things to do in order to call 842-4771." The pupils and teacher prepared the following sequence of steps.

1. Pick up the telephone and hold the receiver to your ear.
2. Listen for the dial tone, a steady humming sound. If you dial before you hear it, you may get a wrong number or no number at all.
3. When you hear the dial tone, place your finger in the hole on the dial for 8. Turn the dial to the right until your finger hits the finger stop. Remove your finger and let the dial go back by itself. It will make a clicking sound.
4. Place your finger in the hole for 4 and turn the dial until your finger hits the finger stop. Remove your finger and let the dial go back again. Continue to dial the numbers 2-4-7-7-1 in the same way.

5. When you finish dialing, wait a moment and you will hear a ringing sound. If you get a beep-beep sound, this means that the line is busy and that you must hang up and wait a few minutes before dialing again. If you hear the telephone ringing, give Mrs. Brown time to answer; let it ring several times.
6. When Mrs. Brown answers the phone, tell her your name and why you are calling.

They practiced in small groups calling Mrs. Mary Brown and other numbers. The manner of performing was discussed by the class and the teacher. Each child also located and wrote the number for the police department, the fire department, the family doctor, and a neighbor.

The children then examined the Yellow Pages. They located the names of plumbers, department stores, grocery stores, shoe stores, etc.

Near the end of the period, the class discussed long distance dialing and the use of area code numbers.

The teacher may want to suggest the following criteria for telephone skills and good manners in telephoning.

CHART 5.4: Telephone Guide

1. Speak clearly.
2. When originating the call, give your name immediately.
3. State the purpose of the call.
4. Keep the telephone message brief and to the point.
5. Answer calls as quickly as possible.
6. When another person is wanted, ask the caller to "Wait just a minute, please," and get the person asked for at once. If it takes a little more time for the person to reach the telephone, explain, "Mother is out in the yard. She will be here in a minute or two."
7. Take any messages accurately or ask if they would please call later. The message should include the caller's name, telephone number, message, and the time the call was received.
8. If you get a wrong number, apologize to the person who answers: "I'm sorry, I have the wrong number." Be polite to anyone who reaches your number in error.

Making introductions and observing social courtesies

Entertaining visitors in the classroom may be upsetting to some children if they have not been prepared for the event. Some children have not received adequate training for such simple courtesies as responding to greetings or making and acknowledging introductions. Before visitors arrive, the teacher should discuss with the class just what is to happen. He may discuss with them such courtesies as greeting visitors at the door, making introductions, the seating of visitors, or serving refreshments.

An excellent time to help children develop self-confidence, assurance, and ease in making introductions and being introduced would be during an open house or similar function. They should be able to put their learning to use in introducing their parents and friends to their teacher and classmates, and in replying when others are introduced to them.

A list of suggestions for making introductions includes:

1. Speak slowly and clearly so that the names can be understood easily. It is all right to ask for a name to be repeated if you did not hear it the first time.
2. Tell something about the persons you are introducing to help them start a conversation.
3. Say, "_____, I would like to introduce _____." Give the name of the person you wish to honor first, such as a woman, an older person, or a person of rank.
4. When being introduced, make a reply, such as "I'm very glad to meet you, _____."
5. To remember the name of a new acquaintance, use it when speaking to him.

The following dialogues may be practiced for other courtesies, such as greeting visitors, seating visitors, or serving refreshments.

1. How to greet visitors at the door: "Good morning. It's good to see you," or "Hello. Won't you please come in?"
2. Offering assistance: "May I take your coat?"
3. Seating visitors: "Mrs. Smith, would you like to sit here?"
4. Serving refreshments: "May I serve you?" "Would you like some punch?"
5. Expressing appreciation for courtesies: "Thank you for showing us your rock collection." "Mr. Brown, we appreciate your telling us about your trip to Europe."
6. Responding to expressions of appreciation: "You are welcome."

Social courtesies should be taught not merely as conventional forms of behavior but as genuine expressions of respect and regard for others. Children should be guided to see that observance of these courtesies makes for good relationships with other people. A sincere, wholesome attitude on the part of the teacher does much to foster similar attitudes in children.

Conducting meetings

There are many meetings of clubs in the elementary school. During a meeting, pupils find it useful to have a chart of the important features of a meeting placed on the wall; the following information will help teachers to develop such a chart.

CHART 5.5: Parliamentary Guide

1. Call the meeting to order.
2. Ask the secretary to read the minutes of the previous meeting.
3. Ask the members for any corrections/additions to the minutes. If there are no corrections or additions, say, "The minutes are accepted as read."
4. Call for and discuss reports from any committees.
5. Call for unfinished business. Ask for a motion, discussion, and vote.
6. Call for new business. Ask for a motion, discussion, and vote.
7. Turn the meeting over to the person in charge of the program for that meeting.
8. After the program, thank the persons concerned and ask for a motion to adjourn.
9. Call for a vote on the motion and tell the group that the meeting stands adjourned.

When motions are in order, a member who wishes to speak stands and speaks when the chairperson calls upon him. If a member wants the group to vote upon his idea, he says, "I move that . . . ." In order to be voted upon, the motion must be seconded. Then the chairperson restates the motion and calls for discussion. Finally he calls for a vote on the motion and announces the result. The chairperson plans the agenda and sees to it that the order of business is followed and that motions are made properly. The secretary is responsible for notices of meetings and keeps records, such as lists of committee members or notes about unfinished business. Most importantly, the secretary keeps the minutes of what is done at the meetings, reporting date, place, time, and kind of meeting; the name of the person presiding; and all motions, whether carried or not.

Conducting interviews

In the intermediate school years, children have occasion to use interviewing techniques. Interviews may be conducted by individuals or small groups of children. To be successful, the interview requires planning ahead of time. Interview techniques can be practiced in the classroom as preparation for the actual experience, with children role-playing as interviewer and interviewee.

The questions to be asked should be designed to bring out the information sought. Questions that are extremely personal or that might cause embarrassment should be avoided. The interviewer should listen carefully and take notes as his questions are answered.

The following bulletin board display suggests an instructional strategy, as well as some points to be noted in evaluating the manner in which the interview is conducted.

REPORTER INTERVIEWS 102-YEAR OLD MAN	FASHION EDITOR INTERVIEWS CLOTHES DESIGNERS
Have you heard or read interviews reported by: 1. television? 2. radio? 3. newspapers? 4. magazines? What do you think are some reasons for interviews?	Guidelines for interviews 1. Make an appointment at the time most convenient for the person to be interviewed. 2. Be polite. 3. Plan questions carefully and state them clearly. 4. Take notes on the answers. 5. Avoid taking too much of the person's time. 6. Thank the person for his kindness in granting the interview.

Interview:
1. a visiting speaker to get information for the school paper.
2. a classmate who has received some unusual honor.
3. a specialist to get information to bring back to class.
4. the principal or a teacher in the school.
5. a person in the classroom or building you know least about and write a report about him or her.

USAGE

Usage refers to the way in which people speak. In the broad sense, effective usage is reflected when the child develops a feeling for the sparkling phrase, the exact word for his needs, the sentence that says precisely what he wants to say as clearly as possible and in a manner suitable to the tone and purpose of the communication. In this section, focus is directed toward particular language forms: words, idioms, and constructions. Two broad labels are applied to these forms or patterns: *standard* (socially accepted) and *nonstandard* (variant).

Dialect differences

Environmental and cultural differences found in the backgrounds of the children in American schools affect the ways in which the children use language. The teacher needs some basic information about the linguistic features of the learner's dialect. Several sources are available for the teacher searching for generalized findings. For example, in a study of 338 children ranging from kindergarten to twelfth grade, Loban isolated some common oral problems among speakers of "standard dialect" and speakers of "social class dialect."[16] A word of caution needs to be given as the reader considers such studies: he must keep in mind that the findings are representative. There will be some speakers of standard dialect who need individual instruction for some oral problem; likewise, while a group may be assigned as influenced by social or regional dialect, there will be individual members of the group who exhibit few, if any, departures from standard English. While it is extremely important for the teacher to be knowledgeable of oral language data pertinent to the children in a given community under his instruction, a few linguistic features in the speech patterns of three distinct groups are presented for consideration.

• *Urban*   Shuy prepared the list on page 170 of some of the characteristic speech patterns in many urban ghetto areas.

Other nonstandard forms may involve subject expression (*John lives in New York.* $\longrightarrow$ John he live in New York.); future form of *be* (*He is sick.* $\longrightarrow$ *He sick.* [meaning "at present"] *He be sick.* [chroni-

---

16. Walter Loban, *Problems in Oral English* (Urbana, Ill.: National Council of Teachers of English, 1966) pp. 47, 49.

WRITTEN EXPRESSION	LINGUISTIC FEATURE	ORAL EXPRESSION
1. John's house	possession	John house
2. John runs.	third-person singular	John run.
3. ten cents	plurality	ten cent
4. He jumped.	past	He jump.
5. She is a cook.	copula	She a cook.
6. He doesn't have any toys.	negation	He ain't got no toys. He don't have no toys. He don't got no toys.
7. He asked if I came.	past conditional question	He asked did I come.
8. Every day when I come he isn't here.	negative *be*	Every day when I come he don't be here.

SOURCE: Roger W. Shuy, "Some Considerations for Developing Beginning Reading Materials for Ghetto Children," *Journal of Reading Behavior* 1 (Spring 1969): 37. Used by permission of National Reading Conference, Inc.

cally]); and use of prepositions *(He is over at his friend's house.* ⟶ *He over to his friend's house.)*[17]

• *Rural*   Stewart studied the speech patterns of Appalachian rural children and found various features, including:

1. Dropped endings of words: *goin', comin', seein'*
2. Lack of distinction in the sound of different vowels before r: *far, fir, car, cur*
3. Elimination of subjects in sentence patterns: *'m' going down town. 'e's doing his work.*
4. Incorrect use of the objective case of pronouns in compound subjects: *me and you, me and my sister*
5. Addition of *n* to possessive pronouns: *his'n, her'n*
6. Distortion of sounds: *cidy* for *city*, *tank* for *thank*; and mispronunciation of words: *duh* for *the*, *tink* for *think*, *terry* for *very*[18]

---

17. William Lobov, *A Study of the Non-Standard English of Negro and Puerto Rican Speakers in New York City* (Washington, D.C.: Cooperative Research Project, U.S. Office of Education, 1968); idem., *The Social Stratification of English in New York City* (Washington, D.C.: Center for Applied Linguistics, 1966); Walter A. Wolfram, *A Sociolinguistic Description of Detroit Negro Speech* (Washington, D.C.: Center for Applied Linguistics, 1969).

18. William A. Stewart, *Appalachian Advance* 4 (September 1969), p. 12.

• *Spanish-American* The child from the home in which Spanish is spoken will likely come to school with a Spanish-American dialect. Facts such as the following would be helpful to the concerned teacher: The Spanish-speaking child who has already learned his alphabet will pronounce the vowels as [ah], [ey], [ee], [ō], [o͞o], not as [ā], [ē], [ī], [ō], [ū]. The Spanish language does not use the voiced *th*, the *z*, the *zh*, or the *j*. The tendency is to substitute the sound in the Spanish language that is most like the missing sound. *Thr-* does not occur in Spanish. The blend of *s* with other consonant sounds *(t, p, k, f, m, n,* and *l)* may present a problem, since Spanish words do not begin with the *s* + consonant sound. A vowel always precedes the *s* when it is followed by a consonant (as *estar* for *star*). The child may have difficulty in pronouncing two consonants together in the final position (as w*asp*, di*sk*, la*st*). Words ending in *r* plus *d, t, l, p,* and *s* may be pronounced without the final consonant (as *car* for *card*). The Spanish letter *h* is silent *(hotel* becomes *otel*). There are only two contractions in Spanish; stress is different; and the Spanish adjectives often follow rather than precede the nouns *(The dress blue is pretty.).*

Some other points of difficulty might be: negation *(Jim is no here.);* agreement of adjectives *(The two boys are bigs.);* omission of subject pronouns *(Is here.);* comparisons *(is more small);* omission of articles *(He is policeman.);* subject-verb agreement *(The girls runs,* or *The girl run.);* possessive adjectives and pronouns *(The book of the boy);* and past tense *(He need help yesterday.).*

Instructional program

Of primary importance in developing self-expression is the manner in which the teacher reacts to the child's dialect. Should the teacher place immediate restrictions on the child's expression, he may only succeed in making the child feel insecure. Teachers must encourage children to express themselves in whatever dialect they have, then lead them gently, by example, toward a more generally accepted (classroom, school, or standard) dialect. The program should be based upon such ideas as:

1. Language is a form of human behavior and it is subject to many variations among its users and to continual change.
2. There are choices and selections to make in the use of language (e.g., *isn't/ain't; as I did/like I did; he doesn't/he don't)* and varying social penalties for particular usage items.

Teachers must encourage children to express themselves in whatever dialect they have, then lead them gently, by example, toward a more generally accepted dialect.

3. There is usage for both formal and informal situations: for formal public address and informal conversations with friends.
4. Usage can be better evaluated as more or less appropriate in terms of the audience and the occasion than arbitrarily as "right or wrong" or "good or bad."

The teacher is likely the most influential speaking model for children outside their home environment. To teach by example, and not by continually saying no, places a responsibility upon the teacher for providing a worthy language model. Children are great imitators, and much of their language is "caught" as well as "taught."

• *Some usage items*   A common cause of ineffective usage instruction may be attributed to the selection and number of items to be taught. Sometimes teachers attempt to "cover" too many items during the year. The following list provides a general selection of usage items to be considered for instructional attention.

Speech Forms Subject to Intensive Teaching in the Elementary School

Verb Forms	*Pronoun Forms*
ain't or *hain't*	my brother, *he* (and other double subjects)
I *don't* have *no*	
learn me a song	*him* and *me* went, Mary and *me* saw, etc.
leave me go	
have ate, have went, have did, *have saw, have wrote,* etc.	*hisself, theirselves,* etc.
he *begun,* he *seen,* he *run,* he *drunk,* he *come,* etc.	*them* books, *this here* book, *that there* book
I *says*	it's *your'n, her'n, his'n, our'n*
he *brung,* he *clumb*	
we, you, they *was*	
was *broke* (for broken)	
was *froze*	
knowed, growed, etc.	

SOURCE: Robert C. Pooley, *The Teaching of English Usage* (Urbana, Ill.: National Council of Teachers of English, 1974), p. 183. Copyright © 1974 by the National Council of Teachers of English. Reprinted with permission.

• *Suggested activities*   An important feature of the above listing is the absence of grade placement for the various items. The reason for that is that forms should be emphasized as needed. Such usages are concrete in nature and easily detected by teachers. The most important factor in allocating specific language usage items to any level should be the performance of the pupils at that level.

An effort must be made to detect common (to group) and specific (to individual) usage facts on which to base instruction. The observation of children's responses during free activity periods, club meetings, and similar occasions when there is uninhibited expression is one of the most productive ways of securing data on oral language patterns. Record-keeping can result from such surveys, as suggested by chart 5.6.

CHART 5.6: Analysis of Nonstandard Usage

Pupils	Verbs	Subject Pronouns	Adjective/ Adverb	Negative	Redundancy	Illiteracies
Agnes	have came	Betty and me	gooder	don't have no	John he	hain't
James						
Donnie						
Lisa						

Nonstandard usages common to most class members and frequently made by pupils in their oral and written expression should be treated with the class as a whole. The other usage items will be dealt with by working in small groups or through individualized instruction. An effort will be made to provide standard usage for the grossly inappropriate speech patterns (severe social penalty) before working on those of a less serious or borderline variety.

More specifically, the following ideas are offered for consideration when teaching standard speech patterns.

1. In the early school years, the teacher should not react in such a way as to make the children feel disapproval or shame when they use a nonstandard speech form. A more constructive approach might be to rephrase the statement so the children have an idea of the approved usage. In anticipation of a usage problem, the teacher

might use the approved form as a question before the children have a chance to use the less approved form. In such ways, the child's habitual language pattern can be altered without trauma. Above all, the teacher remains sympathetic and understanding, giving far more emphasis to suggesting standard substitutes than to condemning the existing usage.

2.   The approach to improving oral usage should be primarily through listening and speaking exercises rather than written ones. In the past, written drill was almost solely relied upon to bring about alteration in oral expression. The tape recorder is an effective device for helping the child hear the "way he talks," and it can be a powerful motivating device for calling attention to usage patterns.

3.   The following example includes some of the more desirable features for teaching an inductive lesson if inappropriate usage of a specific item has been detected by the teacher as common to many of the children.

Item: Use of *saw* and *seen*

a.   The teacher asks the pupils, "What did you see on the way to school this morning?"

b.   Sentences are written on the chalkboard: John saw a fire engine. Mary and Sue saw a bluebird. Jim saw a little kitten.

c.   The children read the sentences aloud while the teacher underlines *saw* in each sentence.

d.   The teacher asks, "Did you see an elephant this morning? Have you ever seen an elephant?"

e.   Sentences are written on the chalkboard: Bill has seen an elephant. Sue has seen an elephant.

f.   The teacher asks other questions and writes replies: John *has seen* a bear. Betty *has seen* the ocean.

g.   The children read the sentences aloud while the teacher underlines *has* and *seen* in each sentence.

h.   The pupils are asked to examine carefully the sentences written on the chalkboard and to note where *saw* was used and where *seen* was used.

i.   Other sentences are composed and written on the chalkboard: We have seen this book. Jim had seen a dog yesterday. They have never seen a real elephant.

j.   The children read the sentences aloud while the teacher underlines *have (had)* and *seen*.

k.   The class discusses the fact that *seen* is used with "helping" verbs, while *saw* does not require them. (The children may suggest that some people say "I seen," "he seen," or "I have saw." Through class discussion of these expressions, the pupils may be guided to see the influence of formal education and the speaking situation upon the language that is used. Further comparison with the best oral and written language causes these expressions to be labeled nonstandard.)

1. The children are given an opportunity to use *saw* and *seen* correctly in oral and written activities.

As many usage lessons as possible should be presented in such an inductive manner. Another example: At the intermediate level, the pupils might be asked to keep a record chart for one day of some usage item, such as *don't* and *doesn't*. They should keep this record not only in the classroom but also outside the classroom. The chart should record the usage, the speaker's probable level of education, the number of persons present in the situation, and the atmosphere (formality of the situation). Observations could then be called for from the data appearing on each child's chart, and generalizations could be made from the total data.

4. Frequent applied and functional practice should be provided for use of the standard form through such occasions as speaking to the class, reporting to a group, storytelling, or participating in drama activities. The pupil must look upon use of words as an integrated part of each language activity rather than as an isolated matter to be practiced only in "language periods." If the results of usage instruction prove disappointing, one reason may be that the child does not have sufficient opportunity to apply his knowledge of usage to *his* own oral and written expressions—but only to textbook and workbook exercises.

5. Aspects of "second language" techniques may be effectively utilized, particularly when the child recognizes that he uses a nonstandard speech form and wishes to participate in activities that will focus upon the standard form. The following steps are an example of this procedure. (It is assumed that the teacher has some basic information about the linguistic features of the learner's dialect—such as those cited on pages 169–171.)

Item: Substitution of *f* for voiceless *th* in the final position (*wif* for *with*, *mouf* for *mouth*, *paf* for *path*)

a. The child recognizes that his nonstandard dialect and the standard dialect are different. (Use a tape recorder and point out that when he says *wif*, he substitutes a sound he hears at the beginning of words like *fan*, *fat*, *fog*, *fight*.)

b. The child hears the standard sound being taught. (Give an oral list of words that contain the voiceless *th* in the final position, such as *with*, *mouth*, *path*, and ask him to discriminate these words from other words—except words like *whiff*, *muff*, *laugh*, etc.)

c. The child discriminates between a sound in the standard dialect and the corresponding sound in the nonstandard dialect. (Identify which sounds are spoken twice in a series to discriminate the voiceless *th* from *f*: *with*, *wif*, *with*; *mouf*, *mouf*, *mouth*; *path*, *paf*, *path*.

d. The child practices reproductions of the standard feature. (Use pattern practice—repeating a series of words, such as *with*, *mouth*, *path*, after each is presented orally. Sentences may be repeated: *John ran down the path with his mouth open.* Later the interfering element /f/

Much technology is now available for teachers of the language arts, such as *The Language Master,* which has numerous possibilities in the oral expression program.

LESSON PLAN: Usage (Syntactical Feature)

Performance Objective:
    The learner adds *he plays fair* to his out-of-school *he play fair.*
Pretest:
    Prepare a list of nonstandard usage forms as the children talk. Choose one specific form for direct attention.
Teaching Suggestions:
1. Write and state both corresponding standard and nonstandard forms. Discuss the differences and help the learner to become aware of these differences. Have him show that he can discriminate between the two forms. For example, he might clap his hands upon hearing the standard form or he might be asked to say both forms. Have him reproduce the standard form orally.
2. Use patterns for concentrated repetition: *he plays fair, she plays fair, John plays fair,* etc.

Mastery or Posttest Suggestion:
    Observe the linguistic pattern under consideration by having the learners engage in a role-playing situation where they discuss the topic of "fair play."
Reteaching Suggestions:
1. Use *The Language Master* for pattern drill—a prerecorded sentence and then the child's repetition.
2. Allow pupil peers to aid each other in modeling and practicing the language pattern.

---

    may be included: *After he ran down the path with his mouth wide open, John began to puff, whiff, and laugh.*)
e. The child uses the standard feature in a meaningful situation. (Use short speaking situations where the child is particularly careful about the feature under consideration.)

    The same procedure as indicated for the phonological interference point may be followed for study of a syntactical feature.[19] One sample is provided above.

---

19. The following references will be useful to the reader interested in understanding syntactical and phonological differences and principles of teaching a second dialect: Gertrude B. Corcoran, *Language Arts in the Elementary School: A Modern Linguistic Approach* (New York: Ronald, 1970), pp. 245–253; Catheryn Eisenhardt, *Applying Linguistics in the Teaching of Reading and the Language Arts* (Columbus, Ohio: Merrill, 1972), pp. 114–126; Kenneth R. Johnson, "Standard English and Disadvantaged Black Children: Teaching Strategies," *Teaching the Language Arts to Culturally Different Children,* ed. William W. Joyce and James A. Banks (Reading, Mass.: Addison-Wesley, 1971), pp. 121–129.

EVALUATION OF ORAL EXPRESSION

Oral language is difficult to evaluate, but the difficulties inherent in measurement should not encourage teachers to make only subjective and cursory appraisals. There is still a need to determine accomplishment, to diagnose the product of individual effort, and to base judgments upon the best possible measurements.

Lack of standardized tests for measuring oral language achievement does not mean that oral language cannot be evaluated. For example, a tape recorder makes it possible for the teacher to record the speech efforts of his class. The speech skills on a tape made at one time of the year may be compared with those made at an earlier date. Other evaluative devices would include teacher-made tests and simple rating scales.

The most practical procedure for a teacher to follow in evaluating oral expression is to make consistent use of checklists to compare expression in a particular situation with the objectives of the speech effort in that situation. A checklist of objectives like the one listed below might be utilized in terms of overall standards for improving speaking skills.

1. Ability to select and organize the content or ideas of a speaking situation
2. Ability to speak with a sincere and courteous attitude and respect for the audience
3. Ability to speak with a suitable voice and use appropriate forms of words that express ideas clearly and accurately
4. Ability to use appropriate posture and body actions

A comparison of the teacher's and child's evaluation will delineate strengths and weaknesses of the learner's oral expression. Checklists such as the following might be used:

Student's Speech Checklist

1. How do I sound?
   a. Is my voice pleasant to hear?
   b. Can others understand the words I say?
   c. Is my voice neither too loud nor too soft?
2. Is my speech interesting to others?
   a. Do I use a variety of expressions and words?
   b. Do I explain things so others understand my ideas?

    c. Do I use language correct for each speaking situation?

    d. Do I remember to take my turn to speak—talking neither too much nor too little?

I can improve my voice and speech by ———————————.

Teacher's Speech Checklist

1. Student's voice
    a. Is the voice pleasant?
      If not, how would you describe it?
    b. Are articulation and enunciation satisfactory?
      If not, what needs to be improved?
    c. Is volume appropriate for each occasion?
      If not, is it too loud or too soft?

2. Student's speech
    a. Does speech show a variety of expressions and vocabulary? If not, what needs improving?
    b. Does speech give evidence of careful thinking? If not, what seems to be the reason?
    c. Is usage acceptable? If not, what faults are most common?
    d. Is there evidence that personality problems hamper speech quality? If yes, what seems to be the problem?

SOURCE: O. W. Kopp, "The Evaluation of Oral Language Activities: Teaching and Learning," *Elementary English* 44 (February 1967): 121–122. Reprinted by permission of the National Council of Teachers of English.

Some teachers have found a flow chart helpful in maintaining a record of individual participation in all of the oral composition activities for identifying skills weaknesses. One way to record this information is to place the names of each class member alphabetically on the left-hand side of a large sheet of cardboard. The first section of the chart could be labeled "Oral Composition Activities" and the second section could be labeled "Skills." As each child participates in the activities, a check could be placed beside the child's name in the appropriate activity square. This would insure that each child had an opportunity to participate in each activity. Those children needing improvement would be identified as they participated in the activities and the kind of difficulty would be marked on the chart. After the identification of the weakness, the teacher could plan more activities for the child that would improve the situation and could mark the activity section as the child completed the tasks.

To probe children's feelings about the specific experiences within the area of oral composition, items may be listed for pupil likes and dislikes. The pupil would check the column that most closely represents his feelings toward the concept, as suggested in chart 5.7:

CHART 5.7: Feelings About Oral Composition

Topic: Oral Composition	*Dislike very much*	*Dislike*	*Like*	*Like very much*
Conversation				
Discussion				
Reporting				
Storytelling				
Pantomime/creative drama, choral reading				
Making announcements				
Giving messages, directions, explanations				
Giving reviews of books, movies, television programs				
Using the telephone				
Making introductions and conducting interviews				
Conducting meetings				

(Similar charts could be developed for other major language arts experiences: listening, literature, written composition, common elements of oral/written expression, grammar, spelling, and handwriting.)

SELECTED REFERENCES

General Professional

Anderson, Paul S. *Language Skills in Elementary Education.* 2d ed. New York: Macmillan, 1972, chapter 2.

Boyd, Gertrude. *Teaching Communication Skills in the Elementary School.* New York: Van Nostrand Reinhold, 1970, chapters 7, 14.

Burrows, Alvina T.; Monson, Diane L.; and Stauffer, Russell G. *New Horizons in the Language Arts.* New York: Harper & Row, 1972, chapter 2.

Corcoran, Gertrude B. *Language Arts in Elementary School: A Modern Linguistic Approach.* New York: Ronald, 1970, chapter 14.

Dallmann, Martha. *Teaching the Language Arts in the Elementary School.* 2d ed. Dubuque, Iowa: William C. Brown, 1971, chapter 4.

Greene, Harry A., and Petty, Walter T. *Developing Language Skills in the Elementary Schools.* 4th ed. Boston: Allyn and Bacon, 1971, chapter 7.

Lamb, Pose, ed. *Guiding Children's Language Learning.* 2d ed. Dubuque, Iowa: William C. Brown, 1971, chapters 3, 4.

Smith, James A. *Adventures in Communication: Language Arts Methods.* Boston: Allyn and Bacon, 1972, chapter 6.

Strickland, Ruth. *The Language Arts in the Elementary School.* 3rd ed. Lexington, Mass.: D. C. Heath, 1969, chapters 7, 8.

Specialized

Brown-Azarowicz, Marjory F. *A Handbook of Creative Choral Speaking.* Minneapolis, Minn.: Burgess, 1970.

Carin, Arthur A., and Sund, Robert B. *Developing Questioning Techniques: A Self-Concept Approach.* Columbus, Ohio: Merrill, 1971.

Colwell, Eileen, ed. *A Second Storyteller's Choice.* New York: Walck, 1965.

Crosscup, Richard. *Children and Dramatics.* New York: Scribner, 1966.

Eisenhardt, Catheryn. *Applying Linguistics in the Teaching of Reading and the Language Arts.* Columbus, Ohio: Merrill, 1972.

Everetts, Eldonna L., ed. *Dimensions of Dialect.* Urbana, Ill.: National Council of Teachers of English, 1967.

Fitzgerald, Burdette S. *World Tales for Creative Dramatics and Storytelling.* Englewood Cliffs, N.J.: Prentice-Hall, 1962.

Gillies, Emily. *Creative Dramatics for All Children.* Washington, D.C.: Association for Childhood Education International, 1973.

Henry, Mabel Wright. *Creative Experiences in Oral Language.* Urbana, Ill.: National Council of Teachers of English, 1967.

Johnson, Kenneth R. *Teaching Culturally Disadvantaged Pupils. Unit 8, Improving Language Skills of the Culturally Disadvantaged.* Chicago: Science Research Associates, 1967.

Lee, Charlotte I. *Oral Interpretation.* 4th ed. Boston: Houghton Mifflin, 1971.

Lewis, Thomas R., and Nichols, Ralph G. *Speaking and Listening: A Guide to Effective Oral-Aural Communication.* Dubuque, Iowa: William C. Brown, 1965.

McCaslin, Nellie. *Creative Dramatics in the Classroom.* 2d ed. New York: McKay, 1974.

McIntyre, Barbara. *Creative Drama in the Elementary School.* Itasca, Ill.: Peacock Publishers, 1974.

Montebello, Mary. *Children's Literature in the Curriculum.* Dubuque, Iowa: William C. Brown, 1973.

Phillips, Gerald M., et al. *The Development of Oral Communication in the Classroom.* Indianapolis: Bobbs, 1970.

Pierini, Mary Francis. *Creative Dramatics: A Guide for Educators.* New York: Seabury, 1971.

Pooley, Robert W. *The Teaching of English Usage.* 2d ed. Urbana, Ill.: National Council of Teachers of English, 1974.

Possien, Wilma M. *They All Need to Talk.* New York: Appleton-Century-Crofts, 1969.

Ross, Ramon. *Storyteller.* Columbus, Ohio: Merrill, 1972.

Saville, Muriel R., and Troike, Rudolph C. *A Handbook of Bilingual Education.* Washington, D.C.: Center for Applied Linguistics, 1970.

Sheldon, William D. *The Reading of Poetry.* Boston: Allyn and Bacon, 1966.

Siks, Geraldine. *Creative Dramatics: An Art for Children.* New York: Harper & Brothers, 1958.

Stewig, John W. *Spontaneous Drama.* Columbus, Ohio: Merrill, 1973.

Walden, James, ed. *Oral Language and Reading.* Urbana, Ill.: National Council of Teachers of English, 1969.

Ward, Winifred. *Playmaking with Children from Kindergarten Through Junior High School.* 2d ed. New York: Appleton-Century-Crofts, 1957.

Zintz, Miles V. *What Classroom Teachers Should Know About Bilingual Education.* Albuquerque: University of New Mexico College of Education, 1969.

LITERATURE

OBJECTIVES	PERFORMANCE RESPONSES
1. **To identify the purposes and forms of literature**	1. Write a paragraph about the forms of literature appropriate for elementary children.
2. **To demonstrate read-aloud story procedures**	2. Select a read-aloud story for an age level of your choice. Share it with a small group of children or peers. Tape your reading and then evaluate it.
3. **To plan a close reading of a piece of literature**	3. Select a picture book, a fiction story, or a poem. Develop a set of questions to be used for close study of it by a group of children.
4. **To learn about magazines and newspapers that are appropriate for children**	4. After examining several children's magazines and newspapers, report their features to the class.
5. **To identify poems that are appropriate for children and to suggest ways of sharing them with the class**	5. Select a read-aloud poem for an age level of your interest. Share it with a small group of children or peers. Tape your reading and then evaluate it.
6. **To select appropriate prose or poetry for special groups**	6. Select an age level and list stories and poems, focusing upon minority groups, that might be recommended for them.
7. **To examine films as one way to introduce literature**	7. If feasible, preview one film appropriate for literature study. Prepare a list of literary concepts associated with it.
8. **To examine a way of organizing literature response stations**	8. Outline a response station plan for a literature project. Utilize your media knowledge.
9. **To identify literature that can be correlated with other subject areas**	9. Select one subject area (social studies, mathematics, science, etc.). Annotate five books and a couple of poems that could be used to develop concepts of the subject area.

10. To gain insight into children's reading interests	10. Make a class survey of books the children read or would like to read. Give an oral report on your findings.
11. To learn about available literature reference books, general booklists, and periodicals	11. Select one source mentioned in the corresponding Objective. Explain its possible use to the class.
12. To acquire understanding about evaluation of a literature program	12. Recommend additional behavioral characteristics (re literature) to be desired on the part of pupils at one school level of your choosing.

Experiences with literature can expand vocabulary, stimulate the imagination, provide the sensitivity and stimulus for writing, whet the appetite for reading, and provoke critical thinking about the world in which we live.

Literature has a very special place in the language arts program since it provides outlets and challenges for children's reading, speaking, and writing, thus furthering appreciation of their cultural heritage of fine writing. Experiences with literature can expand vocabulary, stimulate the imagination, provide the sensitivity and stimulus for writing, whet the appetite for reading, and provoke critical thinking about the world in which we live. As can be noted by the reader, literature is an integral part of practically every chapter in this book, demonstrating its potential to enrich the total language arts program in a wide range of ways.

PURPOSES AND FORMS

While literature is a major integrating experience in the elementary school language arts program, it also has value of its own because it provides new perspectives through vicarious experiences, develops insight into human behavior and wisdom, and provides beauty and inspiration.

A good literature program encourages the development of knowledge about our literary heritage, establishes skills of literary analysis, fosters language skills, enriches content of the curriculum, and stimulates creative activities. The major goal, however, is to promote the experiencing and enjoyment of literature as a means of developing children's reading tastes and lifetime appreciation of fine reading materials.

Literature comes in many varieties: poetry, drama, fiction, and nonfiction. Poetry has numerous forms, such as the ballad, epigram, epic, limerick, lyric, and sonnet. In addition to regular stage plays, drama is often presented through motion pictures, television plays, or scenarios for puppet and marionette shows. Fiction includes novels; short stories; and other short forms, such as animal stories, fables, fairy tales, legends, myths, other-lands-and-other-peoples stories, and realistic stories. Nonfiction includes biographies, essays, historical accounts, journals, letters, personal narratives, and some written speeches and documentaries.

A good literature program will help children to become acquainted with the best of all forms of literature; effort should be made to give children experiences with a variety of literary forms. It should include some of the older classics as well as those excellent, current selections that may become the classics of tomorrow. It should present stories of other times and other places; stories about people like those who live next door; stories that bring chuckles and those that bring tears; stories of fact, fancy, and just plain nonsense. Not every child will respond with equal enthusiasm, but all should have an opportunity to discover literature that has special meaning for them and to read freely along the lines of their own individual interests.

SOME COMPONENTS OF A PLANNED LITERATURE PROGRAM

Many different procedures and activities are used to encourage children to be knowledgeable about and delighted by literature. Storytelling and drama (see chapter 5) have been discussed and will not be repeated in this chapter.

Background and/or knowledge for the teacher that is a prerequisite to developing a good literature program includes:

acquiring a repertoire of stories and poems that brings you pleasure;

knowing the interests and reading levels of the children that you teach;

knowing the books available in your library that meet the interests and reading levels of your children;

establishing a "reading-is-fun" environment;

using some form of literature in your lesson plan every day;

helping children understand the background of the literature they are reading; and

providing time for free discussions on what you have read and what they have read.

Prose

• *Oral reading*   One of the best ways of presenting literature to children is to have the teacher read a story to the class. Primary teachers often have a rocking chair for themselves (or for the child who is to read or tell a story to a group or class). The children seat themselves on the floor around the chair. Oral reading may be preceded by some background information or followed by informal discussion; however, neither the background information nor the discussion needs to be analytical. The pre- or postactivities should be designed to whet curiosity, catch the pupils' attention, clarify meanings of words vital to interpretation, and give purpose to listening.

The enthusiastic teacher knows that one of the best ways to create interest in books is to read to children every day.

Books such as *Mary Poppins* by Pamela L. Traver,[1] *Dick Whittington and His Cat* by Marcia Brown,[2] or *And to Think That I Saw It on Mulberry Street* by Dr. Seuss[3] are examples of good books for reading aloud, as sharing the humor and language adds to the enjoyment of the story. Following are some suggested read-aloud books.

Primary

Aliki, *A Weed is a Flower: The Life of George Washington Carver.* New York: Prentice-Hall, 1965.

Caudill, Rebecca. *A Pocketful of Cricket.* New York: Holt, Rinehart and Winston, 1971.

De Regniers, Beatrice S. *May I Bring a Friend?* New York: Atheneum, 1964.

Emberly, Ed. *Rosebud.* Boston: Little, 1966.

Hader, Berta, and Hader, Elmer. *Two is Company, Three's a Crowd.* New York: Macmillan, 1965.

Hess, Lilo. *Easter in November.* New York: Thomas Y. Crowell, 1964.

Keats, Ezra Jack. *Whistle for Willie.* New York: Viking Press, 1964.

Ness, Evaline. *Tom Tit Tot.* New York: Scribner, 1965.

Sendak, Maurice, *Where the Wild Things Are.* New York: Harper & Row, 1963.

Steig, William. *Amos and Boris.* New York: Farrar, Straus & Giroux, 1971.

Steptoe, John. *Birthday.* New York: Holt, Rinehart and Winston, 1972.

Stevenson, James. *The Bear Who Had No Place to Go.* New York: Harper & Row, 1972.

Intermediate

Bawden, Nina. *Squib.* Philadelphia: Lippincott, 1971.

Byrd, Ernestine. *Ice King.* New York: Scribner, 1965.

Coatsworth, Elizabeth. *The Wanderers.* New York: Scholastic Book Services, 1972.

Fleming, Ian. *Chitty-Chitty-Bang-Bang.* New York: Random, 1964.

George, Jean Craighead. *Julie of the Wolves.* New York: Harper & Row, 1972.

Jarrell, Randall. *The Animal Family.* New York: Pantheon, 1965.

Smith, Vian. *Martin Rides the Moor.* New York: Doubleday, 1965.

Sommerfelt, Aimée. *Road to Agra.* New York: Criterion, 1961.

---

1. Pamela L. Traver, *Mary Poppins* (New York: Harcourt, 1934).
2. Marcia Brown, *Dick Whittington and His Cat* (New York: Scribner, 1950).
3. Dr. Seuss, *And To Think That I Saw It on Mulberry Street* (New York: Vanguard, 1937).

Suhl, Yuri. *Simon Boom Gives a Wedding*. New York: Scholastic Book Services, 1972.

Wojciechowska, Maia. *Shadow of a Bull*. New York: Atheneum, 1964.

(For a comprehensive listing of suggested read-aloud books, see *Let's Read Together: Books for Family Enjoyment*. 3rd ed. Chicago: American Library Association, 1969.)

Teachers should read in natural tones and with expression, but not dramatically. Time should be provided for sharing the illustrations with the children, exploring key words and phrases, and evaluating reactions. It is better to read aloud stories that (1) children cannot easily read for themselves, (2) the teacher personally likes and is thoroughly familiar with, and (3) possess the qualities assigned to the best in literature.[4]

At times a child may ask to read his favorite story to the class or to a small group of children, and at other times the teacher should encourage children to share stories of general interest orally with the group. Older children reading stories to younger ones can be highly beneficial to both groups. No group should be compelled to listen to a poor reader. The teacher must help the reader be well prepared for the presentation of his material. A brief story that is new to the class and presented with visual aids has a good chance of being successful for the reader and for his audience.

• *Free silent reading*   Frequent opportunities for free silent reading should be provided. Children need opportunities to browse through books and magazines in the classroom or library, to find materials that interest them, and then to read silently. Because this type of reading involves free selection, the materials provided by the school must meet the highest standards of literary quality.

• *Recreational reading*   Some teachers have found it helpful to have a definite, regular, and scheduled recreational reading period, separate from the instructional reading time, the free silent reading time, or the literature time. Recreational reading involves introduction of new materials, time for reading, and time for a summary.

---

4. For example, see Dora V. Smith, "The Children's Literary Heritage," *Elementary English* 41 (November 1964): 715–727. See also Elizabeth Guilfoile, "Good Books for Children," *Elementary English* 43 (January 1966): 21–25, 55; Alice Mabel Jordan and Helen Master, *Children's Classics* (Boston: Horn Book, 1967).

During this period of recreation, teachers introduce new books to the class, discuss books that are being read, and provide information about authors or illustrators. During most of the period, the teacher helps slow readers or those who need help with words. He does not interrupt those who are progressing successfully. The final minutes of the class are devoted to sharing interesting ideas and summaries of the books.

Children's preferences are often influenced by the teacher's enthusiasm about a selection of prose or poetry or by other children's likes and dislikes. Enjoyable experiences at school prompt continued reading at home. Since pupils are encouraged to share their at-home reading with the class, parents can play a part by suggesting on occasion that a certain story would be a good one to read or tell to the class; and, of course, the parent's interest in hearing the story read and told is very important. Teachers may further interest parents in at-home reading by sending letters to parents concerning the literature program, encouraging a home library, suggesting reading lists, and recommending specific ways the home can assist with the school's program. Fortunately, there are helpful publications that give parents advice on how to guide children's reading.[5]

• *Close reading/study of literature* The primary purpose of the literature program is the enjoyment of prose and poetry; however, to increase the appreciation of literature, some analysis is necessary. Close reading and study does not mean formal (or informal) literary criticism of every story or poem the child reads. It does mean that the teacher should make systematic inquiry into some of the worthy literature read by children. Usually this is best achieved through discussion with small groups of individuals (six to eight) who have read a story or poem worthy of analysis. Naturally, the teacher should be thoroughly familiar with the material used for literary study.

Items that lend themselves to study by elementary children are genre, plot, setting, theme, characterization, style, format, comparison of stories or poems, and other study criteria. Each will be discussed briefly in turn.

1. Genre: This term means "a distinctive category of literature." While there are different ways of categorizing types of literature, the trend seems to be to provide a classification for children. Huck and Kuhn have classified literary forms into three main categories as follows:[6]

---

5. Annis Duff, *The Bequest of Wings: A Family's Pleasures with Books* (New York: Viking Press, 1941); idem, *Longer Flight: A Family Grows up with Books* (New York: Viking Press, 1955); Anne T. Eaton, *Reading with Children* (New York: Viking Press, 1940); idem, *Treasure for the Taking*, rev. ed. (New York: Viking Press, 1957); Roma Gans, *Reading is Fun: Developing Children's Reading Interests*, Parent Teacher Series (New York: Teachers College Press, Columbia University, 1949); Helen Heffernan and Vivian Todd, *Elementary Teacher's Guide to Working with Parents* (Englewood Cliffs, N.J.: Prentice-Hall, 1969); Nancy Larrick, *A Parent's Guide to Children's Reading* (New York: Doubleday, 1969); Lillian H. Smith, *The Unreluctant Years: A Critical Approach to Children's Literature* (Chicago: American Library Association, 1953).

6. From *Children's Literature in the Elementary School*, 2d ed., by Charlotte S. Huck and Doris Young Kuhn, p. 655. Copyright © 1961, 1968 by Holt, Rinehart and Winston, Inc. Reprinted by permission of Holt, Rinehart and Winston, Inc.

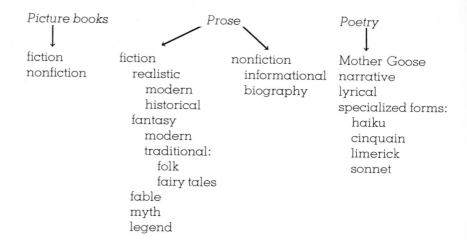

Children profit from knowing some classification pattern, for knowledge of the types of literature will permit them to (a) pursue a particular preference and (b) apply the appropriate criteria for evaluation. This suggests that books lend themselves to various analyses. The following definitions note the key features of some different literary genre:

Picture book: A book in which the pictures are an integral part of the text. Example: *Time of Wonder* by Robert McCloskey.

Prose: A narrative using the ordinary language of man. Example: *The Long Winter* by Laura I. Wilder.

Poetry: A rhythmic composition. Example: *I Went to the Animal Fair* by William Cole, ed.

Realistic fiction: A story, experienced or imagined by the author, that could have happened to real people living in the natural, physical world and social environment. Example: *Old Yeller* by Frederick B. Gipson.

Fantasy: A story rich in imagination. Example: *Charlotte's Web* by E. B. White.

Folktale: A narrative, written or oral, that has been handed down through the years. Example: *Mostly Magic* by Phyllis Fenner.

Fable: A brief tale in which an animal or inanimate object speaks as a human. Example: "The Town Mouse and the Country Mouse" by Aesop.

Myth: A story told to explain natural phenomena. Example: "Jason's Search for the Golden Fleece" by Apollonius.

Legend: A story, coming down from the past, of local heroes. Example: *Legends of the North* by Olivia Coolidge.

Informational book: A book written to give facts. Example: *Where in the World* by Philip Egan.

Biography: A true story about the life of a person. Example: *Carry On, Mr. Bowditch* by Jean Latham.

Narrative verse: A poem that tells a story or relates a particular event. Example: "The Pied Piper of Hamelin" by Robert Browning.

Lyrical poem: A personal or descriptive poem that sings its way into the minds and memories of readers or listeners. Example: "The Swing" by Robert Louis Stevenson.

To bring out the desired information as to genre, ask questions such as the following:

What kind of book was this?

Would you read the opening paragraphs of the book aloud to me to show that this story is of a fantasy type?

2. *Plot:* Plot refers to the plan of a story. It should be substantial, well constructed, and credible. If the plot is original and fresh—not trite or predictable—interest will be high. For historical fiction, the story must be historically accurate; and for biographies, authenticity (a true and accurate picture) is essential.

Questions like the following help the teacher to evaluate the child's understanding of the plot:

What did you discover about this book?

What did it mean to you?

How do events build to a climax?

Even for most historical fiction, the question "Did it tell a good story?" may be asked.

3. *Setting:* An authentic setting will involve the past, present, or future. A specific locale is often described by the author or an implied one may be suggested by dialect and activities. The setting answers the questions of when and where. In a well-written book the setting affects the actions, characters, and theme of the story.

Questions of the following type are used to direct attention to the setting:

Where and when did the story take place?

Did the story capture the spirit and feeling of the place or the age?

How did the author reveal the setting?

4. *Theme:* The theme of a book reveals the author's purpose in writing the story. A good book or story will have a significant, worthy theme and may have a deeper theme—a theme of several layers, so to speak. For example, an obvious theme for *Where the Wild Things Are* might be a story of a boy's dream, but there is also a deeper theme: that is, a mother's way to symbolize love and forgiveness. Even historical fiction usually has a theme.

Here the questions to be asked might include:

What is the "big idea" of this story?
What do you think the author is trying to tell his reader?

5. *Characterization:* A good story will convincingly portray real and lifelike characters who display strengths and weaknesses. Characters come to life by the writer's (a) telling about the person, (b) reporting his conversation with others, (c) giving the thoughts of the character, (d) providing the thoughts of others about the character, and (e) showing the character through his actions. Not all these devices may occur in any one story, but such techniques of characterization enliven children's literature. Too, an author may indicate character development or change through events and reasons. In biographies, a worthy subject is chosen to be the main character. In children's literature, some liberties may be taken with the character, such as the omission of unsavory aspects. At the same time, suitable shortcomings and virtues are recognized.

Questions such as the following help stimulate awareness and attention to characters and events:

How did the author reveal the characters in the story?
If a character changed, what was the change? What caused it? When did it happen?
Are the characters real?

6. *Style:* This term refers to the author's mode of expressing thoughts in words. Of course, the style should be appropriate to plot, theme, and characters. Usually the writer strives for a variety of sentence patterns. Children prefer action and conversation; they do not like too much description or figurative and symbolic meanings. Style includes the author's point of view when he tells the story; he may use his own (first person), the main character's (first person), or the omniscient narrator's (third person) who can reveal the inner thoughts and emotions of the characters.

The following questions are useful for directing attention to the author's style:

What would you say about the way the author wrote?
Did the author tell the story from his own personal point of view?
  Or was he the omniscient narrator?

7. *Format:* Format refers to the size, shape, design of pages, illustrations, typography, paper, and binding of a publication. Particularly with picture books, pictures are an integral part of the text; they help create the mood of the story and show character delineation.

Questions such as the following develop sensitivity to these items:

What are the sizes of the pictures? Why?
What colors are used in the illustrations? Why?
How is the format related to the story?
Do any pictures help to explain the characters?

8. *Comparison of stories or poems:* Frequently it is helpful to ask questions relating two or more stories or poems:

How are they alike?
How are they different?
What is the theme of each?
What are some other stories or poems with the same theme?

In addition to stories or poems with the same or different themes, comparisons are achieved through classical models or through previous works or other works in a series by the same author.

9. *Other study criteria:* There are different study criteria for different types of literature. For example, questions such as the following might be most applicable for a modern fantasy tale:

What are the fantastic elements?
How does the author make the story believable?
Is the story logical and consistent within its framework?
Is the plot original and ingenious?

For informational books, questions such as the following may be asked:

What are the qualifications of the author?
Are the facts accurate?
Is the book up-to-date?
Are differing viewpoints presented?
Is this a general survey book or one of specific interest?

Is there an appropriate amount of detail?

Did it encourage further study and reading on the topic?

Did the illustrations help explain the text?

Did the table of contents, index, headings and subheadings, appendix, and bibliography provide help for you in locating information?

For poetry, items such as the following are important for literary study: rhythm; rhyme and sound (alliteration, assonance, onomatopoeia); imagery (sense, simile, metaphor, allusion, personification); sensitivity to an idea or mood; and forms of poetry (narrative, lyric, limerick, free verse, sonnet).

Paperbacks take up little space, are easily displayed, and, most important, they are read.

• *Book clubs, paperbacks, magazines, and newspapers*   When children become independent readers, membership in a book club may stimulate recreational reading at home. Reading for enjoyment is one of the most important activities that teachers can provide for all elementary school children. The pleasure of owning their own books plus the advantage of having the books come through the mail to their home can create an added stimulus for children to try out their "wings" on new material. Below is a selected list of book clubs:

1. Archway Paperback, Washington Square Press, New York, N.Y. 10020
2. Bookplan, 921 Washington Ave., Brooklyn, N.Y. 11225
3. Catholic Children's Book Club, 260 Summit Ave., St. Paul, Minn.
4. Junior Literary Guild, 177 Park Ave., New York, N.Y. 10017
5. Parent's Magazine Book Club for Beginning Readers, 52 Vanderbilt Ave., New York, N.Y. 10017
6. Scholastic Book Clubs, Englewood Cliffs, N.J., 07632 (See-Saw [ages 5–7], Lucky [ages 7–9], Arrow [ages 9–11])
7. Weekly Reader Children's Book Club, Education Center, Columbus, Ohio 43216
8. Young People's Book Club, 226 North Cass Ave., Westmont, Ill. 60559
9. Young Readers of America (Division of Book-of-the-Month Club), 345 Hudson St., New York, N.Y. 10014
10. Young Folks Book Club, 1078 St. John's Place, Brooklyn, N.Y. 10013

The paperback is now an essential supplementary material in elementary school classrooms. Paperbacks can be made accessible to children in the classroom and in the central school library; they are appealing, easily portable, less formidable, and less expensive than hardback books. The available selection is wide: classics, modern fiction favorites, poetry, series on science and social studies, etc. Two reference sources most appropriate for those who are interested in the use of paperbacks are *Paperback Books for Children*[7] and *Reader's Choice Catalog*.[8]

Magazines and periodicals for elementary school children have been available for several years. Some favorites include:

---

7. *Paperback Books for Children* (New York: Citation Press).
8. *Reader's Choice Catalog* (Englewood Cliffs, N.J.: Scholastic Press).

Children's magazines
and periodicals can
materially contribute to
the education and
enlightenment of boys
and girls.

American Girl	*Ebony, Jr.*
American Junior	*Electric Company Magazine*
Red Cross News	*The Golden Magazine*
Arizona Highways	*Highlights for Children*
Audubon	*Humpty Dumpty Magazine*
The Boy's Life	*Jack and Jill*
Calling All Girls	*National Geographic School Bulletin*
Child Life	*National Parks*
Children's Digest	*National History Magazine*
Cricket	

Many children have interests beyond the topics treated in textbooks and often discover textbook materials are either outdated or insufficient in details. Four sources are footnoted for those who are interested in annotated, selected listings of magazines and periodicals for boys and girls.[9]

Many teachers subscribe to newspapers written specifically for the young. Moreover, children often begin at an early age to read all kinds of articles from the daily, local newspapers, such as comics, sports, society, local news, national news, foreign news, editorials, and columns. Consequently, pupils should know something about newspapers as a medium of information and entertainment and how to read and judge them. Pupils certainly need to be told that just because an item is in print it is not necessarily correct. Children need help in scanning headlines, picking out main points in articles, and reading with an awareness of a newspaper's or a writer's point of view.

As an initiatory activity in the study of newspapers, some teachers give a newspaper-reading survey questionnaire to their class. Developmental activities might include locating examples of the types of materials to be found in a newspaper, comparing neighborhood papers, finding illustrations of stories with accurate or misleading captions, identifying the five Ws and an H in the leading paragraphs, studying how news agencies operate, learning about what a reporter does, finding out about some famous cartoonists, discussing the types of illustrations used, and studying the advertisements. A visit to a newspaper plant may be made or the local editor invited to speak to the class.

Pupils may wish to publish a class newspaper. Activities required in this effort involve pupils in many aspects of the language arts. They plan, discuss, write, and proofread their newspapers, thereby strengthening skills in listening, speaking, writing, spelling, and reading. The collection of news may not always appear on paper; a sketch of a "chalkboard" newspaper is provided on the following page.

---

9. Earl E. Edmondson, "Children's Magazines and Periodicals: A Selective Bibliography," Claremont Reading Conference, Thirtieth Yearbook, 1966, pp. 215–220; Thomas D. Horm et al., "Periodicals for Children and Youth," *Elementary English* 43 (April 1966): 341–358; George W. Norvell, "The Challenge of Periodicals in Education," *Elementary English* 43 (April 1966): 402–408; Nancy Nunnally, "Magazines and Newspapers for Children," *Childhood Education* 42 (April 1966): 517–521.

Weather	Interesting Events	Jokes, Riddles	Lost/Found
Story/Poem			
		Favorite Books	
			Safety Tips

Poetry

Long ago, Goethe wrote, "One ought, every day at least, to hear a little song, read a good poem, see a fine picture, and if it were possible, speak a few reasonable words." If teachers would read a good poem to children every day, the essential elements of rich language use (form, rhythm, words, and subject matter) might be more quickly acquired by the children. The teacher who shares the enjoyment of poetry with children experiences the rewarding satisfaction of seeing young faces light up in response to the beauty of rhythmic words.

Poetry is likely to be neglected because many adults (including teachers) experienced negative teaching of poetry during their school years. For too long, children have been required to memorize inappropriate poems. The required memorization of the same poem by the entire class developed a resistance on the part of many children to further develop poetry reading and study. The child's response to poetry will be influenced strongly by the teacher's response to poetry.

One of the problems in teaching poetry is selecting a suitable poem. A suitable poem should amuse, inspire, move emotionally, or interest intellectually those who are going to hear it or read it. The poem should not only be understandable and enjoyable but should extend the interest of the child to discovering still other poems. When an individual begins reading poems rather than being read to, the teacher must remember to provide him with poems having familiar content and words. Children are more willing to read more difficult and longer poems if their first attempts have been successful and enjoyable.

Teachers of older children often have to overcome a prejudice against poetry. One procedure is to request children to bring to class humorous poems found in periodicals or newspapers. Some children will wish to read their poem aloud to the class, and others may prefer that the teacher or another child share it with the group. After the poem is read, the central idea of the poem can be discussed. Often, older children will compare and contrast the poem with other poems that they know. Another promising approach involves introduction of pupils to such poetry anthologies as *The Birds and the Beasts Were There* and *Beastly Boys and Ghastly Girls* by William Cole (Cleveland, Ohio: World Publishing). And, of course, the limerick is a form that appeals to most children. The classic limerick book is Edward Lear's *The Complete Nonsense Book* (New York: Dodd, 1912). Also valuable is *Laughable Limerick*, compiled by Sara and John E. Brewton (New York: Thomas Y. Crowell, 1965).

• *Poetry reading*   The reading of poetry by a teacher should be a pleasant experience for both the listeners and the speaker. Often, an overly dramatic interpretation of a poem will cause the listener to pay more attention to the manner in which it is being read than to what the poem itself portrays in its own rhythmic pattern. When presenting a poem to the class, a teacher should:

1. select a poem that will interest the listening audience;
2. practice reading the poem before presenting it to the class;
3. speak in a clear, vital, moderate voice, preserving the poem's rhythm;
4. avoid over-dramatization; and
5. provide time for reading the poem more than once to the

A few excellent read-aloud poems include: "Who Has Seen the Wind?" by Christina G. Rosetti, "Mice" by Rose Fyleman, "Eletelephony" and "The Monkeys and the Crocodile" by Laura E. Richards, "The Owl and the Pussycat" by Edward Lear, "Every Time I Climb a Tree" by David McCord, "Godfrey Gordon Gustavus Gore" by William B. Rands, and "Father William" by Lewis Carroll. (Reread the idea for a poetry file in chapter 1 page 11.)

When children start to read poetry orally to other members of their class, the purpose should be to share an enjoyable poetic experience. Each child will read a poem in his own style if he understands the content and knows the vocabulary. Only in the upper-elementary school should rhythm and critical interpretation of the content of a poem be stressed.

• *Poetry by and about special groups*   In the past, literature, both prose and poetry, was focused upon the Caucasian child and his heritage. The children of minority groups in the United States—blacks, Indians, Asians, Jews, and Spanish-Americans—found few books that related to the background of their own culture; consequently, the Caucasian child also received little information about minority cultures. It is important that current programs in children's literature incorporate literature by and about minority groups into the regular literature curriculum as a means of: (1) establishing an awareness of the minority groups' role in our literary heritage; (2) engendering respect for and pride in the contributions made by all authors regardless of race, color, and creed; and (3) promoting understanding and brotherhood through the study of literature.[10]

Some selected volumes that are particularly helpful in the elementary school years include:

Black Literature

Adoff, Arnold, ed. *Black Out Loud*. New York: Macmillan, 1970.

Baker, Augusta. *The Black Experience in Children's Books*. New York: New York Public Library.

Bontemps, Arna. *Golden Slippers: An Anthology of Negro Poetry*. New York: Harper & Brothers, 1941.

Brooks, Gwendolyn. *Bronzeville Boys and Girls*. New York: Harper & Brothers, 1956.

Dunbar, Paul Lawrence. *The Complete Poems of Paul Lawrence Dunbar*. New York: Dodd, 1913.

Hughes, Langston. *Selected Poems of Langston Hughes*. New York: Knopf, 1959.

Red, White, and Black (and Brown and Yellow): Minorities in America. Combined Book Exhibit, Albany Post Road, Briarcliff Manor, New York 10510.

American Indian Literature

Astrov, Margot, ed. *American Indian Prose and Poetry: An Anthology*. New York: John Day, 1972.

Bierhorst, John. *In the Trail of the Wind: American Indian Poems and Ritual Orations*. New York: Farrar, Straus & Giroux, 1971.

Jones, Hettie. *The Trees Stand Shining*. New York: Dial, 1971.

---

10. Dorothy I. Seaberg, "Is There a Literature for the Disadvantaged Child?" *Childhood Education* 45 (May 1969): 508–512; Dora V. Smith, "Selecting Books for Culturally Disadvantaged Children," *Vistas in Reading*, J. Allen Figurel, ed. Proceedings of the Eleventh Annual Convention, vol. 2, pt. 1 (Newark, Del.: International Reading Association, 1967), pp. 406–417.

A Preliminary Bibliography of Selected Children's Books about American Indians. New York: Association on American Indian Affairs.

Literature by and About the American Indian: An Annotated Bibliography. Urbana, Ill.: National Council of Teachers of English.

Chinese and Japanese Literature

T'ang-shih san-pai Schou. *Three Hundred Poems of the T'ang Dynasty.* Translated by Soame Jenyns. London: John Murray, 1948.

Lewis, Richard, ed. *The Moment of Wonder: A Collection of Chinese and Japanese Poetry.* New York: Dial, 1963.

Chinese in Children's Books. New York: New York Public Library.

Eskimo Literature

Lewis, Richard, ed. *I Breathe a New Song: Poems of the Eskimo.* New York: Simon and Schuster, 1971.

Rasmusem, Knud. *Beyond the High Hills: A Book of Eskimo Poems.* Cleveland, Ohio: World Publishing, 1971.

Two other valuable references are: *Near East and Africa*, United States Committee for UNICEF, 331 E. 38th St., New York, N.Y. 10016 and *Multi-Ethnic Books for Young Children* by Louise Griffin, Washington, D.C.: National Association for Education of Young Children, 1970.

City dwellers represent a large segment of our society and many collections of poems about the city are available.

Primary Years

Hoffmann, Hilde. *The City and Country Mother Goose.* New York: McGraw-Hill, 1969

Hopkins, Lee Bennett, ed. *The City Spreads Its Wings.* New York: Watts, 1970

Moore, Lilian. *I Thought I Heard the City.* New York: Atheneum, 1969.

Intermediate Years

Adoff, Arnold, ed. *City in All Directions.* New York: Macmillan, 1969.

Larrick, Nancy, ed. *I Heard a Scream in the Street: Poetry by Young People in the City.* New York: M. Evans, 1970.

Schonborg, Virginia. *Subway Swinger.* New York: William Morrow, 1970.

A prominent issue in literature is the role of women. The frequent model of women presented in books is that of passive acceptance, gentleness, and resignation to domestic accomplishment. The characterization of the girl as a watcher, the "I'll-get-it-for-you" type, cleaning and picking up after the boys, is coming under increasing attention. A good list of old and new favorites is given in *Little Miss Muffet Fights Back: Recommended Non-Sexist Books About Girls for Young Readers.*[11]

• *Poetry collections*   Individual poetry books and the following poetry collections ought to be available on the free-reading table or on the classroom book shelves sometime during the school year.

Association for Childhood Education International, ed. *Sung Under the Silver Umbrella*. New York: Macmillan, 1972.
————. *Told Under the City Umbrella*. New York: Macmillan, 1972.
Austin, Mary C., and Mills, Queenie B. *The Sound of Poetry*. Boston: Allyn and Bacon, 1963.
Brewton, Sara W., and Brewton, John E. *Sing a Song of Seasons*. New York: Macmillan, 1955.
Brewton, John E., ed. *Under the Tent of the Sky*. New York: Macmillan, 1937.
Doane, Pelagie, ed. *A Small Child's Book of Verse*. New York: Walck, 1948.
De Angeli, Marguerite, ed. *Book of Nursery and Mother Goose Rhymes*. New York: Doubleday, 1954.
De La Mare, Walter. *Rhymes and Verses*. New York: Holt, Rinehart and Winston, 1947.
Field, Rachel. *The Pointed People: Verses and Silhouettes*. New York: Macmillan, 1930.
Frost, Robert. *You Come Too*. New York: Holt, Rinehart and Winston, 1959.
Fyleman, Rose. *Fifty-One New Nursery Rhymes*. Garden City, N.Y.: Doubleday, Doran, 1932.
Lear, Edward. *Nonsense Verse*. Boston: Little, 1950.
Livingston, Myra C., ed. *Listen, Children, Listen: Poems for the Very Young*. New York: Harcourt Brace Jovanovich, 1972.
McCord, David. *Far and Few*. Boston: Little, 1952.
Milne, A. A. *Now We Are Six*. New York: Dutton, 1961.

11.   Feminists on Children's Media, P. O. Box 4315, Grand Central Station, New York, N.Y. 10017. See also the entire issue of *Elementary English*, October 1973.

Read, Herbert, ed. *This Way, Delight*. New York: Pantheon, 1956.

Stevenson, Robert L. *A Child's Garden of Verses*. New York: Scribner, 1905.

Teasdale, Sara. *Poems Selected for Young People*. New York: Macmillan, 1938.

Thompson, Blanche, comp. *Silver Pennies*. New York: Macmillan, 1938.

Many poetry collections for young and older readers are now available in paperback.

Aldis, Dorothy. *The Secret Place and Other Poems*. New York: Scholastic Book Services, 1971.

Bisset, Donald H. *Poetry and Verse for Urban Children*. 3 vols. San Francisco: Chandler Publishing, 1968.

Cole, William, comp. *Oh, What Nonsense*. New York: Viking Press, 1969.

De Regniers, Beatrice, et al., eds. *Poems Children Will Sit Still For: A Selection for the Primary Grades*. New York: Scholastic Book Services, 1969.

Hopkins, Lee B. *Faces and Places: Poems for You*. New York: Scholastic Book Services, 1971.

Larrick, Nancy, ed. *Piping Down the Valley Wild*. New York: Delacorte, 1968.

McGovern, Ann, ed. *Arrow Book of Poetry*. New York: Scholastic Book Services, 1971.

Withers, Carl, ed. *Favorite Rhymes from a Rocket in My Pocket*. New York: Scholastic Book Services, 1970.

Not to be overlooked are volumes of poetry written by children for children.

Adoff, Arnold, ed. *It Is the Poem Singing into Your Eyes: Anthology of New Young Poets*. New York: Harper & Row, 1971.

Baron, Virginia Olsen, ed. *Here I am: An Anthology of Poems Written by Young People in Some of America's Minority Groups*. New York: Dutton, 1969.

Barnstone, Aliki. *The Real Tin Flower: Poems about the World at Nine*. New York: Macmillan, 1968.

Hopkins, Lee Bennett, comp. *City Talk*. New York: Knopf, 1970.

Larrick, Nancy, ed. *Green is Like a Meadow of Grass*. Scarsdale, N.Y.: Garrard, 1968.

Lewis, Richard, comp. *The Wind and the Rain*. New York: Simon and Schuster, 1968.

The teacher should be aware of the many films and filmstrips that can be used effectively in presenting poetry. Two major educational film companies are Coronet Films, Chicago, Ill., and Weston Woods, Weston, Conn. Recordings and tapes of poetry for the elementary school may be obtained from Caedmon Records, New York City; Folkways Records, New York City; and Spoken Arts, Inc., New Rochelle, N.Y. Teachers unsure of themselves can learn a great deal from poetry records and will find recordings extremely helpful in presenting a quality poetry program. Finally, two "core" poetry books for the teacher: May Hill Arbuthnot's *Time for Poetry*, 3rd ed. (Chicago: Scott Foresman, 1967) and *The Golden Treasury of Poetry* (New York: Golden Press, 1959), edited by Louis Untermeyer.

• *Instructional suggestions*   All children need to be familiar with many different kinds of poetry: poems about experiences familiar to them; poems of today; poems grasped at first hearing; poems within their reading vocabulary; short poems; poems written to and for children, not "down" to children. Poetry should be used to enrich subjects like music, science, and social studies.

First, a planned poetry program would include a balance of poems of various characteristics as suggested by the following illustrative titles. (For each set, the first poem is more appropriate for the primary school years; the second for the intermediate school years.)

Action
"Indian" by Rosemary and Stephen Vincent Benet
"Dunkirk" by Robert Nathan

Fantasy
"Stocking Fairy" by Winifred Welles
"Day Dreams" by Harry Behn

Humor
"Eletelephony" by Laura E. Richards
"The Panther" by Ogden Nash

Imagery
"Snow" by Dorothy Aldis
"Far and Near" by Harry Behn

Mood
"Tired Tim" by Walter De La Mare
"Otto" by Gwendolyn Brooks

Rhythm
"Hello and Goodbye" by Mary Ann Hoberman
"The Swing" by Robert Louis Stevenson

Story
"The King's Breakfast" by A. A. Milne
"The Mountain Whippoorwill" by Stephen Vincent Benet

Secondly, children enjoy poems about various content topics: everyday happenings ("Bedtime" by Elizabeth Farjeon and "City" by Langston Hughes); the family ("Me Myself and I" and "Thumbprint" by Eve Merriam); interesting people ("My Friend, Leona" by Mary O'Neill and "Portrait by a Neighbor" by Edna St. Vincent Millay); weather and the seasons ("Morning and Afternoon" by Elizabeth Coatsworth and "Something Told the Wild Geese" by Rachel Field); and poems about animals.

Thirdly, children should experience various forms of poetry: ballads ("Beth Gelert" by William Spencer and "The Ballad of the Harp Weaver" by Edna St. Vincent Millay); free verse ("Mouse" by Hilda Conkling and "Fog" by Carl Sandburg); narrative verse ("A Visit from St. Nicholas" by Clement Moore and "Pied Piper of Hamelin" by Robert Browning); lyric ("Where Go the Boats?" by Robert Louis Stevenson and "The Lone Day" by Irene McCleod).

Poetry reading should be introduced at the beginning of the school year by reading three or four humorous poems, followed by a discussion of "Which did you like best?" Gradually during the school year some of the elements of poetry may be brought to the pupils' attention: alliteration, comparisons (similies and metaphors), condensation, contrasts, imagery, mood, repetition, rhythm, suggestion, and symbolism. By the time they understand such elements, the children should be able to respond to poetry with an enthusiastic awareness that will delight both them and the teacher.

As a means of correlating music and poetry, the teacher may select two or three musical records and ask pupils to choose the most appropriate background music for the poem or poems. Later on, the children may be encouraged to undertake the selection of the music for the poem.

When a child finds a poem that he intensely enjoys, memorizing it may enrich the experience, foster a deeper appreciation of the language, and extend his enjoyment. Having the whole class memorize the same selection is not generally recommended, but there may be some favorites that the whole class will want to memorize. The amount of memorization will vary with the individual, but in a good poetry program all children will likely memorize a few poems.

INTRODUCING LITERATURE THROUGH FILM

The content of films, like the content of books, can awaken the child to the world of human experiences and values. One way to begin using films is to choose those based on books read in the language arts program (e.g., *Black Beauty, Johnny Tremain,* or *The Yearling*). Another way is to plan a film program based on a topic that is being studied in the language arts class—such as animal stories (e.g., *Lassie Come Home*). Some introductory activities may help to prepare the pupils for a film and also to stimulate their interest in seeing it. Discussion of a film should center about questions relating to:

> setting, characters, plot
> special or striking effects in the film (music and other background sounds)
> performance of the actors
> other related films or television programs
> recent events that relate to the film
> topics of special interest to the children

Follow-up activities are also valuable: written answers to specific questions, acting out scenes, research projects, illustrations, and prose or poetry writing. The possibilities for activities are limited only by the imagination of the teacher and the children.

The following films have proven effective in the language arts program.

Someday (kindergarten–grade 1), Marlin Motion Pictures, 47 Lakeshore Road East, Port Credit, Ontario (color, 7 min.)

Shape and Color Game (kindergarten–grade 1), Marlin Motion Pictures (color, 8 min.)

Hailstones and Halibut Bones (kindergarten–grade 2), Marlin Motion Pictures (color, 6 min.)

Paddle to the Sea (intermediate), National Film Board of Canada, 1 Lombard St. East, Toronto, Ontario (color, 27 min.)

The Red Balloon, Brandon Films, 221 W. 57th St., New York, N.Y. 10019
(color, 34 min.)
The Golden Fish (intermediate), Brandon Films, (color, 20 min.)[12]

Other films, along with literary concepts implicit in their use, have been suggested by Schwartz.[13]

Films are one aspect of visual literacy. Visual literacy refers to the ability to interpret various symbols, pictures, and other items that send messages in our environment, including color, dance, music, and space. Visual literacy includes (1) reading graphic symbols (signs, maps, charts, graphs, diagrams); (2) interpreting pictures, paintings, photographs, and sculptures; and (3) explaining films and television. One aspect of visual literacy includes action, such as interpreting body language in drama, especially pantomime (see chapter 5, pages 148–150). Television was discussed in chapter 4, pages 117–119.

Some classroom activities that are used to help children achieve visual literacy include:

1. Recognizing ways in which symbols are a form of communication
2. Interpreting a message in a picture (through a sequence, such as telling what is missing in a picture, following picture panels in stories or poems, identifying incongruities in pictures, putting pictures in correct order, explaining a sequence of pictures, and describing sensory qualities in a picture)
3. Interpreting paintings, photographs, and sculptures
4. Interpreting color, dance, music, and space
5. Recognizing effects of print and electronic media

Visual literacy is an emerging concept, built upon strong visual perception at the earliest school level. (See chapter 3, page 74.) Following are some helpful references on visual literacy.

Arnheim, Rudolf. *Visual Thinking*. Berkeley: University of California Press, 1969.

---

12. Ontario Institute for Studies in Education, *The Uses of Film in the Teaching of English*, Toronto 5, Ontario, 1971, pp. 25–37.

13. In her article "Introducing Literature Through Film," *Elementary English* 48 (March 1971): 304–315, Sheila Schwartz suggests "The Perils of Priscilla" (Churchill Films, color, 10 min.); "The Chicken" (McGraw-Hill, b/w, 15 min.); "Catch the Joy," "The Searching Eye," and "Moods of Surfing" (Pyramid, color, 15 min. each).

Birdwhistell, Ray. *Kinesics and Context: Essays on Body Motion Communication*. Philadelphia: University of Pennsylvania Press, 1970.

Fillion, B. "Visual Literacy," *Clearing House* 47 (January 1973): 308–311.

Fransecky, Roger B. *Visual Literacy: A Way to Learn—A Way to Teach*. New York: Association for Educational Communications and Technology, 1972.

Levie, W. H., ed. "Research on Learning from Pictures: A Review and Bibliography." *Viewpoints* 49 (March 1973): 1–91.

Purvis, J. R. "Visual Literacy: An Emerging Concept." *Educational Leadership* 10 (May 1973): 59–68.

Tanzman, J. "Meaning and Importance of Visual Literacy." *School Management* 16 (December 1972): 41.

Van Holt, J. M. "Visual Literacy: A Valuable Communication Tool." *Instructor* 82 (August 1972): 130–132.

Young, F. M. "Visual Literacy Today and Tomorrow: Junior High Art Camp." *Arts and Activities* 73 (February 1973): 44–45.

Some materials produced or published by the Association for Educational Communications and Technology (1201 16th St., N.W., Washington, D.C. 20036) on visual literacy include:

Learning from Pictures (book)
Making Sense Visually and *How Does a Picture Mean* (filmstrips)
Photo-Story Discovery Sets (pictures)
A Visual Fable (filmstrip set)

LITERATURE RESPONSE STATIONS

The role of the literature receiver (reader or listener) is very important within the literature program. The teacher can provide many opportunities for receiver response. An area within the classroom (called response stations or centers) may be established at various times where children may plan for various modes of response.

For example, various working stations were initiated in one classroom after the teacher read *Pinocchio* to the class. Group discussion led to the organization of teams of three to five pupils to share episodes from the book (or to prepare an original Pinocchio episode) with the other class members. Total class planning included (1) a review of various ways of sharing, (2) the need to practice with the tape recorder prior to class presentation, and (3) reference to storytelling criteria discussed earlier in the year.

Initial planning periods were scheduled for group work sessions and copies of *Pinocchio*, both complete and simplified, were available for each team. On succeeding days, time was scheduled for groups to get together. The teacher rotated among the groups as plans evolved and scripts were being prepared. The following work stations were developed:

1. One team decided upon a slide or slide-tape presentation, prepared by the ecktograph (visual recorder) and instamatic camera. The children drew some of their own pictures and also photographed pictures from the book.

2. Another team decided to make a silhouette presentation. Pictures were drawn or traced from the book and then cut out. They told the chosen episode while manipulating the pictures on the overhead projector.

3. A third team drew pictures and taped them together in a sequence. Then the strip was pulled through the opaque projector while the episode was being told.

4. Another group prepared flannelgraph characters—made from construction paper—to be used in their presentation.

5. Another group made puppets of various types: stick, sack, sock, finger. One group made string puppets. The work station contained the following materials: cardboard rolls from wax paper or paper towels, crayons, strings, paste, scissors, paint, boxes for making a stage, etc. They told chosen episodes while manipulating the puppets.

For children who did not choose to participate in any of these classroom presentations, alternate activities were provided, such as the following:

Task Card: Pinocchio

To do this exercise, you may use your thesaurus or dictionary and work alone or with a friend.

Think of words that tell how Pinocchio walked when he
a. ran around old Gepetto's work bench.
b. went to school.
c. went away from the island.
d. looked for old Gepetto.
e. became a real boy.

Literature Activity Card

Go to the literature center. Select a tape, record, filmstrip, video-tape, or film for listening or viewing. You may choose someone to share this with you. When you have finished, fill out a slip and put it in your folder.

Name _____   Date _____
Name of story _____
Author _____
(Check one)   Tape ____ Record ____ Filmstrip ____ Other ____
I saw/listened alone   Yes ____ No ____
I shared this with _____
I (we) enjoyed this   Yes ____ No ____
Other comments:

Literature: Book Report

Go to the nook for bookworms. Select a book to read for fun. Fill out a slip when you have finished and place it in your folder.

Name _____   Date _____
Name of book _____
Author _____
I read the whole book   Yes ____ No ____
I read from page ____ to page ____
Comments:

On various days, the "final" presentations to the class by the groups were videotaped during the actual performance. Later, the children viewed the videotape, evaluating their presentations against previously established criteria for storytelling.

Children's literature provides an excellent springboard for response stations related to art—mural painting, diorama construction, peep boxes, clay modeling, bulletin board displays, mobiles, and wall hangings.

Literature response stations provide opportunities for enrichment items, such as:

1. Art objects (e.g., book-related items): available from F. A. O. Schwarz, 745 Fifth Ave., New York, N.Y. 10022
2. Calendars (e.g., *Winnie the Pooh's Calendar Book*): available from E. P. Dutton, 201 Park Ave. South, New York, N.Y. 10003 or at local bookstores
3. Facsimile editions (e.g., *Kate Greenaway's Alphabet*): available from G. P. Putnam's Sons, 200 Madison Ave., New York, N.Y. 10016
4. Films, filmstrips, records: secure catalog from Weston Woods Studios, Weston, Conn. 16880
5. Note cards, bookmarks: available from Children's Book Council, Inc., 175 Fifth Ave., New York, N.Y. 10010
6. Pictures and poster sets: available for certain authors—e.g., Joan Walsh Anglund, Harcourt Brace Jovanovich, 757 Third Ave., New York, N.Y. 10017; Ezra Jack Keats, Macmillan Publishing Co., Inc., 866 Third Ave., New York, N.Y. 10222; or Brian Wildsmith, Franklin Watts, Inc., 845 Third Ave., New York, N.Y. 10022

LITERATURE FOR ALL CURRICULAR AREAS

The scope of children's literature is constantly expanding as educators become aware of the value of trade books. The library corner is the literature learning center and can take a greater role in the literature program if it is no longer used only for "free reading." Reading, the other language arts, social studies, mathematics, and science can be more fully developed when each is enriched with good literature.

One approach to reading instruction, called *individualized* or *personalized*, has stressed the importance of reading library books. Trade books cover a wider range of personality, emotion, and action than basal readers. Perhaps one of the advantages of the individualized reading approach results from the impact on the reader of encountering many varied sentence patterns; basal readers are generally more restrictive than trade books in their choice of sentence patterns for beginning readers.

The use of an individualized approach to reading has accelerated the production of commercially packaged literature programs such as the following.

Classroom Library Packet. Oklahoma City: The Economy Company, n.d. A twenty-five-volume, boxed set of well-known stories for use at the primary level.

Treasure Chest. New York: Harper & Row, 1966. Thirty-six illustrated children's books for use at the early primary level.

Owl Books. New York: Holt, Rinehart and Winston, 1965. Four sets of children's books: twenty books for preschool through grade 1; forty books for grades 1–2; forty books for grades 2–4; and twenty books for grades 4–6.

Macmillan Reading Spectrum. New York: Macmillan, 1964. A set of thirty different children's books for grades 1–6.

Invitations to Story Time and to Personal Reading. Glenview, Ill.: Scott, Foresman, 1966. Sixteen preschool titles and twenty-five books for each grade 1–6.

Literature provides examples of man's interaction with his environment—a major concern of the social studies. An excellent example of using children's literature in the teaching of social studies has been described by Chambers and O'Brien.[14] Also helpful is the reference source *Literature and Music as Resources for Social Studies*.[15] A valuable source for a list of trade books to supplement and enrich mathematics teaching is *The Elementary and Junior High School Mathematics Library*,[16] as well as similar listings for other curricular areas, such as science and art.[17]

By utilizing children's literature in all curricular areas, teachers will consolidate their teaching efforts. However, children do not profit from the interrelationship of various subject areas when teachers have a literature period and then consistently develop an entirely separate program for each subject.

---

14. Dewey W. Chambers and Margaret H. O'Brien, "Exploring the Golden State Through Children's Literature," *Elementary English* 46 (May 1969): 592–595.

15. Ruth Tooze and Beatrice P. Krone (Englewood Cliffs, N.J.: Prentice-Hall, 1955). See also Helen Huus, *Children's Books to Enrich the Social Studies*, rev. ed. (Washington, D.C.: National Council for the Social Studies, 1966); and Seymour Metzner, *American History in Juvenile Books* (New York: H. W. Wilson, 1966).

16. Clarence Hardgrove (Washington, D.C.: National Council of Teachers of Mathematics, 1968).

17. Hiliary J. Deason, comp., *The AAAS Science Booklist for Children*, 2d ed. (Washington, D.C.: American Association for the Advancement of Science, 1963). See also Kenneth Marantz, ed., *A Bibliography of Children's Art Literature* (Washington, D.C.: National Education Association, 1965).

PERTINENT QUESTIONS ABOUT LITERATURE INSTRUCTION

1. What is the role of interests, preferences, and habits? Elementary school children are influenced by two factors in their selection of reading material: (a) material that is readily accessible to them and (b) the subject-matter of the book. Children cannot learn to read worthwhile literature if they are not exposed to an abundance of good books and magazines at home and in the classroom.

The literature program should be planned to broaden and deepen the children's existing interests, developing new interests and directing undesirable tendencies to more acceptable lines. The most important fact to remember about reading interests is that interests are *learned!* One maxim teachers might find useful is: "A child's interests that he brings to school are our opportunity; the interests he takes from school are our responsibility." Interests of children do not

A well-stocked library can furnish prose and poetry to meet the varied abilities, interests, and needs of each child.

develop out of a vacuum. Children become interested in things because they have been exposed to them.

King has appraised the research on children's reading interests, preferences, and habits and developed the following summaries of factors relating to each.

Summary of Factors Influencing Reading Interests

1. Reading interests tend to change as new interests are developed.
2. Reading interests do not necessarily reflect informational needs.
3. Audiovisual aids may play an important role in changing reading interests.
4. Primary-grade children prefer fairy tales and realistic stories based on everyday activities and animal stories.
5. In the intermediate grades, pupils prefer mystery, adventure, animal stories, family life stories, biographies, sports, science, and social studies.
6. Children appear to be maturing faster in their reading interests.
7. There are few sex differences in reading interests up to age nine.
8. Definite differences in reading interests among girls and boys become apparent after age nine.
   a. Boys read more nonfiction than girls.
   b. Girls read more poetry than boys.
   c. Both boys and girls rank adventure, action, mystery, animal stories, patriotism, and humor high in their preferences.
   d. Boys prefer stories of science, invention, and vigorous action. . . .
   e. Girls will read a book considered to be of interest to boys, but the reverse is seldom true.
9. The reading interests of children who are above average in intelligence mature faster than those of slow learners.

Summary of Factors Influencing Reading Preferences

1. Personal recommendations rank high in determining the selection of reading materials.
2. Pupils read a variety of materials including books, comics, and magazines.

3. They prefer prose form, particularly narrative, to poetry.
4. They prefer stories with a good plot, much action, and humor.
5. They prefer colored pictures to black-and-white ones.
6. Realism tends to be a more important factor in illustrations than color.

Summary of Factors Influencing Reading Habits
1. The amount of reading increases up to the end of the elementary grades.
2. Girls read more than boys.
3. Bright children read considerably more than children with a lower IQ.
4. Home influences are important in establishing reading habits. The amount and quality of reading are related to the number and kinds of books, magazines, and newspapers in the home.
5. Easy access to good school libraries and public libraries is an important influence in establishing desirable reading habits.[18]

2. What aids are available for selecting and evaluating literature materials? Many anthologies, bibliographies, histories, lists, reports, and reviews are available for helping teachers and librarians. A comprehensive guide to book selection aids has been prepared by Haviland.[19]

Some specific reference books, general book lists (usually revised periodically), and periodicals with which the teacher should be familiar are listed below.

Reference Books

American Library Association. *Subject and Title Index to Short Stories for Children.* Chicago: American Library Association, 1955.

Brewton, John E., and Brewton, Sara W., comps. *Index to Poetry for Children and Young People: 1964–69.* New York: H. W. Wilson, 1972.

Eakin, Mary K. *Subject Index to Books for Intermediate Grades.* 3rd ed. Chicago: American Library Association, 1963.

---

18. Ethel M. King, "Critical Appraisal of Research on Children's Reading Interests, Preferences, and Habits," *Canadian Education and Research Digest* 74 (December 1967): 312–326. Used by permission of the publisher.

19. Virginia Haviland, *Children's Literature, First Supplement: A Guide to Reference Sources* (Washington, D.C.: Library of Congress, U.S. Government Printing Office, 1972).

————, and Merritt, Eleanor, eds. *Subject Index to Books for Primary Grades*. 3rd ed. Chicago: American Library Association, 1967.

Eastman, Mary, comp. *Index to Fairy Tales, Myths, and Legends: Supplement 2*. Boston: Faxon, 1952.

Fidell, Rachel, and Fidell, Estelle, eds. *Children's Catalog*. New York: H. W. Wilson.

Field, Carolyn W. *Subject Collections in Children's Literature*. New York: R. R. Bowker, 1969.

Gaver, Mary Virginia, ed. *The Elementary School Library Collection*. Newark, N.J.: Bro-Dart Foundations, 1967–1968.

Mathes, Miriam Snow, et al. *A Basic Book Collection for Elementary Schools*. 7th ed. Chicago: American Library Association, 1960.

Sell, Violet, et al. *Subject Index to Poetry for Children and Young People*. Chicago: American Library Association, 1957.

General Book Lists

Currah, Ann, comp. *Best Books for Children*. New York: R. R. Bowker, 1967.

National Council of Teachers of English. *Adventuring with Books: 2400 Titles for Pre-Kindergarten to Grade 8*. 2d ed. New York: Scholastic Book Services, 1973.

Sunderlin, Sylvia. *Bibliography of Books for Children*. Washington, D.C.: Association for Childhood Education International, 1971.

Periodicals

The Booklist and Subscription Books Bulletin. Chicago: American Library Association.

The Bulletin of the Center for Children's Books. Chicago: Graduate Library School, University of Chicago.

Childhood Education. Washington, D.C.: Association for Childhood Education International.

Elementary English. Urbana, Ill.: National Council of Teachers of English.

The Horn Book Magazine. Boston: Horn Book.

Saturday Review. New York 10036.

School Library Journal. New York: R. R. Bowker.

No reference or review about children's books can substitute for wide reading of books. Teachers must develop criteria for evaluating new books. Trade books may be evaluated in terms of (a) authorship; (b) scope (setting, plot, and theme); (c) characterization; (d) style; and (e) format. Some pertinent questions relating to this area of concern were suggested in a preceding section entitled "Close Reading/Study of Literature." The following questions may help the reader further evaluate a book.

Who is the author and what else has he written? What are his qualifications?

What do you know about the publisher and the editor?

Is the purpose of the book primarily to inform or to spark imagination and thought?

If informational, is the book authoritative and accurate? If inspirational, is it imaginative and perceptive?

Is the plot credible and well constructed through an orderly sequence of events?

Is the setting authentic and consistent with the action, characters, and theme?

Is a worthy theme presented—not necessarily all sweetness and light, but committed to lasting, worthwhile, sound, moral, and ethical principles?

Are the characters convincing? Can the reader identify with their strengths and weaknesses?

Is the writing clear, challenging, inspiring?

Is there a balance between action, description, and conversation?

Are the text, captions, and illustrations woven into an inviting pattern?

Is the total format of the book designed to bring out the desired effect of the text?

What aids are provided in informational books?

How is color used?

The skilled author writes the same way for children as he does for adults. The main difference is in the choice of subject matter: that is, the theme must be appropriate for the experience and background of the reader. Today, more children's books are published than ever before; sometimes it is difficult to see the trees for the forest, but the "giants" are there to be seen by the perceptive reader.[20]

3. *Should reading of books on basic booklists be required?* Some elementary schools have established lists of books for required reading by *all* children at each age or grade level. This practice seems questionable for several reasons:

---

20. More detailed criteria for evaluating children's books may be found in *Children's Literature in the Elementary School*, 2d ed. by Charlotte Huck and Doris Young Kuhn (New York: Holt, Rinehart and Winston, 1968).

a. The needs, interests, and abilities of children at each level are so varied that few books should be read by every child. Almost every teacher has had the experience of seeing one group of children respond enthusiastically to a certain book, while another group at the same level will show little interest in the same book.

b. In every class, there is usually a wide range of reading ability and also varying degrees of maturity and readiness for selections.

c. Some very fine books appeal only to the unusually perceptive reader.

d. Forcing a child to struggle through the reading of a "required" book that does not appeal to him or is too difficult for him is quite likely to pervert the major goal of the literature program, which is to develop a lifelong interest in quality literature.

e. So many good books are available at all reading levels that every child should be provided with books that meet his own needs, preferences, and abilities.

Lists of worthwhile books may be beneficial if the lists are comprehensive and if each child may choose the books he wants to read. Such lists can help children identify books that are readily accessible.

4. What books are available for children with special problems or needs? The following list offers some suggestions.

PRIMARY

INTERMEDIATE

(Appearance Differences)

Beim. *Smallest Boy in the Class*. New York: Morrow, 1949.

Evers. *The Plump Pig*. Chicago: Rand McNally, 1938.

Reyher. *My Mother is the Most Beautiful Woman in the World*. New York: Lothrop, 1945.

Gates. *Sensible Kate*. New York: Viking Press, 1943.

Henry. *King of the Wind*. Chicago: Rand McNally, 1948.

McGinley. *Plain Princess*. Philadelphia: Lippincott, 1945.

(Cultural Differences)

Carle. *Do You Want to be My Friend?* New York: Thomas Y. Crowell, 1971.

Flory. *Ramshackle Roost*. Boston: Houghton Mifflin, 1972.

De Angeli. *Yonie Wondernose.*
New York: Doubleday,
1944.

Politi. *Juanita.* New York:
Scribner, 1948.

Lowe. *Somebody Else's Shoes.*
New York: Holt, Rinehart
and Winston, 1948.

Webb. *Precious Bane.* New
York: New American
Library, 1972.

(Family Differences)

Flack. *New Pet.* New York:
Doubleday, 1943.

Harris. *Little Boy Brown.* Philadelphia: Lippincott, 1949.

Parsons. *Rainy Day Together.*
New York: Harper & Row,
1971.

Morre. *Lucky Orphan.* New
York: Scribner, 1947.

Woodberry. *Come Back, Peter.*
New York: Thomas Y.
Crowell, 1972.

Woolley. *David's Railroad.*
New York: Morrow, 1949.

(Personality Differences)

Cole. *That Pest, Jonathan.*
New York: Harper & Row,
1970.

Viorst. *The Tenth Good Thing
About Barney.* New York:
Atheneum, 1971.

Zolotow. *William's Doll.* New
York: Harper & Row, 1972.

Henry. *Geraldine Belinda.*
New York: Platt, 1942.

Norman. *Climb a Lonely Hill.*
New York: Walck, 1972.

Stolz. *Leap Before You Look.*
New York: Harper & Row,
1972.

EVALUATION OF THE LITERATURE PROGRAM

The quality of a child's reaction to literature can best be judged by an observant teacher who plans for literature in the everyday program and who takes time to be a sensitive and yet critical evaluator of each child's progress.

The following questions will help the teacher in the evaluating process.

1. Is the pupil growing in appreciation of good literature? How do you know?
2. Does he make good use of his time in the library and in free reading of books and periodicals?
3. Does he enjoy storytelling, reading aloud, choral reading, and creative drama?

4. Is he getting to know himself better through understanding and interpreting characters in literature?
5. Is he increasing in his understanding of his own culture and the culture of others through knowledge of the contributions of his own people and people of other lands?
6. How sensitive is he to sounds, rhythms, moods, and feelings as displayed in prose and poetry?
7. How mature is his awareness of the structure and forms of literature, including plot, setting, characterization, and theme?

Answers to these questions may be gained through spontaneous remarks by the pupil to the teacher (e.g., "Do you know any other good books about space travel?"); through directed conversation with the class (e.g., "What books would you like to add to our classroom library?"); and during individual conferences when the pupil has an opportunity to describe books he likes and does not like.

Following are specific behavioral characteristics for children at different grade levels that may be detected by the observant teacher.

Nursery
   know that books have pictures and come in many sizes
   know that a book is read from the front to the back, that the pages go in sequence, and that the words are read from left to right
   look at pictures and understand what they are depicting
   handle books carefully
   enjoy stories and has some favorites
   repeat rhymes, poems, and stories
   begin to use the nursey-school bookshelf or goes to the public library with their parents

Kindergarten
   all of the preceding
   identify with the characters in stories they have heard
   begin to act out characters in stories during free-play
   bring ideas and expression to the pictures in the story
   know their favorite stories by the cover of the book and the illustrations
   know the sequential plot and mood of the story
   enjoy repetitive phrases, sound effects, and pantomiming the action
   clarify and extend concepts of the stories

Primary
 all of the preceding
 know realistic, imaginative, folkloric, and modern stories
 predict what comes next and how the story will end
 name all of the characters
 exchange ideas and respect various opinions
 use the library regularly
 dramatize stories in various ways
 write and illustrate stories
 prepare covers and title pages
 help prepare book exhibits or fairs

Intermediate
 all of the preceding
 apply elements of plot development
 use language from previous stories
 dictate stories using a tape recorder
 read aloud to others
 use various media to enrich reading activities
 exchange books with friends
 identify with the characters and understand the behavior and action of the characters
 relate plot and characters to incidents in their own lives.

Assessment and evaluation can be refined in the field of children's literature when overall purposes are translated into statements of pupil behavior. For one effort at this, see "A Taxonomy of Literary Understandings and Skills," *Children's Literature in the Elementary School*, 2d ed.[21] One pencil-and-paper test of literature appreciation for pupils in grades 4, 5, and 6 is *A Look at Literature*.[22] To determine children's knowledge and background in literature, see Charlotte S. Huck, "Get Children Excited About Books," *Coordinating Reading Instruction*.[23] Two other excellent references include: Martha E. Irwin, "Evaluating Elementary Literature Programs," *Elementary English* 40 (December 1963): 846–849, 888; and Doris Young, "Evaluation of Children's Responses to Literature," *Library Quarterly* 37 (January 1967): 100–109.

21. Charlotte S. Huck and Doris Y. Kuhn (New York: Holt, Rinehart and Winston, 1968), pp. 588–691.

22. *A Look at Literature* (Princeton, N.J.: Educational Testing Service, 1969).

23. Charlotte S. Huck, "Get Children Excited About Books," *Coordinating Reading Instruction*, ed. by Helen M. Robinson (Glenview, Ill.: Scott Foresman, 1971), pp. 114–124.

SELECTED REFERENCES

General Professional

Anderson, Paul S. *Language Skills in Elementary Education.* 2d. ed. New York: Macmillan, 1972, chapter 3.

Boyd, Gertrude. *Teaching Communication Skills in the Elementary School.* New York: Van Hostrand Reinhold, 1970, chapters 12, 13, 16.

Burrows, Alvina T.; Monson, Diane L.; and Stauffer, Russell G. *New Horizons in the Language Arts.* New York: Harper & Row, 1972, chapter 6, 8.

Corcoran, Gertrude B. *Language Arts in Elementary School: A Modern Linguistic Approach.* New York: Ronald, 1970, chapter 12.

Greene, Harry A., and Petty, Walter T. *Developing Language Skills in the Elementary Schools.* 4th ed. Boston: Allyn and Bacon, 1971, chapter 15.

Smith, James A. *Adventures in Communication: Language Arts Methods.* Boston: Allyn and Bacon, 1972, chapter 8.

Strickland, Ruth. *The Language Arts in Elementary School.* 3rd ed. Lexington, Mass.: D. C. Heath, 1969, chapter 17.

Specialized

American Library Association. *A Multimedia Approach to Children's Literature.* Chicago: American Library Association, 1972.

Arbuthnot, May Hill, and Sutherland, Zena. *Children and Books.* 3rd ed. Chicago: Scott Foresman, 1964.

Boyd, Gertrude. *Teaching Poetry in the Elementary Schools.* Columbus, Ohio: Merrill, 1973.

Chandler, Martha H., comp. *A Bibliography of Books for Young Children.* Medford, Mass.: Tufts University Press, 1970.

Cohen, Monroe D., ed. *Literature With Children.* Washington, D.C.: Association for Childhood Education International, 1972.

Coody, Betty. *Using Literature with Young Children.* Dubuque, Iowa: William C. Brown, 1973.

Eakin, Mary K. *Good Books for Children, 1950–65.* 3rd ed. Chicago: University of Chicago Press, 1966.

Fenwick, Sara Innis, ed. *A Critical Approach to Children's Literature.* Chicago: University of Chicago Press, 1967.

Georgiou, Constantine. *Children and Their Literature.* Englewood Cliffs, N.J.: Prentice-Hall, 1969.

Haviland, Virginia, ed. *Children's Books of International Interest.* Chicago: American Library Association, 1972.

————, ed. *The Fairy Tale Treasury.* New York: Coward, 1972.

Hensing, Esther D., ed. *Good and Inexpensive Books for Children.* Washington, D.C.: Association for Childhood Education International, 1972.

Hopkins, Lee Bennett. *Pass the Poetry Please.* New York: Scholastic Book Services, 1972.

Huber, Miriam Blanton. *Story and Verse for Children.* 3rd ed. New York: Macmillan, 1965.

Huck, Charlotte S., and Kuhn, Doris Y. *Children's Literature in the Elementary School*. 2d ed. New York: Holt, Rinehart and Winston, 1968.

Hürlimann, Bettina. *Three Centuries of Children's Books in Europe*. Cleveland: World Publishing, 1968.

Johnson, Edna, et al. *Anthology of Children's Literature*. Boston: Houghton Mifflin, 1970.

Lamb, Pose, ed. *Literature for Children Series*. Dubuque, Iowa: William C. Brown, 1970.

Larrick, Nancy. *A Teacher's Guide to Children's Books*. Columbus, Ohio: Merrill, 1961.

Lonsdale, Bernard J., and Mackintosh, Helen K. *Children Experience Literature*. New York: Random, 1972.

Meigs, Cornelia, et al. *A Critical History of Children's Literature*. New York: Macmillan, 1969.

Montebello, Mary S. *Literature for Children: Children's Literature in the Curriculum*. Edited by Pose Lamb. Dubuque, Iowa: William C. Brown, 1972.

Reid, Virginia M., ed. *Reading Ladders for Human Relations*. 5th ed. Urbana, Ill.: National Council of Teachers of English, 1972.

Robinson, Evelyn R., ed. *Readings About Children's Literature*. New York: McKay, 1966.

Root, Shelton, et al., eds. *Adventuring with Books*. Urbana, Ill.: National Council of Teachers of English, 1973.

Smith, James Steel. *A Critical Approach to Children's Literature*. New York: McGraw, 1967.

Whitehead, Robert. *Children's Literature: Strategies of Teaching*. Englewood Cliffs, N.J.: Prentice-Hall, 1968.

OBJECTIVES	PERFORMANCE RESPONSES
1. To design an early writing experience	1. If feasible, write an experience story dictated by a child or group of children.
2. To plan a way to encourage creative writing	2. Organize an oral presentation, the purpose of which is to motivate creative writing.
3. To demonstrate a way to help children better formulate written expression	3. Develop a lesson for a child or group of children, involving word study of a particular type (e.g., descriptive verbs). Use it with peers or children.
4. To gain insight into rhyming or syllabic poetry writing	4. Introduce one form of rhyming or syllabic poetry writing to a child or class. Evaluate your performance.
5. To illustrate instructional procedures for letter writing	5. Prepare a lesson outline for teaching a particular type of letter writing.
6. To identify and describe features of report writing	6. Make an outline of the section on report writing. Give an oral report to your peers from your outline.
7. To apply ideas of "systematic" instruction to a form of functional writing	7. Develop a systematic lesson (as for "announcement") for either record writing or filling in forms.
8. To identify and recommend procedures for teaching a writing convention	8. Develop an exercise, the purpose of which is to review or introduce one or two principles of punctuation or capitalization.
9. To acquire understanding of the process of evaluating composition	9. Write an analysis of a child's composition based on suggestions given in the chapter.

WRITING CREATIVE PROSE

Teachers today, due to several influences, are giving increased time and attention to creative composition. For the pupil, creative writing, being a high level, mental process, puts the mind in "high gear" and increases awareness. For the teacher, creative writing provides a means for meeting individual differences through better understanding or respect of each child as a person—his thoughts, feelings, and experiences.

Creative writing in schools is neither a luxury allowed by indulgent teachers, nor a form of psychotherapy, but a mode of expression that children practice readily, deriving confidence and writing facility from it.

Some common problems teachers have in teaching creative writing are (1) starting early writing experiences, (2) encouraging written expression, and (3) helping written expression to be better formulated. These problems are discussed in turn.

Creative writing in schools is neither a luxury allowed by indulgent teachers, nor a form of psychotherapy.

Early writing experiences

Two ways of starting children early with writing experiences are suggested below.

• *Experience charts*   Experience charts are recognized as a useful way of preparing children for reading. They also serve in preparing children for written expression in that they are cooperative compositions that require planning what to say, organizing a logical sequence, and choosing the words to convey the exact meaning intended.

When emphasis is centered upon the writing aspects of making a chart, the teacher consciously directs the work with comments and questions, like the following:

How shall we start the chart?
Can someone think of a better way?
Do you like that way of saying it?

The teacher develops a sense of organization by asking other leading questions:

What do we do next?
How should we end?
What title shall we put at the top of the chart?

Through experience chart or story writing, the child senses the following relationship: experience ⟶ speaking ⟶ writing ⟶ reading.

Further discussion of the composition aspects of this writing experience involves the expression of ideas. The teacher develops this aspect by directive questions:

Have we said what we mean?
Is there more that should be said?
Have we put the items on the chart in the proper order?

Through experience charts, children build favorable attitudes toward writing and attain practical experience in such matters as unity of subject matter, organization of thought, choice of words and phrases, and fluency of expression. While the primary emphasis should be upon the matters suggested in the previous sentence, the teacher may call attention to the use of a capital letter at the beginning of a sentence; a period, a question mark, or an exclamation mark at the end; capitalizing proper names of people and places; or commas to separate words in a series.

A cooperatively developed chart in a primary class, (for example, "Our New Book") may be used to illustrate some of the language implications it contains.

CHART 7.1: Experience Chart

> Our New Book
> We have a new book.
> Mrs. Jones, the librarian,
> read it to us on Monday.
> Its title is <u>Petunia</u>.
>
> The story is about a goose who thought she could learn to read by carrying a book under her wing.
>
> How does it end? We won't tell!

The following items may be noted about the above composition from the point of view of mechanics.

1. Capital letters: first word of a sentence, proper names, titles of books, days of the week
2. Period: end of a declarative sentence, abbreviations
3. Question mark: end of a question sentence
4. Apostrophe: contractions
5. Exclamation point: end of an exclamatory sentence
6. Sequence of sentences
7. Paragraphs

Experience writing should mean just what the name implies. It is writing about the experiences children are having or have had. The classroom must be a laboratory where pupils have the opportunity to increase and enrich the range and variety of their storehouse of past and present experiences. Experience writing is often built around the following types of experiences.

1. Trips
2. Activities in the classroom
3. Letters the children dictate
4. Discussions
5. Science experiments
6. Records of plans (such as plans for the day's activities, a trip, etc.)
7. News reports
8. Literary efforts of individuals or groups (as "The First Snake I Ever Saw")

Little attempt should be made to control the children's vocabulary or to provide for repetition of words. This results in one of the chief values of the writing: it serves as a medium for experience with extensive vocabulary for pupils who are at the higher levels of vocabulary development.

To start the written composing process before the children have mastered handwriting and spelling skills, as well as other technical, written expression skills, the beginning step involves the teacher's recording (writing) the children's oral expression. Dictation may be done individually as well as cooperatively by a group of five or six children. Sometimes a teacher may invite individual pupils to compose their own stories and then dictate them privately to him. As each child is telling his story, the teacher may write or type it, placing it on a chart or on the chalkboard. The dictated composition may merit duplication and distribution for reading and analysis by the class. From the organizational point of view, younger children can dictate to older children; parents and aides can be used as scribes. Children's stories can be bound as "books" and the stories can be illustrated.

At the beginning, the written materials should reflect accurately the grammatical, syntactic, and vocabulary features of the child's own dialect. For example, when a child dictates "The dog he look like he sick," this should be recorded exactly as given and not rewritten as "The dog looks sick." Furthermore, Chomsky and Halle lend support to the notion that nonstandard dialectal and phonological features can be adequately represented (perhaps even optimally) with conventional spelling.[1] For example, no attempt should be made to use "eye" dialect, such as *wuz* for *was*. When divergent speakers of English read stories written in standard English, they should be allowed to read these materials in their own dialect. Changing the child's language destroys its integrity and implies that his language is inferior and hence he must be inferior too. "Correcting" the child's language here may also cause a reluctance to dictate or read stories aloud. The language of the classroom constitutes only a fraction of the child's total language environment. Consequently, if classroom language instruction is to make an impact that will result in language modification, it must be viewed as a long-range objective. This objective cannot be effectively implemented by destroying the child's image of the communicative effectiveness of the language he brings with him to school.

It is difficult to recommend a more effective device than experience chart writing for realistic, functional, and constructive learning and teaching. The important language relationships are established effectively in experience writing. This is the relationship of an experience (with its ideas, structure, and inherent significance) to its manifestation first in oral language, then in written form, and finally in reading what has been written. Thus the pupil learns the valuable and necessary contribution that experience makes to speaking, that speaking makes to writing, and that writing makes to reading. Of course, listening is important all through this process.[2]

---

1. Noam Chomsky and Morris Halle, *The Sound Pattern of English* (New York: Harper & Row, 1968).

2. See Virgil E. Herrick and Marcella Nerbovig, *Using Experience Charts with Children* (Columbus, Ohio: Merrill, 1964). This small book shows many effective ways to help pupils understand that words, phrases, and usage conventions are the most expressive and efficient forms of communication.

• *Language-experience approach*   In the language-experience approach, no distinction is made between the reading program and the program for developing the other language arts skills.[3] Full development and growth in any one of these skills hinges upon full development and growth in the other skills. At the beginning of first grade, the teacher encourages opportunities for creative work with crayons, pencils, and paints as well as through the medium of speech. As a child expresses himself through oral language, the teacher summarizes in a sentence or two what he has said and this short composition is written by the teacher as the child watches. Group compositions are also recorded as the children observe. As the teacher writes, he calls attention to items that are important to reading and writing, such as letter formation, association of sounds with symbols, repetition of the same sounds or symbols, and the functions of capitalization and punctuation. These group compositions are used as a basis for discussion. Children read the group compositions as well as their own individual compositions.

As soon as a child expresses a desire to write his own composition, he is given an opportunity to do so. As children reach an independent level in handwriting, they are provided with basic word lists. Soon they develop control over a basic vocabulary through their writing experiences. When children develop in reading ability, they are given increasing opportunities to read from books for interest and research purposes and to do more writing.

Simply stated, the language-experience approach uses this rationale:

What I can think about, I can talk about.
What I can say, I can write.
What I can write, I can read.
I can read what I can write and what other people write for me to read.

Thus it can be seen that writing skills grow directly out of the procedures employed to develop reading facility. Developing facility in writing, in turn, makes a positive contribution to facility in word recognition, speaking, and spelling. Oral language facility increases through reading and writing by means of the dictation of stories and the discussion endemic to the storytelling process. Listening, fostered

---

3. Dorris May Lee and Richard Van Allen, *Learning to Read Through Experience* (New York: Appleton-Century-Crofts, 1963).

by reading good prose and poetry to the children, enables children to develop a sensitivity to language forms.[4]

Sylvia Ashton-Warner describes a somewhat similar approach in *Teacher*, which is a journal of her experiences as a teacher in a New Zealand elementary school.. Miss Ashton-Warner, working with "culturally deprived" Maori children, begins with single words—nothing so elaborate as experience charts. One by one, she asks each child what word he wants. As he suggests the word, she writes it on a card and gives it to him. Almost as soon as the children begin to learn words, they begin what she calls "creative writing." At first they write only their own key words. From this, they move into the stream of autobiographical writing. This autobiographical writing becomes their group reading material. In the reading lesson, they read aloud their own "books" and each other's "books."[5]

Inability to spell the words he wishes to use may hamper the flow of ideas and cause feelings of frustration and defeat in a young writer. Accordingly, the teacher can suggest to the child that he use some of the following procedures.

Spelling Tips for Young Writers

1. Leave a space for the unknown word and continue with writing.
2. Write as much of the beginning of the word as you can.
3. Write the probable spelling on an extra slip of paper. If it looks correct, use it.
4. Think through the story before beginning to write and ask the teacher to list difficult words on the chalkboard.
5. Keep a piece of paper on your desk so that the teacher may quickly write down any word you request.
6. Look up the word in the spelling word box, picture dictionary, or in a reader where the word may be found.
7. Keep a spelling notebook with a separate page devoted to words that you use frequently.[6]

---

4. Russell G. Stauffer, *Directing Reading Maturity as a Cognitive Process* (New York: Harper & Row, 1968).

5. Sylvia Ashton-Warner, *Teacher* (New York: Simon and Schuster, 1963).

6. For further specific and detailed suggestions, see the chapters "Dictated Experience Stories" and "Creative Writing" in Russell G. Stauffer, *The Language Experience Approach to the Teaching of Reading* (New York: Harper & Row, 1970). See also Mary Anne Hall, *Teaching Reading as a Language Experience* (Columbus, Ohio: Merrill, 1970).

Encouraging written expression

• *First-hand experiences*   As indicated in the preceding discussion, first-hand experiences can be the spark that ignites an idea. Close observation, followed by describing or explaining details and relating reactions to an experience, is a foundation stone in composing. Sense awareness is a very important component of expressive composition—listening, looking, touching, tasting, and smelling. For example, increased awareness of feelings and perception come about as children (1) watch snowflakes fall silently, (2) hear a robin serenading its mate, (3) taste the glistening dew drops, (4) feel squishy mud, or (5) smell a field of clover. Questions such as the following may be useful for stimulating sensory awareness.

1. What is the most beautiful thing you have ever seen?
2. What is the most beautiful sound you have ever heard?
3. How does an onion, pepper, candy, ice cream, or a sour pickle taste? Try to describe it.
4. How many different textures can you discover in the classroom? Try to describe them.
5. What is your favorite aroma? Try to describe it so that another person knows what you are describing.

There are other ways of stimulating children toward written expression. These include use of (1) objects; (2) pictures and films; (3) titles (related words, story beginnings and endings); (4) literature; and (5) a writing center. Examples of each of these ways will be discussed in turn.

• *Objects*   An example of using objects to stimulate writing would be a collection of hats brought into the classroom: fireman, cowboy, sailor, sport (baseball, football, etc.). In discussion with the class, encourage the children to think about the possible stories associated with the fireman's hat. Ideas can be expressed orally. Then each child may select one of the other hats as the object of his writing.

• *Pictures and films*   A teacher, adept at photography, could take 35-mm slides of a waterfall. In showing them, he could suggest that the children describe the sounds they would hear if they were in the picture. Art reproductions may also achieve results, as well as the children's own art work. Films like *Paddle to the Sea* (based on the book by Holling C. Holling)[7] often suggest further adventures. Children can react by inventing what might happen next, or at least summarize the story as presented. Sound filmstrips like *Lentil*[8] can be used in much the same fashion. In addition, filmed materials like the following are designed and organized to encourage children to have inventive ideas.

Magic Moments (twenty 16-mm sound films), Encyclopaedia Britannica Educational Corporation, 425 N. Michigan Ave., Chicago, Ill. 60611.

Let's Write a Story, Churchill Films, 662 N. Robertson Blvd., Los Angeles, Calif. 90069.

• *Titles*   At times, a title suggestion may be sufficient to trigger the flow of ideas. Some possible titles are: "Things I Dislike," "A Conversation with My Dog," "My Three Wishes," "What Happiness Means to Me," "My Most Pleasant Evening at Home," or "My Latest Dream." Some children may like pretend biographies, such as "My Life as a Goldfish"; others like topics closer to them, such as "My Favorite Pet."

More often, however, sets of related words or story beginnings and endings may prove more stimulating than titles. An example of a set of related words would be: *bump, dog, bandage, bicycle,* and *smiles.* From these words, children may evolve many different stories.

An example of a story beginning might be: "Bill and John were digging for clams. All at once Bill's shovel hit something that made a hollow sound. It was a shiny, hard object." A story ending: "Bob's older brother said, 'Well, I guess that will be a lesson you will not soon forget.'" *Story Starter Kits* (Boston: Ginn and Company) are commercially available.

• *Literature*   A story such as *Pippi Longstocking*[9] can be followed by written ideas about what else could happen to Pippi. Or a teacher can read a story to the class and stop before reading the end and ask, "What do you think is going to happen? Let's write our own ending." Or children can describe a character in a book, such as Sara in *The Summer of the Swans.*[10]

---

7. National Film Board of America, 680 Fifth Ave., New York, N.Y. 10019

8. Weston Woods Studio, Weston, Conn. 06880

9. Astrid Lindgren, *Pippi Longstocking* (New York: Viking Press, 1950).

10. Betsy Byars, *The Summer of the Swans* (New York: Viking Press, 1970).

After reading *Whistle for Willie*,[11] the teacher might try to stimulate writing by asking: "What if Peter woke up one morning and could not whistle for the dog?" "Someday" may be a natural title for an essay after children have heard or read *When I Am Big*[12] or *Someday*.[13] Different beginnings, different endings, changing of characters, changing of locale—all are opportunities for written expression. Sometimes, only a display of a set of book jackets will serve as a starter for a story. And *Summer Diary*[14] is a book that hasn't been written as yet—the young child is supposed to do just that![15]

After hearing and reading make-believe stories, pupils can be encouraged to tell or write their own fantasy stories. For example, following the presentation of Kipling's *Just So Stories*, children often like to tell or write their own accounts of "why" or "how"—such as how the crow got its caw. With Paul Bunyan or Pecos Pete providing a stimulus, intermediate-level children frequently tell or write their own tall tales. After reading and discussing many fables and studying their characteristics (brevity, animals for characters, presentation of a moral), children may wish to try fable writing. Similarly, reading and study of myths may lead a child to write his own myth. Older children may be introduced to the idea of writing autobiographies by reading a book such as *Life Story*.[16]

• *The writing center*   This is often the place for some of the previously mentioned materials. For example, one fourth-grade teacher had the following materials in the center.

1. A set of pictures
2. A "finish-me" card file (unfinished stories)
3. Varied, interesting objects in a box
4. A chart with cartoons and short newspaper/magazine articles
5. A box of stationery containing interesting letterheads: MGM Studios, NASA, Dr. Albert Einstein, Queen Elizabeth Shipping Lines
6. Notebook paper and ball-point pens in assorted colors, typing paper, a typewriter

---

11. Ezra Jack Keats, *Whistle For Willie* (New York: Viking Press, 1964).

12. Robert Paul Smith, *When I Am Big* (New York: Harper & Row, 1965).

13. Charlotte Zolotow, *Someday* (Harper & Row, 1964).

14. Ruthven Tremain, illus., *Summer Diary* (New York: Macmillan, 1970).

15. See chapter 5 of Mary S. Montebello, *Literature for Children: Children's Literature in the Curriculum* (Dubuque, Iowa: William C. Brown, 1973).

16. Virginia Lee Burton, *Life Story* (Boston: Houghton Mifflin, 1962).

7. Dictionaries and reference books
8. File folder (for work completed at the center)

Worksheets may be placed at the writing center. See the following primary-level example.

Worksheet: Shapes Around Us

1. Go to the viewing center and watch the filmstrip called "A Circle in the Sky!" (Chicago: Coronet Instructional Films, 1970).
2. Listen to the tape of a story called "The Wing on a Flea," *A Book About Shapes* by Ed Emberly. The book is beside the tape recorder and you may look at the pictures while the teacher reads.
3. Go to the art center and get some construction paper scraps.
4. Go to your seat and cut out some shapes that look like the shapes on the bulletin board. Make them different colors and sizes.
5. Paste your shapes on a sheet of paper. Put some on top of each other and try to make an object that looks like an animal or a person.
6. Look at your finished shape and write three sentences about it on a sheet of writing paper.
7. Put your name on the back of both papers and put your shape picture and story on the bulletin board.
8. Read at least three other stories on the bulletin board.
9. Take your picture down and turn it upside down on your desk. Look at it for five minutes and think of things that it reminds you of.
10. Now write three sentences about what it looks like.
11. Put your first story in your folder.
12. Share your second story with others by going to the reading circle and reading it aloud. Put your second story and picture in your folder.

Another item commonly found at the writing center is a set of independent composition activity cards. These may be commercial sets[17] or sets developed by the teacher. An example of one of these cards is illustrated on page 240.

17. For example, *Writing Center* (New York: Holt, Rinehart and Winston, 1971).

Activity Card: Independent Composition—Story Writing

Two boys are running through a field. They are running very fast.
The wind is slapping against their faces. Use the following questions to get some ideas for a story.
    Why are they running?
    Where are they running from or to?
    Are they happy or are they frightened?
    Is something or someone chasing them?

Independent composition activity cards may be developed around a host of ideas: writing a descriptive paragraph about the texture of things pasted on the cards; writing a limerick after studying a sample limerick and its characteristics on a card; completing a story whose first paragraph is given on the card followed by some questions (as illustrated above); using a picture and sentence on the card to begin a story; writing a paragraph that gives a good word picture of a photograph on the card; or writing in response to a problem situation, as shown on page 241.

(A valuable source of ideas for creative writing is *Flair*, Stevensville, Mich.: Educational Services.)

Following are some companies dealing in motivational materials.

Caedmon Records Inc., 505 Eighth Ave., New York, N.Y. (recordings of poetry and stories)

Developmental Learning Materials, 3505 N. Ashland Ave., Chicago, Ill. 60637 (picture series)

Educational Progress Corporation, 8538 E. Forty-first St., Tulsa, Okla. 74145 (plays for reading, sound filmstrips)

Charles E. Merrill Publishing Company, 1300 Alum Creek Dr., Columbus, Ohio 43216 (stories and poems done on tape)

Miller-Brody Productions, 342 Madison Ave., New York, N.Y. 10017 (cassettes, filmstrips, talking books)

Scholastic Magazines, Inc., 904 Sylvan Ave., Englewood Cliffs, N.J. 07632 (posters, record-book sets)

Teaching Resource Films (Educational Enrichment Materials) 86 East Ave., Norwalk, Conn. 16851 (sound filmstrips, records, cassettes)

Activity Card: Independent Composition—Problem Situation

FATHER   JOE

I'M NOT GOING TO PLAY BASKETBALL ANY MORE FOR COACH DOWELL. I HAVE BEEN TO ALL THE PRACTICE SESSIONS AND HAVEN'T BEEN SELECTED FOR THE FIRST TEAM. I'M NOT GOING TO WASTE ANY MORE TIME TRYING.

1. If you were Joe's father, what would you tell him?
2. Why might Coach Dowell not have selected Joe for the first team?
3. Does Joe gain anything by continuing to play even though he isn't chosen for the first team?
4. Is there something you cannot do well? What should you do about it?
5. What things do you do poorly that you would like to do well? Why?
6. Write a paragraph telling your ideas about how you learned to do something well and that you now enjoy doing.

Franklin Watts, Inc., 845 Third Ave., New York, N.Y. 10022 (picture series)

Weston Woods, Weston, Conn. 06880 (poetry, records, films of children's books, sound filmstrips)

(For a comprehensive listing, see chapter 3 of *Content and Craft: Written Expression in the Elementary Schools* by Dorothy G. Hennings and Barbara M. Grant (Englewood Cliffs, N.J.: Prentice-Hall, 1973).

Formulating written expression

Motivation and stimulation alone will not guarantee quality writing. Specific attention must be focused upon aspects of the writing process, such as the use of effective words, ways of describing, and features of originality.

The following two illustrations show how a primary- and a middle-school teacher guided the composing process.

ILLUSTRATION 1

Teacher A believes in early writing, even as early as the first grade. This means that she is willing to accept "incorrect spelling" or "phonetic spelling." She feels that phonetic spelling does not carry over as a fixed way of spelling. She considers the chalkboard the greatest single motivational aid in the classroom (other than the teacher). The chalkboard is lined, since it is for the pupils' use as well as the teacher's. At the beginning of the school year, she permits the children to communicate orally, expressing themselves freely. The pupils are "getting ready" for writing, just as they "get ready" for reading. Ms. A will have read many books to the class by the end of the January school term. Cooperative experience charts will have preceded individual writing. She has found that, contrary to the feeling of teachers of the intermediate years, her pupils like to write if she does not force them to write and if she is not too strict on spelling and punctuation. Below are the steps Ms. A frequently takes in working with her pupils in creative writing:

1. Ms. A leads a discussion relative to a general topic, such as "Birds We Saw on Our Nature Walk." Questions are asked by the teacher, bringing out ideas. Pictures are placed on the bulletin board showing scenes of the topic under consideration.
2. Ms. A then reads aloud a story and a poem related to the topic.
3. She suggests that the pupils might enjoy writing a story about one of the pictures. (She feels that the pictures help them stick to the subject in their short paragraphs.) She asks them to think of a story they would like to write and then to give a title for their writing activity. (She believes that the sharing of titles will give "nonstarters" some ideas and that it will help the writer to stick to the subject.)
4. On a chart, Ms. A writes words that might be needed in the writing activity. She asks the pupils to rely

primarily on phonetic spelling but mentions they may use a picture dictionary or their readers for reference. If necessary, a child may check his spelling from a neighbor's, but this is not too important if the thoughts are good.[18]

5. Ms. A invites about half of the class to go to the chalkboard to write their short stories while the others write at their seats. Ms. A sometimes reminds the class of good ways of beginning a composition with a question, such as "Did you ever . . . ?" rather than "Once upon a time . . . ."

6. As most class members are completing their work, Ms. A has the children read the stories they have written on the chalkboard. Ideas for improvement (and mechanical corrections) are made by class members.

ILLUSTRATION 2

Mr. C teaches ten-year-olds. The following lesson was observed in his classroom. He showed the children several large pictures of people engaged in various activities. Most of the pictures were from magazines. Some were in color, and others were in black and white. No captions or titles were visible.

After a few minutes of silence, the teacher asked the children what they thought of the pictures and if they had any comments about them. The children's responses were typical. Some had seen a few of the pictures before and told where they had seen them. Others reported adventures of their own that were related to one or more of the pictures. Occasionally the teacher turned to a specific picture and asked questions like the following:

What's going on there?
How do you think the man feels?
How can you tell how he feels?
Have you ever felt that way?
What do you think you would do in that situation?

---

18. There is little research into the independent, written vocabulary of first- and second-graders, but the best estimate might be 2,500 words for first-graders and 3,500 for second-graders if pupils have been provided with a good writing program.

How would you describe this picture to someone who could not see it?

After several minutes of discussion, the teacher reminded the children that many books get ideas across to the reader without pictures. He then asked for a few examples from books read recently that told how people felt without using pictures. The children related examples of how they knew characters in books were happy, sad, afraid, or hateful. Some read selections from books they happened to have at their desks.

The teacher returned to the specific pictures and asked the children, "What words could you use to describe the person in this picture? How do you think he feels?" The words mentioned were listed on the chalkboard and the children were encouraged to think of as many synonyms and phrases as possible to explain the situation.

The lesson up to this point had lasted about fifteen minutes. The teacher then invited the children to write stories of their own that told about people—people in situations where they were sad, happy, afraid, uncertain, angry, or otherwise. He told them he hoped they would tell about an imaginary experience or one that had happened to them, but that if they could not, perhaps the pictures of experiences related in the room would give them some ideas. He emphasized the development of stories telling how people feel.

Some children began to write almost immediately. Others would write a few lines, tear up the paper, and start over. After a few minutes, however, all but a very few were writing busily.

When it became apparent that some children could not get started, the teacher went to them and talked with each one quietly, offering encouragement and suggestions.

As the children completed their stories, they were reminded to read them silently to see if the stories sounded natural and if they expressed feelings. They were also reminded to check the list of standards for story writing that the class had previously developed. Many children exchanged their stories and shared comments. Some pupils had not finished their compositions at the close of the period. They were encouraged to complete them so that the stories could be shared with the class.

It is best to discuss aspects of the writing process before, during, and following a particular composition effort. When appropriate, activities such as the following may be helpful if not taught as isolated exercises.

• *Words*   A writer needs words and needs to delight in their use. Many exercises are possible to help children become sensitive to words. Discussion of tired, overworked words, such as *nice, good, pretty,* can bring forth suggestions of more specific words to substitute for them. Lively verbs can help in description. For example, the sentence "The girl walked down the street" could be improved by substituting a more exact verb such as *stumbled, dawdled, ambled,* or *fluttered.* Vivid adjectives and adverbs also help to paint as clear a word picture as possible and can be developed as children suggest words associated with sight, sound, taste, touch, and smell. Newspaper and magazine advertisements use many descriptive words. They can be used to focus pupils' attention upon words that appeal, as suggested by the following task card.

Task Card: Descriptive Words

Study the two advertisements placed on the bulletin board. Pick out the descriptive words used to make the reader want to try the product.

   Pretend you are in advertising and must write an advertisement for a new product. It may be something to eat, drink, wear, play, or some cleaning product. See if you can make it sound like something the reader just cannot do without. Give it a name and illustrate it if you want.

Word charts can be developed with such titles as "Fun Words," "Quiet Words," "Fast Words," "Sleepy Words," or "Words about Sports." Attention can be focused upon synonyms and antonyms; word families *(heart, hearty, heartily, heartless, heartache)*; and foreign language words *(sombrero, petite, salon)*. Worksheets may be prepared for words with different meanings: *I rose from the bed. He smelled the red rose.* Word lists may be developed about occupations *(farmers, mechanics)* or settings *(hospital, sports arena)*. Reread the section about word files in chapter 1, page 12.

Unusual words children glean from their reading can be placed on the bulletin board. Trade books, such as *A Hole is to Dig*,[19] *Ounce, Dice, Trice*,[20] and *Cats Have Kittens, Do Gloves Have Mittens?*[21] can be used for much word play. Use of alliteration, personification, simile, and metaphor add impact. Alliteration and personification are elements in *Joji and the Fog*.[22] Fresh images may be encouraged by completing comparisons (as red as . . . , as bold as . . . , as big as . . . , kittens are like . . . , the beating of the rain is like . . . , the scream of the fire siren is like . . .). Figures of speech may be found in literature. For example, *The Phantom Tollbooth* derives its humor from awareness of words and phrases.[23] Similes and metaphors can be recognized in *White Snow, Bright Snow*.[24] Descriptive phrases abound in *Miracles on Maple Hill*.[25] The flavor of idiomatic phrases pervades in *Strawberry Girl*.[26]

• *Description*   In their writing, children often attempt to give a "picture" of what they are describing. It might be a description of an object, a place, an animal, a person, or an event. The questions to ask about effective description are the "sense" ones: "Can you see it? (Hear it? Taste it? Feel it? Smell it?)" Sensory-oriented exercises are recommended: write your clearest description of the appearance of your bedroom, the sound of the song of a bird, the taste of lemonade, the feel of sand on your toes, and the smell of frying bacon at breakfast.

Specific attributes may be developed for each of the five items—object, place, animal, person, event. For example, as children describe an object, attributes such as the following may be listed on the chalkboard: color, shape, size, weight, texture, temperature, aroma, taste. Attributes for a place might involve animate or inanimate objects in the place and their spacial arrangements, temperature, colors, shapes, and so on. For persons, attributes might include size, weight, facial features, clothing, body characteristics. Similar observation guides may be prepared for animals and events.

---

19. Ruth Krause, *A Hole is to Dig* (New York: Harper & Brothers, 1952).

20. Alastair Reid, *Ounce, Dice, Trice* (Boston: Little, 1958).

21. Cathleen Schurr, *Cats Have Kittens, Do Gloves Have Mittens?* (New York: Knopf, 1962).

22. Betty Lefton, *Joji and the Fog* (New York: Morrow, 1959).

23. Norton Juster, *The Phantom Tollbooth* (New York: Random, 1961).

24. Alvin Tresselt, *White Snow, Bright Snow* (New York: Lothrop, 1965).

25. Virginia Sorenson, *Miracles on Maple Hill* (New York: Harcourt, Brace and World, 1956).

26. Lois Lenski, *Strawberry Girl* (Philadelphia: Lippincott, 1945).

• *Organization*   In considering more complete story writing, other features often deserve attention. For example, suggestions for beginning and ending a story would include attention to such matters as (1) choosing an interest-arousing and suitable topic or idea, (2) giving an interesting title reflecting the major idea or perhaps a key phrase used in the story, (3) planning a good beginning sentence or two that will arouse attention and let the action begin to take place, and (4) preparing a concluding sentence that sums up the experience or sharply ends the action. More specifically, children may avoid such beginnings as "One day . . . ." or "Once upon a time . . . ." by using a variety of phrases:

It was Bill's chance to . . . .
As Susan opened the door to the house . . . .
Tom never dreamed that this was going to be a special day . . . .

Stories can begin with a conversation, with a question, or with other techniques to set the stage for action.

A study of children's literature reveals ways for the writer to "invite" the reader into his story. For example, the pupil might study beginning sentences in such works as *Charlotte's Web* ("Where's Papa going with that ax?");[27] *Roosevelt Grady* ("The Opportunity Class. That's where the bean pickers got put.");[28] or *It's Like This, Cat* ("My father is always talking about how a dog can be very educational for a boy. That is one reason I got a cat.").[29] After such study, one sixth-grade girl started a story in this fashion: "Can you remember when you were so little that you could not reach anything? Well, this is just the problem this small boy is having."

To bring a character to life, the writer needs to tell how he looks, what he does, what he says (and how he says it), what other persons think about the character, and what goes on in the character's own thinking—not necessarily all of these in one story. Such information leads to reasons why the character behaves as he does—the motivation behind his actions. Use of conversation helps to make people seem real and alive. Children can illustrate the several ways characterization may be developed. For example:

1. Stating a fact: "The boy is selfish."
2. Explaining how he does things
3. Describing an event that proves the point

27. E.B. White, *Charlotte's Web* (New York: Harper & Brothers, 1952).

28. Louisa R. Shotwell, *Roosevelt Grady* (Cleveland, Ohio: World Publishing, 1972).

29. Emily C. Neville, *It's Like This, Cat* (New York: Harper & Row, 1963).

4. Comparing him with other selfish persons
5. Using synonyms for the word *selfish*
6. Describing what others say about him

There must be something that makes a scene—an occurrence or event that reveals what, when, where, why, and how things happen. And from this one piece of action—keeping to one idea per paragraph—several actions in a sequence make for a complete story. Pupils must decide the most important details. With a main character, the writer may tell the problem he faces and how he meets it. Putting the events in an order that makes one want to know "what happens next" heightens the suspense value. Before putting together the various pieces of action, the writer must decide whether the story is best told from the point of view of the writer (as a participant in the story), of an observer, or of one of the characters.

Finally, a graph, cooperatively developed with children, may be exhibited to represent a narrative. This graph may represent the introduction (attention-getting beginning, characters, time, and place); problem; mounting action (involving conversation, appropriate words, details); climax or several lesser climaxes; solution to the problem; and ending (short, satisfying).[30]

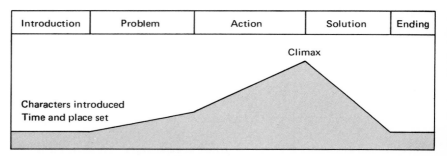

• **Other ideas and materials**   Adequate time is important for quality writing. One time sequence is proposed below.

First Day: Class discussion of the writing assignment may take ten or more minutes and the children's beginning efforts about thirty.
Second Day: Writing may be completed and read aloud to oneself and perhaps to a partner. In terms of evaluative comments, such items as the following may be con-

---

30. Idea from Maxine Schneider, "A Pattern for Story Writing," *Grade Teacher 87* (October 1969); 102–103.

sidered: relatedness of ideas, time sequence, variety in sentence structure, expression of feeling (sensory detail), descriptive power (use of specific words), conversation, and figures of speech.

Third Day: Revision and proofreading take place, the teacher conferring with individuals having difficulty.

Fourth Day: Compositions are read aloud to the class, posted on the bulletin board, or placed in a notebook on the language arts table.

Through such procedures, the pupils discover at the outset that the content of their compositions is important. Children need not worry about punctuation or spelling at this time of first writing. Both thought and manner of expression are important—but there is a time and place for each concern.

Commercially available sets of materials dealing with components of the writing process include:

Composition: Guided ⟶ *Free.* New York: Teachers College Press, Columbia University, 1974. An individualized writing course (twelve-part series) for kindergarten through fourth-grade use.

Composition Through Literature. New York: American Book, 1967. This is a creative writing course for upper elementary and junior high schools. Books A, B, and C are each divided into units, treating the four major types of writing: exposition, narration, argumentation, and description. Each unit is developed on a tripod of literature, composition, and structure.

English Composition. New York: Macmillan, 1968. In this series, for grades 3-8, the emphasis is upon creative and effective writing, step-by-step method of instruction, and self-help features that enable pupils to respond according to their abilities and interests. The series is based upon finding ideas for composition; choosing the right words; organizing words and ideas into larger and larger units; and using the tools of composition—grammar, usage, and mechanics.

Invitations to Speaking and Writing Creatively. Boston: Ginn, 1965. The format, for grades 3-6, is the tear-out workbook. Many unusual writing assignments and suggestions are included. The teacher's manual abounds with suggestions for evaluating the results both academically and psychologically.

Making It Strange. New York: Harper & Row, 1967. This is a creative writing program based on the conscious use of metaphor. Books

1, 2, 3, and 4 correspond to grades 3, 4, 5, and 6. Three forms of analogy are the basis for creative writing: (1) direct analogy—simple comparison; (2) personal analogy—be the thing; and (3) symbolic analogy—compressed conflict.

Thinking and Writing: An Inductive Program in Composition. New York: Prentice-Hall, 1967. This is a program in composition for grades 1–6, based in part on the philosophy of Jean Piaget. Generalizations that are developed include: words and sentences; classification and order; description, beginning explanation; and explanation, interpretation, and argumentation.

Write to Communicate: The Language Arts in Process. Pleasantville, N.Y.: Reader's Digest Educational Division, 1973. This program, for grades 3, 4, 5, and 6, utilizes the process of prewriting, writing, and rewriting. Some components include: motivating the pupil to write; providing copies for peer editing; and furnishing writing forms and media (as awareness posters, workshop posters, phonograph records).

The Writing Bug. New York: Random, 1972. This is an individualized composition program for the middle grades, focusing upon describing, explaining, and storytelling. It includes activity cards, wall charts, filmstrips, cassette recordings, and a teacher's guide.

Writing Skills Laboratories. Chicago: Science Research Associates, 1965. This kit, for grades 4–6, contains individualized instruction combined with sequential writing assignments. The skills are arranged sequentially and the pupil progresses at his own rate, directed to remedial help whenever necessary.

Two excellent sets of filmloops are available for story writing: *Story Starters* (grades 1–3) and *Springboards to Writing* (grades 4–6).[31] In using them with children who lack confidence, it is best to pool the ideas of a whole class. Explain to the children that they are going to view a film to help them write a story. In viewing "House on Fire," for example, ask the first question that appears on the loop—"How could the fire have started?" Collect suggestions from the class (put them on the chalkboard) and repeat the procedure with the other questions supplied. As children begin their stories, tell them they may use any ideas from the chalkboard and encourage them not to worry about punctuation and spelling. Allow time for writing and then encourage the children to share stories by reading them to each other.

---

31. Ealing Films, 2225 Massachusetts Ave., Cambridge, Mass. 02140

Filmstrips or filmloops, presenting provocative "story starter" segments, can be used to stimulate ideas for storywriting.

As children grow in writing experience, the filmed segments may be used more in accordance with individual needs and interests.

Other ideas for the mature writer are presented in chapter 12, pages 449–450.

WRITING CREATIVE POETRY

Poetry writing can help children gain a better understanding of language and writing in general: it involves looking at things accurately, experiencing things acutely, and expressing things lucidly.

The strongest foundation for a poetry writing program is a planned poetry reading and study program that includes a balance of poems of various characteristics, topics, and forms. Through such a program, children become familiar with what poetry is and its varieties of themes and forms. They sense that poems can be about activities (work, play, special occasions); surroundings (home, geographical); reflections (issues of our time, personal concerns); or the arts (literature, art, music, drama). They see that varied forms are possible (couplets, triplets, quatrains, limericks). In terms of syllabic arrangements, five types of poetry writing popular with elementary school children are: haiku, cinquain, lanterne, septolet, and tanka.

Five steps may be recommended as a general procedure for preparing pupils to write various forms of poetry.

1. Reading and study of a well-known poem. (Put it on the overhead projector or the chalkboard.)
2. Reading of a child's poem (perhaps from a previous year) used to convince the children that they, too, can do it; if you have no sample from past years, children enjoy hearing what other children have written (See chapter 6, page 205 for a list of references.)
3. Asking questions to discuss the form under consideration
4. Pooling experiences and opinions by the class members to gather ideas for their own poems
5. Writing suggested, distinctive words, phrases, and ideas on the chalkboard

At this time, the child is invited to move into the creation of his own poem.

Rhyme arrangements

• *Couplet*   A couplet is a simple, two-line, rhymed pattern. A model from literature might be taken from "Cats Have Kittens" or "Jump or Jiggle," both by Evelyn Beyer. Another model might be Christina Rossetti's "What is Pink?" From the first model, a couplet such as the following might result.

If dogs have pups
Do saucers have cups?

From the second Beyer model, noun pairs might be presented for consideration, such as:

Boys _____
Girls _____

From Rossetti, "color" couplets can abound! For example:

What is brown?
The color of the ground.

• **Triplet**   A triplet (or tercet) is a three-line poem that conveys humor and tells a brief story. Following is a triplet prepared by an eight-year-old.

I have a cat.
She sits on a mat.
She looks like a bat.

• **Quatrain**   A quatrain contains four lines with an a, b, a, b rhyming pattern. After reading and study of a number of quatrains ("The Pasture" by Robert Frost is an example), one child wrote:

A bear is funny,
He likes to climb trees,
He likes the honey,
But not the bees.

• **Limerick**   The limerick is a combination of triplet and couplet. The rhyme pattern is 1-1-2-2-1. Three metrical beats are observed in lines 1, 2, 5; and two beats in lines 3 and 4, as noted in the following example.

There was a young lady of Lynn
Who was so exceedingly thin
That when she essayed
To drink lemonade
She slipped through the straw and fell in.
                                        —Anonymous

Syllabic arrangements

• **Haiku**   The classical Japanese haiku, as a general rule, consists of seventeen syllables; is three lines in length; and the first and third lines have five syllables, the second seven. There is no metrical pattern and lines do not rhyme. It contains at least some reference to nature (other than human nature); refers to a particular event (that is, it is not a generalization); and presents that event as happening now, not in the past. As yet, there are no generally accepted criteria for English haiku. It seems obvious, however, that it cannot be exactly the same as Japanese haiku if only because of the difference in language. There is no rule compelling one to follow classical Japanese standards for haiku, but beginners should conform to Japanese standards as far as it is practicable. Pupils using such a strict form before attempting flexibility learn to submit to controls, to observe carefully, to recognize the importance of experience, and to compress their record of a particular moment. If the pupil chooses a simple topic and writes naturally, his own actual experiences serve as subjects for his haiku. Haiku like the following represent average fifth- or sixth-grade results.

Snow falling till dawn.
    Early skiers having fun.
        Winter has begun.

Water trickling over rocks
    bringing life to the forest
        for the bountiful land.

White snow on the ground
    beautiful, so beautiful.
        Then it goes away.

Two books of haiku that teachers and children may find helpful are:

Behn, Harry. *Cricket Songs.* New York: Harcourt, Brace and World, 1964.
Lewis, Richard, ed. *In a Spring Garden.* New York: Dial, 1965.

• *Cinquain*   The cinquain was perhaps influenced by haiku. The pattern frequently used is: first line, one word giving the title; second line, two words describing the title; third line, three words expressing an action; fourth line, four words expressing a feeling; fifth line, another word for the title. An example might be:

Colt
    All legs
        Wobbling, shaking, kicking
            Curious, full of life
                Pony

• *Lanterne*   Here the five lines contain the following numbers of syllables, respectively: 1, 2, 3, 4, 1. Note the visual shape of the Japanese lantern in the following example.

My
dog is
a pretty
German shepherd
dog.

• *Septolet*   The seven lines contain the following number of syllables, respectively: 1, 2, 3, 4, 3, 2, 1. For example:

Quick
Blue-eyed
Pussycat
Frightening jays
From the yard
Proudly
Fast.

• *Tanka*   The tanka is somewhat like an extension of haiku, with a 5, 7, 5, 7, 7 syllable pattern; rhyme and meter are not used. The following poem is an example of this form.

Footprints in the sand
Side by side, the large and small,
Across the damp beach
Tell me that father and son
Have left behind the mother.

Free verse

Examples of free verse include such poems as "Mouse" by Hilda Conkling and "Fog" by Carl Sandburg. Some teachers have reported motivating free verse from *Prayers from the Ark*[32] and *The Creature's Choir.*[33]

Through wide exposure to poetry, along with some attention to

32. Carmen B. De Graztold, *Prayers from the Ark*, trans. by Rumer Godden (New York: Viking Press, 1962).
33. Rumer Godden, *Creature's Choir* (New York: Viking Press, 1965).

analysis of the poet's craft, the child comes to recognize what free verse is and how it differs from prose. It is brief, focusing upon a specific theme, and demands precise usage of words. These words appeal to the senses as well as conveying meaning. Words are patterned in a rhythmic manner (and also sometimes in a rhyming manner) and placed in lines for effect.

Perhaps this kind of verse is the most difficult for elementary school children. Much appeal should be made to the senses. Poems of the "sensations" should be read to children. Sharpness of perception is required.

What do you see in this picture?
What sounds do you hear in the school corridor as we sit silently in our seats?
Describe your favorite flavor of ice cream and let's see if we can guess it?
Let's talk about the feel of a slippery bar of soap.
Can you describe the smell of these various plants and blossoms?

Although free verse follows no regular metrical pattern and recurrence of stress, it is not necessarily formless or unrestrained. Perhaps the teacher will want to begin with two brief sentences, followed by discussion of possible experiences for topics, jotting down ideas, demonstrating the smoothing out and condensing of the ideas, and arranging them in the form of a poem.[34]

Evaluation

In attempting to make valid judgments about the child's work, one must know his age and something about his maturity, background, and experiences. What is considered good poetry for a child of eight may be too immature and unthinking in form and idea for a child of twelve. An expression that is unsatisfactory for a child of wide experience may be judged excellent for an underpriviledged child or a child of limited experience. A poem in which no value is seen may show, by comparison with the child's earlier work, the very sort of individual growth for which the teacher is striving.

Although the standards must be flexible and adapted to the age and grade of the child or the group, there are some specific items to look for that will help the teacher: (1) originality of thought and ex-

---

34. See Moira Dunn, "Writing Poetry in the Elementary School," *Elementary English* 45 (March 1968): 337–341. See also Denis Rodgers, "A Process for Poetry Writing," *Elementary School Journal* 72 (March 1972): 294–303.

pression; (2) choice of words; (3) reflection of what the writer really thinks and feels; (4) clear description that "pictures" a central thought, idea, or pattern; and (5) cadence to the language. If a child's poem has even one of the above mentioned characteristics, it indicates that the poetic spirit is at work and it should be respected.

The child's work must be handled carefully. Pride in work can be developed through praise. Growth takes place in individual or small group conferences where questions are raised.

> How do you feel about this?
> What is a way to narrow the topic?
> Would it be better if the last three words were on a line by themselves?
> What more specific word could be used for this rather vague one?
> What needless words could be deleted?

After such an evaluation session, the child is encouraged to rewrite a final copy if there is to be an audience.[35]

There are several places where children's prose and poetry may be submitted for consideration. A few are listed below.

American Red Cross News
American National Red Cross
Washington, D.C. 20005

Highlights for Children
Editorial Offices
Honesdale, Pa. 18431

Jack and Jill
Curtis Publishing Company
Independence Square
Philadelphia, Pa. 19105

Wee Wisdom
Unity School of Christianity
Unity Village, Mo. 64063

Other ideas and materials

Children might try other forms of poetry writing after reading and study of models: ballads ("Beth Gelert" by William Spencer and "The Ballad of the Harp Weaver" by Edna St. Vincent Millay); narrative verse ("A Visit from St. Nicholas" by Clement Moore and "The Pied Piper of Hamelin" by Robert Browning); and lyrical ("Where Go the Boats?" by Robert Louis Stevenson and "The Lone Dog" by Irene McCleod). And some children may enjoy shaping the arrangement of words to represent their topic. See the example on page 258.

---

35. See chapter 11, "Dignifying Children's Poetic Composition," *Poetic Composition Through the Grades* by Robert A. Wolsch (New York: Teachers College Press, Columbia University, 1970).

A mountain reaches up and comes down to look like an upside down cup.

Books to Motivate Poetry Writing

De Regniers, Beatrice Schenk. *Something Special.* New York: Harcourt, Brace and World, 1958.

Howard, Coralie, ed. *The First Book of Short Verse.* New York: Watts, 1964.

Larrick, Nancy, ed. *Green is Like a Meadow of Grass.* Champaign, Ill.: Garrard, 1968.

Lewis, Richard. *Miracles.* New York: Simon and Schuster, 1966.

O'Neill, Mary. *Hailstones and Halibut Bones.* New York: Doubleday, 1961.

Zolotow, Charlotte. *Some Things Go Together.* New York: Abelard, 1969.

Poems to Motivate Poetry Writing

Brown, Margaret W. "Little Donkey Close Your Eyes"

Carr, Rosemary, and Benet, Stephen Vincent. "Nancy Hanks"

Farjeon, Eleanor. "In the Week When Christmas Comes"

Merriam, Eve. "Catch a Little Rhyme"

Richard, Laura E. "Kindness to Animals"

Films/Records to Motivate Poetry Writing

"Poetry for Me" and "Poetry to Grow On." Monterey, Calif.: Grover Jennings.

"Poems Are Fun" and "Poetry for Beginners." Chicago: Coronet Films.

"An Anthology of Negro Poetry for Young People." New York: Folkway Records.

"Nonsense Verse of Carroll and Lear." New York: Caedmon Recording.

FUNCTIONAL WRITING

If a child has writing experiences only in terms of stories and poetry, he has a restricted composition program. Neglected is the writing of expository prose. A teacher must strive for a balance between creative writing and realistic writing. Each has a significant place in the composition program.

Some situations at the primary and intermediate levels that lend themselves to functional writing situations include:

1. Letters: friendly letters; business letters; social notes of thanks, invitation, sympathy, congratulations
2. Card writing and postcards
3. Reports in content subjects
4. Announcements and notices of events, articles for the school newspaper, items for the bulletin board and exhibits
5. Records of class plans: class activities, events, club minutes, room histories or diaries
6. Forms such as registration slips, examination blanks

In a classroom where many learning experiences are enriching the curriculum, good reasons for writing are not difficult to find. Pupils are active at writing weather reports, making lost-and-found announcements, listing plans, reporting on facts learned, describing how a project was undertaken, writing minutes of club meetings, etc.

Are children learning through these language jobs? A look at the national results of the assessments of educational progress reveals the following statistics for age nine children:

1. While 88 percent of the nine-year-olds wrote an acceptable thank-you note, the success level then dropped to 35 percent who wrote an acceptable invitation to a classroom play, (others omitted date, time, place) and to 28 percent who included all the (six pieces of) information required to address an envelope correctly.
2. When asked to write an announcement about a pet show for the school newspaper, 21 percent wrote announcements including all the required (four pieces of) information.[36]

In terms of appreciating the value of writing, some nine-year-olds were asked whether they had taken any trips away from home

---

36. National Assessment of Educational Progress. National Results. Report 3: *Writing* (Washington, D.C.: U.S. Office of Education: Department of Health, Education and Welfare, 1970), pp. 12, 18, 20.

during the past twelve months, and if so had they performed any writing activities. Seventy-three percent said they had taken a trip, and of these, 78 percent indicated they had performed one or more writing activities. Twenty-three percent said they had sent a postcard; 25 percent said they had written a letter telling about the trip after they got home; 17 percent said they had written a letter while on the trip; 7 percent said they had kept a diary while on the trip; 27 percent said they had made notes about some of the things they saw; 30 percent said they had written a thank-you note to someone they had visited; and 20 percent said they had written a report about the trip after they got home.

Letter writing

Since letter writing is a fundamental job in written composition, it deserves special consideration. Teachers should use only real situations when teaching letter writing, except for practice periods to provide for specific or technical difficulties. There are many situations calling for real letter writing: pupils who are ill or who have moved away, requests for materials, etc.

• *Friendly letters*   Informal discussion should precede letter writing at the primary and intermediate levels. This discussion could cover questions relating to content and form. Though form is important, it should be considered of secondary importance to content. The pupil ought to know that courtesy, informality, humor, expression of opinions and feelings, cheerfulness, and clearness make for interest in friendly letters. The pupil needs to know that he should write a letter naturally and normally, just as he would speak. Letters can be as free and easy as one's speech. (Some people labor to find fancy phrases that serve to obscure plain facts: e.g., "Winter began to salute us" rather than "The weather grew cold.") A letter is an "on-paper" visit and it should sound as if the writer is actually visiting the person to whom he is writing. The pupil should be encouraged to bring his letter-writing jobs to school. If he wants to write a letter to a friend, the teacher ought to make him feel that at school he can get the help he needs.

The mere copying of "standard" letters from a language textbook or workbook seems like a waste of time to the child and generally should be avoided. If proper forms of letters are available during a letter-writing activity, these models may be used for discussing the meanings behind the form. The child should be encouraged to do the job correctly under the teacher's guidance and to develop high standards that come from within so the goals will not be laid aside when he writes without the direct supervision of the teacher.

Checklists posted on the bulletin board or the chalkboard can prove helpful in bringing pupils' attention to mechanical features in letter writing. Information such as the following can be provided for the primary years.

CHART 7.2: Friendly Letter Guide (Primary Years)

A friendly letter has four parts:
    greeting
    body
    closing
    signature

1. Begin the first word in a greeting with a capital letter.
2. Begin each proper name with a capital letter.
3. Put a comma after the last word in the greeting.
4. Begin the first word in the closing with a capital letter.
5. Put a comma after the last word in the closing.

One teacher prepared a learning packet for friendly letter writing at the intermediate level. The front sheet of the packet provided the Why (reasons for writing friendly letters), Objectives, and Self-test. (See page 262.) Some other activities in the learning packet are listed on page 263.

The posttest consisted of two major items. The first item was analyzing a prepared letter, writing the name of each part of the letter on the line beside the part, and properly capitalizing and punctuating the parts. The second item was the assignment of writing a friendly letter, following discussion with the teacher.

For the writing of a friendly letter, the teacher may wish to make use of a source of names of pen pals.

The Christian Science Monitor, Boston, Mass.
The Junior Red Cross, Washington, D.C.
The International Friendship League, 40 Mt. Vernon Street, Boston, Mass. (fifty cents an address)
Parker Pen Company, Janesville, Wisc.

Learning Packet for Friendly Letter Writing (Intermediate Level)

WHY

You will not always be able to communicate orally with the people you need to share thoughts with. Therefore, you need to know how to write a friendly letter that will take your thoughts to distant places.

OBJECTIVES

1. To identify the five parts (as opposed to the four parts taught at the primary level) of a letter and tell what each part contains
2. To review the uses of capital letters and the uses of commas as they are needed in a friendly letter
3. To write a friendly letter as dictated on tape
4. To learn to write an acceptable friendly letter in correct form through practice

   If you feel you can meet the above objectives at this time, take the self-test at the bottom of this page; or if you feel you cannot meet the above objectives at this time, turn to the next page and read the steps to follow to complete this learning experience.

SELF-TEST

1. What are the five parts of a friendly letter?
2. What two things are included in the heading?
3. Correct the following greetings and closings. Write them the way they should be written in a friendly letter.

   dear aunt mary   yours truly   your friend

4. Write a friendly letter to your best friend and tell him (or her) about the birthday party you are going to have.
5. Check your answers with the answer sheet at the end of the packet.

Foreign Correspondence Bureau, P. O. Box 150, Newton, Kans.
Student Letter Exchange, Waseca, Minn. (twenty-five cents an address)
Dyer's Pen-Pal Service Organization, R. F. D. 3, Seguin, Tex.
Youth of All Nations, 16 St. Luke's Place, New York, N.Y.

Additional Activities for Friendly Letter Writing

1. Use the filmstrip projector to watch the filmstrip "Letter Writing for a Reason."[37]
2. Study the diagram, included in the packet, of the parts of a friendly letter. The parts are heading (address and date), greeting, body, closing, and signature. Make your own diagram of the parts of a friendly letter.
3. Complete worksheets A and B in the learning packet. (Worksheet A provided instruction and practice for writing headings and greetings. Worksheet B provided instruction and practice for writing closings and signatures.)
4. Find the tape in the learning packet and the cassette tape recorder on the shelf. Listen to the tape and write the letter as dictated.
5. Write a friendly letter as suggested on worksheet C. (The top of the worksheet provided a sample of the five parts of a letter. The rest of the worksheet was marked off in lines for a letter to be composed to a relative or friend.)
6. Practice writing friendly letters. Choose two of the following:
   a. Write a letter to a friend. Tell your friend about something you have done or seen. Show that you are interested also in what your friend is doing.
   b. Write a letter to your Aunt Sue telling her that you will be able to visit her during Easter vacation. Tell her how long you will be out of school and when you will arrive at her house.
   c. Make up an unusual or funny letter for another classmate and have that friend write an answer to you.
   d. Write a friendly letter to one of your favorite storybook characters.
7. You are now ready to take the posttest. Ask your teacher for a copy of the test.

School Affiliation Service, American Friends Service Committee, 160 N. Fifteenth St., Philadelphia, Pa.
The Canadian Education Association, 151 Bloor St., W., Toronto 5, Canada

37. (Chicago: Society for Visual Education, 1957).

• *Business letters*   The sample business letter below will suggest its six parts and the required capitalization and punctuation items.

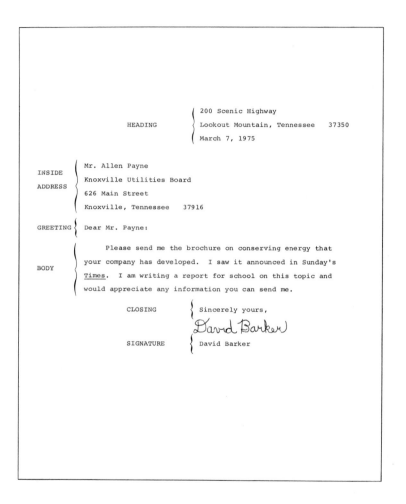

	200 Scenic Highway
HEADING	Lookout Mountain, Tennessee 37350
	March 7, 1975

	Mr. Allen Payne
INSIDE	Knoxville Utilities Board
ADDRESS	626 Main Street
	Knoxville, Tennessee 37916

GREETING   Dear Mr. Payne:

BODY   Please send me the brochure on conserving energy that your company has developed. I saw it announced in Sunday's *Times*. I am writing a report for school on this topic and would appreciate any information you can send me.

CLOSING   Sincerely yours,

SIGNATURE   David Barker

When the time comes to write a business letter, the teacher may distribute mimeographed addresses from *1001 Valuable Things You Can Get Free* (Mort Weisinger, Bantam Books, 1968) or some other source. Business letter writing should include experience with ordering things by mail. (See chapter 12, page 463.)

When letters are ready for mailing, the proper folding of the letter and addressing of the envelope need to receive attention. Approaches to addressing envelopes, with proper punctuation and capitalization, should be illustrated, and appropriate models provided for the pupils.

• *Social notes*   One of the first courtesies a child is taught is to say "Thank you" for gifts or kindnesses. Expressing appreciation is a way of showing consideration for others. It is very easy to say "Thank you" in person; but when it must be written, it seems more difficult. Pupils can be helped to understand that they may put in a letter just what they would say if the person were present. In a letter of thanks, the pupil should mention the thoughtfulness of the other person. For example, he may tell how much he likes a gift he received and what use he is making of it. If a child should happen to receive a gift he does not like, he can still sincerely express appreciation for the kindness that prompted the gift and avoid mentioning his true feeling about the gift itself. There is no excuse for rudeness. Thank-you notes promptly and graciously written indicate good manners and consideration for the feelings of others. Even when thanks are expressed personally, a follow-up note at a later date is a thoughtful gesture.

Letters of invitation should be sincere and cordial. They need to be specific as to the event for which the invitation is issued (party, program, visit to the class) and always give the time, place, and host or hostess.

When a friend is ill or has had a misfortune, a good way to show sympathy is to write a cheer-up letter. Such a letter should (1) say something to show that the writer is sorry he is ill and hopes he will be well soon, and (2) tell him only things that will cheer him or amuse him—do not discuss his illness or the illnesses of others or make mention of unpleasant news that might worry him.

Children have many opportunities to do the kind thing and write a note of congratulations to a friend who has won a contest, received an honor, or had some other good fortune. Children should be aware of such rules as: (1) mention the honor that has been received, (2) say something that shows you are glad he received it, and (3) don't say anything that suggests he was unworthy of it or might have done better.

• *Card writing*   Card writing is a variation of letter writing. Initial instruction may be followed by independent activity at a card writing station, as suggested on page 266.

CARD WRITING STATION

Materials: Large box marked "Thank-You Cards," another marked "Cheer-Up Cards," and a third labeled "Congratulations Cards." Construction paper, crayons, pens, etc.

Directions:

1. Plan a thank-you card for a gift you have received. Fold a piece of construction paper in the form of a card and write the message. Illustrate your card.
2. Plan a cheer-up card for someone who is ill. Design the card. Write the message and put the finished card in the "Cheer-Up" box.
3. Plan a congratulations card for someone who has had some good fortune. Say something that shows you are happy for him.

While there are no specific rules concerning writing of postcards, these points might be suggested:

1. Postcards are less formal than letters.
2. Complete headings are not needed on postcards.
3. Postcards should not be used for very personal or private messages.

A book that teachers and children will find helpful is *The First Book of Letter Writing* by Helen Jacobsen and Florence Mischel.[38] This book discusses the many reasons for letter writing and gives suggestions for various types of letters.

Reports

Children's written work in the content areas (particularly science and social studies) will often take the form of reports. What is usually involved in writing a report? A topic is assigned or chosen, information must be gathered, and the ideas must be organized with major points and supporting details. A need to use reference sources and a bibliography often occurs with report writing. After the first draft is written, it will usually need to be revised and proofread before the final product is prepared. Each of the preceding steps for the initial

---

38. Helen Jacobsen and Florence Mischel, *The First Book of Letter Writing* (New York: Watts, 1957).

draft of a report will be discussed (revision/proofreading appears later in this chapter), suggesting how the various components are best taught in a functional setting, rather than as a series of isolated exercises—although practice and review may be needed on the specific items. Adaptation may be made for age/grade level and experience.

• *Taking notes*   When reading for information on a specific topic in preparation for a written report, the pupil often takes notes to remind himself of ideas. As practice for note taking, a short selection, with a total of 150 to 200 words, could be placed on the overhead projector or chalkboard, with instructions to read and write notes about the topic. Comparison of notes written by the pupils would be encouraged, the discussion concluding with suggestions for note taking, such as:

1. Read the whole selection before beginning to take notes.
2. Take notes only on ideas about the subject.
3. Take notes only on ideas that are important and interesting.
4. Write the notes in your own words, but do not change the meaning; if you cannot do this, use the words of the reference.
5. Do not write notes that you do not understand.
6. Number each note.

• *References*   It is advisable to have the pupils use only one reference source when they begin writing reports; later they can use more than one reference. Reference books with which children should be acquainted include dictionaries, encyclopedias, biographical dictionaries, almanacs, atlases, and book indexes.

• *Bibliographies*   Pupils make lists of books as they gather information from many sources. From the beginning, they are taught to note the source of information or quotation and to give credit to an author whose material they use in their writing. This means they need to learn an acceptable form for recording bibliographical data.

A glance at the bibliographies in several books will quickly establish the fact that there is no single, standard form in general use, although most of the forms vary only in small details. Some schools adopt a single form to be used throughout the system. For the primary years, an author-title listing is probably sufficient. Intermediate-grade pupils should include publisher, place of publication, copyright date, and pages read. Forms like those shown on page 268 have been found acceptable.

CHART 7.3: Bibliography Guide

Primary Years

Earle, Olive. *Robins in the Garden.*

Intermediate Years

Book: Shippen, Katherine B. *Mister Bell Invents the Telephone.* New York: Random, 1952, pp. 75–84.

Periodical: Reese, Bill. "Pass Pointers," *Boys' Life* 49 (February 1959), pp. 40–42.

Encyclopedia: "Basketball," *The World Book Encyclopedia,* vol. B. Chicago: Field Enterprises Educational Corp., 1974, pp. 106–111.

In checking a bibliography he has compiled, the pupil may find it helpful to ask himself the following questions.

Does each entry include
the author?
the publisher?
the place of publication?
the copyright date?
the number of pages read?
proper capitalization and punctuation?

The pupil also needs to learn to use bibliographies prepared by others—the ones he finds in his textbooks, for example. He ought to be able to identify some authors and titles in the lists, to read annotations carefully for clues to the content and usefulness of the books, and to pay particular attention to copyright dates if he is searching for recent information. He should also know how to find out if the books are in the library and where they are located.

• *Organizing*   Using the suggestions for note taking, children should then be able to prepare a set of notes (first collectively with teacher assistance and then individually) from a reference source. Upon completion, the teacher may ask:

How many paragraphs should I make?
What information should go into each paragraph?
In what order should the paragraphs be arranged?

After discussion of these questions, the class members may evolve a cooperative list of ideas, such as:

1. Find what different topics are told about in the notes and list them.
2. After each topic, write the numbers of the notes that tell about that topic.
3. Plan a separate paragraph for each topic.
4. Put the paragraphs in a logical sequence.

The children are learning to list ideas, group them, order the group, write about the ideas in each group (a paragraph), and put the paragraphs in a logical sequence.

• *Making an outline*   Before writing a report, the pupils may be asked to present the report orally. In order to discourage memorization or reading of a report, children should prepare a brief outline that they use in their oral presentation. Outlines are developed with the pupils using the following form:

I. Main topic (most important point—the paragraph idea)
    A. Subtopic (important fact about the main topic)
        1. Detail (thing told about the subtopic)

• *Telling/writing the report*   In presenting a report orally, a good beginning and a good ending must be developed in order to hold the attention of the audience. Examples should be included to add interest and clarify meanings. Some of the material might be presented on a chart or graph. Pictures or realia may be shown as part of the report. Unusual or pertinent vocabulary may be written on the chalkboard or presented on a chart. Group reports may take the form of a panel or dramatic presentation. (The use of review questions for oral reporting is discussed in chapter 12, page 446.)

Scheduling of oral reports is important. Nothing is more boring than listening to one presentation after another, all following a similar pattern. This is eliminated when reports are given as the need arises. At some time, all children will participate in oral reporting, but not all on the same day.

Pupils may be helped by having criteria that they have developed and that they may check as they prepare for their oral reports. The following performance objectives may help the teacher in guiding the children to develop their own set of objectives.

CHART 7.4: Reporting Guide

1. Choose a subject that is interesting to you and to those who will hear the report.
2. Gather information from various sources.
3. Take notes from your reading, putting them into your own words, if possible.
4. Select only the ideas essential to the subject. Arrange the ideas in a logical sequence.
5. Prepare an outline, noting the main and supporting topics.
6. Begin the report with an interesting sentence. Strive for varied ways of presenting the material. Use examples, pictures, objects, and diagrams to make the points clear. Plan an interesting conclusion.
7. Use acceptable sentence patterns and vocabulary, and speak in a clear, conversational tone.

Later, when writing the first draft, the outline is used as a guideline. In doing so, paragraphs are kept to one topic; the sentences within a paragraph tell things in logical order; and when a new topic is introduced, a new paragraph is started.

Instruction in report making should be carried out in a classroom atmosphere where (1) the teacher sets a good example, (2) good audience-speaker relationships are maintained, (3) planning occurs with the child before his performance, and (4) opportunities are provided for improvement of performance through diagnosis and evaluation of individual needs.

An extremely valuable book for interesting and teaching children about report writing is *The First Book of How to Write a Report* by Sue R. Brandt.[39]

Announcements and notices

Various school activities call for written announcements and notices. Such announcements should always include all the information necessary to enable the reader to respond appropriately. The child should always check his written announcements or notices to see if they answer these important questions: Who? What? When? Where? Why? An interesting caption helps to arouse interest. Careful attention must be given to handwriting, for a notice serves no purpose if

---

39. Sue R. Brandt, *The First Book of How to Write a Report* (New York: Watts, 1968).

it is illegible. Moreover, a notice that is attractive in appearance is more likely to be read than a sloppy, carelessly written one.

Notices and announcements should be posted only in places set aside for this purpose and in a manner that does not deface property. They are not to be posted until permission has been granted by the proper authorities. Requesting such permission provides for functional language teaching and learning.

An example of a systematic lesson on oral announcement making is presented in chapter 1, page 17 and it may be adapted to a written announcement experience.

Two related writing activities are news articles and want ads for the school or class newspaper. Both are very direct and to the point. A good guide to writing a news account is to answer the questions: Who (Who is the story about?); What? (What has happened?); When? (When did the event occur?); Where? (Where does the action take place?); Why? (Why did it happen?); and How? (How did it happen?).

For want ad writing, the children may study the columns in the classified ad section of the newspaper.

DOBERMAN PUPPIES—2 red males, ears cropped, pet and show quality. $50. Phone 522-5778 after 5.

When writing a want ad, pupils should include information the buyer will need to cause him to want the article for sale and he should give directions for locating the seller, either by phone or by mail.

Records

Several types of records are kept by elementary school children. Some are group efforts—a class diary or an account of a project or experiment; others are individual records—a record of progress in spelling or of books read. Record keeping can be a valuable learning experience if it is not so lengthy and detailed as to become burdensome.

In a class diary, all pupils assume a share of the responsibility. Since everything that happens cannot be recorded, the pupil must learn to choose the really important items. He learns to be accurate and specific, giving dates and pertinent details. In keeping records of experiments, weather, or similar accounts, each entry should be dated and the information clearly stated in terms meaningful to others.

Records kept by individuals should be simple but accurate. Entries ought to be made regularly in the form agreed upon by the pupils and the teacher.

Filling in forms

Children need to fill out such forms as library cards, the headings of standardized tests, order forms, and subscription blanks. Young children need help in learning to write their full names correctly (not nicknames) and addresses. They should also be able to give and write readily other personal information that is often required: age, date and place of birth, sex, parents' names and occupations, telephone number, height, and weight. Since many forms require the information to be typed or printed, manuscript writing may be put to good use. They need to learn the importance of doing this neatly and correctly. (A learning center for filling in order forms is presented in chapter 12, page 461.)

CONVENTIONS IN WRITING

The mechanics of written expression are considered in this section: capitalization, punctuation, sentence sense, paragraph sense, and manuscript form.

Capitalization

Capitalization is a mechanical element of written language. Courses of study and textbooks in language arts are often quite definite in listing grade requirements in the area of capitalization. However, such listings are merely guides for the introduction of these items; within a classroom there will be considerable variation in capitalization skills. This means that items of capitalization generally listed in the primary years should be mastered before items which are listed for the intermediate years.

• *Instructional items*   A guide to the sequence and placement of capitalization skills is needed by teachers. The following list of minimal capitalization skills is only a suggestion, but it takes into account the needs of children in writing and the relative difficulty of the various items.

Primary years:

1. The first word of a sentence
2. The child's first and last names
3. The name of the teacher, school, town, street
4. The word *I*
5. The date
6. First and important words of titles of books the children read
7. Proper names used in children's writings
8. Titles of compositions
9. Names of titles: *Mr., Mrs., Miss*
10. Proper names: month, day, common holidays
11. First word in a line of verse
12. First and important words in titles of books, stories, poems
13. First word of salutation of an informal note, as *Dear*
14. First word of closing of an informal note, as *Yours* or *Your friend*

Intermediate years:

1. All that is listed for preceding years
2. Names of cities and states in general
3. Names of organizations to which children belong, as Cub Scouts
4. *Mother, Father*, when used in place of the name
5. Local geographical names
6. Names of streets
7. Names of all places, persons, countries, oceans, etc.
8. Capitalization used in outlining
9. Titles when used with names, such as *President* Lincoln
10. Commercial trade names
11. Names of the Diety and the Bible
12. First word of a quoted sentence
13. Proper adjectives, showing race, nationality, etc.
14. Abbreviations of proper nouns and titles[40]

• *Instructional procedures*   There are a number of ways to develop capitalization skills. Certainly the teacher will want to observe the written work of the pupil, noting errors made and possibly tabulating the types of errors as a basis for further teaching and study. Chart 7.5 suggests one method of tabulating.

---

40. Harry A. Greene and Walter T. Petty, *Developing Language Skills in the Elementary Schools*, 4th ed., pp. 259–260. Copyright © 1971 by Allyn and Bacon, Inc., Boston. Reprinted with permission.

CHART 7.5: Analysis of Capitalization Items

PUPIL'S NAMES	First word of a sentence	Proper nouns	Days, months, places, holidays	Titles	First word in a poem	Salutation/ closing of a letter	Official organizations	Brand names	First word of a quoted sentence	Proper adjectives

Self-diagnosis of difficulties should be emphasized. Group and individual dictation drills emphasizing capitalization items that seem difficult for the pupils to master may be used. Pupils should be called upon to check on their use of capital letters on numerous occasions. This not only acquaints the child with irregularities in practice but also with sources commonly used as standards. Group correction of a paper with special reference to capitalization is possible through the use of an overhead projector or the chalkboard. Short, diagnostic tests on the major capitalization skills may be given periodically, followed by practice periods devoted to specific needs. Finally, a five-minute, individualized practice period (proofreading exercise) near the end of the day may be devoted to capitalization errors observed during the day.

Punctuation

Punctuation errors are among the most common mechanical mistakes pupils make in written composition, constituting from one-third to one-half of the total mechanical errors at both the elementary and secondary levels.[41] Puncutation errors persist even in adult writing.

In spite of considerable attention to punctuation, pupils at every grade level show too little improvement in punctuation as they advance through the language arts program. This apparently means that few children have discovered the importance of these items, that they have been inadequately introduced, that there was insufficient review of the items to establish their use, or that insufficient attention was given to their use in genuine writing situations.

• *Instructional items and procedures*　The following is a suggested list of puncutation items that should receive instruction in the elementary school.

Primary years:
1. Period at the end of a sentence which tells something
2. Period after numbers in any kind of list
3. Question mark at the close of a question
4. Comma after the salutation of a friendly note or letter
5. Comma after the closing of a friendly note or letter
6. Comma between the day of the month and the year
7. Comma between name of city and state
8. Period after abbreviations
9. Period after an initial
10. Use of an apostrophe in common contractions such as *isn't, aren't*
11. Commas in a list

Intermediate years:
　　All items listed for previous years
12. Apostrophe to show possession
13. Hyphen separating parts of a word divided at the end of the line
14. Period following a command
15. Exclamation point at the end of a word or group of words that makes an exclamation
16. Commas setting off an appositive
17. Colon after the salutation of a business letter
18. Quotation marks before and after a direct quotation
19. Comma between explanatory words and a quotation

41. R. L. Lyman, *Summary of Investigations Relating to Grammar, Language, and Composition* (Chicago: University of Chicago Press, 1929).

20. Period after numerals and letters in outlines
21. Colon in writing time
22. Quotation marks around the title of an article, the chapter of a book, and a poem or story
23. Underlining the title of a book
24. Comma to set off nouns in direct address
25. Hyphen in compound numbers
26. Colon to set off a list
27. Comma to set off transitional/parenthetical expressions (e.g., yes, no, of course)[42]

The teacher, through study of pupil papers, will note errors made, keeping a record, such as chart 7.6, as a basis for providing needed instruction. (See chapter 12, pages 460, 462 for diagnostic/corrective worksheets for punctuation items.)

CHART 7.6: Analysis of Punctuation Items

PUPIL'S NAMES	Period	Comma	Semicolon	Colon	Quotation Mark	Apostrophe	Question Mark	Hyphen	Underlining

Key: Use numerals (1–27) to correlate with listing of punctuation items on pp. 275–276.

---

42. Greene and Petty, *Developing Language Skills*, pp. 258–259. Reprinted with permission.

The use of intonation is generally taught in chapters on verbal expression or speaking, but intonation may also be taught in chapters on written composition through the use of punctuation. Good writers always try to make their compositions complete in emotional meaning through the use of accurate and meaningful cues that help their readers interpret the emotional impact of what they have written.

The conventional use of punctuation is to give written language clarity and emphasis. The punctuation of writing partially represents the oral intonation of speech. When punctuation is used in this way, it is a guide to the reader for indicating voice signals. If, for example, the written sentence is *I am going.* the reader knows that the utterance is complete, but if the sentence is written *I am going . . . .* the reader knows that only a partial statement has been made. The reason for the differences in the oral reading of the same three words is due to the differences in punctuation.

Intonation includes stress, pitch, and juncture (pause). *Stress* in written composition may be shown by underlining, italics, or capital letters. For example, look at the following variations of one sentence.

1. MARY ate a snail.
2. Mary ATE a snail.
3. Mary ate A snail.
4. Mary ate a SNAIL.

In the first variation, the stress on the word *Mary* immediately indicates that Mary (not anyone else) ate the snail. In variation 2, stressing the word *ate* shows that the act of eating the snail was of great importance. In variation 3, the writer wants to stress that only one snail was eaten. The last variation implies that the writer thought that eating a snail was unusual and that the word *snail* was more important than the other words in the sentence.

There is another use of stress. Some words are spelled the same whether they are used as nouns or verbs. If the word is used as a verb, the second syllable is stressed *(con-tráct, com-bát, fore-árm, ex-pórt).* When the word is used as a noun, the first syllable is stressed.

Pitch is the degree to which a word is pronounced in height (acuteness) or depth (gravity). The degree of acuteness or gravity depends on the rapidity (fastness or slowness) of the vibrations of the sounds. Pitch can be taught to children by making a numerical key showing how the teacher wants certain words in a sentence to be intoned.

Such a key might be
   I   very low pitch (slow)
   II   normal pitch
   III high pitch (fast)
   IV very high pitch (fast), which suggests no control

The following sentences will give teachers some ideas on how to teach pitch and how to develop a key for such teaching.

    IV   I
What! He fell off the roof?

        II
I wish I were a bird.

    I   II
Oh no. I just spilled my soup.

Before a child can write sentences that show the kind of pitch he wants to convey, he will need to use all of the punctuation cues and be able to select words that lend themselves to special contextual emphasis. Writers must learn to use punctuation that is regularly used in pitch and stress in oral language.

The term *juncture* at the elementary school level is simplified to deal with only the primary feature of pauses in oral language. In written language, juncture is identified by punctuation marks indicating pauses of varying lengths that are necessary for communicating the meaning of the sentence.

There are several kinds of juncture. An open, or plus, juncture (+) roughly indicates a word division, like *an ounce* (rather than *announce*). Single bar juncture (/) indicates word group or phrase divisions, like *The man/ in the car/ was laughing*. The double bar juncture (//) marks a more pronounced interruption and is usually thought of as a comma juncture, like *My brother,// who lives in Boston,// came to see me*. The double cross juncture (#) marks a more pronounced interruption and is associated with terminal pitch patterns, like *I am going home.# Are you going with me?#*

The punctuation used for teaching juncture in written composition is not accurate, because written words do not represent oral language as children use it. All three intonation skills work together to improve written communication.

Children can improve their writing ability if they understand that the language they are writing is related to the one they have been speaking all their lives. For advanced pupils in written composition, more detailed instruction in the use of intonation can be obtained from various sources.[43]

Sentence sense

Sentence types are often classified according to purpose: declarative, interrogative, exclamatory, and imperative. Or they may be categorized according to structure: simple (contains subject and predicate); compound (combines two or more simple sentences or independent clauses joined by such words as *and, but,* or, and *nor*); and complex (consists of one or more independent clauses to which is attached a dependent clause that acts as a modifier and begins with a connective such as *if, when,* and *since*).

• *Beginning instruction*   It is not unusual to find children who, at the conclusion of elementary school, do not understand what a sentence is and therefore have difficulty writing good sentences. Yet teachers can begin early to help children understand and write good sentences. In kindergarten or primary years when children dictate stories to the teacher, emphasis can be placed on sentence sense. Suppose the children are telling about a walk in the park. One child may say, "Today we went for a walk in the park." As the teacher writes these words on the chalkboard, he says, "That's a good beginning sentence. What should our next sentence be?"

"We saw some squirrels in the park," suggests another child.

The teacher remarks, "Jan has told one thing about our trip. Who can tell something else?"

"The squirrels were eating nuts," says Bill.

"That is another sentence," comments the teacher. "We will begin it with a capital letter and put a period at the end."

Oral reading also helps pupils to develop sentence sense. As they listen, children discover that changes in pitch and juncture indicate the beginning and ending of sentences. The concept that skills in writing are developed through reading, listening, and speaking has been presented by various writers.[44]

---

43. See Edna Lue Furness, "Pupils, Pedagogues, and Punctuation," *Elementary English* 37 (March 1960); 184–189; J. N. Hook, *The Teaching of High School English,* 4th ed. (New York: Ronald, 1972), pp. 319–349.

44. For example, see John P. Milligan, "Learning About Punctuation in the Primary Grades," *Elementary English Review* 18 (March 1941): 96–98.

Constant comparison between what the child reads and what he reports helps him to sense the concept of one idea separated from others by an initial capital letter and a terminal mark of punctuation. This is the writer's way of showing where he would begin an idea and where he would pause before adding another, if he were talking instead of writing. The teacher, writing at the children's dictation, can do much to strengthen the child's grasp of completeness in sentences.

One-sentence compositions are also helpful. Children may be asked to tell one thing (one sentence) about a picture or object, a pet, a trip, or some topic like "My New Shoes," "My Baby Sister," or "My Favorite Toy." From the one-sentence composition, move to the two- and three-sentence composition as sentence skill develops.

Pupils can be asked to write model sentences based on basic sentence patterns and to experiment with expanding these basic patterns through adding descriptive words, words denoting time and place, etc. They can be led to discover how meaning and emphasis are influenced by the position of these words in the sentence. For example, "The dog chased the cat" can be expanded into "Yesterday, the black dog chased the white cat, Tommy, down the street." Without getting technical about prepositional phrases, infinitives, participles, etc., children can detect open points in the basic patterns where subordinate units and modifiers can be inserted.

• *Further suggestions*   Other suggestions for developing sentence sense throughout the elementary school program have been selected from Greene and Petty:

1. Provide children with ample opportunity for oral composition, especially in the primary grades.
2. Encourage oral expression to form habits of using sentences that make sense, that are clear and complete.
3. Encourage considerable group composing and dictating of letters and other forms of written expression.
4. Encourage children to answer questions with the expression of one complete thought.
5. Provide exercises in which class members are required to distinguish between fragments and complete sentences.
6. Insist on pupils proofreading their own writing.
7. Provide exercises for making sentences out of nonsentence groups of words.
8. Use matching exercises made up of short lists of complete subjects in one column and complete predicates in another.

9. Provide exercises for breaking up run-on sentences into correct sentences.
10. Provide exercises for the organization of sentence elements into their proper relationships.[45]

In spite of such experiences, some children complete the elementary school years still writing fragments. One reason for this is they are often misled by the practices of speech. In speech, sentences lacking the full structure of the pattern are frequently uttered. For example, in reply to the question, "Who is that fellow?" the oral answer might well be "My brother." When an advanced pupil cites a fragment in the work of a professional writer, it can be pointed out that the professional is working on a more subtle and complicated level than the pupil is yet capable of handling. The professional diverges from the norm intentionally—not insecurely or haphazardly or out of ignorance. He does this in particular situations in order to achieve calculated effects. The teacher must emphasize the conventional practices and tell the child that eventually he will learn how and when to depart from the norm.

• *Some sentence difficulties*   The *and* fault, the *run-on* sentence, and the choppy sentence are difficulties frequently found in the writing of older children. The amount of research that has been done in this area is not extensive, but that which has been done is significant. The contributions of Bear and of Symonds and Lee, for example, should influence the teaching of sentence structure in the intermediate years. Bear found that the percentage of run-on sentences written by children tends to increase as their attempts to write complex sentences increase. She found that frequent use of run-on sentences increased from first to fifth grades, where it reached a high point. There was not much improvement in the elimination of this fault between the fifth and eighth grades.[46] Symonds and Lee found that errors in capitalization and punctuation reached a maximum somewhere near the sixth and seventh grades, when pupils are likely to be experimenting with new forms of expression.[47] These findings should not be construed to mean that teachers neglect to help children eliminate difficulties with sentence structure in the intermediate grades. The

---

45. Greene and Petty, *Developing Language Skills*, p. 343. Reprinted with permission.

46. Mata V. Bear, "Children's Growth in the Use of Written Language," *The Elementary English Review* 16 (December 1939): 312–319.

47. Percival Symonds and Baldwin Lee, "Studies in the Learning of English Expression, No. 1. Punctuation," *Teachers College Record* 30 (February 1929): 461–480; idem, "Studies in the Learning of English Expression, No. 2. Capitalization," *Teachers College Record* 30 (April 1929): 686–692.

information could help teachers to realize that difficulties of this type are related to general linguistic and intellectual development and that children cannot be expected to eliminate all such difficulties in any one year.

Some suggestions for correcting the *and* fault could include:

1. Use exercises for developing sentence sense since this fault results from lack of understanding of the sentence.
2. Read aloud or write on the chalkboard a group of sentences joined by *and*s. Let the children point out where each sentence begins and ends. Read again with the *and*s eliminated.
3. Have pupils write paragraphs of three to four sentences. In preliminary discussion, encourage them to be sure to indicate the pause at the end of each sentence.
4. Provide experiences with building sentences of discernible parts: that is, give the pupils kernels, such as "Betty ate," and encourage them to add elements of expansion that tell what, when, where, why, and how the action took place. Pupils might gradually evolve such a statement as "Yesterday while we were at the movies, Betty ate so much popcorn that she became ill." Help them to see how some parts of what they want to say can be put into subordination so that all necessary elements are incorporated in a closely knit sentence of fewer words: "After eating so much popcorn at the movies yesterday, Betty became ill."

Children should be aware of various ways of adjusting run-on sentences: that is, by (1) writing two separate sentences, (2) sentence connector, and (3) subordination.

For example: "Mr. Jones is a good speaker he was chosen to deliver the address."

1. Mr. Jones is a good speaker. He was chosen to deliver the address.
2. Mr. Jones is a good speaker; therefore, he was chosen to deliver the address.
3. Since Mr. Jones is a good speaker, he was chosen to deliver the address.

Some suggestions for avoiding choppy sentences include:

1. Giving practice in improving poor sentences: for example, exercises in which two short sentences are combined into one sentence

2. Reading aloud and writing on the chalkboard a composition composed of choppy sentences (Let the pupils suggest ways of improving it.)
3. Teaching use of connectors other than *and* to add variety to sentences

Paragraph sense

The following dialogue might serve as a good introduction to paragraph writing.

Bill: The sentences in a paragraph tell about one topic.
Betty: Then won't all the sentences be alike?
Teacher: How would you answer Betty's question?

The paragraph indicates the interrelationship of sentences. Through the primary years, the child tells, hears, and sees brief paragraphs—and he writes them. As with the sentence, the pupil learns the concept of the paragraph through practice. Teaching activities in the intermediate years often focus upon ideas such as the following in providing samples of related sentences: finding the main topic, arranging sentences in logical order under the topic, noting quotations in paragraph form, studying paragraphs for key words, and finding details in a paragraph.

Other suggested activities for developing paragraph skills include:

1. Reading paragraphs from science or history books; selecting the topic sentence and main idea
2. Writing one-paragraph compositions telling the story of a cartoon, a picture graph, or a comic strip such as "Peanuts"
3. Clipping and mounting paragraphs from a magazine (The pupils may read them and write the titles and topic sentence on another sheet of paper.)
4. Writing a good beginning sentence for a well-constructed paragraph with a deleted first sentence
5. Writing a good ending sentence for a well-constructed paragraph with a deleted last sentence
6. Presenting a paragraph that includes a sentence that does not help to explain the topic and asking the children to find the unrelated sentence
7. Reading an interesting, correctly written letter to the class;

then rereading it for dictation to see if the pupils can put it into paragraphs correctly

8. Providing opportunities for discussing and listing blocks of ideas before children write a news report

Manuscript form

Neatness, appropriate spacing, even margins, and attractive arrangement of items on the page make written work more pleasing to the eye and more legible. Each year the teacher and children should develop, through discussion, a manuscript form guide. It should vary according to the age and skill of the children involved.

Checking a written report against a manuscript form guide helps in preparing a neat paper.

The following guide, intended for the pupil's use, suggests a manuscript form that was developed in one classroom.

CHART 7.7: Manuscript Form Guide

1. Write your name at the right on the top line of your paper.
2. Write the date at the left on the top line of your paper.
3. Center the title of your report on the third line. Remember to capitalize the important words in your title.
4. Begin the first paragraph of your report on the fifth line.
5. Indent the first word of each paragraph about one inch from the left margin of the paper.
6. Keep a straight margin, about one inch wide, along the left side of your paper. Try to keep about the same margin on the right side.
7. Avoid crowding words at the end of the line.

EVALUATION OF WRITTEN EXPRESSION

Pupil performance in written expression may be appraised through several means. Numerous and multiple devices should be utilized in techniques of evaluation. These include anecdotal records, free and directed observation of the work habits of pupils, collecting samples of the children's written work, checklists, teacher-made and special textbook exercises, application of criteria and standards prepared cooperatively by the teacher and class members, informal interviews, lists of language difficulties in written composition in the classroom or elsewhere, and similar procedures.

Teacher-pupil

Individual revision and proofreading to correct and improve writing is often an onerous task to the child, yet in the final analysis, it is a valuable experience. The following suggestions about revision and proofreading are more appropriate to functional writing than creative writing.

• *Revision*   The teacher may write a paragraph on the chalkboard to serve as a model for illustrating how the process of revision is accomplished. The teacher asks the questions that he hopes pupils will be asking themselves when they examine their own papers with a view toward revision, as suggested in chart 7.8.

CHART 7.8: Revision Guide

1. Does it keep to the subject? Is there a good topic sentence?
2. Is each item interesting to those who read it? Do all details relate to the subject?
3. Has enough been written about the subject?
4. Are sentences in logical order? Is the paragraph well organized?
5. Does each sentence say what it intends to say?
6. Is there a good beginning, a good ending, and an appropriate title?
7. Does the final sentence bring the ideas to a satisfactory conclusion?

• *Proofreading* As with revision, proofreading will not be effectively taught in one lesson but needs to be repeated at intervals. Again, pupils must ask themselves pertinent questions as they examine their own papers. The use of the phrase "their own papers" is used advisedly: little progress is gained by having the teacher proofread his pupils' papers or by having pupils mark one another's papers. The job of proofreading belongs to the child who wrote the composition, and help from others should come only after he has made initial efforts to improve his own paper. Merely mentioning the term *proofreading* or occasionally reminding the child to check his work is insufficient—one must give practical and specific suggestions about what to look for, as in the following proofreading guide.

CHART 7.9: Proofreading Guide

1. As the teacher (or another pupil) reads the sentence, listen and look at each group of words to be sure it is a good sentence. Make sure that you have no run-on sentences.
2. Listen and look for mistakes in punctuation. Be sure that you have put in punctuation marks only where they are needed. Did you end sentences with the mark required?
3. Listen and look for mistakes in word usage. Be sure that you have said what you mean and that each word is used correctly. Is there any incorrect verb or pronoun usage?

4. Look for mistakes in capitalization. Did you capitalize the first word and all important words in the title? Did you begin each sentence with a capital letter?
5. Look for misspelled words. Use the dictionary to check the spelling of any word about which you are not sure.
6. Check legibility of writing and items such as margins, title, indents, etc.

The pupil may find it helpful to reread his composition several times with a different purpose in mind each time. For example:

Proofreading 1:   Reading for sentence sense
Proofreading 2:   Reading for punctuation
Proofreading 3:   Reading to make vague words clearer
Proofreading 4:   Reading for capitalization
Proofreading 5:   Reading for misspelled words
Proofreading 6:   Checking such items as margins, title, and the like

One way to improve proofreading ability is the group correction lesson. The teacher may select a few sentences from pupils' papers (or sentences composed by the teacher) that have errors and copy them on the chalkboard. The same purpose can be served by using the opaque (or overhead) projector or by mimeographing sentences and paragraphs for class discussion and evaluation. Of course, the teacher should include in the presentation the kinds of errors he wishes to bring to the pupils' attention. Then with a group of children, or the entire class, he uses the sentences as a basis of instruction, helping the group to see how to improve these sentences.

Pupils may keep a notebook of rules for punctuation, capitalization, and spelling conventions and this set of rules may be used to help with proofreading. The notebook may be developed as pupils encounter the items during the year; items should, for optimum use, be grouped under such headings as "Capitalization," "Paragraphs," and "Punctuation." Each rule should be stated in precise language and a sample illustrating the rule should be included. For example, "Use a capital letter to begin the first word, the last word, and each important word in the title of a piece of writing—*The Wind in the Willows.*"

Furthermore, the teacher should utilize the findings revealed by proofreading experiences in helping each individual with his particular needs. One way of accomplishing this is to prepare a check-list of technical skills. Opposite each item, the child may tally each time he makes a certain error in his written work. Where there are recurring errors, it is important for the teacher to plan instruction so that appropriate help can be provided. For those needing unusual help (the very slow or the very able), individualized checklists may be provided. Small instructional groups may be organized when only four or five children need help in the same area; and class lessons may be given on skills that appear to be needed by all.

One of the more effective ways to encourage revision and proof-reading is to demonstrate to pupils that progress has been made over a period of time in the skill of written composition. To accomplish this, pupils might keep notebooks or folders in which samples of different kinds of written work are filed periodically, with the dates recorded on the papers. A pupil is strongly motivated when he compares a paper written in September with one written the following December and sees improvement.

(Another classroom example for proofreading is presented in chapter 12, page 443.)

Pupil-pupil

The pupil who writes and receives feedback from only one person, the teacher, is not prepared to communicate in the range of situations that life presents. Classmates should provide one another with feedback rather than receive it only from the teacher.

Class evaluation of work in progress can be evidenced through discussion. Questions such as the following should bring out pertinent information relative to the progress in the work at hand:

What are we trying to accomplish?
To what extent have we reached our goals?
What difficulties have we encountered?
Are we spending our time productively?

There should be group discussions where everyone examines his own efforts and reports on his difficulties. Sessions can be held where the class helps to identify the strengths and weaknesses in a group project and where individual projects—reports, stories, poems—are offered for group reactions. Of course, the use of group appraisal needs to be developed with some care, as there are some possible dangers: for example, unfair criticism can result from personal rivalry.

Not every lesson has to include evaluative criticism. For example, whenever creativity is the purpose of the lesson, the teacher should keep criticism to a minimum. However, many of the lessons devoted to functional written expression would include some helpful evaluation so that each pupil will be aware of his current needs and be reminded of standards previously established.

In the early part of the year, the teacher might well offer most of the evaluative suggestions so that the children will know what to strive for; they tend to notice trivial points and often fail to see the more fundamental qualities that make language either effective or ineffective. The teacher is naturally more discriminating. He will take care not to overcriticize the slower child; he will give favorable comments and praise, but only when it is merited; he will avoid destructive criticism and give positive comments. He will not say, "That was a poor story introduction," but will say, "What might be a better story introduction?"

Pupils should be introduced to evaluation suggestions gradually. At first, they may consider a single standard. For the sake of variety, the pupils may choose one of their members to be the critic for that day. From time to time, the teacher might introduce new methods of evaluation; for instance, the use of a guide sheet to be checked may give the children a more objective basis for criticism.

To initiate pupils into the role of critics, the following criteria may be helpful.

1. In the early stages, children should restrict their suggestions to the evaluative standards that have currently been established; the teacher should supplement this with further evaluation.
2. The teacher should help pupils to become more adept in detecting the really commendable and the essentially weak features of a composition, rather than concentrating on trivialities.
3. Children should always give favorable comments first.
4. Pupils should give helpful reactions—suggestions for improvement of weaknesses. Negative criticism is out of place.

Individuals may keep such records as diaries of activities, samples of work, lists of goals achieved, needs, or reports given. A survey of these records and lists by the child or a small group will supply considerable evidence about pupil progress.

The following list includes a few additional devices that have proved helpful to pupils:

1. List your greatest strengths and weaknesses in various aspects of language.
2. Regularly check progress toward certain goals on a rating scale.
3. Identify skills that need to be improved.

Helping children to develop powers of self-evaluation and self-direction is part of everything the teacher does.[48]

SELECTED REFERENCES

General Professional

Anderson, Paul S. *Language Skills in Elementary Education*. 2d ed. New York: Macmillan, 1972, chapter 6.

Burrows, Alvina T.; Monson, Diane L.; and Stauffer, Russell G. *New Horizons in the Language Arts*. New York: Harper & Row, 1972, chapter 9.

Dallmann, Martha. *Teaching the Language Arts in the Elementary School*. 2d ed. Dubuque, Iowa: William C. Brown, 1971, chapter 5.

Greene, Harry A., and Petty, Walter T. *Developing Language Skills in the Elementary Schools*. 4th ed. Boston: Allyn and Bacon, 1971, chapter 8.

Lamb, Pose. *Guiding Children's Language Learning*. 2d ed. Dubuque, Iowa: William C. Brown, 1971, chapter 6.

Smith, James A. *Adventures in Communication: Language Arts Methods*. Boston: Allyn and Bacon, 1972, chapter 9.

Strickland, Ruth. *The Language Arts in Elementary School*. 3rd ed. Lexington, Mass.: D. C. Heath, 1969, chapters 13, 14.

Specialized

Applegate, Mauree. *Easy in English*. New York: Row, Peterson, 1960.

————. *Winged Writing*. New York: Harper & Row, 1961.

————. *Freeing Children to Write*. New York: Harper & Row, 1963.

Armour, Richard. *Writing Light Verse and Prose Humor*. Boston: Writer, 1958.

Arnstein; Flora J. *Children Write Poetry: A Creative Approach*. 2d ed. New York: Dover, 1967.

————. *Poetry in the Elementary School*. New York: Appleton-Century-Crofts, 1962.

---

48. See Nita Wyatt Sundbye, "Evaluation of Children's Compositions," *The Language Arts in the Elementary School: A Forum for Focus*, ed. Martha King et al. (Urbana, Ill.: National Council of Teachers of English, 1973), pp. 220–232.

Braddock, Richard, et al. *Research in Written Composition.* Urbana, Ill.: National Council of Teachers of English, 1963.

Burrows, Alvina T., et al. *They All Want to Write: Written English in the Elementary Schools.* New York: Holt, Rinehart and Winston, 1964.

Carlson, Ruth Kearney. *Writing Aids Through the Grades: One Hundred Eighty-Six Developmental Writing Activities.* New York: Teachers College Press, Columbia University, 1970.

Conrad, Lawrence H. *Teaching Creative Writing.* New York: Appleton-Century-Crofts, 1937.

Decker, Isabelle M. *One Hundred Novel Ways with Book Reports.* New York: Scholastic Book Services, 1969.

Hennings, Dorothy G., and Grant, Barbara M. *Content and Craft: Written Expression in the Elementary School.* Englewood Cliffs, N.J.: Prentice-Hall, 1973.

Holmes, John. *Writing Poetry.* Boston: Writer, 1960.

Hook, J. N. *Writing Creatively.* 2d ed. Boston: D. C. Heath, 1967.

Mearns, Hughes. *Creative Youth.* New York: Doubleday, 1929.

National Council of Teachers of English. *Let the Children Write.* Urbana, Ill.: National Council of Teachers of English, 1967.

Petty, Walter T., and Bowen, Mary E. *Slithery Snakes and Other Aids to Children's Writing.* New York: Appleton-Century-Crofts, 1967.

Pratt-Butler, Grace K. *Let Them Write Creatively.* Columbus, Ohio: Merrill, 1973.

Staudacher, Carol. *Creative Writing in the Classroom.* Palo Alto, Calif.: Fearon, 1969.

Stegall, Carrie. *The Adventures of Brown Sugar.* Urbana, Ill.: National Council of Teachers of English, 1967.

Walter, Nina W. *Let Them Write Poetry.* New York: Holt, Rinehart and Winston, 1962.

Wolsch, Robert A. *Poetic Composition Through the Grades.* New York: Teachers College Press, Columbia University, 1970.

Vocabulary Development and Reference Skills

**VOCABULARY DEVELOPMENT
AND REFERENCE SKILLS**

OBJECTIVES	PERFORMANCE RESPONSES
1. **To apply ways of developing children's vocabularies**	1. a. Locate a contextual clue to the meaning of a word that is introduced in an elementary school textbook. Present the clue to a child or small group. b. Prepare an introduction to a lesson on metaphor for a child or small group. c. Select one trade book about words for use with a pupil or class. Plan a presentation around it and evaluate your performance.
2. **To explain and demonstrate a component of semantics**	2. Take the word *man* and help children become aware of the subtle word meanings that exist in the English language.
3. **To formulate plans for dictionary use**	3. a. Suggest how you would handle the problem of looking up the spelling of *cinnamon* in a dictionary. b. Prepare a presentation of one of the beginner or junior dictionaries to a child or class.
4. **To create instructional exercises for one other reference source**	4. Use the index of an elementary school English textbook to prepare a worksheet that develops one of the suggested reference skills.

There are many skills that are closely related to both oral and written expression. Some of the rhetorical skills (such as sentence construction) are discussed in the preceding chapter concerning written expression. The use of some sources of information has been explored in the preceding chapters on oral expression, literature, and written expression. This chapter treats other common elements of oral and written expression: vocabulary, semantics, lexicography, and other reference sources.

VOCABULARY DEVELOPMENT

The position of an individual in society may be determined by the extent of his knowledge of words and how to use them in a manner appropriate to a particular time, place, and situation. The intelligent, mature, well-educated individual is familiar with words like *rip off*, *far out*, *bombed out*, *cool*, *right on*, *super*, *funky*, and *chalk up*. He may find these words useful on some occasions, but if his vocabulary were limited to such expressions, he would find himself severely handicapped.

Vocabulary may be defined as the stock of words used by a person, class, or profession. Almost every individual uses several different vocabularies, all having much in common, yet each distinctly different. The most basic of these vocabularies are often designated as hearing, speaking, reading, and writing. Words are symbols of ideas; to express and communicate ideas, one needs facility in the use of words. Teachers must give attention to developing the vocabularies of each child through carefully planned instruction and, to do so, must be aware of what words are (verbal representations of concepts) and how concepts are formed.

Words are labels; they are used to communicate experiences. A word is not the thing nor the experience itself. The word *dog* is not a dog at all—it is a label for the animal we so designate. Many words stand for abstractions, for which there may be no concrete referent in reality. Such words would include *beauty*, *intelligence*, *depression*. The social group from whom experiences arise and from whom words are learned shapes the language and thoughts of its members. Thus, the Eskimo has many words for snow, whereas people from warmer climates have fewer words for it. Words influence how we see our world and what we may think of it. Even though abstract descriptions may bear little or no resemblance to reality, they can be a powerful determinant of our thinking and our behavior.

Since vocabulary development is so closely related to abstract thinking, the teacher is concerned with the number, the breadth, and the depth of concepts with which pupils have some acquaintance. For concept development, the individual should have actual experiences with the concrete object, person, idea, or event—mainly through sense impressions. From a series of experiences, accurate discrimination of essential and nonessential characteristics of the object (person, idea, or event) must be made. Further examples help to insure adequate learning of the concept.

The teacher's responsibility includes both a *quantitative* approach to vocabulary (particularly for children whose environmental circumstances have not equipped them to conceptualize clearly or to verbalize adequately) and a *qualitative* approach (a broadening and deepening of the children's listening-speaking vocabulary by teaching them ways to make fine discriminations in the use of words in different situations).

Ways to develop vocabularies

There are numerous ways of helping children to acquire knowledge of many words and proficiency in their use. As yet, there is insufficient evidence to show which methods of vocabulary instruction work best at different age levels and with pupils of varying degrees of ability. The resourceful teacher will find many opportunities inherent in classroom activities.

• *Firsthand experiences*   A varied background of firsthand experiences, field trips, and excursions is profitable at all grade levels. Concrete experiences permit the words to be associated with real situations; consequently, schools should try to extend the experiences of children. The nature and quality of the educative experiences that children meet, both inside and outside the classroom, are primary factors that determine speaking, writing, reading, and hearing vocabularies.

Experiences should be followed by oral and written accounts and descriptions. Teachers need to see that the new words derived from these experiences are understood and made vivid and clear. Without follow-up, a child's recollection or understanding is likely to be incomplete or inaccurate. Observation and experience alone will not increase vocabulary. Unless the teacher focuses upon words for the object or situation, answers questions, and discusses the experience, the child has no way to acquire the new words that the experi-

A field trip, such as to a museum, provides an opportunity for increasing the child's stock of words.

ence could furnish. Discussion provides an opportunity to correct misunderstanding and wrong concepts. For example, it is not sufficient to tell a child that *frantic* means "wild." He may try to pick some frantic flowers!

Teachers should try to discover what experiences the children lack, because children learn early to conceal their inadequacies by silence. Studies have indicated that many pupils, even after several years of schooling, may not know where the farmer gets eggs or that a bank may be something other than a place where they store their money. One teacher reported that many nine-year-old pupils in a class in a depressed urban area had no idea of the meaning of *dandelion*. Children should always be encouraged to ask questions and not be subjected to ridicule if some of the questions seem absurd.

Of course, all direct experiences need not be of a field trip nature, nor can all experiences be direct ones. Vicarious experiences (films, for example) provide for vocabulary growth. Storytelling and oral reading by the teacher are also valuable ways of imparting experience.

All of the experiences of the school day can be utilized toward broadening the child's vocabulary if the teacher is aware of the opportunities: the sharing period, the daily news period, group work period, free conversation, discussion time. The environment and activities of the school will lead the teacher to discover other similar avenues for experiences that develop new concepts and new vocabulary.

• *Books*   Books are another significant source of vocabulary growth, particularly books that provoke questions and discussion. Pupils need a variety of interesting, easy-to-read books so that new words and ideas can be learned from the context. In choosing new vocabulary words, the teacher might ask pupils the following questions:

> What words in the selection can be interpreted by examining the context?
> Why are certain sentences interesting to read?
> What words or phrases encountered in today's reading seem particularly well chosen?
> What are some descriptive words in today's reading?

As with direct experiences, it is important to encourage the pupil to ask questions about words that he does not understand.

• *Context clues*   Children who read extensively can learn many words just through use of context. Wide reading provides the opportunity for context to illuminate word meaning when it is essential to the on-flow of thought. Through a variety of reading material, the reader can begin to recognize the subtleties and varied meanings of words.

Reading authorities have emphasized the importance of developing effective use of context.[1] Classroom experience and research suggest that lack of skill in using context is quite prevalent among elementary school pupils, but that instruction in the use of context aids seemed helpful.[2]

---

1. For example, see Paul McKee and William K. Durr, *Reading: A Program of Instruction for the Elementary School* (Boston: Houghton Mifflin, 1966), pp. 258–268; George D. Spache, *Reading in the Elementary School*, 3rd ed. (Boston: Allyn and Bacon, 1973), pp. 495–501; and Albert J. Harris, *Effective Teaching of Reading* (New York: McKay, 1962), pp. 220–221.

2. For example, see William S. Gray and Eleanor Holmes, *The Development of Meaning Vocabularies in Reading* (Chicago: University of Chicago Press, 1938); and Janice Mantle Harrison, "Acquiring Word Meaning Through Context Clues" (Master's thesis, Ohio State University, Columbus, 1960).

Chart 8.1 below suggests various types of contextual aids to word meanings.[3]

CHART 8.1: Contextual Aids to Word Meanings

Type	*Explanation/Example*
1. Typographical aids	parentheses or footnotes
2. Grammatical aids	appositives (The *epidermis*, the outer layer of skin, protects from germs.)
3. Substitute words	synonyms and antonyms (What can you do to *mitigate*, or lessen, the miseries of a cold?)
4. Word elements	roots, prefixes, and suffixes
5. Figures of speech	(The soldiers, *numerous as the sands in the sea*, march forward.)
6. Pictures, diagrams, charts	
7. Inference	(Because of the mountain ranges and the cold climate, the amount of *arable* land is limited.)
8. Experience clues	(The crow cawed *raucously*.) Understanding of the last word depends upon the reader's experience of hearing a crow's harsh voice.
9. Comparison/contrast words	(Is John *clumsy* or is he *agile*?)
10. Summary clues	(John will be here soon for he is usually very *punctual*.)
11. Familiar expression	(He kept his *cool*.)
12. Example	(Put an *antiseptic*, such as alcohol, on the skin.)

The above are the kinds of aids that pupils often encounter and that need to be presented and practiced if contextual analysis is to become an important means of vocabulary growth. Contextual usage can be developed through planned, thoughtful, and intelligent guidance, just as the ability to use other means for vocabulary growth is developed through carefully planned instruction. It is desirable to teach children to read an entire sentence (or the remainder of a paragraph) before attempting to derive the meaning of an unknown word.

---

3. A. Sterl Artley, "Developing the Use of Context," *Developing Vocabulary and Work-Attack Skills*, A Report of the Eighteenth Annual Conference and Course on Reading (Pittsburgh: University of Pittsburgh, 1962), pp. 91–98; Constance M. McCullough, "Context Aids in Reading," *The Reading Teacher* 11 (April 1958): 225–229; Lee C. Deighton, *Vocabulary Development in the Classroom* (New York: Teachers College Press, Columbia University, 1959).

Context generally reveals only one of the meanings of a word to the reader.

"THE RULER WAS 12" LONG"

The practice of immediately stating, "Look it up in a dictionary," is poor one. It would be better to say, "Try to find a clue to the meanin of the word through the context." Time should then be provided fo discussion of how the meaning was arrived at through context.

The structure of the phrase, sentence, or paragraph often serve as a clue to the meaning of what is written. Rhetorical aids are als guides to reading comprehension of a paragraph, conjunctions an certain adverbs being very common links.

Pupils do not always derive correct meanings of words from th context. Context invariably *determines* the meaning of a word bu does not always reveal its meaning. Context generally reveals onl one of the meanings of a word to the reader. Also, context seldor clarifies the whole of any single word meaning. Vocabulary growt through use of context is a gradual one. Finding one clue here an another there, fitting them together, and making tentative judgmen and revising them later are required.

Some representative commercially prepared materials on cor textual clues are footnoted.[4]

• *Visual and other instructional aids and materials*   Visuc aids should be utilized frequently, not only to illustrate words tho have been used but to suggest other words. Remember, howeve that discussion must accompany seeing.

Programmed materials, in booklet form, or a machine can be used to teach vocabulary.[5] Single concept, language filmloops ca be used for self-study aids.[6] The new filmloops can be operated b any child and viewed individually or projected on the screen fo group viewing. There are specially prepared records for vocabular development.[7] Mason has described television's contributions t vocabulary development in children.[8] Of course, films and filmstrip

---

4.   A. A. DeVitis and J. R. Warner. *Words in Context: A Vocabulary Builder*, 2d ed. (New York: Appleton-Centu Crofts, 1966); Richard A. Boning, *Using the Context*, *Book A* (New York: Barnell Loft, 1973); Olive Niles et al., *Tact in Reading, I and II* (Chicago: Scott Foresman, 1965).

5.   Two volumes, prepared by the Center for Programmed Instruction for the U.S. Office of Education, *Progra '69* and *The Use of Programmed Instruction in U.S. Schools*, survey in detail available programs and their uses the schools. Both are available from the Superintendent of Documents, U.S. Government Printing Office, Washir ton, D.C. 20402. To keep abreast of current developments, the center publishes a bimonthly bulletin, *Programm Instruction*, 365 West End Ave., New York, N.Y. 10024.

6.   "Words and Ideas Series." Sterling Educational Films, 241 East 34th St., New York, N.Y. 10016.

7.   Morris Shrieber, ed., "An Annotated List of Recordings in the Language Arts" (Urbana, Ill.: National Coun of Teachers of English, 1964).

8.   George E. Mason, "Television's Contributions to Vocabulary Development in Children" (Boston: Allyn an Bacon, Teachers Service Division Bulletin, No. 124, 1966).

are available for use upon occasion on such topics as *Build Your Vocabulary*[9] or *Increase Your Stock of Words.*[10]

Other instructional aids and materials include the thesaurus and trade books. In addition to many children's dictionaries, beginning thesauri are now available to help children enrich their vocabularies, find substitutes for overused words, and develop an awareness of the flexibility and power of language.[11] The thesaurus may supply such alternatives as *march, stride, stalk, lurch, saunter,* and *clump* for a word to describe how a person walks. Individuals are helped in their word selection by special illustrative sentences, pictures and illustrations, or explanations that dramatize the meaning of a particular word. Special attention may be given to certain word entries: "umbrella words," such as *cute, nice;* slang words, such as *goof-ball, hip;* overworked words, such as *love, hate;* and sets of words, such as *pride* of lions, *gaggle* of geese. Some word histories may also be provided. Following is a list of some trade books about words.

Asimov, Isaac. *Words from the Myths.* Boston: Houghton Mifflin, 1961.
Christ, Henry. *Winning Words.* Boston: D. C. Heath, 1963.
Ernst, Margaret. *More About Words.* New York: Knopf, 1951.
————. *Words: English Roots and How They Grow.* 3rd ed. New York: Knopf, 1954.
Fadiman, Clifton. *Wally the Word Worm.* New York: Macmillan, 1964.
Funk, Charles. *Hog on Ice and Other Curious Expressions.* New York: Harper & Brothers, 1948.
Higgens, Helen Boyd. *Noah Webster, Boy of Words.* Indianapolis: Bobbs, 1961.
Krauss, Ruth. *A Hole Is to Dig: A First Book of Definitions.* New York: Harper & Brothers, 1952.
————. *Open House for Butterflies.* New York: Harper & Brothers, 1960.
Lambert, Eloise, and Pei, Mario. *The Book of Place Names.* New York: Lothrop, 1959.
Mathews, Mitford McLeod. *American Words.* Cleveland, Ohio: World Publishing, 1959.
Minteer, Cathine. *Words and What They Do to You.* New York: Harper & Brothers, 1952.

---

9. Chicago: Coronet Films.

10. Chicago: Society for Visual Education.

11. W. Cabell Greet et al., *In Other Words: A Beginning Thesaurus* (grades K–2) and *Junior Thesaurus: In Other Words* (grades 6 and up) (Chicago: Scott Foresman, 1969, 1970).

O'Neill, Mary. *Words, Words, Words*. New York: Doubleday, 1966.

Povensen, Alice, and Povensen, Martin. *Karen's Opposites*. New York: Golden Press, 1963.

Proudfit, Isabel. *Noah Webster, Father of the Dictionary*. New York: Messner, 1942.

Rand, Ann, and Rand, Paul. *Sparkle and Spin: A Book About Words*. New York: Harcourt, Brace and World, 1957.

Reid, Alastair. *Ounce, Dice, Trice*. New York: Little, 1958.

Severn, Bill. *People Words*. New York: Washburn, 1966.

Shipley, Joseph T. *Playing With Words*. Englewood Cliffs, N.J.: Prentice-Hall, 1960.

Van Gelder, Rosalind. *Monkeys Have Tails*. New York: McKay, 1966.

Webster's New Dictionary of Synonyms. Springfield, Mass.: Merriam, 1968.

White, Mary Sue. *Word Twins*. New York: Abingdon, 1961.

• **Content areas**   In every subject field, teachers should develop vocabulary carefully. They need to be sure that words met in elementary mathematics, health, science, and social studies have real significance. The importance of this cannot be overemphasized. Children's understanding of concepts is often vague and inaccurate. Note the vocabulary demands made upon the pupil by the following sentences taken from elementary mathematics, science, and social studies textbooks.

> *Mathematics:* The polygon in picture A has four straight sides. Its opposite sides are equal and also parallel. It has four right angles. This polygon is a rectangle.
>
> *Science:* Between Mars and Jupiter, there are a great many small planets called *asteroids*. There are more than a thousand of these, and each follows its own path or orbit around the sun. Comets and meteors are also members of the solar system.
>
> *Social Studies:* On a high plateau of Central Africa live millions of black people. They live four thousand feet above the sea, just at the equator.

The vocabulary problem is more acute in textbooks than it is in general reading material. The selection of textbooks that avoid complicated verbiage and explain new terms clearly when they are introduced is one important way of reducing the vocabulary problem to teachable proportions.

Each of the content areas has a vocabulary of its own that must be learned. One cannot expect a pupil to understand without assistance such technical terms as *commutative*, *factor*, and *perimeter* in arithmetic and similar technical terms in other subjects. Whenever an important new concept is introduced, there is need for a detailed explanation.

• *Oral and written expression*   Teachers should encourage variety in oral and written expression. A conscious effort needs to be made by teachers to encourage use of words that express thought exactly, rather than words that perform omnibus service.

Many children fall victim to the insidious habit of using a small number of stock adjectives and adverbs and fail to develop a command of vocabulary that can express finer shades of meaning. If a party is described as "lousy," it would be profitable to ask the child to describe more exactly the way in which the party was lousy. Was it *boring, dull, dreary, disappointing*? Discussion is one of the better ways of awakening children to the desirability of stating their meanings with precision.

A task card, focusing upon the same idea, may be prepared. See the example below.

Task Card: Descriptive Words

Directions: Here is a paragraph with some underlined words. See if you can substitute synonyms for the underlined words. A list of substitute words is given to help you.

The children were playing a <u>noisy</u> game and mother smiled as she watched them <u>jump</u> around. She was happy to have her <u>children</u> home with her. Father had been <u>delayed</u> in town that evening and he was late in <u>getting</u> home.

(cavort   family   arriving   detained   rowdy)

Worksheets like the following may also be helpful in encouraging use of more descriptive words.

Worksheet: Descriptive Words

1. For each of the following questions, circle the appropriate word or words. Add a word if needed.
    a. What kind of day is it today?
        (stormy, pleasant, calm, rainy, snowy, bright, dull, clear, brilliant)
    b. What is the sky like today?
        (overcast, cloudless, hazy, somber, darkening, threatening, sunny)
    c. What is the wind like today?
        (gusty, gentle, moderate, howling, whispering, tingling, cold, chilly, biting)
2. Here are some words that can be used to describe a way of walking. Choose ten and use each one in a sentence.
    (hurried, ran, raced, strolled, waddled, limped, stumbled, crawled, leaped, hopped, trudged, trotted, pranced, stamped, stormed, skipped, galloped)
3. Use different words for *said* in ten sentences.
    (whispered, shouted, screamed, laughed, cried, giggled, praised, scolded, bragged, grumbled, argued, answered, announced, agreed, stated, suggested, objected, asked, replied, inquired, remarked, explained)
4. Various words can be used in place of some "overworked" words. Add as many as you can to the list.

    a. nice: kind, pleasant, helpful, _____
    b. great: enjoyable, amusing, _____
    c. got: collected, found, gathered, _____
    d. bad: awful, _____

• *Teacher-model*   The teacher can use new words, sometimes in reading aloud, sometimes in providing explanations. New words used in oral reports may be taught also.

Particularly in the primary years, when most pupils are mainly occupied with developing recognition of words already in their understanding, reading, and speaking vocabulary, the teacher needs to read and tell many stories to the group. In reading to children, it is inadvisable to simplify the vocabulary. After reading a story, new words may be discussed and in later retelling or dramatization, the use of the new words should be encouraged.

Pupils are great imitators and if the teacher employs good vocabulary, they tend to approach his level of expression. The tendency to "talk down" to boys and girls is a hindrance rather than a help.

* ***Morphology study***   Such study includes antonyms, synonyms, homonyms, homographs, root words, figures of speech (metaphor, simile, personification), exaggerations, word associations, and inflectional devices. The slight differences of meaning, especially with synonyms, can be given some attention. For example, "What is the difference between *large, huge,* and *enormous?*" would be an appropriate question for a pupil in the intermediate years.

Following are some games and activities for the study of synonyms, antonyms, and homonyms.

1. Paste words such as *happy, big,* and *sad* on several soup cans. Cut out small cards to play the game. Children think of a synonym, write it on a card, and drop it into the appropriate can.
2. "Synonym concentration" for two to four players: First, shuffle synonym cards (with even numbers of synonyms) and spread them out face down. The first player turns up two cards. If they are synonyms, he takes them. If not, he turns them face down again. Each player, in turn, tries to match two synonyms. The game is played until all cards are paired.
3. A story may be composed, with instructions to use synonyms to replace the underlined words. For example:
   One day a <u>little</u> girl was <u>walking</u> down the <u>street</u>. She <u>saw</u> a coin lying on the sidewalk. She <u>looked</u> all around but no one was there, so she <u>picked up</u> the coin.
4. "Antonym-O" can be played like Bingo. The caller reads words, and the players cover the antonyms on their cards. The first player to complete a row is the winner and the next caller.
5. A series of homonyms, such as *pail* and *pale,* can be listed on a worksheet. The child writes a sentence using each correctly; for example, *The pale boy was carrying a pail of water.*

Homonyms are words that are pronounced alike but differ in meaning and spelling (as *to, too, two*). *Homographs* are words that are spelled alike but differ in derivation, meaning, or pronunciation (as *bow* meaning "the forward part of a ship" and *bow* meaning "a ribbon tied in loops").

A knowledge of the meaning of some of the more common Latin and Greek roots found in many English words is helpful. Pupils can easily learn roots like *port*, meaning "to carry," and *fac* or *fic*, meaning "to make." From one of the roots, it is possible to build up a family of words. Such a family might be *porter*, *import*, *export*, *deport*, *report*, *transport*, *portable*, etc.

Children should be helped to identify figurative language, as such language often poses problems for them. Following are some examples of expressions that may not be interpreted correctly by pupils.

> The villagers think that the stranger is a wolf in sheep's clothing. *(metaphor)*
> She had cheeks like roses. *(simile)*
> The Sun smiled when Tony's bird escaped from the cat. *(personification)*

Probably the best way to develop a real understanding of figurative or indirect language is through practice in paraphrasing. The attempt to restate another's thoughts in clear, unambiguous language of one's own is a crucial test of whether the thought has really been understood.

A sample worksheet appropriate for study of figures of speech is given on page 307.

Before individual use is made of such figure-of-speech worksheets, several days of whole-class and small-group instruction is appropriate. A teaching procedure such as the following might be used:

1. The teacher introduces one of the figures of speech—metaphor, simile, personification—for whole-class brainstorming (about ten minutes).
2. A team of around five pupils brainstorms the figure of speech (five to ten minutes).
3. Each child writes his own sentence using a figure of speech (five minutes).
4. The children read their sentences to each other in teams (about five minutes).

Worksheet: Figures of Speech

Metaphor	Simile	Personification
His voice was a fog horn.	His feet were as cold as ice cubes.	The Stone nestled against the tree.

A. Complete the following:
    (Metaphor)
    1. The fire siren _____.
    2. The high steeple _____.
    3. The diesel engine _____.

    (Simile)
    4. She was as happy as _____.
    5. The cat's fur was like _____.
    6. The bell was as loud as _____.

    (Personification)
    7. The Jet _____.
    8. The Water _____.
    9. The Firecracker _____.

B. Find five figures of speech in the story folder on the reading table. Write them on a sheet of paper and give the meaning of each.

C. Try to illustrate three figures of speech.

D. Make up your own figure of speech and illustrate it.

5. Each team selects one figure of speech to read to the class (about five minutes).
6. The children listen to the teacher read their figures of speech (two to three minutes).

Understanding of *exaggerations*, as in tall tales, colloquial expressions, and regional dialects, is best developed through wide reading and discussion.

Pupils become more aware of word associations as they write compositions. They may find listing words helpful: "happy" words,

"sad" words, "beautiful" words, "exciting" words, words describing sounds, and the like. The major purpose of this kind of exercise is to clarify the meanings of words through bringing out important relationships between ideas. As the children grasp these relationships, their understanding of the words becomes more accurate.

The study of inflection (that is, meaningful changes of form to show certain grammar relationships) includes such concepts as contractions, possessives, prefixes, and suffixes. The teacher should identify elements with which the class members have difficulty and plan an instructional program on that basis. When studying contractions, ask:

What is a contraction?
Is *don't* a contraction?
Is *do not* a contraction?
Am I using a contraction when I say, "She isn't at home"?

Then read phrases like the following for identification of contractions.

here's Tom   toys in boxes
cannot go   they're playing ball

An instructional bulletin board can serve for teaching and practicing contractions, as suggested on page 309.

When studying possessives, ask, "What does *possessive* mean? What does *showing ownership* mean? Does *boy's book* show ownership?" Then read phrases like the following for identification of possessives.

children's game   honest firemen
serious people   dogs' tails

When studying prefixes and suffixes, discuss:

What is a prefix?
What is the prefix in *disobey*? How is the prefix spelled?
What is the suffix in *helpful*? How is the suffix spelled?

Then read words like the following, asking the children to write the prefixes or suffixes they hear.

rethink   dwelling
unnamed   murmured
disagree   sillier
submarine   pouches
pretest   ugliest

An activity card can serve as the focus for teaching and practice of prefixes and suffixes, as suggested below.

---

prefix

    dis- ⟶

    pre- ⟶

suffix

    -er ⟶

    -ly ⟶

1. **Put base words from the envelope with one of the prefixes or suffixes above.**
   (Note: Appropriate base words would include *like, please, card, color, view, paid, test, strong, hard, fast, love, slow, friend,* etc.)
2. **Use the new words in sentences.**

In studying prefixes and suffixes, one researcher found that 24 percent of the words in Thorndike's *Teacher's Word Book* can use prefixes and that fifteen of these prefixes account for 82 percent of the total number of prefixes.[12] Below is a list of these fifteen prefixes.

ab	from	*in*	into
ad	to	*in*	not
be	by	*pre*	before
com	with	*pro*	for, onward
de	from	*re*	back
dis	opposite	*sub*	under
en	in	*un*	not
ex	out		

---

12. Russell G. Stauffer, "A Study of Prefixes in the Thorndike List to Establish a List of Prefixes That Should Be Taught in the Elementary School," *Journal of Educational Research* 35 (February 1942): 453–458.

The preceding prefixes have fairly constant meanings, and a person who knows the more common prefixes can frequently make a close guess as to the meaning of the word, particularly when it is in a meaningful context. The rarer prefixes are also worth knowing, but probably should be for individual study or for incidental consideration in connection with learning of particular words that contain them.

The problem of teaching the meanings of suffixes is somewhat more complicated. The most common suffixes include *-ing*, *-ed*, *-er*, *-ly*, *-(e)s*, *-tion*, and *-y*. This problem has been dealt with in detail by Thorndike, who pointed out that most suffixes in English have several different meanings, and that teaching the most common meanings may create confusion.[13]

• *Other recommended activities*   The following items may be listed in vocabulary notebooks: new words heard in conversation or discussion, adjectives that are vivid and effective, new words encountered in general reading, descriptive words heard over radio or television, words that can be substituted for overworked or "tired" words, and new uses of old words.

Through activities like the following, special types of vocabulary lists may be encouraged by the teacher.

1. Read a story or poem aloud and ask pupils to pick out the words that "make a noise" (*squeal*, *purr*, *growl*, etc.).
2. Let a child, while blindfolded, remove an unknown object from a grab bag and describe its shape, size, and weight.
3. Have individuals feel, then describe, the texture of such materials as sandpaper, cotton batting, sponge, and silk.
4. Bring to class bottles of vanilla and lemon extract, peppermint, oil, and other kitchen flavorings. Let several children taste them and then describe the taste.
5. Let pupils smell the bottles mentioned in number 4; then describe the odors.

A learning station is also an appropriate means of providing children with further experience in classifying words into descriptive categories.

---

13. Edward L. Thorndike, *The Teaching of English Suffixes* (New York: Teachers College Press, Columbia University, 1941).

Learning Station: Sensory Words

Things I Taste ice cream	*Things I See* rainbow	*Things I Feel* fur
Sounds I Hear whistle		*Things I Smell* lemon

Directions:
1. Write ten words under each of the headings above. One example is provided for each heading.
2. Think of some other titles (categories) and list as many words as you can that fit the categories.
3. When finished, put your papers in the "Words" folder on the table.

Pupils need to recognize the usefulness and desirability of a large vocabulary. A "Learn a New Word Each Day" campaign could be employed. The teacher who is sensitive to word values and enthusiastic about encouraging children to develop their vocabularies may at times put a new word on the bulletin board with directions to answer such questions as:

What does it mean?
How is it pronounced?
How would you use it in a sentence?

Encouraging the children to make use of the new word two or three times during the school day would be an important part of this activity.

(One book that is a good source of activities for vocabulary development is *Anchor*, Educational Service, Inc., P. O. Box 219, Stevensville, Mich. 49127.)

SEMANTICS

Increasing vocabularies is an important task, but responsible and humane use of words is perhaps even more important. The power of words for both good and evil has long been recognized, but to date little has been done at the elementary school level toward a systematic study of semantics. Semantics is the study of what language does

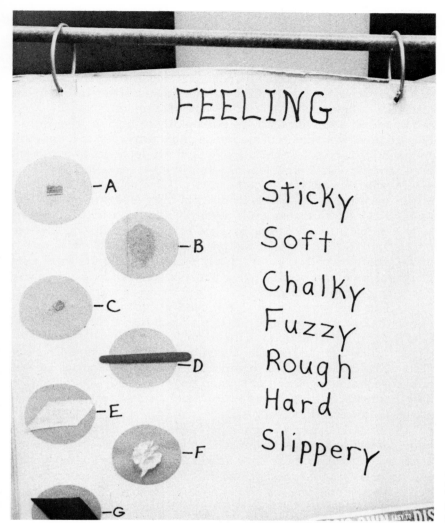

FEELING

Sticky
Soft
Chalky
Fuzzy
Rough
Hard
Slippery

−A
−B
−C
−D
−E
−F
−G

A chart, with a collection of items and a question, "How does each one feel?", can evoke many descriptive words.

for and to people—what words stand for in the world of reality and what purposes they serve in our relations with others. What should be taught about semantics and how might it be taught? The following suggestions provide a partial answer to this question.

1. Understanding symbols: Symbols may be nonlinguistic: expressive gestures, traffic lights, road signs, flags, emblems. Language itself is a symbol, along with its derivatives: shorthand, Morse and other codes, Braille alphabets, the symbols of mathematics, and so on.

   2. Understanding referents: A *referent* is something that refers or is referred to. For communication to occur, there must be an agreed-upon meaning for the referent—an accepted meaning for the sender and receiver. It is at this point that much of the confusion of communication can be traced, particularly of multi-referent words. For example, what different meanings might *run* have for a baseball player, a stocking salesman, a playwright? Understanding a referent often involves gleaning meaning from the context—verbal, social, emotional, or historical.

   In addition to the problems cited in the preceding paragraph, there are terms without tangible means of referential support: *generosity, patriotism, truth, happiness, goodness, democracy, justice, cooperation.* What such a term means will depend upon who uses the word, what this person values, his purpose for using the word, and his definition of the word. When a writer or speaker uses such terms, it is necessary to pause and think: "Here is a word worth examining. What does this person mean? Is it used to stir emotion or express opinion? Does the word mean to him what it seems to mean to me? Do I really understand what he is saying?"

   3. Understanding the denotative meaning of a word: This appears to be a fairly straight-forward concept, but dictionaries are not published frequently enough to keep up with all the new words (or new meanings of words)—particularly technical words—nor do they generally contain slang expressions.

   4. Understanding the connotative meaning of a word: Connotation refers to suggested or implied meaning associated with a word apart from the thing it explicitly names. This is one of the more difficult aspects of understanding words, for there are so many words that have multiple and/or changing connotations. For example, a generation or so ago the word *square* carried the connotation of true, honest, and forthright when used in describing a person; today, the same word is used to describe a person who is socially inept and out of touch.

   5. Understanding euphemisms: Euphemism is the substitution of an agreeable expression for one that may offend or be unpleasant: e.g., *mortician* for *undertaker.* The word *plump* is less offensive than *fat,* and *slender* is more pleasing than *skinny.* Euphemisms require constant updating, as they occur in usage long before they appear in dictionaries.

6. *Understanding functional shift: Functional shift* requires an understanding not only of connotative shifts, but also shifts in parts of speech, as a change from a verb to a noun; for example: *They walk to the bus stand each day,* or *Joe went for a walk.* A sample independent activity card, dealing with functional shift, is illustrated below.

Activity Card: Functional Shift

Did you know that the same word can be used to mean two different things? Look at these two sentences:

  The grocer *ground* the coffee.

  The *ground* was too hard to plow.

There are many such words. For example: *leaves, circle, judge, weeds, perch, worry, fall, bruise.* Can you write a pair of sentences using each word as a noun and then as a verb?

---

7. *Understanding the purposes of slang and various groups who use slang:* An activity could be the compiling of slang words and expressions used by class members and defining the slang words in standard language. Discussion could include who uses these expressions, when they are appropriate, and special slang used by different groups—ethnic, geographical, age, occupational.

8. *Understanding technical language:* Technical terms are important, for people are increasingly exposed to technical fields such as space, medicine, and ecology.

9. *Understanding all forms of affective language:* Social adjustment and consumer wisdom are absolutely vital to everyone, as they affect every aspect of life. It is important to realize that every form of communication contains a bias because the sender is expressing the concept from one subjective viewpoint and the receiver is accepting it from another subjective viewpoint. When the two viewpoints are not clearly understood, confusion and/or propagandizing results. Children should know that catchwords and slogans, such as *brotherhood of man,* and *good citizen,* can produce stock reactions.

  That words can be used to state personal opinion, rather than fact, must be instilled in children at an early age. Children (and adults) must be taught to ask for evidence when hearing a statement such as "That government official is crooked." It must be recognized that there is considerable difference between "Bill is lazy," and "Bill seems lazy to me."

Appropriate activities for teaching about affective language include scrutiny necessary to distinguish between propaganda or opinions and facts; study of newspapers and magazines to locate examples where writers use opinion or scientific fact; and analysis of propaganda techniques found in writing and speaking, such as name-calling, glittering generality, transfer, testimonial, plain folks, and bandwagon. Too, listening to a television commercial provides an opportunity to discuss "sell" words and phrases.

LEXICOGRAPHY

What is a dictionary?

To give more understanding and appreciation of dictionaries, elementary school pupils could profitably learn about how words get selected for a dictionary; how dictionary making has changed since the days of the famous dictionary-maker, Samuel Johnson; and how dictionaries are made.

• *Dictionary making*   Many children are unaware that a dictionary cannot contain all the words of the language: there are just too many words and some of them are special words only used by a small group of persons. An unabridged dictionary in the classroom or library and the abridged dictionaries used by the class members should help in understanding some of the differences in dictionaries. The history of Samuel Johnson, author of the first dictionary of the English language, and a study of a facsimile page of *A Dictionary of the English Language* (1755) would interest children. Point out the way Johnson liked to use long words to explain simple ones and the way he let his personal feelings creep into definitions of words almost as if the words belonged to him alone. A similar study of Noah Webster, the first American dictionary maker, and his early dictionaries would be equally interesting.

Today's dictionaries, of course, are not made by one man. Many *readers*, who live in all parts of the country, help by reading newspapers, magazines, books, scientific journals, and other print media. As the readers work, they look for new words, new meanings for

O B D

OA'RY. *adj.* [from *oar.*] Having the form or use of oats.
  His hair transforms to down, his fingers meet,
  In fkinny films, and fhape his *oary* feet.   *Addifon.*
      The fwan with arched neck,
  Between her white wings mantling, proudly rows
  Her ftate with *oary* feet.   *Milton.*
OAST. *n. f.* A kiln. Not in ufe.
  Empty the binn into a hog-bag, and carry them imme-
  diately to the *oaft* or kiln, to be dried.   *Mortimer.*
OATCA'KE. *n. f.* [*oat* and *cake.*] Cake made of the meal of
  oats.
  Take a blue ftone they make haver or *oatcakes* upon, and
  lay it upon the crofs bars of iron.   *Peacham.*
OA'TEN. *adj.* [from *oat.*] Made of oats; bearing oats.
  When fhepherds pipe on *oaten* ftraws,
  And merry larks are ploughmens clocks.   *Shakefp.*
OATH. *n. f.* [aith, Gothick; að, Saxon. The diftance be-
  tween the noun *oath*, and the verb *fwear*, is very obfervable,
  as it may fhew that our oldeft dialect is formed from different
  languages.] An affirmation, negation, or promife, corrobo-
  rated by the atteftation of the Divine Being.
  Read over Julia's heart, thy firft beft love,
  For whofe dear fake thou then did'ft rend thy faith
  Into a thoufand *oaths*; and all thofe *oaths*
  Defcended into perjury to love me.   *Shakefpeare.*
  He that ftrikes the firft ftroke, I'll run him up to the
  hilts as I am a foldier.
  —An *oath* of mickle might; and fury fhall abate.   *Sha.*
  We have confultations, which inventions fhall be publifhed,
  which not: and take an *oath* of fecrecy for the concealing of
  thofe which we think fit to keep fecret.   *Bacon.*
  Thofe called to any office of truft, are bound by an *oath*
  to the faithful difcharge of it: but an *oath* is an appeal to
  God, and therefore can have no influence, except upon thofe
  who believe that he is.   *Swift.*
OA'THABLE. *adj.* [from *oath.* A word not ufed.] Capable
  of having an oath adminiftered.
      You're not *oathable*,
  Altho' I know you'll fwear
  Into ftrong fhudders th' immortal gods.   *Shakefpeare.*
OATHBREA'KING. *n. f.* [*oath* and *break.*] Perjury; the vio-
  lation of an oath.
  His *oathbreaking* he mended thus,
  By now forfwearing that he is forfworn.   *Shak. Hen. IV.*
OA'TMALT. *n. f.* [*oat* and *malt.*] Malt made of oats.
  In Kent they brew with one half *oatmalt*, and the other
  half barleymalt.   *Mortimer's Hufb.*
OA'TMEAL. *n. f.* [*oat* and *meal.*] Flower made by grinding
  oats.
  Oatmeal and butter, outwardly applied, dry the fcab on the
  head.   *Arbuthnot on Aliment.*
  Our neighbours tell me oft, in joking talk,
  Of afhes, leather, *oatmeal*, bran, and chalk.   *Gay.*
OA'TMEAL. *n. f.* An herb.   *Ainfworth.*
OATS. *n. f.* [aten, Saxon.] A grain, which in England is
  generally given to horfes, but in Scotland fupports the people.
  It is of the grafs leaved tribe; the flowers have no petals,
  and are difpofed in a loofe panicle; the grain is eatable.
  The meal makes tolerable good bread.   *Miller.*
  The *oats* have eaten the horfes.   *Shakefpeare.*
  It is bare mechanifm, no otherwife produced than the
  turning of a wild *oatbeard*, by the infinuation of the particles
  of moifture.   *Locke.*
  For your lean cattle, fodder them with barley ftraw firft,
  and the *oat* ftraw laft.   *Mortimer's Hufbandry.*
  His horfe's allowance of *oats* and beans, was greater than
  the journey required.   *Swift.*
OA'TTHISTLE. *n. f.* [*oat* and *thiftle.*] An herb.   *Ainf.*
OBAMBULA'TION. *n. f.* [*obambulatio*, from *obambulo*, Latin.]
  The act of walking about.   *Dict.*
To OBDU'CE. *v. a.* [*obduco*, Latin.] To draw over as a co-
  vering.
  No animal exhibits its face in the native colour of its fkin
  but man; all others are covered with feathers, hair, or a
  cortex that is *obduced* over the cutis.   *Hale.*
OBDU'CTION. *n. f.* [from *obductio*, *obduco*, Latin.] The act
  of covering, or laying a cover.
OBDU'RACY. *n. f.* [from *obdurate.*] Inflexible wickednefs;
  impenitence; hardnefs of heart.
  Thou think'ft me as far in the Devil's book, as thou and
  Falftaff, for *obduracy* and perfiftency. *Shakefpeare's Henry* IV.
  God may, by a mighty grace, hinder the abfolute com-
  pletion of fin in final *obduracy*.   *South's Serm.*
OBDU'RATE. *adj.* [*obduratus*, Latin.]
1. Hard of heart; inflexibly obftinate in ill; hardned; impe-
  nitent.
  Oh! let me teach thee for thy father's fake,
  That gave thee life, when well he might have flain thee;
  Be not *obdurate*, open thy deaf ears.   *Shakefpeare.*
  If when you make your pray'rs,

O B E

  God fhould be fo *obdurate* as yourfelves,
  How would it fare with your departed fouls ?   *Shakefp.*
  Women are foft, mild, pitiful, and flexible;
  Thou ftern, *obdurate*, flinty, rough, remorfelefs.   *Shakefp.*
      To convince the proud what figns avail,
  Or wonders move th' *obdurate* to relent;
  They harden'd more, by what might more reclaim.   *Milt.*
  Obdurate as you are, oh! hear at leaft
  My dying prayers, and grant my laft requeft.   *Dryden.*
2. Hardned; firm; ftubborn.
  Sometimes the very cuftom of evil makes the heart *obdu-
  rate* againft whatfoever inftructions to the contrary.   *Hooker.*
      A pleafing forcery could charm
  Pain for a while, or anguifh, and excite
  Fallacious hope, or arm th' *obdurate* breaft
  With ftubborn patience, as with triple fteel.   *Milton.*
  No fuch thought ever ftrikes his marble, *obdurate* heart;
  but it prefently flies off and rebounds from it. It is impoffible
  for a man to be thorough-paced in ingratitude, till he had
  fhook off all fetters of pity and compaffion.   *South.*
3. Harfh; rugged.
  They joined the moft *obdurate* confonants without one in-
  tervening vowel.   *Swift.*
OBDU'RATELY. *adv.* [from *obdurate.*] Stubbornly; inflexibly;
  impenitently.
OBDU'RATENESS. *n. f.* [from *obdurate.*] Stubbornnefs; in-
  flexibility; impenitence.
OBDURA'TION. *n. f.* [from *obdurate.*] Hardnefs of heart;
  ftubbornnefs.
  What occafion it had given them to think, to their greater
  obduration in evil, that through a froward and wanton defire
  of innovation, we did conftrainedly thofe things, for which
  confcience was pretended ?   *Hooker, b.* iv.
OBDU'RED. *adj.* [*obduratus*, Latin.] Hardned; inflexible;
  impenitent.
  This faw his haplefs foes, but ftood *obdur'd*,
  And to rebellious fight rallied their pow'rs
  Infenfate.   *Milton's Paradife Loft, b.* vi.
OBE'DIENCE. *n. f.* [*obedience*, Fr. *obedientia*, Latin.] Obfe-
  quioufnefs; fubmiffion to authority; compliance with com-
  mand or prohibition.
  If you violently proceed againft him, it would fhake in
  pieces the heart of his *obedience*.   *Shakefpeare's K. Lear.*
      Thy hufband
  Craves no other tribute at thy hands,
  But love, fair looks, and true *obedience*.   *Shakefp.*
  His fervants ye are, to whom ye obey, whether of fin
  unto death, or of *obedience* unto righteoufnefs.   *Rom.* vi. 16.
  It was both a ftrange commiffion, and a ftrange *obedience*
  to a commiffion, for men fo furioufly affailed, to hold their
  hands.   *Bacon's War with Spain.*
      Nor can this be,
  But by fulfilling that which thou didft want,
  Obedience to the law of God, impos'd   }
  On penalty of death.   *Milton's Paradife Loft, b.* xii.
OBE'DIENT. *adj.* [*obediens*, Latin.] Submiffive to authority;
  compliant with command or prohibition; obfequious.
  To this end did I write, that I might know the proof of
  you, whether ye be *obedient* in all things.   *2 Cor.* ii. 9.
      To this her mother's plot
  She, feemingly *obedient*, likewife hath
  Made promife.   *Shakefp. M. W. of Wind.*
  He humbled himfelf, and became *obedient* unto death.
                                          Phil. ii. 8.
  Religion hath a good influence upon the people, to make
  them *obedient* to government, and peaceable one towards
  another.   *Tillotfon, Serm.* 3.
  The chief his orders gives; th' *obedient* band,
  With due obfervance, wait the chief's command.   *Pope.*
OBE'DIENTIAL. *adj.* [*obedientiel*, Fr. from *obedient.*] Accord-
  ing to the rule of obedience.
  Faith is fuch as God will accept of, when it affords fidu-
  cial reliance on the promifes, and *obediential* fubmiffion to the
  command.   *Hammond.*
  Faith is then perfect, when it produces in us a fiduciary
  affent to whatever the gofpel has revealed, and an *obediential*
  fubmiffion to the commands.   *Wake's Prep. for Death.*
OBE'DIENTLY. *adv.* [from *obedient*] With obedience.
  We fhould behave ourfelves reverently and *obediently* towards the Divine Majefty, and juftly and charitably towards
  men.   *Tillotfon.*
OBE'ISANCE. *n. f.* [*obeifance*, Fr. This word is formed by cor-
  ruption from *abaifance*, an act of reverence.] A bow; a cour-
  tefy; an act of reverence made by inclination of the body or
  knee.
  Bartholomew my page,
  See dreft in all fuits like a lady;
  Then call him Madam, do him all *obeifance*.   *Shakefpeare.*
  Bathfheba bowed and did *obeifance* unto the king: 1 *K.* i. 16.

18 K   The

A page from Samuel Johnson's *A Dictionary of the English Language* (1755) reveals differences with today's dictionaries. (See, for example, the definition of *oats*.)

old words, changes in spelling, and changes in usage. Each time a reader sees a new word or a change in meaning, spelling, and usage of an old word, he writes it down on a special card known as a *quotation card*. He copies the passage in which the word is used, giving the source, the date, and other data. The cards are then sent to a main office where they are carefully placed in a central file.

When quotation cards for a new word begin to show up in large numbers, the dictionary editor watches his files to determine how widely the word is being used, how it is being used, and who is making use of it. Before a new word goes into a dictionary, it is accurately defined by language scholars, phoneticians advise about its pronunciation, and experts in special fields supply facts about the word.

• ***Description versus prescription***   Should dictionary-makers record English as it is actually used by people in their everyday writing and speech (that is, *descriptive*) or as some people think the language should be used according to a set of rules (that is, *prescriptive*)?

Pooley attempted to answer this question. Although he was concerned specifically with the controversy surrounding the introduction of *Webster's Third New International Dictionary*, his comments are appropriate for children's dictionaries.

> These are two conflicting views of what a dictionary ought to be, and upon the publication of the *Third International*, these two views came into sharp conflict. The first view is that a dictionary is a standard or norm to maintain the purity and correctness of the English language. It is a book of reference to settle disputes and to answer differences. It is an Emily Post of words and idioms. What the dictionary upholds is good English—what the dictionary condemns is bad English. . . .
>
> There is, however, a second view of what a dictionary ought to be, a view that has been growing in recognition and support in recent years. This view that a dictionary is a scientific, unbiased, wholly objective record of the English language as it has been in the past and as it is at the moment of forming the dictionary . . . must be duly set down.[14]

---

14. Robert C. Pooley, "Dictionaries and Language Change," *Language, Linguistics, and School Programs*, Proceedings of the Spring Institutes, 1963, of the National Council of Teachers of English (Urbana, Ill.: National Council of Teachers of English, 1963), pp. 75–76.

One of the prescriptive characteristics of *Webster's New International Dictionary, Second Edition* is usage labels such as *Slang, Dial.* (dialect), and *Colloq.* (colloquial). *Webster's Third*, on the other hand, is not particularly concerned with artificial notions of correctness or superiority. It aims at being descriptive, not prescriptive; recognizing that language changes and that change is normal; accepting spoken language as the standard language; basing correctness upon usage, all usage being relative. Such an approach permitted use of illustrative quotations from *Time* as well as from *Spectator;* heavy reliance upon oral speech as well as written words; and setting of the year 1775 as the year of obsolescence.

The concept of a dictionary as something other than the final arbiter of correctness in our language is a difficult concept for children to grasp, even those at the intermediate level. However, the teacher who helps children to realize the true role of a dictionary is helping them to respect rather than to fear it.

• ***The dictionary as a source book***   With this understanding, pupils use the dictionary as a source book for the study of the English language. Urgings of linguists for more knowledge about the language can be met partly through correct usage of a dictionary. For example, a pupil can learn about the stability of consonants and the variance of vowels through study of the pronunciation key (a set of arbitrary symbols for phonemes). He can gain insight into the way the language grows and changes by detecting variant spellings (e.g., *taboo* or *tabu*). He can learn about different pronunciations for the same word [e.g., *either* $\longrightarrow$ ēthə(r) or īthə(r)]. He can discover that some words have more than one meaning and can function as more than one part of speech.

The uses of a dictionary

One of the most helpful listings of useful criteria in dictionary selection was written a few years ago by Murray and should be consulted by teachers when selecting a picture dictionary for the beginning years or a junior dictionary for the intermediate years.[15] Following is a list of dictionaries for children.

Barnhart, Clarence L., ed. *The Thorndike-Barnhart Junior Dictionary*. New York: Doubleday.

---

15.   C. Merrill Murray, "Selecting an Elementary School Dictionary," *Elementary English* 34 (May 1957): 293–297.

————. *The World Book Dictionary*. Chicago: Field Enterprises Educational Corp.

Basic Dictionary of American English. New York: Holt, Rinehart and Winston.

Clemons, Elizabeth. *The Pixie Dictionary*. New York: Holt, Rinehart and Winston.

Courtis, Stuart, and Watters, Grenete. *The Illustrated Golden Dictionary*. New York: Golden Press.

Funk and Wagnalls. *The Standard Junior Dictionary*. New York: Funk and Wagnalls.

Intermediate Dictionary of American English. New York: Holt, Rinehart and Winston.

Monroe, Marion, and Greet, Cabelle. *My Little Pictionary*. Chicago: Scott Foresman.

————. *My Second Little Pictionary*. Chicago: Scott Foresman.

Moore, Lillian. *The Golden Picture Dictionary*. New York: Golden Press.

O'Donnell, Mabel, and Townes, W. *Words I Like to Read and Write: A Picture Dictionary for Beginners*. New York: Harper & Row.

New Picture Dictionary. Dayton, Ohio: George A. Pflaum.

Oftedal, Laura, and Jacob, Nina. *My First Dictionary*. New York: Grossett and Dunlap.

Reed, Mary, and Osswald, Edith. *My First Golden Dictionary*. New York: Golden Press.

Walpole, Ellen. *The Golden Dictionary*. New York: Golden Press.

Watson, Aldren A. *Very First Words to Read and Write*. New York: Holt, Rinehart and Winston.

Webster's Elementary Dictionary. Springfield, Mass.: Merriam.

Webster's New World Dictionary: Basic School Edition. New York: Prentice-Hall.

Whitman, Doris, ed. *The Word Wonder Dictionary*. New York: Holt, Rinehart and Winston.

Winston Dictionary for Schools. New York: Holt, Rinehart and Winston.

Wright, Wendell. *The Rainbow Dictionary for Young People*. Cleveland, Ohio: World Publishing.

• *Dictionary skills*   A knowledge of alphabetical order is basic to the use of a dictionary. Early in the school program (and sometimes before), children begin to recognize the letters and to learn letter names. Soon thereafter, most children know the consecutive order of the letters. To use a dictionary efficiently, the child must be

Through use, children learn that a dictionary is far more useful than serving only as a source for checking spelling.

able to recall quickly whether a letter comes near the beginning, the middle, or the end of the alphabet, and whether a certain letter comes before or after another letter. Games can be used to develop this kind of quick recall. As they begin to understand the alphabetical arrangement of words, children may be given lists of words to put in alphabetical order. Begin with lists in which each word starts with a different letter, progressing to lists of words starting with the same letter, and then to mixed lists as the children begin to understand arrangement by second and third letters.

Practice in putting words in alphabetical order may precede locating words in a dictionary. When the child has some understanding of the alphabetical arrangement of words, he can be introduced to guide words as aids to locating the words he needs.

Skill in locating words is only the beginning of mastery of the dictionary. The child must also be able to interpret and use the information he finds. He needs to learn the main parts of a dictionary entry:

1. Entry word (usually in boldface)
2. Pronunciation (usually enclosed in parentheses; letters used in respelling for pronunciations represent sounds assigned to them as explained in the pronunciation key)
3. Label (shows use or meaning is limited to a particular region or level of usage)
4. Definition(s)
5. Illustrative sentence (shows how a word is used in a sentence)
6. Part-of-speech label (usually an abbreviation naming functions of the word)
7. Inflected forms
8. Etymology (tells the language where the word came from and its meaning)
9. Run-on entry (entry word with suffix)
10. Idioms (special definitions)

The following list of dictionary skills and the approximate grade levels at which they are usually introduced should be adapted to individual needs.

Primary years
1. Learning the names of letters, recognition of each.
2. Learning the alphabet
3. Learning the location of letters in the alphabet with relation to each other
4. Arranging words alphabetically, beginning with different letters, beginning with the same letter
5. Appreciation of the dictionary as a tool and as an interesting source of information

Intermediate years
1. All of the above
2. Understanding that a dictionary is built on alphabetical order by first, second, and third letters
3. Familiarity with the relative position of letter sections: d's come in the first quarter, y's in last quarter
4. Using guide words to locate material on a page
5. Understanding that words are listed by plain forms
6. Using a dictionary to find the correct spelling of a word
7. Learning the use of diacritical markings and key words as aids in pronunciation
8. Learning the meaning and use of accent marks

9. Learning the meaning and use of respelling to show pronunciation
10. Learning the meaning and the use of syllabication
11. Using the definition best suited to the context
12. Using a dictionary for correct use of homonyms
13. Using a dictionary as a key to various meanings of a common word
14. Understanding abbreviations in a dictionary
15. Using synonyms and antonyms to clarify meaning
16. Using a dictionary to get related forms, irregular plurals, and irregular verb forms
17. Using cross references for additional information
18. Understanding the significance of word derivation, prefixes, and suffixes
19. Learning about special features of a dictionary[16]

Exercises like those on page 324 can be used to provide instruction for the items mentioned above. They are listed roughly in sequential order from the primary to the middle school years.

Certainly, more than one dictionary will enhance the instructional program. If you look up just two words, *cupboard* and *entertainment*, in the newest Webster's and the newest Thorndike-Barnhart, you will note different diacritical marks, syllabic divisions, and phonetic respellings. While a particular page or copies of the same dictionary may be helpful for a specific lesson, children are denied significant learning about language if only one dictionary is used exclusively in the classroom. What often results is talk about "what *the* dictionary says," "*the* meaning of a word," "*the* correct respelling of the word," and the like.

• *Dictionary-related activities and topics*   Below are more advanced activities and topics to encourage vocabulary growth.

1. Building lists of synonyms and antonyms (such as listing as many ways as can be found in which sports writers tell that a team was defeated)
2. Improving colorless paragraphs by using words with sensory appeal and lively action words
3. Tracing the derivations of words (as days of the week, months of the year)

---

16. Adapted from a listing in Iowa Elementary Teachers Handbook, vol. 3, *Reading* (Des Moines: Iowa State Department of Public Instruction, 1944). Used by permission.

Dictionary Exercises

1. Ask the pupils to consider the dictionary in three parts: A–G, H–Q, and R–Z. Provide a list of words and have the pupils decide in what part of the dictionary each word may be found: beginning, middle, or end.
2. Give several word pairs and ask what initial letters are used in each pair (e.g., *cat–king; circle–soap; jacket–gingerbread*).
3. Write several pairs of words on the chalkboard, asking which word in each pair comes first in the dictionary.

    above   hill   race
    across   hunt   rabbit
4. Use a page from a dictionary to explain the purpose of guide words.
5. Prepare an exercise, asking the pupils to list words they expect to find between the guide words.

    flew–food   read–room
6. Present an example of a dictionary entry, along with respelling [e.g., *en-ve-lope (en'-və-lōp)*]. Teach the use of the pronunciation key (not memorization of diacritical marks), indicating that in *en* the e has the same sound as in the word l<u>e</u>ss; that ə carries the same sound of the e you hear in kitt<u>e</u>n; and that o has the same sound as you hear in fl<u>o</u>w. Point out the accent mark and the marks which suggest syllabication. Provide a list of four to six words, asking for pronunciation.
7. Ask the children to look up a word with several different meanings, such as *play*, and write a sentence for each of its meanings.

4. Listing common prefixes and suffixes along with basic root words
5. Examining the dictionary for new words
6. Making a study of how places got their names (*chester, burg, ton, mont, ville, ford, haven, land, port, field, hill*)
7. Listing slang words and idioms (*rap, hassle, goof off, pealing out, bummer, slick, jiving, foxy*)
8. Discussing the finer shades of the meaning of words, as *difficult, arduous*
9. Discovering ways our vocabulary grows and changes:
    a. Different names in different parts of the country for common objects, as *sack, bag, poke*

b. Place names now incorporated into common nouns (as *millinery* from Milan, *frank* from Frankfurt, *calico* from Calcutta)

c. People's names that have become common words (*Colt, Levi*) and names that have been incorporated into our vocabulary (*pasteurize, vulcanize, forsythia, silhouette, iris, voltage, saxophone, macintosh, panic*)

d. Ways Greek and Roman mythology have influenced English vocabulary (*mercury, volcanoes, herculean*)

e. Meanings that sports have contributed to words (*baskets, spare, fly, love, crawl, tackle, iron*)

f. Greek and Latin forms that occur in English words:

Greek		*Latin*	
auto	self	*aqua*	water
bio	life; living things	*audi*	hear
geo	earth; land	*bi*	two; twice
gram	thing written	*inter*	among; between
graph	to write	*multi*	many
logy	kind of speaking	*ped*	foot
	or reasoning	*post*	behind; after
meter	measure	*super*	above; over
peri	around	*visio*	sight; seeing
phon(o)(e)	sound; voice		
phot(o)	light		
tel(e)	far; far off		

Here is a suggested activity (for one of the items in 9f) that can be meaningful to intermediate level children.

Questions of the Day

1.	What do these words have in common?	telephone
2.	Try to define each word, using the dictionary if needed.	telegraph
		television
3.	What do you think *tele-* of each word means?	telescope
		telephoto
4.	How many other examples of words beginning with *tele-* can you give?	telepathy

---

From a growing appreciation of what a dictionary is and increasing competence in its use, boys and girls become intrigued with the magic of words and the beauty and richness of the English language.

OTHER REFERENCE SKILLS

In addition to dictionary skills, other reference sources should be considered at the elementary school level. Such items as the following are appropriate for study of general books, encyclopedias, almanacs, atlases, and biographical dictionaries.

Books
1. Cover data of book (title, author)
2. Table of contents
3. Index (main topics, alphabetical order, subtopics, page numbering, cross references)
4. Glossary
5. Appendix
6. Index

Encyclopedias
1. Volumes (guide letters and numbers)
2. Topics (alphabetical order)
3. Guide words
4. Cross references
5. Index

As children search for populations of cities, historical events, current events, or sports news, they frequently turn to an up-to-date almanac (e.g., *World Almanac, Book of Facts,* and *Information Please Almanac*). Again, facility in the use of an index is an important tool, as it is with use of the type of information found in an atlas. Children frequently need to find information about famous persons and in the process should become familiar with biographical dictionaries, such as *Who's Who in America, The Junior Book of Authors, American Men in Science,* and *Current Biography.* Another important reference source is *Bartlett's Familiar Quotations.*[17]

---

17. Raedeane M. Nelson, "Getting Children Into Reference Books," *Elementary English* 50 (September 1973) 884–887, 896.

SELECTED REFERENCES

General Professional

Burrows, Alvina T.; Monson, Diane L.; and Stauffer, Russell G. *New Horizons in the Language Arts.* New York: Harper & Row, 1972, chapter 10.

Corcoran, Gertrude B. *Language Arts in the Elementary School: A Modern Linguistic Approach.* New York: Ronald, 1970, chapter 10.

Dallmann, Martha. *Teaching the Language Arts in the Elementary School.* 2d ed. Dubuque, Iowa: William C. Brown, 1971, chapter 6.

Greene, Harry A., and Petty, Walter T. *Developing Language Skills in the Elementary Schools.* 4th ed. Boston: Allyn and Bacon, 1971, chapter 10.

Strickland, Ruth. *The Language Arts in Elementary School.* 3rd ed. Lexington, Mass.: D. C. Heath, 1969, chapter 10.

Specialized

Deighton, Lee C. *Vocabulary Development in the Classroom.* New York: Teachers College Press, Columbia University, 1959.

Petty, Walter T., et al. *The State of Knowledge about Teaching of Vocabulary.* Urbana, Ill.: National Council of Teachers of English, 1968.

Vocabulary Lists

Buckingham, B. R., and Dolch, Edward W. *A Combined Word List.* Boston: Ginn, 1936.

Dale, Edgar, et al. *Children's Knowledge of Words.* Columbus: Ohio State University, Bureau of Educational Research and Service, 1960.

Dolch, Edward W. *Teaching Primary Reading.* Champaign, Ill.: Garrard Press, 1941, chapter 10.

————. "Needed Vocabulary," *Elementary English* 38 (December 1960): 530–534.

Durrell, Donald, and Sullivan, H. P. "Vocabulary Instruction in the Intermediate Grades," *Elementary English Review* 15 (April 1938): 146–148, 158, 179–185.

Fitzgerald, James A. "An Integrating Basic Communication Vocabulary," *Elementary English* 40 (March 1963): 283–289.

Gates, Arthur I. *A Reading Vocabulary for the Primary Grades.* New York: Teachers College Press, Columbia University, 1935.

————. *A List of Spelling Difficulties in 3,876 Words.* New York: Teachers College Press, Columbia University, 1937.

Horn, Ernest. *A Basic Writing Vocabulary: 10,000 Words Most Commonly Used in Writing.* University of Iowa Monographs in Education, no. 4. Iowa City: University of Iowa Press, 1926.

Rinsland, Henry D. *A Basic Vocabulary of Elementary School Children.* New York: Macmillan, 1945.

Thorndike, Edward L., and Lorge, Irving. *Teacher's Word Book of 30,000 Words.* New York: Teachers College Press, Columbia University, 1944.

GRAMMAR

Grammar

OBJECTIVES	PERFORMANCE RESPONSES
1. **To differentiate the major features of three kinds of grammar**	1. Consider the sentence *The boy kicked the ball.* Make grammar comments about it from each point of view; traditional, structural, transformational.
2. **To identify and recommend grammar concepts for the elementary school level**	2. Examine an elementary school language arts textbook. What is the nature of the grammar content: topics, scope, sequence, and teaching suggestions?
3. **To describe and demonstrate instructional procedures for (a) parts of speech, (b) sentence study, and (c) sentence expansion and restructuring**	3. Plan a lesson for one grammar concept related to each of the following: parts of speech, sentence patterns, sentence expansion and restructuring.

Grammar is a careful description and analysis of the structure of a language—its sound structure, word structure, phrase and sentence structure. The following explanation of grammar is presented to encourage the reader to explore all avenues that promote the child's growth in power to use language.

KINDS OF GRAMMARS

Two major figures in traditional grammar, which had its foundations in the eighteenth century, were Joseph Priestly and Robert Lowth. Structural grammar, which held sway in the United States from about 1925 to 1960, is generally based upon such theories as those expressed by Leonard Bloomfield in *Language*.[1] The transformational movement began with Noam Chomsky's *Syntactic Structures*.[2]

Language arts teachers are generally aware of traditional grammar but unfamiliar with structural grammar and transformational-generative grammar. Contemporary language arts textbooks incorporate some of each kind of grammar, since each has implications for the teaching of English. The latter two grammars are not as new or as different from traditional grammar as a superficial glance might indicate. These three grammar approaches are complementary rather than competitive.

Traditional grammar

Traditional grammar is the collection of grammatical principles and rules that (with variations and modifications) have been used by teachers for many years. Some features of traditional grammar and comments about the features are listed below.

1. Parts of speech: There are seven to ten parts of speech, depending upon the taxonomy of different grammarians: (noun, pronoun, verb, adjective, adverb, preposition, conjunction, article, infinitive, and interjection). Critics point out unsystematic definitions: for example, nouns and verbs are defined according to *meaning;* prepositions, adverbs, and adjectives according to *function.*

2. Functions of parts of speech: For example, parts of speech can serve several different functions. A noun may be a subject, a

---

1. Leonard Bloomfield, *Language* (New York: Henry Holt, 1933).

2. Noam Chomsky, *Syntactic Structures* (The Hague, The Netherlands: Mouton, 1957).

Ideas about root words
and inflected words are
a part of the description
and analysis of the
structure of words.

direct object, a subjective complement, an indirect object, or an object of a preposition.

3. Terms and explanations of larger units: Phrases, clauses, and sentences—particularly the subject-predicate concept of a sentence are covered in traditional grammar. Sentences are categorized according to *function:* (declarative, interrogative, imperative, and exclamatory) and *structure* (simple, compound, complex).

4. Sentence expansion (by modification, subordination, and coordination)

5. Diagramming: See the example below.

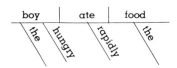

6.   Parsing: Parsing means to analyze a word grammatically as to form and function in a sentence. For example, *ate* in the preceding diagram is an irregular, transitive verb; active voice; indicative mood; past tense; singular number, third person; subject of the verb is *boy*.

Structural (descriptive) grammar

Some features of structural grammar and comments about the features are listed below.

1.   Basic significant sounds: The smallest distinctive sound element in a language is a phoneme: /b/ in *bit*, /p/ in *pit*. About forty vowel and consonant phonemes have been identified in the English language.

2.   Secondary phonemes: In addition to vowels and consonants, English uses phonemes of stress, pitch, and juncture.

3.   Basic grammatical units: The smallest meaningful units of language, called morphemes, range from noun plurals to larger units such as *boy*. The word *worker* is composed of two morphemes: *work*, a free morpheme, and *er*, a bound morpheme. (A bound morpheme cannot stand alone as a meaningful unit.)

4.   Form classes: These form classes resemble the four major parts of speech: nouns, verbs, adjectives, and adverbs. Form class words may change *form* to indicate a change in meaning: for example: *boy, boys*.

5.   Function (structure) words: These include (a) noun markers or determiners (articles, possessives, demonstratives, such as *a, my, this*); (b) prepositions; (c) auxiliary verbs (such as *am, are, is*); (d) modals (such as *may, can, will*); (e) intensifiers or qualifiers (such as *very, considerable*); and (f) conjunctions (coordinating and subordinating).

6.   Definitions according to position, form, and function: For example, a noun is a word that:

a.   takes certain endings (to show plural number or possession).
b.   often appears with certain function words (determiners) preceding it.
c.   occupies a certain position (such as after a determiner, before a verb).

Below is a group of sentences containing some nonsense words. Through a knowledge of position, form, and function, can you identify the nonsense words as "nouns" or "verbs"? Can you tell whether the verb is transitive or intransitive and how the noun is used: subject, direct object, indirect object, or predicate noun?

> A bargung moppels its ritbuck.
> Several bargungs moppeled their ritbucks.
> Two doolers gave the gotging some lavery.
> Every brark is an unboodle.
> A brark can opperlize those gratorps.

7.   Sentence patterns: Structuralists speak in terms of sentence patterns, although they differ in their conceptions of these patterns.[3] One set, proposed by Lefevre and Lefevre, is illustrated below.[4]

Pattern One:
  N-V (noun-verb) *The balloon descended.*
  N-V-ad (noun-verb-adverb) *Mary drove slowly.*
  N-V-adj (noun-verb-adjective) *The man turned purple.*
Pattern Two:
  N-V-N (noun-verb-noun) *The cowboy saddled his horse.*
Pattern Three:
  N-V-N-N (noun-verb-noun-noun) *Dad called Mary a tomboy.*
  N-V-N-adj (noun-verb-noun-adjective) *Ruth painted the room white.*
Pattern Four:
  N-Lv-N (noun-linking verb-noun) *My boss is an Irishman.*
  N-Lv-ad (noun-linking verb-adverb) *Anne has been here.*
  N-Lv-adj (noun-linking verb-adjective) *The apples were sweet.* (Other words commonly treated as linking verbs include *feel, seem, appear, look, become, remain, taste, smell, sound*)

8.   Additional concepts: Structuralists have emphasized that (a) language is systematic, (b) every language has its own grammar, and (c) a living language changes. Stressing that speech is the primary form of language, they have pointed out differences between spoken and written language. They have distinguished between the speech patterns unique to an individual *(idiolect)* and those belonging to geographic regions and social classes *(dialect)*. They have em-

---

3.   For example, see Verna L. Newsome, *Structural Grammar in the Classroom* (Oshkosh: Wisconsin Council of Teachers of English, 1961); and Enola Borgh, *Grammatical Patterns and Composition* (Oshkosh: Wisconsin Council of Teachers of English, 1963).

4.   From *Writing by Patterns*, by Helen F. and Earl A. Lefevre. Copyright © 1965 by Helen F. Lefevre and Earl A. Lefevre. Reprinted by permission of Alfred A. Knopf, Inc.

phasized various levels of usage (standard, nonstandard, etc.). In addition, they have recognized functional varieties: that is, suiting language to the situation.

Transformational-generative grammar

Grammarians of the transformational school differentiate in meaning the terms *competence* and *performance*. The first term refers to the individual, unconscious knowledge of grammar. This refers to the ability of the native speaker to understand grammatical sentences and to detect ungrammatical sentences: *Wash the dishes before leaving*, versus *Leaving before dishes the wash*. He interprets sentences even though elements may be missing: *Bill was a good athlete and so was Tom (a good athlete)*. He realizes that two or more sentences may have the same meaning: *The attorney did the work*, and *The lawyer did the work*. He understands that a sentence can be ambiguous: *Flying planes can be dangerous*.

Performance, on the other hand, signifies the actual use a person can make of this knowledge at any particular stage of his development.

Surface structure and *deep structure* are two important terms in transformational grammar. The form of a sentence—what you read or hear—represents the surface structure. The meaning of a sentence is the deep structure—the underlying set of semantic relations expressed in the sentence. For example, the surface structures of *He refused to tell the story because he was afraid to*, and *He refused to tell the story because he was afraid to tell the story*, are different, but both sentences have the same deep structure. The surface structure, *Bill was puzzled by Marie*, has an underlying deep structure, (PASSIVE) *Marie puzzled Bill*. *Transformations* have converted the deep structure into the surface structure—in the latter case a passive transformation. This transformation interchanged the noun phrases *Bill* and *Marie*; *was*, a form of *be*, has been introduced; and the preposition *by* was inserted before *Marie*. *Marie* is the "deep subject" of the structure, although *Bill* is the "surface subject."

The general tenet of transformational-generative grammar is that English possesses a finite set of rules that describe the operations by which basic structures are combined and modified into an infinite number of sentences. A sentence is composed of two parts, the *noun phrase* and the *verb phrase*. Phrase-structure rules state that the components of a sentence may be written as:

1. Sentence ⟶ Noun Phrase + Verb Phrase (S ⟶ NP + VP). A sentence consists of a noun phrase plus a verb phrase.

2. NP ⟶ $\begin{cases} \text{Determiner} + \text{Common Noun} \\ \text{Proper Noun} \\ \text{Pronoun}^5 \end{cases}$

   This rule states that a noun phrase may be composed of a determiner (article, demonstrative, or possessive) and a noun (count, mass, collective, concrete, or abstract); a proper noun; or a pronoun (personal or indefinite).

3. VP ⟶ Auxiliary + Verb Expression. A verb phrase may be written as an auxiliary and a verb expression. (The VP may contain a variety of combinations as noted below.) Simple, declarative, active sentences may be described by the phrase structure rules as given above. Basic sentences follow such patterns as:

   The girl laughed.
   The girl is a nurse.
   The girl frightened her brother.
   The girl has a bicycle.
   Apples are good.
   Father bought the boy a coat.
   The gymnast seems tired.

   Basic sentences have a fixed order—the subject is followed by the predicate. A basic sentence such as *The girl laughed*, might be represented by a "tree diagram," as follows.

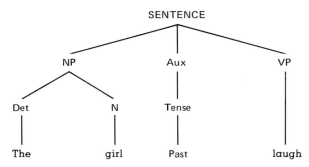

4. Auxiliary ⟶ Tense + (Modal) + (Aspect).[6] The auxiliary may only be an indicator of tense or it may include a modal aspect.

---

5. Tense $\longrightarrow$ $\begin{Bmatrix} \text{Present} \\ \text{Past} \end{Bmatrix}$

6. Modal $\longrightarrow$ *(can, may, will, shall, must, could, might, would, should).*

7. Aspect $\longrightarrow$ *(have + -en) + (be + -ing).* The *-en* form refers to a form of the verb or *be,* when *have + -en* is added to a VP: that is, a past participle such as *eaten.* The *-ing* form is the form of the verb or *be,* when *be + -ing* is added to a VP: that is, a present participle such as *playing.*

8. Verb expression $\longrightarrow$ $\begin{Bmatrix} \text{Verb nontransitive} \\ \text{Verb transitive} \end{Bmatrix}$

9. Verb nontransitive $\longrightarrow$ $\begin{Bmatrix} \text{Verb} \\ \quad \text{intransitive} \\ \text{Verb} \\ \quad \text{linking + complement} \end{Bmatrix}$

V_i, or verb intransitive, is a verb that needs nothing else to make a VP, as *walk, go, run, stand.* V_l, or verb linking, is a verb that is followed by an adjective, such as *remain, seem, is, feel.*

10. Verb transitive $\longrightarrow$ V + NP.

V_t, or verb transitive, is the way a verb is used when followed by an object NP, as *see, kick, hit, throw.* Thus the model of a "tree diagram."

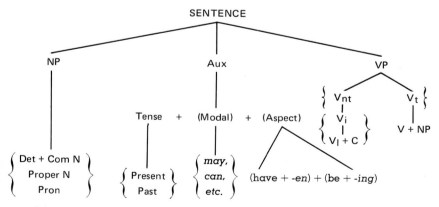

More complicated structures are described by means of "transformation structure" rules. See how the deep structure (QUESTION)

The girl (tense) *laugh,* is transformed into a surface question, *Did the girl laugh?*

1. Q + NP + tense + VP (deep structure)
2. Tense + NP + VP (inflection adjustment: *laughed* to *laugh*)
3. Tense + *do* + NP + VP (addition of *do*)
4. Did the girl laugh? (question transformation)

Transformations may consist of addition, deletion, rearrangement, substitution, and combination. Following are some transformed sentences.

(NEGATIVE) The boy does not sell papers.
(PASSIVE) Papers are sold by the boy.
(NEGATIVE-PASSIVE) Papers are not sold by the boy.
(QUESTION) Does the boy sell papers?
(NEGATIVE-QUESTION) Doesn't the boy sell papers?
(NEGATIVE-PASSIVE-QUESTION) Aren't papers sold by the boy?

Other common transformations include:

(REQUEST) You do the dishes. $\longrightarrow$ Do the dishes.
(THERE) A cat is on the bed. $\longrightarrow$ There is a cat on the bed.
(POSSESSIVE) John has a cat. The cat is lively. $\longrightarrow$ John's cat is lively.

GRAMMAR CONCEPTS IN THE ELEMENTARY PROGRAM

Concepts such as the following are frequently a part of the content of elementary school language arts textbooks.

I. Phonology
   A. Sounds and their representations
   B. Intonation
II. Morphology
   A. Root words, prefixes, suffixes
   B. Inflected forms, affixes, functional shifts
III. Form class and structure words
   A. Form classes
      1. Nouns (forms, positions, functions, kinds)

        a. Noun phrases (functions of)
        b. Pronouns (personal, indefinite, etc.)
    2. Verbs (forms, positions, functions, kinds)
        a. Verb phrases (functions of)
        b. Tense (present, past, etc.)
        c. Voice (active, passive, etc.)
    3. Adjectives (forms, positions, functions)
    4. Adverbs of location, time, manner (forms, positions, functions)
    B. Function (or structure) words
        1. Determiners (articles, possessives, demonstratives)
        2. Prepositions
        3. Auxiliary verbs and modals
        4. Conjunctions (coordinating and subordinating)
        5. Intensifiers (or qualifiers)
IV. Syntax
    A. Word order
    B. Component parts of a sentence
        1. Subject
            a. Types of
            b. Subject patterns
        2. Predicate
            a. Types of
            b. Predicate patterns
    C. Subject-verb agreement
    D. Sentence types
    E. Sentence patterns
    F. Transformations (negative, interrogative or question, passive, etc.)
    G. Modification (by noun, adjective, verb, adverb)
    H. Expansion (coordination, subordination)

Formal analysis, with its attendant concentration upon terminology, is not the best grammar curriculum for young children.

The preceding list might seem to suggest a heavy classroom emphasis upon analysis and formalistic procedures. This is not the case. The most effective program for the elementary school emphasizes *experience* (use) with language. Formal analysis, with its attendant concentration upon terminology, is not the best grammar curriculum for young children.

Under any circumstances, the instructional program should take into account such important understandings and concepts as the following:

1. The child begins school with an intuitive grasp of language structure.
2. Spoken expression is a distinct form of communication (as contrasted with written expression).
3. A distinction needs to be maintained between grammar (description and analysis of the language) and usage (conventions of language; choice of forms appropriate to content and situations).
4. Despite slow but constant change, English is systematic in many ways and recurrent patterns abound. However, there are irregular features of the language.
5. The structure of each language is unique and must be described in its own terms. For example, English possesses a flexible nature: sentence elements may be manipulated to evolve different ways of saying the same thing or to express subtle shades of meaning.
6. No single system for describing the language is adequate in all respects.
7. Advances in linguistic scholarship will need to be studied in terms of curriculum revision.

INSTRUCTIONAL PROCEDURES

In contrast to the traditional approach of "explaining it to the child" (which gives little encouragement to his thinking or to his originality), the recommended strategy for teaching grammar involves permitting a child to make his own observations, share his findings, and finally form his own tentative generalizations or "rules." As the reader analyzes the content of the following worksheets, he will notice that they are based on deductive reasoning. (Only the lesson plan on pronouns uses an inductive method.) Not only does the pupils' active involvement in the development of the lessons create a good learning situation, but their participation also enables the teacher to gauge their grasp of the situation.

Most of the materials in this section would be more appropriate for the upper school years, except the few noted as suitable for the early school years. Moreover, most of the lessons are of a "summary" or "review" nature, involving more concepts than would normally be presented at any one time in an initial presentation. The purpose of these worksheets is to acquaint the reader with grammar concepts commonly presented during the elementary school years.

Parts of speech

• *Noun*

Worksheet: Noun

Examine the five sentences.
Decide how the underlined words
are alike or different.

The <u>boy</u> sings well.
The <u>girls</u> ran fast.
The <u>man's</u> coat was gray.
His <u>glasses</u> were broken.
Those <u>cats</u> purr loudly.

1. What do the -s or -es added to some of the words indicate?
2. What does the -'s added to one of the words indicate?
3. How many of the words are preceded by the words *the, his,* or *those?*
4. Can you make a statement about some of the words "fitting" in certain positions, but not in others?
5. Would any of the underlined words fit in the blank below? The _____ was (were) lost.
6. Would any of the underlined words sensibly replace the word *oogle* in the sentence *The oogle ran fast?*
7. The underlined words are all nouns. Try to make a statement that defines a noun.
8. Write five sentences and underline the nouns in each sentence.

• *Pronoun*   Pronoun study includes personal, possessive, indefinite, and demonstrative pronouns. The following lesson plan is a systematic or mastery type, which would follow exploratory lessons on the pronoun.

LESSON PLAN: Pronouns and Their Antecedents

Performance Objective:
   Given pronouns and their antecedents in written expression, the pupil indicates his understanding of the concept by stating the sentence relationship it signals.

Pretest:
   Give the pupils sentences such as, *The boy is a good student. He is also a fine athlete.* (At least five such sets of sentences should be used.) Ask the pupils to indicate to whom or what the *pronoun* refers in each case. The idea to get across here is that the pronoun can stand for and mean the same thing as another word in the preceding sentence. Criterion for mastery is 100 percent.

Teaching Suggestions:
   List at least five pronouns on the chalkboard: e.g., *they, he, himself, it.* Ask for their meanings. Establish the fact that these words stand for other referents.

Mastery or Posttest Suggestions:
   1. Write about five sets of sentences of this nature: *The boy is a good student. _____ is also a fine athlete.* Give instructions to fill in the blanks with a pronoun.
   2. The suggestions provided in the pretest may also be used for the posttest.

Reteaching Suggestions:
   1. Prepare short sentences in which each pronoun has an antecedent. Circle each pronoun and ask the learner to underline the word for which it stands.
   2. With sentences such as those suggested above, underline the antecedents and ask the pupils to circle the pronouns that stand for the antecedents.
   3. Write some pronouns of the type mentioned in "Teaching Suggestions." Ask for things each pronoun could stand for.

• *Verb*

Worksheet: Verb

The children walk to school each day.

1. Use Kevin's suggestion to show that you understand what he means.
2. Write three other forms of *walk*, as Sue suggested, to show that you understand her idea.
3. Does Sue's idea work with a word such as *move*?
4. Can *walk* be used in the blank in Jenny's test sentence?
5. To what form class does the word *children* belong? How does this help suggest the function of *walk*?
6. What other clues are provided that might help Jim to tell if *walk* is a verb?
7. Write two sentences to show that some words (such as *walk*) can be used as either nouns or as verbs.
8. Does an irregular verb, such as *see*, form the past by adding *-d* or *-ed* to the stem?
9. How many forms do the following irregular verbs have? What are they?

Stem	Sing.	Past	Pres. Part.	Past Part.
set	sets	set	setting	set
sit	sits	sat	sitting	sat
do	does	did	doing	done

10. What is the difference between regular and irregular verbs?

The same procedure as the one on page 343 can be used to explore other verb concepts, such as:

1. Kinds of verbs (action, auxiliary, linking)
2. Forms of auxiliaries (helping verbs)
    a. *Be: be, am, are, is, was, were, being, been*
    b. *Have: have, has, having, had*
    c. Modals: *can, could shall, should, will, would, may, might, must*
        When used as an auxiliary, forms of *be* are followed by a present *(-ing)* participle or a past *(-en)* participle; forms of *have* are followed by a past participle; and forms of modals are followed by the simple form (stem) of the verb.
3. Comparing past participle and past tense (Most -*en* forms are the same as the -*ed* form.)
4. Tense and number (sing. or plur.) of auxiliaries

• *Adjective*

Worksheet: Adjective

What other words could replace the underlined words to make sense in these sentences?
A.   The <u>old</u> house was vacant.
B.   The house is very <u>old</u>.

1. Both sentences above begin with *the,* which is an article. What is a more general term for *article*?
2. Between what two kinds of words does the adjective come in sentence A?
3. What is the function or purpose of an adjective?
4. One test for an adjective is if it can fill both blanks in the following sentence:
        The _____ toast is very _____.
5. Another test for an adjective is whether it can be compared. For example:

Positive	*Comparative*	*Superlative*
old	older	oldest
beautiful	more beautiful	most beautiful

Use this test for the words you substituted for the underlined words in sentence A.

6. In sentence B, the verb *is* is a linking verb—its function is to join the subject *(house)* with the adjective *(old)* that follows. Other linking verbs are *become, seem, remain.* Which words are used as adjectives below?
   a. The roses are beautiful.
   b. The water seems warm.
   c. John became tired.
7. In what two positions may adjectives be found?
8. In sentence B, the adjective follows the word *very.* Another test is to insert the word *very* before the underlined words in the following sentences to see if the sentences still make sense. Which underlined word is an adjective?
   a. The <u>three</u> boys went on a picnic.
   b. The <u>noisy</u> boys went on a picnic.
9. Use the three adjective tests to see if any of the underlined words in the following sentences can be classified as adjectives.
   a. The <u>toy</u> car is red.
   b. The <u>galloping</u> horse ran away.
   c. The <u>stolen</u> car was found.
   d. The <u>blond</u> girl is my sister.

• *Adverb*

Worksheet: Adverb

Which of the words in parentheses would fit the blank in the sentence below?

> Betty did her work _____.
> (quickly, yesterday, pretty, here)

1. Which of the four words make sense in the sentence?
2. Which one tells "How?" "In what way?" "Where?" "When?"
3. Can any of the adverbs *(quickly, yesterday, here)* be compared as adjectives are compared?

4. Does the adverb come before or after the verb in the sentence?
5. What statement can you make about the position of adverbs after studying these examples?
   a. Joe opened the package *carefully*.
   b. Joe *carefully* opened the package.
   c. *Carefully*, Joe opened the package.
6. Here is a test for adverbs: *Tom rode his bike* _____. What are some adverbs that could be used to fill in the blank?
7. Use the three adverb tests suggested in exercises 2, 3, and 4 to see that the words you suggested in the test sentence in item 6 are used as adverbs.
8. One pupil said he sometimes had trouble telling an adjective from an adverb. He studied the sentences below written by the teacher.

     The girl is <u>tall</u>.
     The girl is <u>here</u>.

   Which underlined word is an adjective and which is an adverb?

     The candy is <u>hard</u>.
     Bill plays <u>hard</u>.

Note: The concept of modification has many different ramifications. For example, in addition to nouns being modified by adjectives, nouns can also be modified by nouns, present participles, past participles, and prepositional phrases. Verbs, which are modified by adverbs, can also be modified by prepositional phrases, adjectives, nouns, and other verbs. See the following sentences:

Joe ran *rapidly*. (adv.)
Joe ran *over the bridge*. (prepositional phrase)
Joe ran *home*. (noun)
Joe came *running*. (verb)

• *Preposition*

Worksheet: Preposition

After Tim made his statement, three children asked questions about prepositions. What do you think is the answer to each question?

1. Write nine sentences using a different preposition in each one.
2. Amy wrote this sentence to help her answer her question:
    > Mother went to the store.

    Write enough sentences to help you decide upon an answer.
3. One classmate said *no* to Amy's question and wrote these sentences on the chalkboard:
    > Soon Bill came *by*.
    > Then he came *in*.

    What would you say about Amy's example sentence?
4. What is the noun in the prepositional phrase in Phyllis's sentence?
5. Why is it important to know the answer to Phyllis's question?
6. One pupil wrote this sentence to help him answer Tony's question:
    > The car in the garage was bright red.

    What noun is modified by the prepositional phrase? What is the position of this noun in relation to the prepositional phrase?

Basic sentence patterns

In the beginning school years, sentence patterns should be taught by example rather than by linguistic description. The order and function of words in a sentence can be informally taught by starting with a simple statement such as *The car stopped.* Very young children enjoy the challenge of describing *where, when, how,* and *why* the car stopped. Children can learn to sense the "nounness," "verbness," and descriptive qualities of words as the words function in expressing their ideas.

The following two worksheets provide some indication of the nature of the content found in recently published language arts textbooks for primary level children.

Worksheet: Subject-Predicate

Question of the Day: Using the sets of words in box A below, how many sentences can you make? For B? For C?

A

NP	VP
Snow	is green.
Bill	was hit by the ball.
The tree	is sweet.
He	is white.
Sugar	works.

B

NP	VP
Girls	ride horses.
Some cars	are pretty.
They	are here.
The cats	work.
The boys	are in the street.

C

NP	VP	
He	sings	a car.
A bird	were	down the street.
The ducks	wants	outside.
A girl	are	softly.
They	lives	happy.

The preceding exercise lends itself to exploring other sentence concepts. Following are some suggested concepts.

1. Word order
2. A simple subject may contain more than one noun; a simple predicate may contain more than one verb.
3. Complete subject, complete predicate
4. Functions of subject (doer of action, receiver of action)
5. Predicate types (intransitive verb, transitive verb): After the verb *be*, the following may be used: adverb, prepositional phrase, adjective, subjective complement
6. Subject-verb agreement
7. Transformations

Worksheet: Sentence Classification

A. Close the door, Jim.
B. Did you read about the exciting race?
C. Bill has a new red bicycle.
D. What a beautiful day!

1. How would you answer the question asked by Mr. Garcia?
2. Which of the four sentences is the same type as the teacher's?
3. What punctuation mark is used at the end of sentence B?
4. Sentences A and C both end with a period. How do they differ from one another?
5. What does the exclamation point used at the end of sentence D suggest?
6. Find four sentences in your textbook or another book that represent the four types given above.
7. Write sentences to illustrate the four sentence types (A, B, C, and D).
8. One pupil said she thought that an exclamation mark should be used at the end of sentences A and C. What might she have been thinking?
9. Another pupil said, "Not every sentence that asks a question should have a question mark at the end. If it is said with great feeling, an exclamation mark would be used instead." Is she correct?
10. Write a statement about each of the following types of sentences:

    statement (sentence C above)
    question (sentence B above)
    exclamation (sentence D above)
    command (sentence A above)

In the upper elementary school years, children can be asked to identify sets of sentences according to patterns or build fragments into sentences according to some particular pattern, such as the ones listed below.

S-V (subject-verb)
S-linking verb-adj./adv.
S-V- direct object
S-V- two subjective complements
S-linking verb-subjective complement

Exercises can be developed that compare and contrast sentences having different patterns and excerpts from articles and stories may be examined from the point of view of sentence patterns used. Excerpts from the child's own writings may be studied for examples of sentence patterns.[7]

7. Pose Lamb, *Linguistics in Proper Perspective* (Columbus, Ohio: Merrill, 1967), pp. 109–120.

Sentence expansion/restructuring

In the early elementary school years, children enjoy taking a basic NP and VP and testing various sentence patterns. The basic subject and verb, such as *Rabbits hop*, can be expanded. To these, they can add descriptive elements. The NP may be expanded to *The big gray rabbits* and the VP may be expanded to *hop merrily through the grass*. Thus, the expanded sentence would read *The big gray rabbits hop merrily through the grass*. Such basic subject-verb elements as the following may be used for expansions:

Car crashed
Horse galloped
Boy climbed

In the upper elementary school years, pupils can be asked to write sentences following basic patterns and to experiment with expanding these basic patterns through modification elements. For example, *The girl saw a dog*, can be expanded into *Yesterday, the tall girl, who lives next door, saw Bob's dog, Spotty, in the park*. They can discover open points in the basic patterns where subordinate

Expanding the basic sentence is the easiest way of showing children the structure of sentences.

units can be inserted. For example, modifiers can be inserted before the subject, after the subject, and after the verb.

Sentence-combining (combining two or more related sentences into one sentence) can start in the primary years. One method of teaching this is for the teacher to display sentences, such as the following, on an overhead projector.

The boy fell down.
The boy was young. $\longrightarrow$ The young boy fell down.

After he has asked the children to notice what was done, the teacher may orally give a series of such short sentences, e.g., *The dress had pockets. The dress was red*, etc., and call for individual answers. When the point seems clear to most of the children, they may respond in unison.

At another time, attention could be directed at compounding the predicate, utilizing a procedure similar to that suggested below.

The man put out the light.
The man went to bed. $\longrightarrow$ The man put out the light and went to bed.

Without knowing the term *relative clause*, children can respond to combining sentences like the ones below.

The dog barked.
The dog was sitting at the door. $\longrightarrow$ The dog, who was sitting at the door, barked.

Additional combining could include:

Possessives:
Bill has a dog.
The dog is gentle. $\longrightarrow$ Bill's dog is gentle.

Appositives:
Clara is my youngest sister.
She went to California. $\longrightarrow$ Clara, my youngest sister, went to California.

At the intermediate level, coordinators, subordinators, and sentence connectors may be used. Coordinators (also called coordinating conjunctions) include such words as *and, but, for, nor, or, yet*. Some pairs (*both . . . and, either . . . or, neither . . . nor, not only . . . but also*) are sometimes called correlatives. Subordinators (also called subordinating conjunctions) include such words as *after, as if, because, before, if, since, so that, than, unless, until, when, whether, while*. Sentence connectors are words like *however, moreover, nevertheless*, and *therefore*.

Coordination:

The phone rang. ⎫
No one answered it. ⎭ ⟶ The phone rang, but no one answered it.

Subordination:

The wind was strong. ⎫
The leaves fell to the ground. ⎭ ⟶ The leaves fell to the ground because the wind was strong.

Sentence connection:

I am not going to the movie. ⎫
I am going to the dance. ⎭ ⟶ I am not going to the movie; however, I am going to the dance.

A sample instructional worksheet on combining related ideas into one sentence follows.

Worksheet: Sentence-Combining

A. The boys were planning a trip. ⎫ ⟶ _____
    The boys were excited about it. ⎭

B. Bill rode his bike to school today. ⎫ ⟶ _____
    Joe rode his bike to school today. ⎭

C. They walked up the hill. ⎫ ⟶ _____
    They walked down the hill. ⎭

D. Sue likes to visit her uncle. ⎫ ⟶ _____
    He lives in Arkansas. ⎭

E. The television program was good. ⎫ ⟶ _____
    It was too long. ⎭

F. Joe ate three sandwiches. ⎫ ⟶ _____
    He was hungry. ⎭

The set of sentences shown above was written in one class. Later the children rewrote the sets of related ideas into six single sentences.

1. John noticed that each sentence in A had the same subject. He used the subject only once in writing one sentence that combined the related ideas of the two sentences. What might the one sentence have been?

2. B was rewritten by combining the subjects of the two sentences. What was the combined sentence?
3. C was rewritten by combining the endings of the two sentences. What might be the one sentence?
4. Agnes rewrote D as one sentence, replacing one of the words with *who*. What word might that be?
5. Tony used a coordinating conjunction, such as *and, but, for, nor, or, yet*, in connecting the sentences in E. Which conjunctions best show the relationship between the two closely related ideas?
6. Ben used a subordinating conjunction, such as *after, because, before, since, unless, until, while*, to connect the sentences in F. Which conjunctions best show the relationship between the two closely related ideas?

Children need lots of practice with many different kinds of sentences. Following is an activity that even the very young child finds enjoyable.

Cut out seven cards and write each of the following words on a separate card: *Sometimes I eat when I go home*. Mix the cards, giving one each to seven children, asking them to come to the front of the room and make as many different sentences as they can. There are many different ways that these seven words can be combined. The purpose of this activity is to show the children that sentence elements can be reordered.

Another way to show how sentences are structured is through transformations. After experience with putting together active sentences, pupils can soon detect how active sentences are transformed into passive ones. *The boy bought an apple*, becomes *An apple was bought by the boy*. (The object is transferred into the subject position, the subject is moved to the end of the sentence after the word *by*, and a form of the verb *to be* is inserted before the past participle of the original verb.) Likewise, the statement can be transformed into a question, *Did the boy buy an apple?* or *Was an apple bought by the boy?* Negative transformations may be made: *The boy did not buy an apple*.[8]

Following is a lesson idea on transformations.

---

8. For other activities and strategies on applied linguistics see Samuel J. Keyser, "The Role of Linguistics in the Elementary School Curriculum," *Elementary English* 47 (January 1970): 39–45; and Bernare Folta, *Three Strategies for Revising Sentences* (Terre Haute: Indiana Council of Teachers of English, n.d.).

Worksheet: Sentence Transformations

A. He is a good student. $\longrightarrow$ He is not a good student.
B. He ate the hotdog. $\longrightarrow$ He did not eat the hotdog.
C. He is leaving. $\longrightarrow$ Is he leaving?
D. He left. $\longrightarrow$ Did he leave?
E. You wash the car. $\longrightarrow$ Wash the car.
F. You are friendly. $\longrightarrow$ Be friendly.
G. A box is in the cabinet. $\longrightarrow$ There is a box in the cabinet.
H. John found a dime. $\longrightarrow$ A dime was found by John.
I. Mr. Gray has a new car. } My softball hit Mr. Gray's new
    My softball hit the car. } $\longrightarrow$ car.

1. How does the sentence on the right in A differ from the one on the left.
2. Which is the negative sentence in B? What was done to the other sentence in B to derive the negative sentence?
3. What words have been rearranged to change the first sentence in C to a question?
4. What helping verb has been added to rewrite the sentence in D? What was done about the verb form?
5. What word is left out in the sentence on the right in E, which is a request?
6. In the second sentence in F, how has the verb been changed?
7. What was done in rewriting the sentence in G?
8. Three things were done in rewriting the sentence in H. What were they?
9. In I, two sentences have been combined into one sentence. What was done to indicate the possessive form of *Mr. Gray* in the sentence on the right?
10. Transform each of the following sentences as directed:

    Tom is here. $\longrightarrow$ (NEGATIVE)
    Jim threw the ball. $\longrightarrow$ (NEGATIVE)
    She is singing. $\longrightarrow$ (QUESTION)
    Jane laughed. $\longrightarrow$ (QUESTION)
    You rake the leaves. $\longrightarrow$ (REQUEST)
    You are helpful. $\longrightarrow$ (REQUEST)
    A pencil is in the desk. $\longrightarrow$ (THERE)
    A baseball broke the window. $\longrightarrow$ (PASSIVE)
    Bill has a dog. }
    My book fell on the dog. } $\longrightarrow$ (POSSESSIVE)

SELECTED REFERENCES

General Professional

Anderson, Paul S. *Language Skills in Elementary Education.* 2d ed. New York: Macmillan, 1972, chapter 8.

Boyd, Gertrude. *Teaching Communication Skills in the Elementary School.* New York: Van Nostrand Reinhold, 1970, chapter 9.

Corcoran, Gertrude B. *Language Arts in the Elementary School: A Modern Linguistic Approach.* New York: Ronald, 1970, chapter 9.

Greene, Harry A., and Petty, Walter T. *Developing Language Skills in the Elementary Schools.* 4th ed. Boston: Allyn and Bacon, 1971, chapter 11.

Lamb, Pose. *Guiding Children's Language Learning.* 2d ed. Dubuque, Iowa: William C. Brown, 1971, chapter 12.

Smith James A. *Adventures in Communication: Language Arts Methods.* Boston: Allyn and Bacon, 1972, chapter 12.

Strickland, Ruth. *The Language Arts in Elementary School.* 3rd ed. Lexington, Mass.: D. C. Heath, 1969, chapter 15.

Specialized

Department of Public Instruction. *Teaching English Language and Grammar.* Madison: Wisconsin English Language Arts Curriculum Project, 1967.

Francis, W. Nelson. *The Structure of American English.* New York: Ronald, 1958.

Hill, Archibald A. *Introduction to Linguistic Structures: From Sound to Sentence in English.* New York: Harcourt, Brace and World, 1958.

Hook, J. N., and Crowell, Michael G. *Modern English Grammar for Teachers.* New York: Ronald, 1970.

Pooley, Robert C. *Teaching English Grammar.* New York: Appleton-Century-Crofts, 1957.

Roberts, Paul. *Modern Grammar.* New York: Harcourt, Brace and World, 1968.

Sledd, James. *A Short Introduction to English Grammar.* Chicago: Scott Foresman, 1959.

Stageberg, Norman C. *An Introductory English Grammar.* New York: Holt, Rinehart and Winston, 1971.

Thomas, Owen P. *Transformational Grammar and the Teacher of English.* New York: Holt, Rinehart and Winston, 1965.

Spelling

OBJECTIVES	PERFORMANCE RESPONSES
1. **To differentiate the role of utility and sound-letter relationships in the spelling program**	1. Prepare a list of spelling words on the basis of some phoneme-grapheme relationship. State the generalization to be achieved.
2. **To identify the major features of the test-study and corrected-test technique**	2. Present a list of spelling words to a class or small group of children, utilizing these techniques.
3. **To plan methods to study spelling words**	3. Prepare a set of four to six study exercises to accompany the spelling list in Performance Response 1 or 2.
4. **To describe procedures for instilling purpose and desire to be a good speller**	4. Prepare a spelling game, stating objectives, materials, and procedures.
5. **To introduce important spelling rules**	5. Using an inductive approach, teach one important spelling rule to a small group (children or peers).
6. **To demonstrate a proofreading strategy**	6. Prepare material that would be required for one of the fourteen lessons presented in the proofreading unit.
7. **To determine a child's spelling level**	7. Using one of the suggested ways, determine the level of spelling material appropriate for an individual.
8. **To design modifications for types of spellers (poor, average, and above-average)**	8. a. Check the learning modality of a child. b. Collect written papers from an elementary school classroom. Analyze the most common kinds of errors. c. Plan a systematic, or mastery, lesson for one of the kinds of errors located. d. Prepare a set of three to four learning center activities for the kind of error.

SELECTION AND GRADE PLACEMENT OF WORDS

Most of the word lists in today's spelling books are structured to make full use of two important factors: (1) frequency of use in writing and (2) sound-letter relationships. These factors are discussed in turn.

Utility

Some spelling programs are based on the theory of social utility: that is, words are selected on the basis of their importance in the different spelling activities of life. There are a number of investigations about spelling vocabulary, but perhaps the most important one is by Ernest Horn.[1] He studied letters of bankers, excuses written to teachers by parents, minutes of organizations and committee reports, letters of application and recommendation, the works of well-known authors, letters written in magazines and newspapers, personal letters, business letters—a total of five million words and 36,000 different words. From this, the most important 10,000 words were selected as basic words, according to these criteria:

1. The total *frequency* with which the word was used in writing
2. The *commonness* with which the word was used by everyone, regardless of sex, vocation, geographical location, educational level, or economic status
3. The *spread* of the word's use in different kinds of writing
4. The *cruciality* of the word as evidenced by the severity of the penalty attached to its misspelling
5. The probable *permanency* of the word's use
6. The *desirability* of the word as determined by the quality of the writing in which it was used

---

1. Ernest A. Horn, *A Basic Writing Vocabulary—10,000 Words Most Commonly Used in Writing,* University of Iowa Monographs in Education, First Series, no. 41 (Iowa City: University of Iowa Press, 1926). See also Henry A. Rinsland, *A Basic Vocabulary of Elementary School Children* (New York: Macmillan, 1945). This is a basic writing vocabulary as determined by words used most often by children in and out of school situations; and James A. Fitzgerald, *A Basic Life Spelling Vocabulary* (Milwaukee, Wis.: Bruce Publishing Co., 1951). This is a basic spelling vocabulary of 2,650 words that are used most often by children in and out of school and words that will be used by them as they develop from childhood to adulthood. This list is of great value to curriculum makers; it should interest those who wish to evaluate the vocabularies of their spelling books or who desire a valid core spelling vocabulary.

Spelling with flannel-board letters provides another mode of learning for some children.

Horn suggested the following criteria for introducing these basic words in the spelling program:

1. The most important words should be introduced in the beginning grades and those of lesser importance in the later grades.
2. The simplest words should be introduced in the beginning grades and the more difficult words in the later grades.
3. Those words that are used often or needed in the curriculum activities of children should be introduced when appropriate.

As to the difficulty of the words presented at a grade level, words may vary greatly in the degree of difficulty for pupils. There are insufficient data in this area at present; the best answer is determined through prestudy tests for each pupil, which reveal just which words he should study among those of greatest importance. Also, there is a need to adjust the spelling load to the ability of the learner.

Justification for the social utility approach to selection and grade placement of words is evident when two factors are considered: (1) the permanence of the words and (2) the amazingly small number of words used in the average person's writing vocabulary. In attempting to determine how long the 5,000 words most commonly used in writing had been in existence, Horn stated:

Less than 4 percent of these words have come into the language since 1849, and less than 10 percent have come in since 1749. More of these words were in the language before 1099 than have come into the language since 1799.[2]

The data in figure 10.1 indicate approximate percentages of total words in writing accounted for by a certain number of words.

FIGURE 10.1: Approximate Percentage of Total Words Commonly Used in Writing

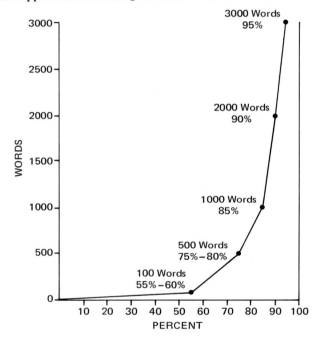

The preceding data suggest that an increase in the number of words beyond 3,000 does not result in a proportional increase in spelling power in writing done by the average child or adult.

So which words should be studied and learned? Normally, those

---

2. Ernest A. Horn, "The Validity and Reliability of Adult Vocabulary Lists," *Elementary English Review* 16 (April 1939): 134.

in a basic spelling list, supplemented by individual lists based upon needs and errors. No one spelling book can adequately fulfill the spelling requisites of written composition, but most leading spelling books contain words that are selected with care. As shown in figure 10.1, a pupil must know the spelling of about 3,000 words in order to know how to spell about 95 percent of the words he will need in his writing. Time is wasted in school by requiring children to learn words that are seldom needed in writing. The practice of using content area terms as a source of spelling words should be carefully evaluated, because these words may seldom be written by many of the children. Content area words that are important and are used frequently in writing should be presented as a part of the spelling curriculum. In making decisions as to the importance of such words, teachers should check them against word lists—Horn's, Fitzgerald's, or Rinsland's.[3] The practice of arbitrarily increasing the size of the spelling vocabulary will be frustrating and discouraging to the slow learner who should spend his energy in attempting to learn the most important and necessary words. For the same reason, using a reading vocabulary as a basic source for spelling is not justified.

Phoneme-grapheme correspondences

Some linguists have emphasized that speech sounds are central to spelling instruction. Mastery of the correspondence of sounds (phonemes) of the language and letters (graphemes) used to represent them is considered essential to the spelling process. Symbols for the smallest distinct meaningful units of sounds are called phonemic symbols. Not all linguists agree on the identification and number of the sounds and are, of course, influenced by their own pronunciation. Furthermore, there is a lack of agreement in sound symbolism—as a study of various dictionaries will quickly reveal.

A chart of sound-spelling, or phoneme-grapheme, correspondences is provided below. While the data will not be correct in all details for all dialects of English, it may be used to gain some idea of the major spelling patterns of English. (Some common variant spellings of the English sounds can be detected from this chart as well.)

---

3. Horn, *A Basic Writing Vocabulary*; Fitzgerald, *A Basic Life Spelling Vocabulary*; and Rinsland, *A Basic Vocabulary of Elementary School Children*.

CHART 10.1: English Phoneme-Grapheme Correspondences

I. Consonants

	Initial	Medial	Final
p	*pin*	sli*pp*er, pi*p*er	ni*p*
t	*tin*	si*tt*er, Pe*t*er, deb*t*or	fi*t*, recei*pt*, deb*t*
č or t∫	*ch*in, *c*ello	*c*at*ch*er, rap*t*ure	cat*ch*, ri*ch*
k	*c*an, *k*itten, *ch*asm, *qu*ick	pa*ck*er, ba*k*er, li*qu*or	sa*ck*, brea*k*, opa*que*
b	*b*in	ru*bb*er, tu*b*a	ni*b*
d	*d*in	la*dd*er, so*d*a	pa*d*, shoul*d*
ĭ or dʒ	*j*ug, *g*entle	le*dg*er, sol*d*ier, wa*g*er	ba*dge*, ra*ge*
g	*g*o, *gh*etto	bi*gg*er, ti*g*er	ra*g*
f	*f*in, *ph*oto	ba*ff*le, tou*gh*er, si*ph*on, hei*f*er	li*f*e, rou*gh*, cu*ff*
θ	*th*in	e*th*er	pa*th*
s	*s*in, *ps*alm, *c*enter, *sc*ience	pa*ss*er, ra*c*er	pa*ss*, thi*s*
š or ∫	*sh*in, *s*ure	sma*sh*er, spe*ci*ous, omni*sci*ent, o*c*ean, pa*ssi*on, na*ti*on	la*sh*
v	*v*ein	fli*vv*er, mo*v*er	wa*v*e
ð	*th*en	ei*th*er	ba*th*e
z	*Z*en	lo*s*er, bla*z*er, no*zz*le	rou*s*e, dog*s*, ja*zz*
ž or ʒ	———	mea*s*ure, a*z*ure, delu*si*on	———
m	*m*an	ha*mm*er, ta*m*er, co*mb*er	ha*m*, autu*mn*, to*mb*
n	*n*ip, *kn*it, *gn*aw	si*nn*er, fi*n*er	pi*n*, sig*n*
ŋ	———	si*ng*er, dri*n*k	si*ng*
r	*r*ed, *wr*eck, *rh*etoric	bea*r*er, hu*rr*y	he*r*, bu*rr*
l	*l*ong	fi*ll*ing, sai*l*or	ha*ll*, meta*l*
y	*y*et	Saw*y*er	sa*y*
h	*h*ot, *wh*o	a*h*ead	———
w	*w*et, (*wh*ere)	sho*w*er	co*w*

II. Vowels

iy or i	beat, beet, receive, receipt, grieve, belief, machine, ski, quay, key, scene, be, people, Caesar, happy
i or ɪ	bit, build, hymn, busy, women, give, England
ey or e	bait, mate, may, maid, grey, straight, gauge, break, weigh, rein
e or ɛ	bet, head, said, friend, leisure, many, leopard
æ	bat, laugh, have
uw or u	boot, lute, blue, flew, lose, loose, flu, fruit, through, who, canoe
yuw or yu	beauty, mule, few, you, view
u or ʊ	good, bull, wolf, should
ow or o	boat, vote, show, shoulder, beau, though, sew, yeoman, go, woe
ɔ	dog, bought, taught, taut, law, broad, water, walk
a	not
ay or ai	bite, fight, my, flies, buy, bind, guile, height, stein, eye, aisle
ah	father, ah, mirage
aw or au	about, plow, bough
ɔy	Boyd, noise, adroit
⎰ ə¹ or ʌ¹	but, blood, enough, won, love
⎱ ə²	butter, bottle, metal, pleasure, soda, sailor, cherub, barrel, carrot, spirit, ocean
ar	cart, heart
er	pair, pare, pear, there
ir	ear, here, beer
ɔr	oar, floor, war, pour, hoarse, horse, bore
ur	poor
yur	pure, Muir
ər¹	her, shirt, word, lurk, pearl, Byrd, journal

¹stressed
²unstressed

SOURCE: © 1969 by Harcourt Brace Jovanovich, Inc. and reprinted with their permission from *Reading: A Linguistic Perspective* by Ronald Wardhaugh.

• *Applications*   To some linguists, many English words are spelled in a regular manner: that is, they find the phoneme-grapheme correspondence reliable. Hodges and Rudorf report data suggesting that the phonemes of the 3,000 words most frequently used in children's writing are regularly represented by certain graphemes approximately 80 percent of the time.[4] Linguists generally recommend that the child's first experience with spelling should be with regular words. Such an approach would mean that pupils would learn to transfer the spelling of one word to the spelling of related words. For example, once a child had learned to spell *all*, he would be encouraged to discover that he can now spell many words—*ball, call, fall, hall, tall, halls, calling, called, taller, tallest.*

Hall, while acknowledging that not all of our words are written with regular or consistent spelling, would divide the spelling words into three main types according to phoneme-grapheme correspondence: the regular (like *stop*), the semiregular (like *play*), and the irregular (like *come*). He would present lessons with the "short sounds" of the vowels *(hit, set, bat, hot, but)*. Then he would contrast this with the long vowel–consonant–silent-e pattern *(met-mete, hat-hate, kit-kite, not-note, cub-cube)*; and finally he would present the "long sounds" of the vowels *(able, be, idle, go, unit)*. The consonants and the consonant blends and digraphs would be systematically and sequentially developed. Hall also emphasizes different ways of representing the same sound (the *f* sound spelled with *f, ff, ph, gh*) and different sounds represented by the same letter (as *a* in *add, dollar, May*).[5]

Worksheet: Spelling

A	B	C
mouse	crowd	below
south	flower	arrow
proud	bow	follow
pound	bowl	
sound	powder	
count	plow	
mountain		
round		

In some words, the vowel sound heard in *owl* is spelled with _____ and in other words it is spelled with _____. *Ow* also spells the _____ sound.

---

4. Richard E. Hodges and Hugh Rudorf, "Searching Linguistics for Cues in the Teaching of Spelling," *Elementary English* 42 (May 1965): 527–533.

5. Robert A. Hall, Jr., *Sound and Spelling in English* (Philadelphia: Chilton, 1961).

The influence of dialect upon spelling is an important point to consider. From recent studies, it appears that spelling errors are not similarly patterned in all dialects. The chart of Phoneme-Grapheme Correspondences is less applicable to some dialects than to others. At the least, caution should be maintained in utilizing any packaged program distributed nationwide that is based upon patterns of sound-symbol relationships. Given a spelling program based upon phonological patterns, an alert teacher should detect deviate pronunciations. The teacher should also be aware of the possibility of his own dialect varying significantly from that of the majority of his class.

Lamb presents five spelling patterns often recommended by linguists for study by elementary school children.

Pattern	Examples	Exceptions
C-V-C (short vowel)	cat drip dent	
C-V-C + e (long vowel, silent e)	save hive drove	love have give come
C-V-V-C (long first vowel)	rain leaf coat need	relief break
C-V + r (controlled, preceding vowel)	far bird clear bore	heard burn third
C-V (long vowel)	go be by	to do too[6]

Exceptions (and many are very common words) are noted above to caution the reader. After the generalization is operational for most of the children, the exceptions, their frequency and significance, can be discussed. No pattern should be taught as foolproof.

---

6. Pose Lamb, *Linguistics in Proper Perspective* (Columbus, Ohio: Merrill, 1967), pp. 79–84.

SUGGESTED PROCEDURES FOR TEACHING SPELLING

Within the specific spelling instruction period, an efficient program gives consideration to the manner of presenting new words to be taught, the pupil's study procedures, review and testing, and helping the child acquire and maintain an interest in spelling.[7]

Presenting new words

A preliminary test of the words in the lesson should be given before the pupil begins his direct study. It is important that the child make no alterations in the first spelling, for until he can spell a word correctly on the first attempt and without hesitation, he does not sufficiently know the word. This teaches him how to test his own spelling ability adequately.

• *Test-study plan*   The test-study plan of spelling instruction has proved to be very effective. It consists of the following features.

1. A preliminary term or monthly test is given to determine the general level of spelling achievement of individuals within the class.
2. A test on each weekly (or other instructional period) assignment is given before instruction is begun on that assignment. Sometimes the test is preceded by the teacher pronouncing each word as the pupils look carefully at it. Following this, the pupils pronounce the words themselves. . . .
3. The words that each pupil misspells on this pretest are identified by the child and become his study list for the lesson.
4. In learning to spell each word, each child uses the steps in learning to spell each word that have been worked out by the class or by the teacher and himself if modifications have been necessary to fit his particular needs.
5. A mid-lesson test is given to determine progress made since the pretest. A final weekly, or lesson, test shows the total progress made during the lesson and identifies words for later review.

---

7.   The host of suggestions that follow are based on a solid research foundation, as cited by Thomas D. Horn, "Spelling," *Encyclopedia of Educational Research*, 4th ed. (New York: Macmillan, 1969), pp. 1282–1299.

6. Each child keeps his own record of spelling achievement on a chart or similar device.

7. Any words that the child misspells on the final test are recorded by him in a special review word list.

8. Each child studies the words in his review list in the same manner as he studied them in their original presentation.

9. At regular intervals, testing of the review words for each child is done until all such words are mastered.

10. A final term or monthly test is given to measure the progress made since administration of the first test.[8]

• ***Corrected test technique***   According to Thomas Horn, the corrected test technique alone will contribute from 90 to 95 percent of the achievement resulting from the combined effect of pronunciation exercise, corrected test, and study.[9] If this is true, the corrected test appears to be the single most important factor contributing to achievement in spelling. This procedure requires the teacher to spell aloud slowly—letter by letter—each word administered on the pretest. The pupil follows with his eyes, marking each word either as correct or incorrect. The corrected test technique is advocated to provide maximum learning opportunities, not to make less work for the teacher. Since the corrected test appears to be so potent a learning factor, it should be utilized during spelling periods in such ways as to insure its maximum effect.

In the corrected-test approach, the child checks his spelling of each word as the teacher presents it orally on a letter-by-letter basis. This provides the child with the opportunity to use his auditory sense in developing a perception of the correct spelling. However, with the increased emphasis on the use of multi-sensory experiences in the development of a perceptual image, it seems logical to add to this procedure the opportunity to utilize the visual sense in the corrected-test approach as an aid to the development of a more accurate perception of each word. One way this might be done would be to present each word on an overhead projector, asking the child to check his spelling of the word against the word appearing on the screen. If his word is misspelled, it is checked wrong. After checking the spelling of a word, the child is instructed to look at the word on the screen

The corrected test appears to be the single most important factor contributing to achievement in spelling.

---

8. Harry A. Greene and Walter T. Petty, *Developing Language Skills in the Elementary Schools*, 4th ed., pp. 398–399. Copyright © 1971 by Allyn and Bacon, Inc., Boston. Reprinted with permission.

9. Thomas D. Horn, "The Effect of the Corrected Test on Learning to Spell," *Elementary School Journal* 47 (January 1947): 277–285.

and carefully follow along as the correct spelling is read by the teacher.[10]

Pupils' study procedures

The teacher must give careful attention to the pupils' methods of study and their use of the study period. The study period should be a learning period. Only those children who made errors in the pre-test should be required to study spelling words; but the others need not be excused from subsequent tests. Effective study requires that each child work only on his own difficulties; so locating the difficulties

A child's list of words frequently used in writing effectively relates spelling instruction and written expression.

10. Jerry N. Kuhn and Howard H. Schroeder, "A Multi-Sensory Approach for Teaching Spelling," *Elementary English* 48 (November 1971): 865–869.

must be the first step. Following is a list of steps the children might follow when studying the spelling of a word.

1. Pronounce the word clearly to yourself.
2. Carefully copy the word, noting how the sounds in the word are represented by the letters.
3. Look at your copy and say the letters twice.
4. Cover the word or close your eyes. Pretend you are writing the word on paper twice.
5. Write the word on paper without looking at your book or the copy you made.
6. Check your word. Did you spell it correctly?
7. If you missed the word, go over all the steps again. When you are sure you can spell the word, study the next word.

Effective study exercises should be utilized on the days following the pretest and prior to the final test. Following is a sample lesson plan.

LESSON PLAN: Five-Day-Spelling Plan

Monday:
Pretest and corrected test technique
Tuesday:
Give exercises that attach meaning and imagery to the spelling words. Phrasing exercises (the writing of each word in two or three phrases) are helpful. For example, if the word is *cover*, phrases might be *box cover* or *cover the answers.* Another type of exercise would be to provide the phrase and then have the pupils write only the spelling word. They could also practice adding affixes to the word, making a list of these words (*covering, covers, covered, uncover,* etc.).
Wednesday:
Written expression. Sentences may be composed, using each word in the lesson in a sentence. Sentences may be expanded or shortened by adding or subtracting modifying words. Self-testing is also an effective exercise.
Thursday:
Partners. Pupils could dictate each word to their partners and vice-versa. Then they would correct their spelling words together, recording and studying all misspelled words.
Friday:
Final test. Misspelled words are correctly written in the pupils' spelling notebooks for continued review and testing. Achievement is marked on a progress chart.

Review and testing

Review periods are needed in the teaching of spelling. Each pupil should voluntarily review words that he misspells frequently (words he has in his spelling notebook) and provisions need to be made for incidental review.

Testing is also important. There can be several tests in connection with each lesson. A single correct spelling must not be taken as a true measure of the child's ability to spell a word. Dictation is one way to test spelling. A dictation exercise, such as a group of sentences, a story, a description, or an explanation, should include the most basic and commonly used words. Words are not used by themselves in actual practice, but in context; therefore, sentence or paragraph dictation may be a satisfactory type of practice that will establish the spelling of a word as an unvarying habit. Some dictation may be given every day, even if it is only three or four brief sentences.

Pupil interest

Each child should develop a "spelling consciousness" and an interest in spelling. Following are some suggestions for maintaining spelling interest.

1. The teacher, by his attitude, emphasizes the importance of spelling.
2. The teacher uses efficient, business-like methods in teaching spelling.
3. He encourages in the class a spirit of mutual pride and co-operation in spelling achievement.
4. Each pupil is provided with a definite and efficient method of learning to spell words.
5. The teacher insists upon careful, exact, neat work.
6. Each pupil sees his progress and maintains an individual progress chart.
7. The teacher calls attention to the importance of accurate spelling in ordinary, daily life.
8. Opportunities to spell in written work are provided.

SPELLING GAMES AND ACTIVITIES

Games and activities can help children learn many basic ideas about components of the language arts. They give children variety in the way they handle a topic, allow them to actively participate in the learning process, and provide repeated exposures without becoming tiresome. Other side learnings include learning to follow directions, becoming observant, and learning cooperation. Games are most effective when they

1. meet a specific objective or purpose;
2. are planned for a small group of children; and
3. are a part of the program, rather than a "reward."

An example of a spelling game is provided below.

SPELLING RUMMY (2–4 players)

Objective:
  To reinforce the meaning and spelling of common homonyms.

Preparation:
  Make a set of twelve three-by-five-inch cards that contain homonym words (*male, bear, sun, pair, two, be, wood, meet, cent, dear, one, sale*). Make another set of twelve cards that contain their homonyms (*mail, bare, son, pear, to (too), bee, would, meat, scent, deer, won, sail*). Make a key so players can check answers as needed.

Directions:
  1. The dealer shuffles the cards and deals three to each player. He puts the remaining cards face down to make a draw pile and turns up the top card.
  2. Players check their cards for matching pairs. These are put face up on the table and a sentence given for the correct usage of each. If pairs or sentence usage is incorrect, the player continues to hold cards.
  3. The first player draws either the top card from the discard pile or one from the draw pile. If he completes a pair, he makes a sentence for each of them. If correct, he discards a card and puts it face up on the discard pile.
  4. Play continues with each player taking his turn in order.
  5. When a player wants a card below the top card in the discard pile, he can take it only if he takes all the cards above it, too.
  6. Play continues until one player is rid of all of his cards.

7. A point is scored for each matching pair a player makes with a correct usage of each word in a sentence.
8. The winner is the player with the most points after a given number of rounds have been completed.

Following is an example of a spelling activity.

LETTER COMBINATION OY

Objective:

To provide practice with the letter combination oy as in *boy*

Directions:

Write the word for each of the following definitions, making sure that the word includes the oy spelling.

a. a feeling of happiness _____
b. something for a child to play with _____
c. to disturb or irritate _____
d. to accompany for protection _____
e. something that lures or entices _____
f. to put an end to _____
g. to make use of _____
h. to take pleasure or satisfaction in _____

Procedure:

A small group (four to six) is given definitions of words that contain the oy spelling. Children try to supply as many words as possible independently; comparison and discussion of answers then may be encouraged.

One excellent source for spelling games is Anderson and Groff's *Resource Materials for Teachers of Spelling.*[11] Commercial "Spelling Learning Games" kits are also available.[12]

SPELLING RULES

The trend in the elementary school has definitely been one of teaching fewer spelling rules. However, there is, as yet, considerable dif-

---

11. Paul S. Anderson and Patrick J. Groff, *Resource Materials for Teachers of Spelling* (Minneapolis: Burgess, 1968).

12. (Chicago: Lyons and Carnahan).

ference of opinion among authorities as to the number and kind of rules to be taught.

Ernest Horn suggests that only such spelling rules be taught as apply to a large number of words and have few exceptions. For example:

1. Words ending in silent e usually drop the final e before the addition of suffixes beginning with a vowel, but they keep the e before the addition of suffixes beginning with a consonant. Illustration: *make–making; time–timely.*
2. When a word ends in a consonant and *y,* change the *y* to *i* before adding all suffixes except those beginning with *i.* Do not change *y* to *i* in adding suffixes to words ending in a vowel and *y* or when adding a suffix beginning with *i.* Illustration: *baby, babies, babying, play, played, playing.*
3. Words of one syllable or words accented on the last syllable, ending in a single consonant preceded by a single vowel, double the final consonant when adding a suffix beginning with a vowel. Illustration: *run–running; begin–beginning.*
4. The letter *q* is always followed by *u* in common English words. Illustration: *quick, queen, quiet.*
5. English words do not end in *v.*
6. Proper nouns and most adjectives formed from proper nouns should begin with capital letters.[13]

A "cloze procedure"[14] can be used for testing knowledge and application of Horn's six rules through use of such sentences as:

1. The girl was mak_____ a cake.
2. Bill was play_____ with a ball.
3. Susan was run_____ down the street.
4. Two pints is the same amount as one q_____art.
5. Do you believ_____ that story?
6. The new boy's name is _____ack.

In teaching the few important rules, Brueckner and Bond suggested the following series of steps.

1. Select a particular rule to be taught. Teach a single rule at a time.

---

13. Ernest A. Horn, "Spelling," *Encyclopedia of Educational Research,* 3rd ed. (American Educational Association, 1960), p. 1345. Reprinted by permission of The Macmillan Company.

14. Idea is adapted from the cloze procedure—use of context clues—in checking reading comprehension. In a reading passage, every "nth" word is omitted, the reader supplying the missing word. In spelling, particular letters are omitted. For further information on the cloze technique, see Eugene Jongsman, *The Cloze Procedure as a Teaching Technique* (Newark, Del.: International Reading Association, 1971).

2. Secure a list of words exemplifying the rule. Develop the rule through the study of words that it covers.
3. Lead the pupils to discover the underlying generalizations by discussing with them the characteristics of the words in the list. If possible, the pupils actually should formulate the rule. Help them to sharpen and clarify it.
4. Have the pupils use and apply the rule immediately.
5. If necessary, show how the rule in some cases does not apply, but stress its positive values.
6. Review the rule systematically on succeeding days. Emphasize its use and do not require the pupils to memorize a formalized statement.[15]

PROOFREADING

As elementary school teachers know, carelessness, indifference, and failure to proofread are major causes of errors in written work.

Proofreading exercises are designed to develop in the child a firm habit of attention to detail. Proofreading should begin early, and by the third grade, a more formal approach to proofreading can be presented.

The following Fourteen Lesson Program suggests some instructional techniques in developing proofreading habits.

I.   Introduce the idea of proofreading.
  A. After viewing a film (or something else appropriate), pupils write a paragraph reviewing the content of the film.
  B. Say to the children: "As you write, if you are unsure about the spelling of a word, put a small check above the word. Then, after you finish writing, go back and try to think of the correct spelling. If you can, draw *one* line through the word and correct it above. If you cannot, just leave the check above the word. Be sure to check back over *every word* when you go back over your paper. After you are finished checking and correcting spelling, write 'Proofread for Spelling' *under* your paragraph. I will call for all papers at the end of ten minutes."

---

15. Leo J. Brueckner and Guy L. Bond, *The Diagnosis and Treatment of Learning Difficulties* (New York: Appleton-Century-Crofts, Copyright © 1955), p. 373. Reprinted by permission of the publisher.

II. Do dictionary lessons on alphabetizing, use of guide words, finding synonyms, etc.

III. Use a Common Sounds Spelling Chart to help find unknown words. (Chart to give all major sounds and ways sounds are spelled)

   A. Order this chart from a publisher of spelling textbooks or prepare your own from a dictionary page.

   B. Give a list of unknown words to spell and have the class use techniques of check-guessing, use of dictionary, and the chart.

IV. Construct and display a How to Proofread Chart outlining techniques to be used over and over again. The items:

   A. Place a check mark over any guess *when* written.

   B. After the work is completed, go back and check guesses and correct any errors.

   C. Draw *one* line through corrected words and correct it above it.

   D. In correcting words:

      1. Use spelling rules.

      2. Use a Common Sounds Spelling Chart.

      3. Use a dictionary, making use of guide words, a file of frequently used words, or a chart of frequently misspelled words.

   E. Write "Proofread for Spelling" at the end.

V. Give exercises in looking for and correcting spelling errors in a teacher-prepared story. Include common errors for the particular grade level. Emphasize techniques.

VI. Give exercises in writing a dictated paragraph, emphasizing check guessing and all proofreading techniques. Always allow time for the proofreading process.

VII. Proofread a book report. Emphasize techniques. This is the initial opportunity for students to proofread their own work.

VIII. Give another dictated paragraph. Emphasize checking every guess, no matter how slight the guess.

IX. Give spelling-list (twenty words) exercises. Words should be appropriately difficult according to the ability of the children. Emphasize the proofreading task.

X. Proofread the second individually prepared copy—a summary of a story.

XI. Proofread a second spelling list.

    XII.   Individually proofread a friendly letter. Give time for proof-reading and point out that there should be *no* spelling errors.

    XIII.   Write an original story as a culminating activity to this proofreading unit. Emphasize techniques.

    XIV.   Continue to call attention to the chart each time children are handing in written materials (check for spelling accuracy).[16]

As inferred from the above suggestions, proofreading is a visual task which focuses upon the spelling errors of the writer. Misspelling words that appear on basic spelling lists must be rigorously overcome. Notice (steps V and VI) that pupils start with some common sets of materials and exercises and then the materials become differentiated: that is, their own (step VII). Notice the statements about "providing time" for proofreading, correction, and recopying. These activities must be an integral part of instruction—perceived as important by teachers and children. Additional emphasis can be focused upon proofreading by declaring "Special Proofreading Week" or "Special Proofreading All Written Work Day." Finally, an individual teacher, focusing on this skill, may produce some improvement, but to be most effective, there needs to be a total, school-wide program of proofreading.

GROUPING FOR SPELLING INSTRUCTION

As one observes the wide differences in spelling achievement within a single grade level of children (for example, in a fourth grade class, there is often a range of five or six grade levels in spelling achievement), it is evident that the teacher must give serious consideration to ways of adjusting instruction to meet the varying needs of children in this area of study. Fortunately, spelling lends itself well to individualization.

    Why do children have such differing levels of spelling skills? Several factors are responsible: ability, ways of learning, and rates of learning. Each factor must be considered in designing a more individual program. One type of program calls for grouping—arrang-

---

16. Carl Personke and Lester N. Knight, "Proofreading and Spelling: A Report and a Program," *Elementary English* 44 (November 1967): 768–784.

ing the children in groups for the poor spellers, the average spellers, and the above-average spellers.

Determining levels

It is not difficult to determine a child's spelling level, since evidence can be found on almost every piece of written work that is turned in to the teacher. Standardized tests are certainly unnecessary in the primary years and are not essential at the intermediate level. However, if there is need for such testing, the following tests may be recommended:

Morrison, J. C., and McCall, W. A. *Morrison-McCall Spelling Scale.* Yonkers-on-Hudson, N.Y.: World Publishing, 1923. This scale contains eight lists of fifty words each; the teacher selects any of these lists for a spelling test. Grade and age norms are provided (from first grade up to the college freshman level).

Kottmeyer, William. "Diagnostic Spelling Test." *Teacher's Guide for Remedial Reading.* Rev. ed. New York: McGraw-Hill, 1959, pp. 87–90. This spelling test will yield information about phonetic power in spelling. Results give suggestions as to spelling level and placement.

Another way of finding individual instructional levels has been proposed by Burrows and others. First, a spelling list from each grade's speller is needed. A sample of 20 to 25 words is selected from each grade's list. (If there are 250 words in the grade's total list, selecting every tenth word provides an unbiased sample of 25 words, for example.) Second, in testing the class to determine spelling levels, each child should have sheets of paper on which he can put 20 to 25 words in a column. Each word on the first-grade list is pronounced once, the pupils writing it on their paper. Third, children who spell 70 percent or more of the first-grade words correctly are tested again, using the second-grade level list. Testing continues (perhaps on other days) until all children spell less than 70 percent of a list correctly. The following distribution represents a likely occurrence in a second-grade classroom:

Number of Children	Instructional Level
5	1
12	2
8	3
5	4

This means there would be four spelling groups, with each assigned to an appropriate level.[17]

Instructional procedures

A general procedure, based upon levels of achievement, could include the following seven steps:

1. Spelling instruction would be initiated, using the test-study and corrected test (self-correction) techniques. On Monday, each group is administered a list of twenty words taken from the master spelling list. The teacher has four lists (grades 1, 2, 3, and 4) and reads one word from each list in turn. The children in group 1 spell the first word; the group 2 children spell the second word; those in the third group spell the third word; and those in the fourth group, the fourth word.

2. When the four lists are dictated, the corrected test technique is begun. Each child is given a typed copy of the words he was asked to spell (group 1 must have five copies of the list and so on). The child checks his spellings against the list, finding his own misspellings.

3. Each misspelled word is studied immediately, as previously suggested.

4. On Wednesday, the same procedure for Monday is followed. (All pupils spell the same words again even if they had no misspelled words on Monday.) If a child spells all words correctly on both days, he is finished for the week. If a child misses the same word on Wednesday that he missed on Monday, he studies it again on Thursday.

5. The test is given again on Friday for those who do not spell all words correctly on both Monday and Wednesday.

6. Additional delayed-recall checks are made monthly. (The words missed in the preceding four weeks are used again in the test-study procedure.)

7. Instruction is varied by giving the more able spellers supplementary words for spelling or they are given a new list on Fridays. For the slowest learners, reduction of the number of words per week is recommended (one-half or fewer of the lesson words).

• *The poor speller*   Seven special points should be considered in teaching the poor speller.

1. Present a limited number of words each week (perhaps five to ten).

---

17. Alvina T. Burrows, Dianne Monson, and Russell L. Stauffer, *New Horizons in Language Arts* (New York: Harper & Row, 1972), pp. 245–248.

2.   For the spelling words, use only the most common words in writing, the most basic words. These are the words that appear earliest in a graded spelling textbook series. A list proposing the words of highest frequency use is presented in chart 10.2.

CHART 10.2: First 100 Words in Order of Frequency

1.	I	21.	at	41.	do	61.	up	81.	think
2.	the	22.	this	42.	been	62.	day	82.	say
3.	and	23.	with	43.	letter	63.	much	83.	please
4.	to	24.	but	44.	can	64.	out	84.	him
5.	a	25.	on	45.	would	65.	her	85.	his
6.	you	26.	if	46.	she	66.	order	86.	got
7.	of	27.	all	47.	when	67.	yours	87.	over
8.	in	28.	so	48.	about	68.	now	88.	make
9.	we	29.	me	49.	they	69.	well	89.	may
10.	for	30.	was	50.	any	70.	an	90.	received
11.	it	31.	very	51.	which	71.	here	91.	before
12.	that	32.	my	52.	some	72.	them	92.	two
13.	is	33.	had	53.	has	73.	see	93.	send
14.	your	34.	our	54.	or	74.	go	94.	after
15.	have	35.	from	55.	there	75.	what	95.	work
16.	will	36.	am	56.	us	76.	come	96.	could
17.	be	37.	one	57.	good	77.	were	97.	dear
18.	are	38.	time	58.	know	78.	no	98.	made
19.	not	39.	he	59.	just	79.	how	99.	glad
20.	as	40.	get	60.	by	80.	did	100.	like

SOURCE: Ernest A. Horn, *A Basic Writing Vocabulary.*

Particular attention should be given to Horn's list. Three little words—*I, the,* and *and*—account for 10 percent of all the running words in print. Anyone who spells these three words correctly is automatically a 10 percent correct speller. Only ten words—*I, the, and, to, a, you, of, in, we,* and *for*—account for 25 percent of all the running words in the average adult writing vocabulary. Only 100 words—the words listed by Horn—account for 65 percent of the running words written by adults.[18]

Kyte and Neel derived what they term a *core vocabulary* in spelling to provide the minimal essentials for various instructional

---

18.   See also Rinsland, *A Basic Vocabulary of Elementary School Children* for the first 254 words of highest frequency use.

programs.[19] For example, a core list of words mastered by children who are slow learners or who have considerable difficulty in learning to spell assures better writing performances by children with these handicaps than will occur when they struggle to master 3,000 or 4,000 words. The core list was constructed through the use of the findings in the two monumental studies by Horn and Rinsland, combining the words that occur most commonly both in adults' and children's writing. (Ernest Horn detected the words used in writing by adults, and Rinsland listed the words used by children.)

Following are some other useful word lists.

Breed, Frederick S. *How to Teach Spelling*. Dansville, N.Y.: F. A. Owen Publishing Co., 1930.

Buckingham, B. R. *Buckingham Extension of the Ayres-Spelling Scale*. Bloomington, Ill.: Public School Publishing Co., 1918.

Dolch, E. W. *Better Spelling*. Scarsdale, N.Y.: Garrard, 1942, pp. 257–270.

Gates, Arthur I. *A List of Spelling Difficulties in 3876 Words*. New York: Teachers College Press, Columbia University, 1937.

3. To supplement a list of basic words—or replace it if deemed desirable by the teacher—each child should develop an individual word list. Each child keeps his own spelling notebook, with the pages alphabetically labeled. Here are some appropriate kinds of words for the notebooks:

    a. Words the child asks the teacher to spell for him in his writing tasks

    b. Words the child has to look up to use in his writing

    c. Words misspelled on papers turned in

    d. Special content words (for writing purposes, not spelling mastery)

4. Check the child's method of learning—visual, auditory, kinesthetic—and teach the child to study the word lists in the most productive way for him. The *Mills Learning Method Test* is designed to compare the effectiveness of various learning methods: visual, auditory, kinesthetic, and combined.[20] The "Gates-Russell Spelling Diagnostic Tests" have, as a part of the test, a separate section that is

---

19. George C. Kyte and Virginia M. Neel, "A Core Vocabulary of Spelling Words," *Elementary School Journal* 54 (September 1953): 29–34.

20. Robert E. Mills, *Mills Learning Method Test* (Ft. Lauderdale, Fla.: The Mills Educational Center, 1970).

Maintaining a personal spelling notebook is one excellent way to individualize spelling instruction.

designed to compare the effectiveness of the same learning methods as used in the *Mills Learning Method Test.*[21]

The study procedures on page 371 indicate ways to study from a visual or auditory mode. These include "picturing" the words by the visual learner; for the auditory learner there is heavy emphasis upon saying the word aloud, writing what he says, underlining syllables, learning unphonetic parts, and the like.

For the kinesthetic, or motor, learner, Fernald advised the teacher

21.   A. J. Gates and D. H. Russell, *Diagnostic and Remedial Spelling Manual: A Handbook for Teachers* (New York: Teachers College Press, Columbia University, 1937).

to write the word with a crayon in big letters on a piece of paper, using the "tracing" technique described below.[22] The teacher

    a.   Keeps two fingers in contact with writing (index and second finger, fingers kept stiff).

    b.   Says the word.

    c.   Says each part without distortion on the initial stroke of each syllable as each syllable is traced.

    d.   Crosses *t*'s and dots *i*'s from left to right.

    e.   Says each syllable as each syllable is underlined.

    f.   Says the word.

    g.   Repeats (a) through (f) until the child appears ready to do it himself.

The word is traced by the child, following the procedure noted, until he can write the word without the copy. Then he checks his word against the original copy. If he is correct, he writes the word again and checks it again. He is encouraged to write the word correctly two successive times. If he is unsuccessful, he should keep trying until he can do it correctly. He should always rewrite the entire word if an error is made; erasures or other corrections are not permitted. Retention of the word is checked the following day.

The kinesthetic learner should not have words spelled aloud to him nor should he be asked to spell orally. He should be discouraged from copying a word from the chalkboard but should learn it first by tracing. The parents should be informed of the procedure used at school so they may follow the same routine at home.

5.   Try to categorize the types of spelling errors made by the poor speller—not just isolated words he misspells. For a rapid method of collecting samples of a pupil's tendencies to spelling errors, Spache's spelling errors tests are recommended.[23] Two separate tests for use in grades 2 through 4 and 5 through 6 are offered, each test providing opportunities for the committing of twelve common types of spelling errors:

    a.   Omission of a silent letter *(bite ⟶ bit)*

    b.   Omission of a sounded letter *(and ⟶ an)*

    c.   Omission of a doubled letter *(arrow ⟶ arow)*

    d.   Addition by doubling *(almost ⟶ allmost)*

---

22. Grace M. Fernald, *Remedial Techniques in Basic School Subjects* (New York: McGraw-Hill, 1943), chapter 13.

23. George D. Spache, *Spelling Errors Test* (Gainesville: University of Florida, n.d.).

e. Addition of a single letter *(dark ⟶ darck)*
f. Transposition or reversal *(ankle ⟶ ankel)*
g. Phonetic substitution for a vowel *(bead ⟶ beed)*
h. Phonetic substitution for a consonant *(bush ⟶ buch)*
i. Phonetic substitution for a syllable *(flies ⟶ flys)*
j. Phonetic substitution for a word *(bare ⟶ bear)*
k. Nonphonetic substitution for a vowel *(bags ⟶ bogs)*
l. Nonphonetic substitution for a consonant *(bottom ⟶ botton)*

6. Maintain individual spelling error charts in order to further individualize the work. For example, the twelve common types of errors suggested in number 5 above could be charted showing the child's name and error type or types.

7. Maintain a high level of interest and a desirable attitude toward spelling. On page 372 some important ideas about pupil interest, which must be convincingly presented to the poor speller, were suggested. Some evidences of interest and attitude toward spelling have been delineated by Brueckner and Bond.[24] Evidences of lack of interest include:

a. Avoidance of writing or reluctance in writing
b. No apparent effort to check the spelling of new words
c. Reluctance to use a dictionary to look up spellings about which the pupil is uncertain
d. Resentment of criticism of spelling in other written work

Evidences of a good attitude toward spelling include:

a. Experimenting by writing words on scratch paper
b. Requests of a pupil for help in spelling of difficult words
c. Proofreading to detect slips, lapses, and misspellings
d. Eagerness and promptness with which the study of new words is begun
e. Satisfaction with evidence of improvement in spelling

• *The average speller*   The average speller uses the regular instructional program. The following five specific points may be incorporated as features of the program.

1. Use pairs of pupils with similar spelling achievement; they should also have the ability to study together words missed from the

24. Brueckner and Bond, *The Diagnosis and Treatment of Learning Difficulties*, p. 353.

basic list. Again, good study procedures should be emphasized, including the corrected-test technique.

2. Maintain individual word files (or notebooks) of words that need to be studied. This file may include other content area words, the learner's personal "word demons," and other words he may want to learn to spell. Frequent review will be made of the words.

3. Check for the types of errors made. Knowledge of the most common types of errors at the various school levels is important to keep in mind. For example, the most common errors made in the primary years are:

    a. Mispronunciation *(pospone* for *postpone)*
    b. Confusion of words similar in sound *(were* for *where)*
    c. Omitting or inserting "silent" letters *(stedy* for *steady)*
    d. Transposition of letters *(form* for *from)*

Certain kinds of spelling errors require different correctional procedures. For example, when a pupil misspells a phonologically irregular word (such as *again* or *guess*), visual image should be stressed. Incorrect spelling of homonyms *(their, they're, there; your, you're; know, no)* suggests a need to emphasize meanings and perhaps teaching by word groups. Lack of knowledge of important rules may cause incorrect spelling of such words as *coming, getting, studying,* and *tired.* Accurate speaking and listening would be stressed with words such as *February, which, athlete, pin.* Visual image and pronunciation may be helpful procedures where transposition of letters could occur *(girl, goes, first, from* written as *gril, gose, frist, form). Stars* may appear incorrectly as *stors* due to poor handwriting. Errors involving double consonant letters likely can be improved through stressing visual imagery, while errors with medial consonant letters would suggest a need to emphasize pronunciation and learn about unstressed vowels.

4. Record types of errors to pinpoint specific weaknesses and give direction to individual and small-group instruction. Where needed, systematic lessons may be presented. An example is provided for one particular type of spelling error.

LESSON PLAN: Spelling—Silent e Principle

Performance Objective:
  Given a word illustrating the silent e principle, the learner spells other words illustrating this principle.

Pretest:

Use sets of words like the ones provided below as a spelling test. The word in parentheses is to be used as a model by the child as he spells the other words in the row.

(ride)	1. wide	2. slide	3. five	4. drive
(ate)	1. late	2. plate	3. gave	4. save
(cake)	1. fake	2. rake	3. shake	4. take
(home)	1. nose	2. close	3. rope	4. rode

Criterion for mastery is 100 percent correct.

Teaching Suggestions:

1. If the learner is unable to meet the criterion in the pretest, write the sets of words in vertical columns on the chalkboard. Tell him to pronounce each word and then ask: "What vowel letter is in the middle of each word in the set?" "Is the vowel sound long or short?" "What letter is at the end of each word?" "Does the letter at the end represent any sound?" Lead to the generalization that when a one-syllable word ends in silent e, the preceding vowel is a long sound.

2. Direct the learner's attention to the following arrangement of words, noting similarities and differences in spelling and pronunciation.

not	Tim	mad	hid	rid	rod	slid
note	time	made	hide	ride	rode	slide

Mastery or Posttest Suggestion:

The pretest can be used as the posttest, using the same procedures and criterion for mastery.

Reteaching Suggestion:

Direct the learner's attention to the similarities in the sets of words in the pretest.

---

5. Provide much practice or use of spelling words through written expression and maintain a progress chart to indicate improvement that is taking place in spelling.

• *The above-average speller* The above-average speller may expect several modifications in his program. The teacher may:

1. Excuse the child from formal spelling instruction if he can spell 90 percent or more of the month's or semester's word list correctly.

2. Have the pupil keep a word file for his writing purposes.

3. Permit the pupil, if he so desires, to continue into higher-level basic word lists or to study some specialized writing vocabulary (social studies, science, etc.).

4. Challenge the child in such ways as the following:
    a. Assigning bonus lists of words not included in the basic spelling list (Such words, though not used as frequently as the words selected for the basic spelling list, are important for the capable speller who is likely to do more than an average amount of written work.)
    b. Encouraging the child to make extensive use of his spelling in functional and creative writing
    c. Encouraging the child to make interesting and worthwhile diversions in the field of linguistics (For example, exercises could focus upon word origins, which are absorbing to children.)
    d. Listing spelling words that may be spelled correctly in more than one way, as *catalog, catalogue*
    e. Keeping individual lists of new words that the child would like to learn how to spell
    f. Using words in written sentences to show varied meanings of words in the spelling list
    g. Finding the root words in larger words
    h. Adding prefixes and suffixes to root words and writing an explanation of their effect on meaning
    i. Making charts of synonyms, antonyms, homonyms, contractions, and abbreviations
    j. Listing derivatives of words found in the weekly spelling list
    k. Learning the spelling of words from units of work
    l. Preparing dictation exercises for the class
    m. Learning plurals, particularly of troublesome words
    n. Selecting and marking out "silent" letters frequently mispronounced
    o. Compiling a list of words with different *gh* sounds: e.g., *enough, graph, though, sleigh, taught, night.*

(See chapter 12, page 451, for more ideas for the advanced speller.)

Other materials and suggestions

Spelling experts are attempting to provide individualized or multi-level programs, and their content should be examined for ideas. Two such commercial publications are:

Ginn Individualized Spelling Program, Ginn, 191 Spring St., Lexington, Mass. 02173.

Follett Spelling Program, Follett Publishing, 1010 W. Washington Blvd., Chicago, Ill. 60607.

Other sets of materials—more laboratories or kits—that will provide ideas are:

Continuous Progress in Spelling (one for primary and one for intermediate), Economy Co., 1901 N. Walnut, Oklahoma City, Okla. 73105.

Spelling Laboratory, Science Research Associates, 259 E. Erie St., Chicago, Ill. 60611.

On My Own Spelling (grades 3–6), D. C. Heath, 125 Spring St., Lexington, Mass. 02173.

Some teachers are trying out a spelling learning center concept, an area where activities and experiences are designed to teach a specific area of knowledge. A learning center is therefore structured and preplanned to include assessment (pre- and post-) and direct teaching-learning activities. The pretest helps uncover what skills and abilities each child possesses and where he should be placed within the sequence of tasks to be learned. After the pretest, the teacher is ready to determine the specific skills that will be presented in the learning center. Posttests are established after each major portion of the learning sequence, so that the child can be directed to additional tasks for further reinforcement and moved to a more advanced set of tasks.

In order to provide for the child's progression through the tasks with a minimum of teacher assistance, learning centers often contain: (1) a task box with directions for each task arranged sequentially from easiest to most difficult; (2) a box for individual folders for each child containing his specific tasks within the center, a record of tasks accomplished, and any worksheets he may have completed; (3) a teacher-alert box with folders of children who have reached the "check-with-teacher" point in specific directions; (4) a materials box with any materials or apparatus necessary for the learning tasks; and (5) a checking station, with answers to specific exercises or tasks that the child is to correct himself, providing immediate reinforcement of correct or incorrect work.

One second-grade teacher pretested her class and learned that all but a few had established the phoneme-grapheme correspondence in simple consonants at both the beginnings and endings of words. A few of the children had some knowledge of short and long vowels, but the majority seemed to be lacking this skill. The teacher decided to give small-group help to the children who needed consonant work and to set up a spelling learning center, beginning with short vowel sounds, for other members of the class.

She then planned some activities that included the following examples:

Activity 1, Vowels:
A list of words illustrating one short vowel phoneme-grapheme correspondence is presented (taken from a spelling book or class list, etc.). The child looks at each word, reads it, and notes the visual similarities of the words. He then listens to a tape of the correct pronunciation of each word as he looks at it. The vowel sound is then identified. The child makes a list of five words (from a class list, his workbook, his imagination—depending upon the child and his ability). With a partner, the child shares and discusses the words, noting visual and oral-aural examples of the sound.

Activity 2, Baseball:
Two teams, consisting of one to four children each, are chosen by the teacher. A baseball diamond and four markers are set up in the classroom. The pitcher directs a word at the batter. If the word has the proper vowel sound, the batter must spell it. If he succeeds, he has a hit and moves to first base. If he does not, he is out. If the word has the wrong vowel sound, the batter may call "ball." Two correctly identified balls constitute a hit. If the batter recognizes the word as a ball, calls it as such, yet spells it correctly, he has a double. Three outs and the team retires. The side with the greatest number of runs wins.

Activity 3, Crossword Puzzle:
Meanings are provided for words on the list. Children fill in the correct word in the puzzle. Correct copy at the checking station.

Activity 4, Be A Detective:
Proofread for words with proper phoneme-grapheme correspondence misspelled in a letter. This requires identification of the word and a correction of the letter.

Various games and activities of this nature may be employed for each short vowel sound. Depending on the children and their abilities, the teacher may check after each sound-spelling relationship or after all have been presented. Children are routed either to further reinforcement (possibly of a kinesthetic or tracing nature) or to new concepts or enrichment after checking. Children with knowledge of some of the sounds are placed within the sequence of tasks according to their demonstrated skills on the pretest. This center would help establish phoneme-grapheme correspondence and a process (proofreading).

SELECTED REFERENCES

General Professional

Anderson, Paul S. *Language Skills in Elementary Education*. 2d ed. New York: Macmillan, 1972, chapter 7.

Boyd, Gertrude. *Teaching Communication Skills in the Elementary School*. New York: Van Nostrand Reinhold, 1970, chapter 5.

Corcoran, Gertrude B. *Language Arts in Elementary School: A Modern Linguistic Approach*. New York: Ronald, 1970, chapter 8.

Dallmann, Martha. *Teaching the Language Arts in the Elementary School*. 2d ed. Dubuque, Iowa: William C. Brown, 1971, chapter 8.

Greene, Harry A., and Petty, Walter T. *Developing Language Skills in the Elementary Schools*. 4th ed. Boston: Allyn and Bacon, 1971, chapter 12.

Lamb, Pose. *Guiding Children's Language Learning*. 2d ed. Dubuque, Iowa: William C. Brown, 1971, chapter 8.

Smith, James A. *Adventures in Communication: Language Arts Methods*. Boston: Allyn and Bacon, 1972, chapter 11.

Strickland, Ruth. *The Language Arts in Elementary School*. 3rd ed. Lexington, Mass.: D. C. Heath, 1969, chapter 16.

Specialized

Anderson, Paul S., and Groff, Patrick J. *Resource Materials for Teachers of Spelling*. 2d ed. Minneapolis: Burgess, 1968.

Boyd, Gertrude, and Talbert, E. Gene. *Spelling In The Elementary School*. Columbus, Ohio: Merrill, 1971.

Greene, Harry A. *The New Iowa Spelling Scale*. Iowa City: Bureau of Educational Research, 1960.

Hanna, Paul R., et al. *Spelling: Structure and Strategies*. Boston: Houghton Mifflin, 1971.

Hildreth, Gertrude. *Teaching Spelling: A Guide to Basic Principles and Practices*. New York: Holt, Rinehart and Winston, 1955.

National Conference on Research in English. *Research on Handwriting and Spelling*. Edited by Thomas D. Horn. Urbana, Ill.: National Council of Teachers of English, 1966.

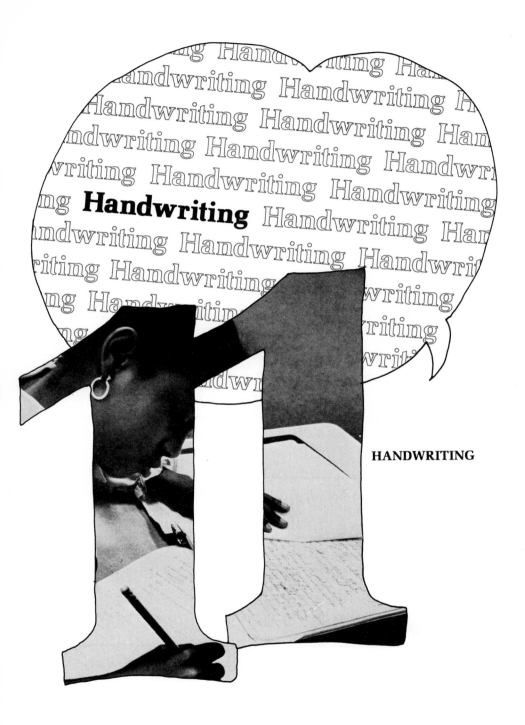

Handwriting

HANDWRITING

OBJECTIVES	PERFORMANCE RESPONSES
1. **To identify signs of handwriting readiness**	1. Recommend a list of activities for a child who lacks handwriting readiness.
2. **To become aware of at least three types of basic handwriting materials**	2. Prepare a class report on a scope and sequence chart of one commercial handwriting program.
3. **To design a manuscript mastery type lesson**	3. Utilize features of a perceptual-motor approach to teach a manscript lesson to a small group of children or peers.
4. **To gain insight into common manuscript errors and difficulties**	4. Select what might be a major difficulty in manuscript writing and outline procedures to alleviate it.
5. **To formulate plans for a cursive handwriting lesson**	5. Utilize features of a perceptual-motor approach to teach a cursive lesson to a small group of children or peers.
6. **To gain insight into common cursive errors and difficulties**	6. Select what might be a major difficulty in cursive writing and outline a set of procedures to alleviate it.
7. **To describe appropriate positions for right- and left-handed writers at a desk**	7. Demonstrate appropriate positions— seating, paper, and pencil—for right- and left-handed writers at a desk.
8. **To describe appropriate positions for right- and left-handed writers at the chalkboard**	8. Demonstrate appropriate positions for right- and left-handed writers at the chalkboard.
9. **To acquire understanding about a handwriting learning center**	9. Develop one activity for a handwriting learning center, citing objectives, materials, and procedures.
10. **To supply ideas for instilling purpose and desire to be a good writer**	10. Outline a lesson plan that focuses upon motivational aspects.
11. **To assess the merit of handwriting**	11. a. Score a child's handwriting against a standardized handwriting scale.

b. Collect written papers from an elementary school classroom. Analyze the most common types of handwriting errors and record them in chart form.

12. To probe a child's attitude toward handwriting	12. Score a child's response to the semantic differential scale on page 433.

Handwriting is viewed as a tool for communication, not as an end in itself. The goal of handwriting instruction today is to teach children to write legibly and with a purpose. Legibility calls for neatness and reasonable adherence to conventional letter forms while permitting individual variations.

Research indicates that the whole-class approach, which dominated handwriting instruction for so many years, may actually be a waste of time for many pupils. This time could be much more profitably spent in some other area of the increasingly crowded curriculum.

Increased use of the typewriter, duplicator, and other mechanical aids have not eliminated the need for handwriting; many situations in business, professional, and personal life still call for handwritten work. The teaching of handwriting is still important, and the school must not evade its responsibility for teaching children this skill.

Legibility calls for neatness and reasonable adherence to conventional letter forms while permitting individual variations.

SOME BASIC PREMISES IN THE TEACHING OF HANDWRITING

The handwriting program that attempts to meet children's needs takes into account the following basic premises:

1. The primary purpose of handwriting is to express meaning. The pupil should have a purpose for writing, even in the earliest stages of writing instruction. He may at times need help and practice on specific letters, but the basic motivation for improving his skill is a strong desire to express and communicate. (Direct handwriting instruction or practice periods need not be too long—fifteen to twenty minutes per day at the primary level and about ten to fifteen minutes per day at the intermediate level.)

2.   Because handwriting is a skill that is used in all other curricular areas, attention must be given to it as needed throughout the school day. Special handwriting periods are usually desirable to reach and maintain the desired efficiency level, but the instruction and practice provided should be based on the needs of children in practical writing situations.

3.   The objectives of handwriting instruction include helping pupils (a) recognize and accept the importance of good handwriting, (b) develop pride in and a critical attitude toward their own handwriting, (c) acquire suitable speed in handwriting and learn to adjust speed to purpose, and (d) develop habits of neatness and orderly arrangement in written work.

4.   Individuality in handwriting is to be respected, though courtesy requires enough conformity to prevent inconvenience and misunderstanding on the part of the reader. Improving handwriting does not necessarily destroy individuality. The teacher should help the child find and develop the style of handwriting that is best for him.

GROWTH PATTERNS AND READINESS IN HANDWRITING

The physical growth of children should be taken into consideration in planning the program of handwriting instruction. The growth patterns of children as they relate to handwriting may be briefly summarized as follows:

1.   Handedness has usually been established between ages five and seven. Most children in this age group, however, have not fully developed coordination of the smaller muscles of the hands and fingers. Some irregularities in handwriting may be expected, and standards should not be unreasonably high. Frequent use of large areas, such as the chalkboard, permits use of the better coordinated large muscles.

2.   Coordination of smaller muscles has improved by the time the child reaches the ages of eight to ten. Writing is reduced in size and it becomes more uniform in quality.

3.   By the end of the elementary school years, the average child can produce handwriting of good quality at an acceptable rate of speed.

Since the growth patterns of children vary, not every child will be ready for handwriting instruction at exactly the same time. The teacher should be able to identify and help the child who is ready.

Following are some indications of when a child may be taught to write.

   a. He has spontaneously shown an interest in learning to print his own name.
   b. He has developed facility in the use of scissors, crayons, paint brushes, and pencils in a variety of informal activities.
   c. He can copy simple geometric or letter-shaped figures.
   d. He has established handedness.
   e. He has participated in composing and sending written messages.
   f. He senses a personal need to learn to write.
   g. He can be introduced to a writing program that is geared to his level of maturity.[1]

Children who lack readiness for handwriting need activities that will prepare them for the experience. They need to develop not only physical readiness, but also an understanding that writing is more than a mechanical skill. The readiness criteria listed above provide clues to the types of activities that promote handwriting readiness.

HANDWRITING MATERIALS

Appropriate use of commercial handwriting materials for teachers and pupils can do much to promote interest in handwriting. Every teacher should have a teacher's handwriting manual. General teaching procedures, goals to be achieved, chalkboard writing, analysis of letters, and sample lesson plans are discussed in most teacher guidebooks. Until instructional material that is more suitable to the individualized approach proposed in this chapter is available, the teacher is obliged to *adapt* the material found in the manuals. Teacher guidebooks, too often designed for formal, whole-class work, contain helpful and important suggestions for teachers, but they are not to be used in a slavish, word-for-word manner and should not be so interpreted.

---

1. Althea Beery, "Readiness for Handwriting," *Readiness for Reading and Related Language Arts*, A Research Bulletin of the National Conference on Research in English (Urbana, Ill.: The National Council of Teachers of English, 1950). Used with permission of The National Council of Teachers of English.

The teacher should also secure a copy of the scope and sequence chart that often accompanies basic material adopted for pupil use. A close study of this kind of chart will reveal an overview of many features of the handwriting program for the various books (grades K–8):

kinds of writing	letter forms
basic habits	rhythm-fluency
paper rulings	applied uses
writing tools	refinement skills
elements of legibility	evaluation

The teacher can use this information to get a brief overview of the handwriting program at one particular level, as well as the programs in the preceding and following levels. With this information, the teacher can diagnose what should have been learned previously and what still needs attention; thus he can provide the kind and amount of instruction needed to care for the varied differences found among pupils.

The pupil's handwriting workbook is a convenient source of practice materials. The teacher, after an inventory of individual needs of pupils, may select and use the parts of the workbook that provide instruction on particular difficulties. There is little justification for assigning the same practice lesson to all pupils unless it is actually needed by all. There is less justification for assigning pages in the workbook to be completed while the teacher is busy with other chores. In such cases, the pupils are simply slavishly using "copybooks" and there is little or no instruction taking place. Published handwriting materials are useful, but they do not relieve the teacher of the basic responsibility of instruction.

TEACHING MANUSCRIPT

Manuscript is a writing form that uses simple curves and straight lines to make unjoined letters. (See page 400 for Manuscript Alphabet.) Cursive is a writing form with the strokes of the letters joined together and the angles rounded. (See page 407 for Cursive Alphabet.)

After much discussion and study of the relative merits of manuscript and cursive writing, most authorities agree that manuscript writing has definite advantages for initial instruction and that the addition of cursive writing should be made before the beginning of the fourth grade. According to Herrick, there are three major arguments supporting the use of manuscript symbols for initial instruction.[2] (1) The motor development and eye-hand-arm coordination of the young child enable him to form straight vertical lines and circles (the basic forms of manuscript writing) more rapidly and legibly than the complex cursive forms. (2) The manuscript writing symbols are similar to those the child is learning to read, so there is no need for him to learn to read two forms of written language at the time when his responsibilities for learning are already overwhelming. (3) Manuscript writing is more legible than cursive writing.

The fact that a large majority of school systems (84 to 89 percent) have adopted the manuscript form for beginning writing is evidence that these arguments have been accepted by teachers.[3]

A sample of manuscript letters recommended by one commercial system of handwriting is shown in chart 11.1.

Initial instruction

Primary level teachers are responsible for giving the child a good start in handwriting and for helping him develop desirable attitudes toward it. The following suggestions, modified from a listing by Shane, Mulry, Redding, and Gillespie, may prove helpful in overall planning for writing instruction in the primary years.

1. Beginning handwriting attempts should be characterized by large, free strokes rather than confined within narrow, lined spaces. Chalkboards, easels, or large sheets of paper may be used. Since the small-muscle control of most five- and six-year-olds is limited, the use of the large muscles in these initial handwriting attempts should be encouraged to avoid strain and fatigue.

2. Folds, between which letters are to be formed, may be made on unlined paper until children become adept at writing between lines.

3. As skill increases, lined paper may be introduced for those children who are coordinated enough to use lined paper. The beginning space between lines is usually about one inch. Some teachers like to use commercially available

---

2. Virgil E. Herrick, "Children's Experiences in Writing," *Children and the Language Arts*, ed. Virgil E. Herrick and Leland B. Jacobs (Englewood Cliffs, N.J.: Prentice-Hall, 1955), pp. 271–272.

3. Frank N. Freeman, "Survey of Manuscript Writing in Public Schools," *Elementary School Journal* 46 (May 1946): 375–380; Ada R. Polkinghorne, "Current Practices in Teaching Handwriting," *Elementary School Journal* 47 (December 1946): 218–224.

CHART 11.1: Manuscript Alphabet

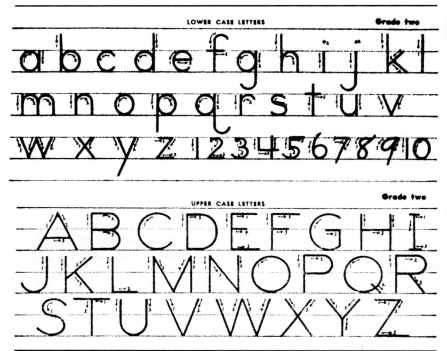

paper which has a dotted or light-colored line as a guide for the height of the lowercase letters.

4. When children are working at their desks, they should have a sample of the handwriting task before them. Since eye-hand coordination in these early stages is still developing, too much strain is imposed by looking up and down and back and forth at the chalkboard. As children become more skillful, they may copy from the chalkboard, but they should be seated near the sample and facing it.

5. When pupils begin to write on lined paper, they may use a large beginner's pencil. Research suggests that standard-sized pencils are all right to use, too, depending upon the teacher's and pupils' personal preferences.

6. It is important that the teacher's handwriting be firm, bold, and exact. Teachers who lack certainty and ease in manuscript writing should try to perfect this skill.

7. Primary rooms should have a permanent alphabet and a sample of Arabic numerals visible for easy reference. These may be printed on tagboard by the teacher or purchased commercially.

8. The teacher studies the children's written work for clues to their needs and progress. He provides practice situations to help children cope with troublesome letters. He often works with small groups on several different writing tasks and gives individual help when needed.

9. Attention should be given to spacing between letters and words in each writing experience.

10. The same general procedures that are followed in teaching manuscript forms may be employed in teaching children how to write numerals. As they do their arithmetic lessons, number pages in their booklets, write telephone numbers or dates, or make calendars, children should be taught where to start and how to form the numerals.[4]

Teachers need to be aware of the danger of allowing children to write without supervision at the beginning. Without supervision, some incorrect practices may become firmly fixed. Teachers should observe the children closely as they begin developing handwriting skills to see that proper habits are established. This will do much to eliminate the need for remedial work later on.

It is also important that handwriting procedures be individualized from the beginning. The child should be helped to evaluate his own work and to find his own errors. He should not be required to practice repeatedly forms he has already mastered. Only errors made by practically everyone should be taken up by the entire class.

Chalkboard writing

Writing on the chalkboard is enjoyable for the children and easily supervised by the teacher. Guidelines ruled on the chalkboard are helpful. Capital letters may be made about three inches high, with proportionally-sized lowercase letters. The following suggestions for chalkboard writing should prove helpful.

1. Face the chalkboard and stand comfortably.
2. Stand far enough back to allow good arm movement and to allow adequate visualizing of letters and words.

---

4. Harold G. Shane et al., *Improving Language Arts Instruction in the Elementary School* (Columbus, Ohio: Merrill, 1962), pp. 372–374.

3. Hold an eraser in the left hand for easy use (right hand for left-handed children).
4. Keep the writing near eye level. (If the chalkboard in the room is too high, a low platform or stepstool may be needed so children can reach it.)
5. Hold the elbow close to the body.
6. Use a half-length piece of chalk. Hold the chalk about one inch from the writing end between the thumb and first and second fingers. The second finger will rest upon the chalk, differing somewhat from holding a pencil. The inner end of the chalk will point to the center of the palm of the writing hand.

Recommended stance at the chalkboard and chalk-holding position are illustrated in figure 11.1 below.

FIGURE 11.1: Recommended Stance at the Chalkboard and Chalk-Holding Position

Practice through a functional approach

The handwriting needs of young children include writing their own names, addresses, and telephone numbers; writing dates; keeping records, such as a weather chart; writing labels and captions for objects, charts, and pictures; and writing letters, notices, announcements, and simple stories. A study made by Rose indicates that the functional approach to teaching beginning handwriting produces better results than work with individual letters.[5]

This approach does not rule out instruction concerning letter forms; it also takes into account pupil difficulty with individual letters. The sample lesson plan given below represents a mastery or systematic type lesson for the manuscript letter g.

LESSON PLAN: Manuscript: Lowercase *g*

Performance Objective:
Given a known word including the letter g, the learner forms the letter according to instructions for good manuscript form.

Pretest:
Write (in manuscript) the word *good* on the chalkboard. Ask the learner to write it carefully several times on his paper. If the learner's g is of medium or poor formation, continue with the teaching suggestions.

Teaching Suggestions:
1. Have the learner visually analyze the g on the chalkboard, answering such questions as: "Which part is made first?" "Which way do you move your pencil to make the circle?" "How wide is the lower part?" "Where does it finish?"
2. Have the learner make four or five g's, describing the process as he writes.
3. Ask the child to analyze g, j, and q, answering such questions as "Which two letters are alike?" "How are g and q different?" Then the learner can make g, j, and q.

Mastery or Posttest Suggestions:
The learner, after making four or five g's, may analyze his letters by answering such questions as, "Am I moving my pencil the right way to make the circle?" "Is the lower part as wide as the circle?" "Does the lower part end high enough?"

Reteaching Suggestions:
1. Instruct the learner to write the words *glad* and *age* after they have first been written on the chalkboard by the teacher.
2. Ask the learner to write the sentence *I am going to go*, after it has been written on the chalkboard.

---

5. Timothy Edward Rose, "Beginning Handwriting" (Master's Thesis, University of Iowa, Iowa City, 1950).

Perceptual-motor

Furner described a program of primary level handwriting instruction in which the perceptual-motor nature of learning is emphasized. Her main point is that instruction in handwriting should build perception of letters and their formation as a guide for motor practice, rather than emphasizing only the motor aspect. The following points summarize her specific instructional recommendations.

1. Involve pupils in establishing a purpose for each lesson.
2. Provide many guided exposures to the formation of letters: e.g., focus attention upon different aspects of the formational process in subsequent trials in order to assist the child in building a mental image of the letter form.
3. Encourage a mental as well as a motor response from each child during the writing process: e.g., have the child describe the process as he writes or have him visualize or write a letter as another child describes it. This procedure makes use of multi-sensory stimulation.
4. Stress self-correction by emphasizing comparison and improvement rather than writing many samples.
5. Provide consistent letter-form models. The teacher's writing should conform to the style adopted by the school.
6. Keep expectations regarding the quantity of writing consistent with what the children can realistically produce. (For example, Furner found that the average first grader can write only sixteen to seventeen letters per minute. This amounts to only about thirty words in ten minutes.)[6]

Frequent types of manuscript errors and difficulties

Teachers might give special attention to the following findings.

1. Lewis and Lewis reported a study of errors in the formation of manuscript letters by first-grade children.

   a. The most frequent type of error was *incorrect size*. While this error was distributed among all letters, it was more frequent with the descenders, *p, q, y, g,* and *j*.

      Examples: *p q y g j*

---

6. Beatrice Furner, "Recommended Instructional Procedures in a Method Emphasizing the Perceptual-Motor Nature of Learning in Handwriting," *Elementary English* 46 (December 1969): 1021–1030; 46 (November 1969): 886–894; and 47 (January 1970): 61–70.

b. The letter forms most frequently *reversed* were N, d, q, and y.

Examples: N b p x

c. *Partial omission* occurred most frequently in m, U, and I.

Examples: m U I

d. *Additions* were most frequent with q, C, k, m, and y.

Examples: q C k m x

e. *Incorrect relationship of parts* was generally common, occurring most frequently with k, R, M, and m.

Examples: K R M m

f. *Incorrect placement relative to line* was a common error with descenders and a less frequent error with the other letters.

Examples: See a.

g. The letter forms most frequently misshaped were j, G, and J.

Examples: j C J

h. In general, errors were most frequent in letter forms in which curves and vertical lines merge: J, U, f, h, j, m, n, r, u. Errors were least frequent in the letter forms constructed of vertical lines or horizontal and vertical lines: E, F, H, I, L, T, i, l, t.[7]

2. In manuscript form, common reversal problems involve d and b, q and g, s and y, and capital N. Most reversals can be avoided by careful initial teaching and by supervised early writing attempts. Instruction calls for emphasizing the correct beginning point, correct direction of motion, and correct sequence of multi-part letters. Chalk-

---

7. Edward R. Lewis and Hilda P. Lewis, "Which Manuscript Letters Are Hard for First Graders?" *Elementary English* 41 (December 1964): 855–858.

board practice is highly recommended for the elimination of possible reversal errors. In addition, the confusion caused by presenting similar letters such as *d* and *b* is easily reduced by separating by a week or more the teaching of these two letters. Other teaching suggestions include:

a. Associate a strong *b* and *d* sound with words as the letter is taught: *b* in *boy* and *d* in *dog*.
b. Build a close association between formation of *a* and *d*.
c. Make the letter *b*, saying "b right."
d. Associate lowercase *b* with capital *B*. (Capital B is seldom reversed.)
e. Associate formation of lowercase *h* with *b* (seldom confused with *b*).
f. Use the kinesthetic approach—tracing of letters.
g. Associate formation of capital and lowercase *c*; capital and lowercase *s*.
h. Accompany the *N* with "sharp top always to the left."

TEACHING CURSIVE WRITING

A few school systems continue to teach only manuscript writing in the intermediate years, but before the beginning of the fourth grade, the transition has usually been made from manuscript to cursive. The evidence concerning the alleged superiority of cursive writing over manuscript writing is inconclusive. It is argued that cursive writing can be done with greater speed than manuscript writing, but it has also been shown that legibility decreases with great increases in speed. Some handwriting experts assert that there is not as much opportunity for individuality in the manuscript form as in cursive. Social pressures favor the teaching of cursive forms, for many adults feel that manuscript is "printing" and not really "writing." A sample of cursive letters recommended by one commercial system of handwriting is shown in chart 11.2.

Initial instruction

There is no generally accepted agreement concerning the exact time when cursive writing should be introduced. Strickland says that the second grade appears to a number of people to be too early for two reasons. First of all, children still have not developed enough

CHART 11.2: Cursive Alphabet

CURSIVE HANDWRITING GRADE 4

A B C D E F G H I J K L M
N O P Q R S T U V W X Y Z
a b c d e f g h i j k l
m n o p q r s t u v
w x y z   1 2 3 4 5 6 7 8 9 10

THE ZANER-BLOSER COMPANY, COLUMBUS, OHIO

SOURCE: The Zaner-Bloser Company, Columbus, Ohio. Used by permission of the publisher.

muscular coordination to master cursive writing easily; therefore, an excessive amount of time must be spent learning it. Secondly, children have just reached the stage in which they can enjoy manuscript writing and are beginning to be prolific writers. Adding a new form of writing at this time cuts off interest in creative writing as it is beginning to flower and makes the whole problem of writing more difficult.[8] Herrick says that, in general, the time necessary for making the transition decreases as the transition period is postponed from second grade to third grade.[9]

There is a readiness for the transition just as there is for beginning writing. Not all pupils are ready at the same time; some will be by the middle of the second grade, others should wait until the latter part of the third or the beginning of the fourth grade. Most children, however, develop a readiness for cursive writing sometime during the second or third year of school. Evidence of this readiness includes

---

8. Ruth G. Strickland, *The Language Arts in the Elementary School.* 3rd ed. (Boston: D. C. Heath, 1969), p. 380.
9. Herrick, "Children's Experiences in Writing," p. 273.

(1) the ability to write manuscript letters well from memory, (2) the ability to read cursive writing from the chalkboard and from paper, and (3) a desire to learn cursive writing.

Many teachers begin teaching pupils to read cursive writing early in the second school year by writing a few words on the chalkboard in cursive form—names, the date, the days of the week, or a simple sentence.

Following are some differences to point out between cursive and manuscript writing.

1. In cursive writing, the letters of each word are joined and the pencil is not lifted until the end of the word.
2. The letter *t* is crossed, and the *i* and *j* are dotted after completion of the word in cursive writing instead of after completion of the letter in manuscript writing.
3. In cursive writing, spacing between letters is controlled by slant and connective strokes, not by the shape of the letters, as in manuscript.
4. Cursive writing has slant, while manuscript is vertical.
5. The writing paper may be placed straight on the desk for manuscript, while the paper is slanted for cursive writing.

Four to six weeks of daily instructional periods of fifteen to twenty minutes are usually sufficient for the transitional instructional period. Some teachers have found the following more specific suggestions helpful in initial lessons with cursive letters.

1. Start with one type of stroke, such as used in the words *cat, in, cup,* or *it,* and indicate four steps from manuscript to cursive.

a. Manuscript

b. Manuscript
(letters joined by dashes)

c. Non-slant cursive

d. Cursive

2. Begin with words containing letters that are practically alike in both alphabets except for beginning and ending strokes:

for example, the lowercase letters *a, c, d, g, h, i, l, m, n, o, p, q, t, u,* and *y* and the capital letters *B, C, K, L, O, P, R,* and *U.*

3. Give attention to letters that do not follow regular manuscript strokes, like *s* and *r;* also *b, e, f, k,* and *z,* which do not join easily with other letters.
4. Devote some time to crossing *t's* and *x's* and dotting *i's* and *j's.*
5. Use the chalkboard for much initial work. The suggestions for chalkboard writing on pages 401–402 are applicable to cursive writing as well as to manuscript; the only exception is that for cursive writing, pupils write directly in front of the right shoulder (or in front of the left shoulder, if left-handed).
6. Use pupil spelling words for practice in handwriting class, giving a much greater proportion of time to lowercase letters than to capitals. (Ninety-eight percent of the letters that pupils write will be lowercase.)

During this transitional period, the children may continue to use manuscript writing for some work, especially that done without close supervision by the teacher. Skill in manuscript should also be maintained throughout the elementary school years and used when this style of writing is more appropriate for the work being done. The continued use of manuscript even through adulthood is becoming more and more prevalent.

Later instruction

The following lesson attempts to illustrate some desirable procedures that may be incorporated in the cursive writing program. An analysis of some of the instructional procedures of the lesson follows the description.

Six questions about handwriting were listed on the bulletin board under the caption "Is Your Handwriting Good?" The six questions were:

1. Are all the letters started in the correct way?
2. Are the letters formed correctly?
3. Are the letters the proper height?
4. Are the letters a good size?
5. Are the letters and words spaced correctly?
6. Do the letters rest on the line?

The teacher began the lesson by saying, "For our handwriting study today, let's take out the papers you wrote yesterday. I looked at your papers but did not put any marks on them. Look at the writing on your papers and try to select some letters that need attention."

The children listed many different letters and after some discussion, class attention was finally centered on the capital letter G.

Then the teacher asked, "What in particular do you notice about the first stroke of this letter?" The fact that part of it is a loop was verified by consulting the capital G on the wall chart. The children watched the teacher form the letter several times as he focused upon different aspects of the process. It was then suggested that pupils compare their capital G with the one on the wall chart, followed by practice of the letter. During this time, the teacher moved quietly about the room checking with individual children.

The lowercase letter *r*, which had also been mentioned by a number of children, was considered next. It was pointed out that *r* in the words *morning* and *worm* was different from the *r* on the wall chart. The teacher wrote the word *color* on the chalkboard and asked, "If you are not careful in writing the *or*, what will it become?" Several children verbalized the formational process for *r* in their own words. All the children then engaged in a brief exercise in writing *r*'s singly and in words. The teacher next wrote a *w* on the chalkboard and stated, "I am going to read what the spelling book says on the formation of *w*."

After similar attention to the word *winter*, the pupils' attention was directed to the bulletin board. They used these six questions in an evaluation of their own writing. In reference to question 3, examples of three heights of letters were cited: *t, h, e*.

The last five minutes of the fifteen-minute period were devoted to free practice; each pupil was encouraged to work on one of the six questions that he found the most troublesome. The teacher also said, as this free practice period got under way, "I'll come around to help you." As the teacher moved quietly about the room, he talked with individual pupils.

Some instructional procedures of the preceding lesson include:

1. An appropriate mental attitude for learning was sought by involving the children in establishing the problem for the lesson.
2. The general method of instruction attempted to build perception of letters and their formation as a guide for motor practice, rather than emphasizing only the motor aspect of handwriting.
3. Perceptual abilities—accurate perception of letter forms and the various general formational features—were stressed through comparing the child's model to the desired one.
4. Children were encouraged to build a mental image of the letters and other features of writing (such as spacing and size).
5. Children were asked to watch the formation of a letter several times, the teacher focusing on different aspects of the formational process.
6. Children were encouraged to verbalize the formational process of the letters.
7. Multi-sensory stimulation was provided through visual, auditory, and kinesthetic exposure, rather than just visual, as in a handwriting book.
8. Self-correction was stressed by giving the child a means of comparing his procedures and the desired ones.
9. Emphasis was placed on comparison and improvement rather than writing numerous samples.
10. Consistency of letter formation occurred through noting letter forms on wall charts and in the spelling textbook.
11. Finally, care was taken to deemphasize speed of writing and to supervise carefully the children's practice.

After the period of basic instruction, work in cursive writing becomes more individualized. Some children will need little further practice. Others may need to work toward improving formation of certain letters, spacing, alignment, or slant.

Pen work should be introduced only when the pupils are capable of writing acceptably with a pencil. For some pupils, this may mean grade 3; for others, grade 5. The fountain pen is useful, but the ballpoint pen is favored by many persons. Handwriting is a practical skill, and it would appear reasonable to teach children to write well with the implements they will be using most often.

Frequent types of cursive errors and difficulties

The following listing is useful in helping children correct errors and illegibilities in handwriting.

1. Newland found that four types of errors are responsible for most illegibilities:
   a. Failure to close letters
   b. Closing looped strokes *(l* like *t;* e like *i)*
   c. Looping nonlooped strokes *(i* like *e)*
   d. Straight-up strokes rather than rounded strokes *(n* like *u;* c like *i;* h like *b)*[10]
2. Four letters, *a, e, r,* and *t,* cause about 45 percent of errors of illegibility.
3. The Arabic numerals 5, 0, and 2 are most often written illegibly.[11] Other problem numerals are 7, 9, and 6.
4. One research includes *n, o, s,* and *v* in the group of letters causing difficulty.[12] Still another research indicates that *h, i, k, p,* and *z* represent 30 percent of all illegibilities. Horton found that 12 percent of errors occur with *b, c, i, l, m, n, u, v,* and *x.*[13]
5. Often it is not individual letter formation, but letter combinations, that causes difficulty. Some difficult combinations are:
   b (followed by *e, i, o, r,* or *y)*
   e (followed by *a, i, s)*
   f (followed by *r)*
   g (followed by *r)*
   n (followed by *g)*
   o (followed by *a, c, i, s)*
   v (followed by *e, i)*
   w (followed by *a, c)*
6. Some teachers have found that cooperatively developed teacher-pupil charts, such as chart 11.3, are helpful in summarizing special points to check in cursive writing.

---

10. T. Ernest Newland, "An Analytical Study of the Development of Illegibilities in Handwriting from Lower Grades to Adulthood," *Journal of Educational Research* 26 (December 1932): 249–258.

11. T. Ernest Newland, "A Study of Specific Illegibilities Found in the Writing of Arabic Numerals," *Journal of Educational Research* 21 (March 1930): 177–185.

12. S. L. Pressy and L. C. Pressy, "Analysis of 3000 Illegibilities in the Handwriting of Children and Adults," *Educational Research Bulletin* 6 (September 1927): 270–273; Donald H. Rollistin, "A Study of the Handwriting of College Freshmen" (Master's Thesis, University of Iowa, Iowa City, 1949).

13. Lowell W. Horton, "Illegibilities in the Cursive Handwriting of Sixth Graders," *Elementary School Journal* 70 (May 1970): 446–450.

CHART 11.3: Handwriting Guide

a. When joining *b, c, o,* and *w* to another letter, you do *not* come to the baseline before beginning the next letter.

Examples: *be on welcome*

b. Be sure the lower parts of *y* and *z* extend the same distance below the baseline. (also *f, g, j, p, q*)

Examples: *zoo yes*

c. The letters *r* and *s* have tips that make them a little taller than letters like *o* or *e*.

Example: *rose*

d. The letter *f* is the only one that has a lower and upper loop.

Example: *fall*

e. Remember that *d* and *t* are taller than *a* and shorter than *l*.

Examples: *bad late last*

f. When you write *a, d,* and *g,* be careful to close them. (also *o, p, q, s*)

Example: *adage*

g. The letters *b, f, h, k,* and *l* have tall loops and are about the same height as capitals.

Examples: *b B f F h H k K l L*

h. When these capitals begin words, they do not join the next letter: *D, F, L, O, P, Q, T, U, W,* and *X.*

Examples: *Don Frank Louise*

i. Letters beginning with overcurves are *m, n, v, x, y,* and *z.*

Examples: *m n v x y z*

j. Letters beginning with undercurves are *e, i, p, r, s, t, u,* and *w.*

Examples: *e i p r s t u w*

k. Letters that begin above the baseline are *a, c, d, g, o,* and *q.*

Examples: *a c d g o q*

l. Letters that extend below the baseline are *f, g, j, p, q, y,* and *z.*

Examples: *f g j p q y z*

RIGHT- AND LEFT-HANDED CHILDREN

Manuscript

Wide-spaced paper is advisable for the beginning writer. It is sometimes recommended that both right- and left-handed pupils place the paper on the desk perpendicularly in front of them and pull the downstrokes toward themselves. Enstrom has found that many teachers feel this placement is not natural, interferes with visibility, causes pupils to turn their hands over on the side, tilt their heads excessively, and hunch over their work. He suggests some procedures to aid in preventing these practices. (1) Have the right-handed pupil slide his horizontally placed paper somewhat to the right on the desk. (2) Instruct the pupil to hold back approximately one inch on the pencil with one finger resting on top. (3) Be sure that the desk is not too high for the pupil. (4) Have the paper for the left-handed pupil slanted to the right at about a thirty degree angle.[14]

Cursive

Almost every classroom will have at least one and possibly two or three children who are left-handed.[15] Our system of handwriting

---

14. Eric A. Enstrom, "Paper Placement for Manuscript Writing," *Elementary English* 40 (May 1963): 518–522.

15. George C. Carrother, "Left-handedness Among School Pupils," *American School Board Journal* 14 (May 1947): 17–19.

has been developed for the majority who are right-handed. As a result, the left-handed child will often develop improper handwriting habits that impede his speed and quality. This need not happen if the teacher will make adjustments for the left-handed child. Following are some suggestions for helping the left-handed pupil.

a. Place the writing paper clockwise about thirty degrees or more. (This is more crucial than any other factor in determining success or failure in writing with the left hand.)
b. Keep the elbows reasonably close to the body.
c. Direct the blunt end of the pencil or pen so that it points to the left shoulder.
d. Hold back from the writing point at least one-fourth inch farther than a right-handed writer. (A rubber band or other marker placed around the pencil or pen at this point will serve as a reminder.)
e. Sit at a desk that is adjusted comparatively low so that it is possible to see where the point of the pencil or pen touches the paper.[16]

In addition, the authors of this book would like to suggest two other procedures that may help the left-handed writer to make the proper adjustments from the beginning. (1) The writing paper should be placed toward the left side of the desk for both manuscript and cursive writing; and (2) the pupil, if it seems impossible for him to slant his writing to the right, should be permitted to write vertically or to slant to the left.

In a few cases, the teacher may be faced with the problem of determining hand preference where handedness is not firmly established. If handedness is established, there is little justification for attempting to change it; but an unsure or ambidextrous child should be carefully encouraged to use his right hand for ease in social and work situations. If a child has established awkward left-handed habits, he should be helped to improve; and if the poor habits are firmly entrenched, a great deal of help may be necessary. In such cases, the pupil may need lots of writing practice at the chalkboard, and he may have to be excused from most of the paper work for a while so that he will not revert to old habits that seem at the time to be more efficient.

---

16. Enstrom, "The Extent of the Use of the Left Hand in Handwriting and the Determination of Relative Efficiency of the Various Hand-Wrist-Arm-Paper Adjustments," *Dissertation Abstracts*, vol. 27, no. 5 (Ann Arbor: University of Michigan, 1957).

Recommended paper and pencil positions for right- and left-handed writers are illustrated in figure 11.2.

FIGURE 11.2: Recommended Paper and Pencil Positions for Right- and Left-Handed Writers

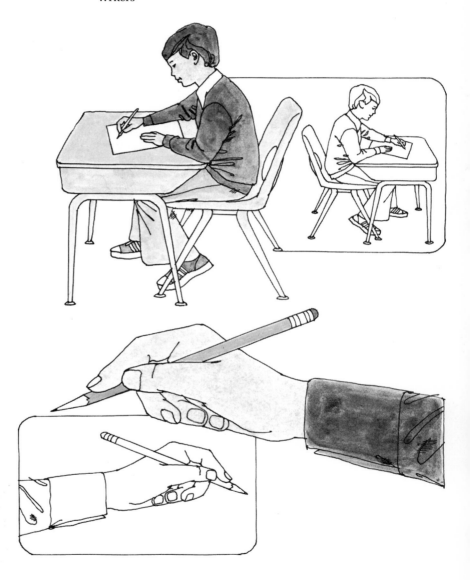

HANDWRITING LEARNING CENTER

One fourth-grade teacher decided to utilize aspects of the learning-center approach to provide some of the handwriting instruction for a period of six weeks. The materials used and some of the activities associated with these materials should provide many ideas for those interested in further development of this approach.

Activities, instruments, and materials utilized in this learning center are supported by research in handwriting done in the past decade.[17]

1. Folders were provided for each child so that the children had a specific place to store their writing activities. Inside each folder were three sets of evaluation sheets for maintaining a record of the formation of each letter of the alphabet (lower- and uppercase) as well as for each numeral. These evaluations occurred at the beginning, middle, and conclusion of the six-week period. The folder also contained a sheet for recording the score on three writings of the standard evaluation scale that accompanied the basal handwriting series. Finally, the folder contained a checklist for the pupils to evaluate their own handwriting, such as the one on page 418.

2. Three transparencies, showing the entire alphabet (upper- and lowercase and the numerals), were provided. Three sheets of paper, corresponding to the lines on these transparencies, were included in each child's folder. The child could place the transparency over his own alphabet writing and check.

Three other transparencies were available to use in checking the pupils' handwriting on regular notebook

---

17. For example, see Joseph S. Krzesni, "Effect of Different Writing Tools and Papers on Performance of the Third Grades," *Elementary English* 48 (November 1971): 821–824. (He found the use of ball-point or felt-tip pens improved performance of third-graders by 33 percent.) Two outstanding bibliographies of research in handwriting cite references that confirm other ideas proposed for the center: Lowell Horton, "The Second *R*: A Working Bibliography," *Elementary English* 46 (April 1969): 426–430; and Eunice Askov, Wayne Otto, and Warren Askov, "A Decade of Research in Handwriting: Progress and Prospect," *Journal of Educational Research* 64 (November 1970): 100–111. (Ideas confirmed in these two references include the use of evaluation scales by both teachers and pupils; the selection of appropriate practice materials based upon exhibited, individual needs revealed through diagnostic evaluation; attention to image-development of the letters and numerals; relating of letters and numerals on the basis of common elements; provision for various modes of learning—tracing, copying, "feeling"; the effects on writing performance of specific positions of the parts of the body; and the emphasis upon functional reasons for handwriting, with considerable attention upon motivational aspects.) Another interesting medium for handwriting instruction is described by Mary Anne Strahan in "Film Loops to Teach Handwriting," *Instructor* 80 (May 1971): 70–71.

Checklist: How Well Do I Write?

A. Here is how I write when I am in a hurry:
    (Write: "This is a sample of my writing when I am in a hurry.")
    _____

B. Here is how I write when I do my best writing:
    (Write: "This is a sample of my best writing.")
    _____

C. I would grade my hurried writing: (Circle one.)
        excellent   good   fair   poor
    I would grade my best writing: (Circle one.)
        excellent   good   fair   poor

D. Here is my analysis of my handwriting:
    (Put a check in the appropriate blank.)   YES   NO
    1. Slant
        Do all the letters have the same
        slant?   _____   _____
    2. Spacing
        Are the spaces between letters and
        words uniform?   _____   _____
    3. Size
        Are all letters with tall loops almost
        a space tall *(b, f, h, k,* and *l)*?   _____   _____
        Are *d, p,* and *t* about ⅔ space tall?   _____   _____
        Are other lowercase letters approxi-
        mately ⅓ space tall?   _____   _____
    4. Alignment
        Do all the letters touch the baseline?   _____   _____
    5. Loops
        Are *b, f, h, k,* and *l* (upper-loop letters)
        well formed?   _____   _____
        Are *g, j, p, y,* and *z* (lower-loop
        letters) well formed?   _____   _____
    6. Closing
        Are *a, d, g, o, p, q,* and *s* closed?   _____   _____
    7. Roundness
        Are *h, m, n, v, x, y,* and *z* rounded on
        top?   _____   _____
    8. Retraces
        Are *a, d, i, m, n, r, s, t, u, v,* and *w*
        retraced?   _____   _____
    9. Endings
        Do all my words end with good
        finishing strokes?   _____   _____

SOURCE: *My Handwriting Quotient* (Madison, Wis.: W. A. Sheaffer Pen Co., 1960).

When children evaluate their handwriting against a checklist for good handwriting, they are learning to assume responsibility for locating their specific weaknesses as a basis for improving hand-writing performance.

paper. These consisted of three separate paragraphs. The pupil wrote one of these paragraphs and then placed the transparency over his paper to see how nearly his writing coincided with the sample.

Another transparency with about thirty-degree diagonal lines was available so that the pupils could check their slant and spacing.

3. A copy of the grade level handwriting booklet was separated and each page placed inside a clear, plastic envelope. When a pupil had a particular need, he would use the appropriate page of the handwriting booklet.

4. A box of file cards, entitled "Points to Remember About Each of the Letters," was prepared. Each letter (upper- and lowercase) and numeral (0–9) was written on a card. In this way, several pupils could make use of the file at the same time. Samples are provided on page 420 for one letter and one numeral.

File Card: Cursive *a*

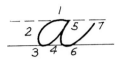

1. Starts flat parallel to the headline and baseline
2. Round back
3. Rather sharp turn at the baseline
4. Upstroke is rather flat
5. Closed at the top with a retraced stroke
6. Turn #6 and turn #3 look alike
7. Finish stroke ends with an undercurve about the same height as the letter.

Numerical count: 1-2
Descriptive count: Around up-down up

SOURCE: *Points to Remember About Each of the Letters of the Alphabet* (Columbus, Ohio: Zaner-Bloser, n.d.), p. 4. Used by permission of the publisher.

File Card: Numeral *3*

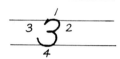

1. Start with slight check like 2
2. A round head smaller than used in 2
3. Small closed loop at right angles to the slant line
4. A free swing resting on the baseline; stop with the pen on the paper
    The numeral *3* requires considerable curve. Be careful to swing the ending stroke far enough to the left so as to show main slant with the beginning loop.

Numerical count: 1-2-3
Descriptive count: Dot-circle-circle

SOURCE: *Points to Remember About Each of the Letters of the Alphabet,* (Columbus, Ohio: Zaner-Bloser, n.d.) p. 58. Used by permission of the publisher.

5.　A file of activity cards stressing the different strokes and features of letters (as noted in the preceding checklist) was available in the center. Each card contained the name of the stroke or letter feature, an illustration of the stroke, letters or groups of letters using the feature, and an activity for the child to perform. (Children selected for themselves the activity cards they needed for practice.) An example is provided below.

Activity Card:　Connecting Stroke

The check-stroke ending to an undercurve beginning is a little tricky, especially when connecting with the letters *e, i, u, r,* and *s.* Check stroke is the short, retraced motion before making the ending stroke on *b, o, v,* and *w.*

oil our ore be veal
write brown will

Practice making these letter combinations on your own paper and then use each in one or more words.

6.　A set of large tracing cards, one for each upper- and lowercase letter, was available at the learning center. These cards were made by using wide-ruled paper with a middle line dividing the writing space into halves, so that the formation of the letter was easy to visualize. Each card had the letter written five times on the top line and one time on each of the following lines. (The card was covered with transparent contact paper and drymounted on posterboard.) The cards permitted the children to trace the letter as well as to finish filling in the page with the same letter. Using felt-tip pens, the writing done by the children could be erased after each use.

7.　Clay and pencil-sized wooden dowels were provided so that the pupils could trace and form letters in clay and "feel" the letters with their fingers. Wooden blocks about one-half inch thick and six inches square were covered with transparent contact paper so that the clay could be pressed on them and then removed.

8.   One set of upper- and lowercase letters was cut from sandpaper and then pasted on index cards. One letter, with strokes indicated, was pasted on each card. Pupils could feel the letters with their fingers and listen to the "sounds" of the letters as they traced over them with a wooden dowel pencil. Another set of blank sandpaper cards (sandpaper strips pasted on index cards) was in the activity file so that pupils could write with the dowel pencil and listen to the "sounds" of their letter formations.

9.   A special file, called "Additional Activities," was provided so that the pupils could have a functional purpose for a handwriting activity: for example, "Use your best cursive handwriting to write the words to your favorite song." These were tasks to be completed in one's best handwriting.

10.   Several charts, like the ones listed below, were posted in the area of the learning center.

> A chart naming, illustrating, and showing the uses of each of the different strokes
> A chart classifying each of the upper- and lowercase letters according to its strokes and the type of letter
> A chart presenting an evaluation scale appropriate for the particular grade level
> A chart presenting handwriting errors and ideas on how to correct them
> A chart illustrating the correct positions for writing with the right hand, writing with the left hand, and writing on the chalkboard

Handwriting equipment of various kinds was kept at the center. For example, one dozen ball-point pens were provided, largely for motivational purposes. These were to be used instead of pencils at times. One dozen felt-tip pens were also placed in a box at the center. Chalk (white and colored) was available for chalkboard writing.

MAINTAINING INTEREST IN HANDWRITING

Beginning pupils are usually eager to learn to write. When the time comes for the addition of cursive writing, interest is high because this form of writing seems more "grown-up" than manuscript. However, there are times when interest lags and practice seems dull. Extra motivation or a different procedure to give freshness to instruction is needed at these times. Handwriting periods should be varied rather than follow a routine pattern. Some lessons will be functional, others will involve analysis and practice, and some will deal with the historical development of handwriting. The following suggestions may prove useful in adding interest to handwriting lessons.

1. Study of the historical development of handwriting adds interest and increases appreciation for handwriting as a tool. Below is a list of several excellent books on this topic for children.

Cahn, William, and Cahn, Rhoda. *The Story of Writing*. Irvington-on-Hudson, N.Y.: Harvey House, 1963.

Gourdie, Tom. *The Puffin Book of Lettering*. Baltimore, Md.: Penguin Books, 1961.

Hofsinde, Robert (Gray-Wolf). *Indian Picture Writing*. New York: William Morrow, 1959.

Irwin, Keith Gordon. *The Romance of Writing*. New York: Viking Press, 1957.

An overhead projector is an excellent aid for building accurate letter perception and focusing upon different aspects of letter formation.

McCain, Murray. *Writing*. New York: Farrar, Straus & Giroux, 1964.

Norling, Josephine. *Pogo's Letter, a Story of Paper*. New York: Holt, Rinehart and Winston, 1946.

Ogg, Oscar. *The Twenty-Six Letters*. Rev. ed. New York: Thomas Y. Crowell, 1971.

Russell, Solveig P. *A Is for Apple and Why: The Story of Our Alphabet*. New York: Abingdon Press, 1959.

2.   Pride in workmanship is often more stimulating than formal practice. Opportunities for such workmanship are found in writing letters, records of work accomplished, announcements for the bulletin board, articles for the school paper, poems, plays, or stories. All these demand neat and legible handwriting.

3.   The opaque projector is a useful aid in motivating the class to analyze handwriting. Samples of handwriting may be projected on the screen for study and discussion of their good and poor qualities. (These samples should not come from class members.) An overhead projector is a good means for giving instruction in the beginning points of letters, the direction of movement, and the shapes of strokes.

4.   Rating handwriting in work done in the other content areas gives emphasis to the importance of writing. All writing should be purposeful.

5.   Interest in improving writing can be stimulated by asking questions like:

What is your best letter?
What letter is most difficult for you?
How is handwriting useful to you?
What use do you think you will make of handwriting as an adult?

6.   Charts giving suggestions for handwriting can be made. One example is suggested below.

CHART 11.4: Reminders for Manuscript Writing

1.   Make all letters with straight line segments and circles.
2.   Move from left to right in making letters.
3.   Make all capital and tall letters two spaces high and small letters one space high.
4.   Space letters close together.
5.   Space words one finger apart on ruled paper.

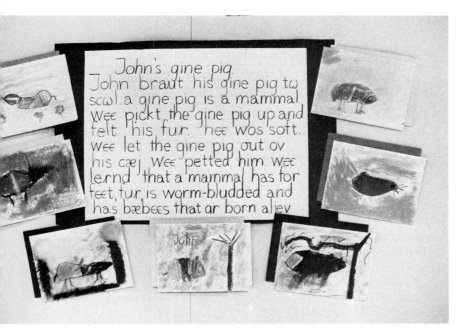

When the child is introduced to beginning reading and writing through the Initial Teaching Alphabet, a few variant letter formations are utilized.

7. Bulletin boards, displaying pupils' work or other materials related to handwriting, may be prepared. Each child should have an opportunity to display his work once or twice during the year.

8. A study of various handwriting tools (e.g., pens, pencils) and of various styles of writing and their special uses can be most interesting and provide ideas for some bulletin board displays.

9. Having pupils' handwriting papers rated by someone outside the classroom—the principal or another teacher—adds interest.

10. Teacher enthusiasm and respect for good handwriting is of prime importance. The teacher should strive to present a good model of handwriting for the pupils. He will find that individual variations in his own writing are likely to be imitated by the children. A positive approach, with praise used more liberally than reproach, is much more likely to produce enthusiasm and good work from boys and girls.

EVALUATING HANDWRITING

The most important criterion for evaluating handwriting is its legibility. Speed is also important but should not be stressed to the point where it interferes with legibility. As has been noted previously, letter formation is the chief factor affecting legibility, but spacing, alignment, slant, and line quality must also be taken into account.

Standardized merit scales

Some instructional effort needs to be expended in developing and encouraging the use of aspirational (how I would *like* to write) and normative (how I *do* write) models. One way of doing this is through the use of handwriting scales.

Several commercial scales have been developed for measuring the general quality of handwriting. These usually consist of samples of handwriting arranged in order of merit with a certain value assigned to each. The child compares a sample of his writing with those on the scale and decides which one it most closely resembles, giving it the rating indicated. Some well-known and widely used scales for measuring the quality of cursive writing are the "Thorndike Scale for the Measurement of Merit of Handwriting,"[18] "The Ayres Handwriting Scale,"[19] and *The American Handwriting Scale*.[20] "The Freeman Handwriting Scales" are available for both cursive and manuscript.[21] *Conrad Manuscript Writing Standards* may be used in evaluating manuscript writing.[22] Two evaluation scales (one for a primary year and one for an intermediate year) are shown on pages 427–428.

HOW TO EVALUATE WRITING WITH A SCALE

I. Procedure
   A. Teachers may write the sentences given in the scale on the chalkboard.
   B. Pupils practice writing the example several times.
   C. Pupils then may be asked to write the sentence carefully on another sheet of paper.
   D. At the end of two minutes, papers may be collected and graded.

---

18. Edward L. Thorndike, in *Thorndike Scale for Measuring the Handwriting of Children* (New York: Teachers College Press, Columbia University, 1910).

19. Leonard P. Ayres, *A Scale for Measuring the Quality of Handwriting of School Children*, Bulletin No. 113 (New York: Division of Education, Russell Sage Foundation, 1912).

20. Paul V. West, *The American Handwriting Scale* (Schaumburg, Ill.: Palmer Company, 1929).

21. Frank N. Freeman and the Zaner-Bloser staff, *Handwriting Measuring Scale, Grades 1–9* (Columbus, Ohio: Zaner-Bloser, 1958).

22. Ruth Conrad, *Conrad Manuscript Writing Standards* (New York: Teachers College Press, Columbia University, 1929).

CHART 11.5: Evaluation Scale (Manuscript)

Specimen 1 — High for Grade 2
Similar manuscript writing may be given a mark of A, and writing better than
this may be evaluated accordingly.

Farmers are good friends. They grow some of our food.

Specimen 2 — Good for Grade 2
Similar manuscript writing may be given a mark of B.

Farmers are good friends. They grow some of our food.

Specimen 3 — Medium for Grade 2
Similar manuscript writing may be given a mark of C. The average speed for this grade
is about 30 letters per minute.

Farmers are good friends. They grow some of our food.

Specimen 4 — Fair for Grade 2
Similar manuscript writing may be given a mark of D.

Farmers are good friends. They grow some of our food.

Specimen 5 — Poor for Grade 2
Similar manuscript writing may be given a mark of E, and writing poorer than this
may be evaluated accordingly.

Farmers are good friends. They grow some of our food.

SOURCE: "Expressional Growth Through Handwriting," *Evaluation Scale, Manuscript Writing*, by the Zaner-Bloser staff. (These specimens are the average of each rank.) Used by permission of the publisher.

CHART 11.6: Evaluation Scale (Cursive)

Specimen 1 — High for Grade 5
Similar cursive handwriting may be marked A, and writing better than
this may be evaluated accordingly.

I live in America. It is good to live where you have freedom to work and play. As an American, I support my country and what it stands for.

Specimen 2 — Good for Grade 5
Similar cursive handwriting may be marked B.

I live in America. It is good to live where you have freedom to work and play. As an American, I support my country and what it stands for.

Specimen 3 — Medium for Grade 5
Similar cursive handwriting may be marked C. The standard speed for this grade
is about 60 letters per minute.

I live in America. It is good to live where you have freedom to work and play. As an American, I support my country and what it stands for.

Specimen 4 — Fair for Grade 5
Similar cursive handwriting may be marked D.

I live in America. It is good to live where you have freedom to work and play. As an American, I support my country and what it stands for.

Specimen 5 — Poor for Grade 5
Similar cursive handwriting may be marked E, and writing poorer than this
may be evaluated accordingly.

I live in America. It is good to live where you have freedom to work and play. As an American, I support my country and what it stands for.

SOURCE: "Expressional Growth Through Handwriting," *Evaluation Scale, Cursive Handwriting,* by the Zaner-Bloser staff. (These specimens are the average of each rank.) Used by permission of the publisher.

II. Grading
  A. Classify the papers roughly into three groups, calling them good, medium, and poor.
  B. Beginning with the "good" group, compare each paper individually with the specimens of the scale. If it is equal to any of the specimens, give it the grade assigned to that specimen. If it is better than the top specimen, give it a grade of A+.

Informal devices

Many informal devices are used to determine quality in handwriting and to locate specific weaknesses.

• *Letter form*   To check letter formation, a card with a hole a little larger than a single letter cut in the center is used. The card is moved along a line of writing so that the letters are exposed one at a time. Illegible or poorly formed letters stand out clearly and may be noted for further practice.

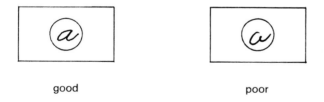

good   poor

For manuscript and cursive writing, lines are drawn along the tops of letters to see if they are of proper height and uniformly written as suggested in the particular handwriting program.

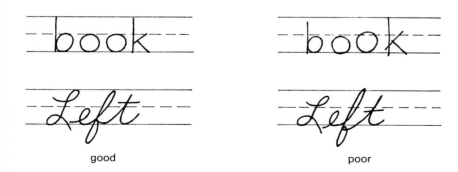

good   poor

• *Spacing*   In manuscript, a space of about one letter (small o) between letters—with adjustments to the series of letters used—is desirable, with a bit more space between words and sentences. The spacing should be uniform throughout. In cursive writing, there should also be a space of about a small letter between letters and slightly more space between words and sentences.

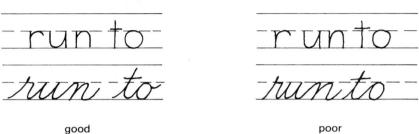

good   poor

• *Alignment*   A rule is used to check alignment; a line should be drawn touching the base of as many of the letters as possible.

good   poor

• *Slant*   Slant applies only to cursive writing. Lines of a straight or uniform slanting nature may be drawn through the letters and the letters marked that are off slant. (Some handwriting experts recommend "slant" as a way of making manuscript writing more individual and attractive, thereby encouraging its continued use.)

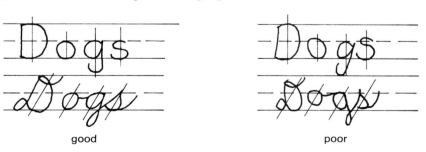

good   poor

• *Line quality*   To check line quality, an examination of the evenness of writing pressure is made. The same consistency is desirable, rather than a mixture of light and heavy, thick and fine writing.

      good   poor

Other suggestions and materials

As far as possible, the child should appraise his own handwriting. The time of critical examination would be preceded by a group or class discussion on the qualities of good writing and ways of discovering and correcting weaknesses. The child then becomes aware of the need for good handwriting and alert to finding and correcting his errors. Keeping a folder of dated samples of his work throughout the year helps the child to see his progress (or lack of it).

The teacher may use the child's handwriting folder in checking his progress and planning the program of instruction he needs. A file with a card for each pupil showing his strengths and weaknesses is also helpful to the teacher. Individual checklists kept by the pupil in his notebook to show progressive levels of achievement may be maintained. An illustration of a progress chart appears on page 432.

Rate measures may be accomplished by counting the total number of letters written by a pupil in a two-minute period and dividing this number in half. Emphasis on speed is not only useless but harmful until letter formation becomes secure. Pupils need to develop firm handwriting skills that can be maintained with a reasonable degree of speed. Pupils are well advised to make satisfactory adjustments in quality and speed to the various handwriting situations in which they find themselves. Norms in speed should not be used as arbitrary standards for all children.

There are several good diagnostic charts available. One such device is the Zaner-Bloser *Chart on Handwriting Faults and How to Correct Them.*[23] It gives specific ideas for detecting handwriting

---

23. Frank N. Freeman, *Chart on Handwriting Faults and How to Correct Them* (Columbus, Ohio: Zaner-Bloser).

CHART 11.7: Handwriting Progress

	October	November	December
Letter size and form			
Spacing between letters			
Spacing between words			
Spacing between sentences			
Alignment			
Slant			
Line quality			
Letter joinings			
Letter endings			
Margins and arrangement			
Neatness			
Position			
Speed of writing			

Key: NI—Needs improvement; S—Satisfactory

Name of pupil _____

weaknesses and helpful suggestions for correcting the defects discovered.

The Zaner-Bloser Company also has specially prepared materials for close analysis of individual letter formation of both manuscript and cursive.[24] These materials should be helpful for individuals who need to improve letter forms. Also, various professional books provide listings of defects in handwriting and their possible causes.[25] When extremely poor handwriting habits are acquired by certain pupils, it may be necessary for the teacher to prepare special worksheets. These worksheets may be needed for such items as specific numerals; specific manuscript or cursive letters; difficulties noted in letter combination, spacing of letters and words, slant, or alignment. Examples of such worksheets may be found in various sources.[26] For one example, see chapter 12, page 445.

---

24. Parker Bloser, *Our Print Letters and How We Make Them* (Columbus, Ohio: Zaner-Bloser); idem., *Our ABC's and How We Improve Them* (Columbus, Ohio: Zaner-Bloser).

25. For example, see Harry A. Greene and Walter T. Petty, *Developing Language Skills in the Elementary Schools*, 4th ed. (Boston: Allyn and Bacon, 1971), p. 461.

26. For example, see Paul C. Burns, *Improving Handwriting Instruction in Elementary Schools*, 2d ed. (Minneapolis: Burgess, 1968), pp. 105–111.

Again, part of the evaluation program should include attention to attitude measurement. One simple instrument is called the *semantic differential technique*. This instrument is made up of a list of bipolar adjectives weighted on a seven-point scale. The name of the concept is written at the top of the set of scales. A sample, general scale (again, specific activities may serve as the item to be rated) is shown in chart 11.8. The child is asked to place a check in proper relation to the word that best tells his feeling.

CHART 11.8: Semantic Differential Scale—Handwriting

1.	good	___	___	___	___	___	___	___	bad
*2.	distasteful	___	___	___	___	___	___	___	agreeable
3.	pleasurable	___	___	___	___	___	___	___	painful
*4.	hazy	___	___	___	___	___	___	___	clear
5.	important	___	___	___	___	___	___	___	unimportant
6.	sweet	___	___	___	___	___	___	___	sour
7.	valuable	___	___	___	___	___	___	___	worthless
*8.	negative	___	___	___	___	___	___	___	positive
*9.	unpleasant	___	___	___	___	___	___	___	pleasant
10.	nice	___	___	___	___	___	___	___	awful
*11.	meaningless	___	___	___	___	___	___	___	meaningful
12.	wise	___	___	___	___	___	___	___	foolish
13.	high	___	___	___	___	___	___	___	low
*14.	unsuccessful	___	___	___	___	___	___	___	successful
*15.	tense	___	___	___	___	___	___	___	relaxed

The scale may be weighted in the following manner for asterisked bipolar adjectives:

$$-3 \quad -2 \quad -1 \quad 0 \quad 1 \quad 2 \quad 3$$

The scale would be reversed, however, for all other sets, as follows:

$$3 \quad 2 \quad 1 \quad 0 \quad -1 \quad -2 \quad -3$$

Add the plus scores and subtract the sum of the minus scores. A high positive score indicates a positive attitude.

Finally, there are sets of handwriting materials that may be helpful in individualizing the program: for example, *Penskills I* and *II*.[27] Further ideas for the child of superior writing ability are presented in chapter 12.

---

27. *Penskills, I* and *II* (Chicago: Science Research Associates).

SELECTED REFERENCES

General Professional

Anderson, Paul S. *Language Skills in Elementary Education.* 2d ed. New York: Macmillan, 1972, chapter 4.

Boyd, Gertrude. *Teaching Communication Skills in the Elementary School.* New York: Van Nostrand Reinhold, 1970, chapter 4.

Corcoran, Gertrude B. *Language Arts in Elementary School: A Modern Linguistic Approach.* New York: Ronald, 1970, chapter 11.

Dallmann, Martha. *Teaching the Language Arts in the Elementary School.* 2d ed. Dubuque, Iowa: William C. Brown, 1971, chapter 7.

Greene, Harry A., and Petty, Walter T. *Developing Language Skills in the Elementary Schools.* 4th ed. Boston: Allyn and Bacon, 1971, chapter 13.

Lamb, Pose. *Guiding Children's Language Learning.* 2d ed. Dubuque, Iowa: William C. Brown, 1971, chapter 7.

Smith, James A. *Adventures in Communication: Language Arts Methods.* Boston: Allyn and Bacon, 1972, chapter 10.

Specialized

Andersen, Dan A. "Teaching Handwriting," *What Research Says to the Teacher:* no. 4. Washington, D.C.: National Education Association, 1968.

Arnold, Gwen F., et al. *Handwriting in Wisconsin.* Madison: School of Education, University of Wisconsin, 1951.

Blair, Glenn Myers. *Diagnostic and Remedial Teaching.* Rev. ed. New York: Macmillan, 1956.

Brueckner, Leo J., and Bond, Guy L. *Diagnosis and Treatment of Learning Difficulties.* New York: Appleton-Century-Crofts, 1955.

Burns, Paul C. *Improving Handwriting Instruction in Elementary Schools.* 2d ed. Minneapolis: Burgess, 1968.

Gray, William S. *The Teaching of Reading and Writing: An International Survey.* Chicago: Scott Foresman, 1956.

Herrick, Virgil, ed. *New Horizons for Research in Handwriting.* Madison: University of Wisconsin Press, 1963.

Horn, Thomas D., ed. *Research on Handwriting and Spelling.* Urbana, Ill.: National Council of Teachers of English, 1966.

Myers, Emma Harrison. *The Whys and Hows of Teaching Handwriting.* Columbus, Ohio: Zaner-Bloser, 1963.

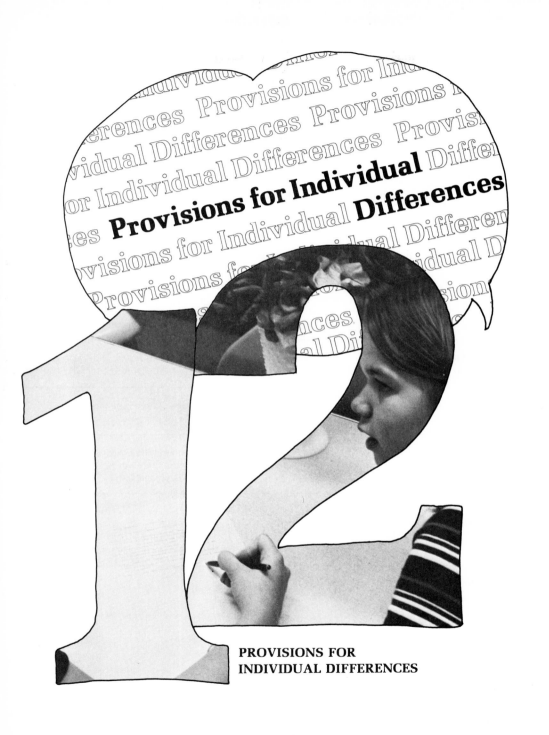

PROVISIONS FOR
INDIVIDUAL DIFFERENCES

OBJECTIVES	PERFORMANCE RESPONSES
1. **To identify plans for differentiation of instruction**	1. Examine an elementary school language arts textbook. What provisions are made for different instruction for the advanced and slower-learning child?
2. **To assess features of within-class instruction**	2. Cite what, in your opinion, are the strongest and the weakest features of the proposed within-class instructional plan.
3. **To plan other aspects of differentiation**	3. a. Prepare an enrichment language arts activity worksheet for a selected child or group of children. b. Design a corrective worksheet for a child needing special help with numeral formation. c. Develop a set of review or summary questions for a topic in a current language arts textbook for children.
4. **To demonstrate adjustments and modifications for the language-gifted**	4. Sketch a bulletin board plan for a group of language-gifted children.
5. **To formulate plans for other special children**	5. Design one specific language arts activity to be used by one type of special child.
6. **To design corrective work**	6. Prepare an analytical test and some illustrative, follow-up exercises for some technical language skill.
7. **To identify materials that provide for individual differences**	7. a. If feasible, examine one of the sets of materials cited on pages 462–463. b. Sketch a sample learning center display as illustrated in this chapter.

It is no secret that the language ability of individuals varies greatly. In spite of this variation, it is common practice for all pupils to use the same instructional materials and to be assigned the same tasks. In view of the obvious need for an adjustment of instruction, every plan should be given careful consideration.

This chapter delineates a comprehensive plan, with accompanying specific details, for one approach to differentiated instruction. Chapter 13 discusses alternative organizational plans proposed for enhancing teaching and learning effectiveness.

PLAN FOR WITHIN-CLASS INSTRUCTION

One teacher's procedure for adjusting instruction to meet individual needs is given below.

It is no secret that the language ability of individuals varies greatly.

After a few days of studying oral composition in one third-grade class (specifically directed at storytelling), the teacher said, "Your experience with the inventory test (teacher-made or textbook-prepared), class-developed standards, and our study of the past couple of days indicate that most of you can profitably spend some time improving your ability at storytelling. You should work on such items as speech patterns, outlining a story, organizing events in sequence, making a good beginning, and using interesting words. Here is a special worksheet that suggests some advanced, independent exercises and activities. Look at it to see if you want to do the exercises now or whether you first want to become more familiar with the ideas suggested in our textbook about storytelling." After examination of the worksheet and the book exercises, the teacher said, "I'm going to work the first part of the period with those interested in the textbook exercises. If you wish to work with me, put the worksheet in your folder. You may want to try it later. Those wishing to work with the worksheet may proceed."

Allowing a child to determine whether he feels able or wishes to do an exercise or activity is one of the commendable features of this type of planned, differentiated instruction. When other basic ideas of oral composition are treated, the teacher will continue to give the children a choice of exercises, and in each situation the supplementary worksheets would contain independent, more advanced work. Following is an example of one of these worksheets.

Worksheet: Becoming a First-Rate Storyteller

1. You and a friend record your pronunciation of these words with a tape recorder. Then listen to the tape, noting the differences in pronunciation between you and your friend.

again	depths	governor	poetry
arctic	dictionary	height	probably
attached	drowned	hollow	pumpkin
burst	elm	lion	rinse
creek	evening	memory	such
crept	every	numerator	tune
deaf	family	partner	vanilla
denominator	geography	poem	window

2. List five words you have read or heard that are rarely used today. How many "picturesque" words have you encountered recently? List five of them.

	Old words	*Picturesque words*
Example:	fetch	bookworm
	_____	_____
	_____	_____
	_____	_____
	_____	_____

The filmstrips "Times and People Change Words" and "Roots and Shoots" may help give you some further ideas about old and picturesque words.[1] Also check the trade book *Heavens to Betsy and Other Curious Sayings*.[2]

3. Listen to the record story of *The Hundred Dresses* by Eleanor Estes. Note the voice patterns. Then tell the portion of the story you liked best to a friend, trying to keep your voice flexible.

4. Work with a partner and develop a pantomime of Robert Browning's "The Pied Piper of Hamelin."

5. Prepare a short speech on different ways of "talking" (such

---

1. "Time and People Change Words" and "Roots and Shoots." (Chicago: Society for Visual Education, 1954).
2. Charles E. Funk, *Heavens to Betsy and Other Curious Sayings* (New York: Harper and Brothers, 1955).

as Morse Code). A good reference source is *Communication: From Cave Writing to Television* by Julie F. Batchelor.[3]

6. Prepare a favorite fairy tale (e.g., "The Princess on the Glass Hill") to tell to a small group.
7. Prepare a story (e.g., one of *Aesop's Fables* or one of the *Just So Stories*) to tell to another class member.
8. Give an oral review of a movie or a TV program to a partner. Ask your partner to use the checklist for evaluation that is found on the language arts table. Then listen to his movie or TV review and evaluate his performance.

For a part of the period, the teacher may discuss these projects and ideas with interested pupils. He may suggest that, although it is desirable to attempt all the items on the worksheet, it is not required. Pupils should be complimented on good work and their efforts often shared with the entire class. After two levels of work (average and advanced) have been fairly well established, the third level should be added for particular phases of the topic under consideration for the slower-learning children.

OTHER ASPECTS OF DIFFERENTIATION

Special worksheets comprise only a part of the program of providing differentiated instruction. Some differentiated study was presented by means of study charts. Sometimes, differentiation involves the use of textbooks other than the adopted one, commercially published programmed materials, and the like. Aspects of the overall program include (1) provision for differing levels of work in the regular assignment, (2) additional exercises or enrichment suggestions provided by the textbook program (or teacher-made), (3) special language arts bulletin boards and displays, (4) special programs for pupils in need of corrective or remedial instruction, and (5) reviews and summaries. Each will be discussed briefly.

Regular assignments

Of all the various aspects of the differentiated program, this is probably the most important one. Initial presentations on a topic or concept (including the use of pretests or inventories) lend themselves to whole-class activity. Individualized activity would be util-

---

3. Julie F. Batchelor, *Communication: From Cave Writing to Television* (New York: Harcourt Brace, 1953).

ized by the child after he has participated in the initial stages of the group presentation. As soon as it is apparent that a pupil has grasped the major content intended for the total group, he would be excused to work individually or in another manner. For example, the class could work as a unit in listening to a pupil's oral report, preparing a written composition (such as completing a story read in part to the class), practicing a usage item needed by all or most of the class members, or taking Monday's pretest in spelling. In these situations, children with both limited and considerable language ability could work on the same assignment. The variation would take place within the lesson itself and in the follow-up study sessions. More advanced pupils would have an opportunity to make more complete contributions, but the class would not be separated into groups; each pupil would work at his own level of achievement on the same topic. This frees the teacher of the necessity of preparing several lesson plans and, therefore, makes for a good learning situation. Children of lesser ability profit from suggestions of superior-achieving pupils, and the latter gain from the exercise of presenting their thoughts clearly. High morale is maintained when the class works together in this fashion.

After introductory study of a new language arts concept or idea, additional follow-up will likely be needed. At this point, instructional strategies may involve the use of small groups. For example, an intermediate-grade teacher has received a set of written compositions, one from each pupil. After correcting the compositions, he bases the next day's lesson on these corrections, making a list of the following items:

1. Weaknesses in ideas, organization of thoughts, use of descriptive words or phrases, revision and proofreading
2. Errors in capitalization, punctuation, sentence sense, or paragraph sense
3. Spelling difficulties
4. Usage problems
5. Handwriting deficiencies

Then he would make a list of the names of class members, indicating who had difficulty in the above items and which items were general for the class.

From a list like this, a teacher will be able to keep track of his class members, be able to assign appropriate study materials, and retain a record for later evaluations as other compositions are written. In effect, the teacher teaches only what needs to be taught and only to those needing it. Pupils who know how to write correctly are not held back by those who need extensive help. Items, like those described above, can be isolated, analyzed, and taught individually and in groups.

Enrichment

After several worksheets of the type suggested earlier have been introduced, a limited number of others dealing with various ideas (not necessarily related to the topic under study) may be placed on the language arts table.

Independent activities can be developed rather easily for (1) study of language concepts through references to children's books, (2) unusual ways of sharing books, (3) creative writing efforts, (4) study of advanced dictionary skills, (5) spelling games and activities, (6) historical development of many aspects related to handwriting, (7) language games related to listening or vocabulary development, or (8) library research on a variety of topics.

Following are some examples of the types of materials teachers may develop for enrichment purposes. Occasionally, there should be a discussion of the material prepared by children in response to the ideas. The discussion may be carried on with an individual, a small group, or the class as a whole.

Activity Card: History of Words

WHY IS "WHERE GO THE BOATS?" CALLED A LYRIC POEM? — TEACHER

WOULD IT HELP IF I KNEW THE HISTORY OF THE WORD LYRIC? — OPAL

SOMEWHERE I READ THAT IN OLDEN DAYS A POET READ HIS POEM WHILE SOMEONE PLAYED SOFTLY ON A LYRE. THAT IS AN INSTRUMENT LIKE A SMALL HARP—SOMETHING LIKE THE AUTO HARP WE USE IN OUR CLASS! — SHIRLEY

From such a discussion, the children decided a lyric poem would be a melodic one, with feeling, and perhaps suitable for singing or musical accompaniment.

Here are some other words with interesting histories. See if you can write a short story about each one.

curfew   gargantuan   robot
boycott   lilliputian   yahoo

Worksheet: Language in Literature

A. Do the following:
1. Go to the listening center.
2. Read "The Pied Piper of Hamelin" by Robert Browning.
3. Listen carefully to the record of "The Pied Piper of Hamelin."

B. Answer these questions and do these exercises.
1. What does *pied* mean?
2. Who do you think the Pied Piper was?
3. Why did the mayor "quake with consternation"?
4. What do you think the Pied Piper looked like? The city of Hamelin?
5. Choose four or five other children who have heard this record. Prepare a round-table discussion to present to the class on the topic, "Do you think the ending is happy or sad? Why?"
6. Write a story about what you think the children of Hamelin found on the other side of the door in the mountain.

Activity Card: Homonyms

Can You Find the Errors?

1. Some of the underlined words in the paragraph below are used incorrectly. Cross through each incorrect word and write the correct word above it.

> Pete picked a <u>flour</u> from a bush by the <u>rode</u> but <u>threw</u> away the <u>bury</u>. He <u>new</u> they were poison even though they <u>seemed</u> harmless. Just then he <u>herd</u> a <u>grown</u> from under the bushes.

2. Write a paragraph or a story using the words below; use some words correctly and some incorrectly. Then ask a friend to find your errors.

sent	ring	not	wood	bear	steak
cent	wring	knot	would	bare	stake

Activity Card: Proofreading

Proofread this paragraph. Then rewrite it, making the necessary corrections.

Bill and Mary fond a babe robin wich fell out of it's nast they took it hom and put it in a box they dug upon worm's and fed it One Day wen the robin body was strong the children took it to the park and set it fre mother said you have done a good ded

---

Additional ideas for enrichment activities include:

    playing word games
    using Roget's *Thesaurus* or some other book of synonyms
    writing the same message or story in several forms for different
        audiences, different effects, etc.
    rewriting a story to have an opposite ending, different setting,
        or different characters
    writing unusual titles or captions for cartoons, pictures, or news
        items
    telling a story entirely through pictures, cartoons, photographs,
        or drawings[4]

Special materials

Pupil participation in the preparation of instructional materials often creates interest and understanding. It is desirable for children to select an idea that is best suited to their ability. Following are some topics for bulletin board displays:

    "Listening Games"
    "Variations in Speech" (lists of words associated with different
        dialects)
    "Anecdotes" (for telling aloud)
    "Guess Who" (riddles or illustrations about book characters)
    "News"
    "How to Give a Good Report"

---

4. E. Paul Torrance, *Role of Evaluation in Creative Thinking* (Minneapolis: Bureau of Educational Research, University of Minnesota, 1964).

Attractive language arts bulletin boards can also be instructional—as noted by these reminders for punctuation marks.

"Creative Writing"
"Announcements and Reports"
"A New Word for Today" (or a crossword puzzle)
"My Best Handwriting"

The teacher can use the language arts table to assist in differentiation of instruction by placing items like the following on it: poetry books, a daily journal maintained by the class, a story box for children's contributions, language games, and trade books about the study of language.

Corrective instruction

Providing special corrective exercises for slower learners is a major part of a differentiated program of instruction. Pupils need to recognize deficiencies; test results need to be discussed with individuals; and then corrective learning procedures should be offered on a voluntary basis. There needs to be a favorable attitude toward any corrective study. Even then, the pupils will devote only a part of the language arts time to this activity and will continue to participate in most regular class activities when new ideas or concepts are introduced. Following is a worksheet designed for corrective instruction.

Worksheet: Cursive α

1.   Write this word and see how well you can make the α.

road

   a.   Where does α begin?
   b.   Is α closed or open?
   c.   Is the up-stroke retraced or looped?
   d.   Does the concluding stroke sit on the baseline?
2.   Make a row of α's. Make each one look like the one at the beginning of the row.

α

3.   Look at the letters at the right.
   a.   Are α and *d* the same width?
   b.   What is the only difference between α and *d*?
   c.   Write α, *d*, and o on the next line.
4.   Write the words below, making good α's.

draw gave

5.   Write the sentence below, making your α's correctly.

I had to read it again.

6.   Are you now making better α's?
   a.   Are you closing all your α's?
   b.   Are you retracing, not looping, the up-stroke?
   c.   Does the connecting stroke sit on the baseline?
   d.   Do any of your α's look like o's, u's, or *i*'s? (They *should not*.)

The teacher must give frequent attention to pupils using corrective materials, get them started, discuss the materials, and encourage them as much as possible by showing an interest in what they are doing. Sometimes, the more able class members can successfully assist those engaged in corrective work. The pupils are encouraged to use lots of the special worksheets and to redo some worksheets several times. Some workbooks contain parts, though not specifically designed for corrective work, that may serve quite well for some deficiencies. Some programmed materials are also suitable.

Reviews

Review procedures are utilized after intensive study of a particular topic in such a way that they can be of benefit to both the slower-learning and the faster-learning child. Sets of thought-provoking questions over the major topics of the year should greatly enhance a program of differentiation.

An illustrative set of review questions for the topic of oral reporting is provided below:

1. How do you select a topic for reporting?
2. What is the most difficult problem you have in gathering information on a topic from several sources?
3. How do you take notes, organize them in outline form, and then state them in your own words?
4. If you were helping another child with a report, what is the most important information you could give him about collection and organization of material?
5. What makes a good beginning and a good ending for a report?
6. What are the roles of the speaker and listeners when a report is being given?
7. What are some features of a good oral report?

Features and implications of a suggested program

Distinct features of the proposed program are summarized as follows. First, the pupils work together on the same topic, so they are kept in one group. This is particularly true when new topics or ideas are introduced, mastery exercises are provided, tests administered, and other such activities performed. Even when most work for the period is differentiated, all the children may participate in some common activity. This allows the teacher to devote his time to one major class preparation. Second, by letting the pupils choose their work,

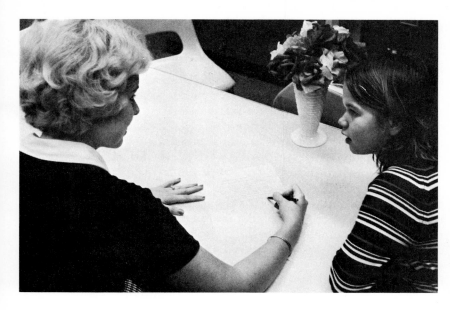

A set of thought-provoking questions, following study of a language arts topic, can be useful in helping the child review his knowledge of important aspects of the topic.

many of the undesirable features of grouping are diminished. The stigma and feeling of resentment of being with a particular group is reduced. Third, the needs of the faster-learning child are met without utilizing materials designed for use in succeeding years. Fourth, the quality and availability of materials for differentiation will be major factors in whether or not the program is successful. Unfortunately, few commercial materials of this nature are available, so teachers, individually or in groups, will have to produce them.

The development of such materials seems justified in terms of the purpose—to give children an opportunity to work with materials at a level and at a rate that is in keeping with their abilities. The possibilities for such adjustments are evident in every facet of the language arts field: speech, oral composition, literature, written composition, usage, spelling, and handwriting. Where a program of this nature is in existence, learning will be achieved on all levels.

IDEAS FOR THE LANGUAGE-GIFTED

The mentally gifted child in the elementary school language arts program needs guidance, as do all children, although it may be a different kind of guidance from that required by the average or slow learner.

Characteristics and needs

A teacher must be alert to those who may be superior language pupils. Let us imagine a teacher of ten-year-olds who soon after school began in September has given the class a standardized achievement test. The teacher would already have studied the pupils' cumulative records and noted their choices of trade books or reference books during the first few days or weeks of school. A study of the achievement test records will now assist the teacher in planning a broad outline of a program for the advanced. He will note the children who scored considerably above grade level on the test. Whether called talented, bright, superior, a fast learner, or gifted, these children likely can progress at a rate of one-and-a-quarter or more years within one calendar year as compared to the average child, who makes one year of mental growth for each year of his life. Any available tests of intelligence (individual or group) might provide further clues to identification. In daily observation, it will be seen that usually the gifted will finish assignments before the others. Of course, there are underachievers among the gifted. And there are several factors that might interfere with the recognition of the gifted—physical defects, emotional instability, and poor study habits. Too, some gifted tend to be nonconformists and "irritate" the teacher, causing them to be considered "brats" rather than "brains."

Each language-gifted child is, of course, different. But there are some characteristics that they seem to have in common: (1) interest in books and reading; (2) a large vocabulary, with an interest in words and meanings; (3) the ability to express themselves verbally in a mature style; (4) enjoyment of activities usually liked best by older children; (5) curiosity to know more, making use of the dictionary, encyclopedia, and other reference sources; (6) a long attention span in conjunction with initiative and an ability to set goals and plans; (7) a high level of abstract thinking; and (8) a creative talent with a wide range of interests.

These advanced, language-oriented pupils have the same basic needs as all children in terms of acceptance and affection. They have the same need for the basic language tools as others, but here it will be a matter of difference in degree and in timing from the average. They need to work at their own level regardless of other members of the class, and they need some teacher direction and guidance even though they are capable of directing many of their own activities. Where a skill is needed, it should be taught them. They are ready for long-term projects and should have the opportunity to pursue their interests and hobbies—and broaden them. They need to be encouraged to think critically and to use this ability in their work. In attending to such specially mentioned needs as suggested, the teacher must not overlook the need for all-around development of the child—and this involves being accepted, having friends, possessing a feeling for others, and working as a team member.

Suggested instructional procedures

Within the language arts program, there are many opportunities at every age level to provide differentiation of instruction. To suggest some general approaches, one idea would be to supply the classroom with a variety of books and allow the pupils to read widely. Some follow-up techniques from this type of environmental setting might be: (1) encouragement of storytelling to classmates and to other classes of stories and books read, perhaps with suitable background music and sound effects; (2) promotion of dramatization (perhaps puppet or shadow-play) of stories read; (3) utilization of art and construction activities, such as making dioramas, illustrating favorite books, making murals and posters about books; and (4) initiation of a literature club where pupils set their own goals and rules.

Special long-term, enrichment projects may be developed for use throughout the school year. One example of such a project might be an in-depth study of the newspaper, the radio, television, or other communication media.

Special language arts bulletin boards (anecdotes, cartoons, news, reports, word trees, etc.) and language arts displays (child's poetry, creative writing, etc.) may be developed by the children themselves.

More specifically, other opportunities for the language-gifted may be categorized under oral and written composition, spelling, and handwriting. Each will be discussed briefly in turn.

• *Oral and written composition*   These expressive phases of the language arts, liberally supported by a strong literature program, can provide many opportunities for the gifted child. Since output is so dependent upon input, a stimulating environment of books in the classroom should aid immeasurably in providing the best possible learning situation. Library or trade books, encyclopedias, and general references dealing with arithmetic, language arts, social studies, science, fiction, and poetry should be specifically selected and maintained in the classroom library. Even more such books should be provided in the centralized school library. While the emphasis may be upon challenging the talented to do research for language arts assignments during the "language arts period," there is no need for study to be restricted solely in that direction. (Topics for supplemental research could include "What is the Newberry Prize?" "What are the names and uses of diacritical marks, and how did they come into usage?" "What is the history of the word *shibboleth?*" and "What is *Roget's Thesaurus* and how is it used?") Pupils can be encouraged to maintain a notebook specially designed to hold the reports on these topics and to use the information should they be called upon for it.

Poetry should play a particularly useful role in the program for the advanced learner. Since poetry often uses language that is figurative, it may help to develop the child's ability to look below the surface—to "read between the lines." Talented pupils may be encouraged to read poetry to other children, write original poems, make a bulletin board display of their favorite or original poems, participate in choral reading, memorize their favorite poems, or compose music for their favorite poems.

As an outgrowth of a strong literature background, creative writing of prose and poetry deserves special consideration as a suitable activity for the language-gifted child, who is capable of developing more comprehensive thought and expression than the average child. He should be encouraged to note how other writers create word pictures and express their ideas effectively. A wide range of choice in vocabulary and variety in sentence structure should also be emphasized in original written composition.

Larom described an experiment that he conducted with sixth graders that might be used with the more advanced to teach them some of the characteristics of good writing. Larom taught the group to (1) use lots of description; (2) choose "live" verbs; (3) "render a happening" by injecting emotions, sensory impressions, and reactions to events into an account of an incident; (4) avoid omitting vital parts of the plot; (5) build suspense; (6) reveal character in a variety of ways; (7) provide motivation for actions in the plot; (8) maintain a constant viewpoint instead of switching from first to third person; and (9) develop a theme through the actions and characterizations in the story.[5]

In word study, advanced exercises using a dictionary may be developed, covering topics such as (1) synonyms and antonyms, (2) derivation of words, (3) "new" words, (4) slang words, and (5) etymology. Language games should be available for pupil use: Scrabble, anagrams, crossword puzzles, etc.

---

5. Henry V. Larom, "Sixth Graders Write Good Short Stories," *Elementary English* 37 (January 1960): 20–23.

• *Spelling*   A number of specific suggestions may be offered to those interested in challenging the gifted pupil in the area of spelling: (1) bonus words, (2) maintenance of personal spelling lists, (3) study of the history of words, (4) listing rare or newly coined words, and (5) spelling games.

• *Handwriting*   Books, films, filmstrips, and similar sources are valuable references for children who are interested in the study of handwriting. Topics such as the following can be introduced through these media: (1) history of handwriting; (2) study of writing surfaces; (3) production of newspapers, magazines, and books; (4) history of handwriting instruments; (5) writing letters to foreign correspondents; and (6) comparing handwriting.

SPECIAL CHILDREN

The socially disadvantaged

The socially disadvantaged child has been restricted in what he has seen, heard, touched, and tasted; he is lacking in certain experiences. Several pertinent features should permeate the program for the socially disadvantaged. First, concern must be focused upon the child's self-concept. While this is important in all teaching and learning situations, it is crucial where the child may have acquired a poor self-image. (See chapter 1, page 18.)

A listening climate should pervade the classroom. It is most important that the teacher be a good listener to the child. Teachers frequently are guilty of half listening or ignoring what the child is trying to tell them, and this undoubtedly has an impact on the child's view of the importance of listening. (Read *Nobody Listens to Andrew* by Elizabeth Guilfoile.)[6] Listening attitudes and experiences must be put to use in the classroom through conversations among pupils, activities at the listening center, and individual, teacher-pupil conferences.

Oral expression should be encouraged—through concrete experiences, role-playing, the use of educational media, learning centers, and reading to children and asking them questions on what they have heard.

Rich, concrete experiences, in which there is an explicit aim to name and to discuss, should be a major factor in the language arts

---

6. Elizabeth Guilfoile, *Nobody Listens to Andrew* (Chicago: Follett, 1957).

program. Particular provisions should be made for many speaking activities following each new experience.

Role-playing can be utilized in numerous ways. (For example, see chapter 5 for the acting out of ideas.) Role-playing is a good stimulus for discussion and appeals to the child's love of action. He will enjoy talking about the scenes he has acted out or has seen other children dramatize. He finds this quite exciting and is often keenly articulate in the discussion period that follows role-playing. Later, the teacher may be able to arouse considerable discussion merely by reminding the children of the incident acted out on a previous occasion.

Mechanical programmed materials may be especially effective with some disadvantaged children. Other visual aids (e.g., the magnetic board, word puzzles) could be used for stimulating thinking. An activity center in the classroom may provide opportunities for making recordings or filmstrips.

Study of their heroes helps pupils to gain a sense of their own worth. The lives and careers of heroes—from Clara Barton to Booker T. Washington—might well serve as subjects for oral and written compositions.

The school library can offer valuable services for the child. Whenever possible, the children's interests—sports, adventure stories, science fiction, etc.—should be utilized. A library with a large collection of books representing a variety of subjects can satisfy the interests of every child. A good picture book collection is particularly valuable. Books with appealing illustrations and a brief, simple text can be introduced to children not yet able to read; this can encourage them to select books in the library to take to their classrooms for the teacher to read to the class or to small groups. The librarian can supplement books with filmstrips and films, storytelling, and recordings.

The speech-impaired

Although many teachers assert that they are not speech teachers, they cannot escape being teachers of speech. When teaching the language arts, speech is taught, directly or indirectly, in almost every lesson.

• *Developmental speech activities*   Teachers are often concerned about the incidence of "baby talk." Should the child who enters school using "baby talk" be referred to a speech therapist? By focusing attention too early on the child's speech, the child may become self-conscious and refuse to talk. The teacher should try to encourage distinct enunciation and pronunciation from the very start without making the child self-conscious about his language. Many speech problems are due to nothing more serious than immaturity and will disappear in time.

The value of group training for young children to provide practice in speech and the ability to hear accurately correct articulation has long been established.[7] The teacher of young children can make training of this type incidental to the presentation of rhymes, stories, and songs. After observing and listening to the children, the teacher may plan more formal lessons, organized around the speech sounds that seem to be defective.

Some of the most common types of errors are readily identifiable to the teacher who has trained himself to listen: *w* for *r* and *l*, *th* for *s*, voiced *th* for *z*, *f* for *th*, *d* for the voiced *th* and *g*, *b* for *v*, *s* or *ch* for *sh*, and *t* for *k*.[8]

Every experience in which oral language is used may become an opportunity for informal speech development. For many children, a social situation encourages them to talk freely and results in increased self-confidence and independence, which is reflected in rapidly increasing speech control.

When a child continues to use substitutions, omissions, distortions, or additions of sounds, the teacher must create exercises to sensitize his ear and provide a variety of opportunities to help him practice the correct sound. For children who lisp, the teacher should emphasize ear training and give an explanation of the articulation of the correct sound, followed by recitation of words, phrases, and sentences containing the sounds causing difficulty.

The teacher should also be alert to monotonous voice patterns. Here, children may listen to storytelling records in which voices are flexible. Stories, like *The Three Bears* or *The Hundred Dresses*, in which a variety of emotions are depicted, may be utilized. The children should have a feeling of belonging to a group where relative freedom of expression is encouraged. In every case, they should be complimented on successful improvement of speech patterns.

• *Corrective speech activities*   Sometimes the regular classroom teacher will discover pupils in his class who have severe speech

---

7. A. T. Sommer, "The Effect of Group Training upon the Correction of Articulatory Defects in Preschool Children," *Child Development* 3 (June 1932): 91–107.

8. Margaret C. Byrne, *The Child Speaks: A Speech Improvement Program for Kindergarten and First Grades* (New York: Harper & Row, 1965).

difficulties requiring treatment by a speech therapist. Although these children may go to a special person for help, the classroom teacher still has the responsibility of working with the child during the major part of the school day. This is appropriate, since the teacher is the best person to assist the child in his "carry-over" of newly learned speech habits; and again, speech must be integrated into his normal, everyday activities. Classroom teachers who hope to be successful in helping these children must be aware of each child's particular speech needs.

Eisenson and Ogilvie list some special qualifications classroom teachers should possess.

1. His own speech and voice must be worthy of imitation.
2. He must have a discerning ear so that he can recognize articulatory and vocal errors (such as hoarseness, nasality, breathiness, or too-high pitch) that the children are making.
3. He must have an accurate knowledge of how the American-English vowels and consonants are made.
4. He must be able to plan a program of speech improvement for all the children. Whereas only 5 percent have need of speech correction, almost all children have need of speech improvement.
5. He should have enough knowledge of speech correction to reinforce the teaching of the speech therapist. He must, therefore, be able to understand the aims, objectives, and procedures of the speech therapist.
6. He should be able to identify those pupils in his class who need speech help.[9]

Common disorders: Articulartory disorders are by far the most common type of speech disorder among school children, and it is in this area that the classroom teacher can accomplish the most. A disorder of articulation may exist when a child persists in one or more of the following practices:

1. Substitutes one sound for another (e.g., *whittle* for *little*)
2. Omits a sound (e.g., *pane* for *plane*)
3. Distorts the sound (Sounds of *s*, *z*, and *r* are the most commonly distorted ones.)

Some of these articulatory distortions are the result of neuro-muscular or structural malfunctions, such as cleft palate, cleft lip,

---

9. Jon Eisenson and Mardel Ogilvie, *Speech Correction in the Schools*, 2d ed. (New York: Macmillan, 1963), pp. 26–27.

cerebral palsy, or extreme malocclusion of the teeth. The help of specialists will be required for physical defects, but many speech problems are due to immaturity and to factors in the child's environment.

The classroom teacher needs to help pupils to distinguish the differences in sounds. The pupil must be "bombarded" with the proper sound of the *s, z, th, sh,* or whatever sound causes difficulty. His ear must recognize the sound and distinguish it from other sounds. The pupil should begin to learn the sound in isolation or in short simple words. The child should work on only one sound at a time and only at specific times. If he is corrected constantly during the day, he may begin to resent correction and revert to his former indifference to sound.

Perhaps one of the most constructive steps the teacher can take is to assist in developing healthy attitudes in the child, his parents, and his peers toward the handicap, relieving anxieties and tensions and enhancing his environment at school and at home. This may be more important than more formalized speech assistance.

Complex disorders: Stuttering is one of the most complicated and difficult speech problems. The stuttering child may have silent blocks during which he is unable to produce any sound, or he may repeat a sound, a word, or a phrase. He may prolong the initial sound of a word. Along with this, the child may show signs of excessive muscular strain, such as blinking his eyes.

It is normal for the child from the ages of two to six to repeat a sound, a word, or a phrase forty or fifty times for every 100 words. If no undue attention is focused on the child's speech during this period of nonfluency, maturation will usually enable him to overcome repetition.

When stuttering occurs in the classroom, it is wise for the classroom teacher to face this problem in a rather indirect way. It is equally important for the classroom teacher to realize that there is no such thing as "perfect speech." In adult speech, many nonfluencies are accepted as normal speech. The parents' help in eliminating sources of tension is also important.

The safest suggestion to the classroom teacher with regard to helping a child who stutters is "Don't." Do not ask him to stop and start over, to slow down, to speed up, to take a breath; this may only make him more concerned about the way he is talking and may cause him to stutter more. Do not deny him the right to recite in class—speaking should be made a rewarding experience for the pupil as often as possible. In fact, the pupil should be encouraged to talk and to keep on talking even if he stutters. Help him to develop confidence in his speaking ability. As far as possible, treat the child as if he had no stuttering problem. Accept and react to his stuttering as you would to normal speech and help the other members of the class to develop this same attitude of acceptance.

Others

Many other "special" children may be found in most public school classrooms: for example, the slow learner and the child with visual impairment, hearing impairment, or some other physical handicap. Most of the procedures and materials recommended in this book are effective with special children when reasonable adjustments are made for the particular difficulty. Furthermore, the recommendations for individualization of instruction and the de-emphasis upon arbitrary age-grade standards made in this and other current books help to focus upon each child's individual educational needs. The interested reader should refer to the selected references at the conclusion of this chapter and to other specialized sources for further in-depth study of children who have special difficulty.

Following are some general practices that may be emphasized when teaching special children.

1. The teacher's attitude toward a child is of paramount importance. Special children require much encouragement and understanding.

2. Special children need to realize success in their undertakings. Progress charts are a visible form for noting improvement.

3. Concrete and first-hand experiences are always a safe beginning point for instruction. Audio-visual materials can also be very helpful as a teaching strategy. Various modes of learning need to be presented: for example, the tracing, or kinesthetic, approach for handwriting and spelling instruction. And taping an assignment might be preferable to a written report for a visually handicapped child.

4. An extended readiness period is needed for each task. For the slow learner, many readiness activities are needed in preparation for manuscript writing. Activities that help to develop eye-hand coordination, such as construction with tools, drawing and painting, clay modeling, and coloring, are helpful.

5. One instructional item should be presented at a time. Instead of teaching "oral expression experiences" in a combined or unified manner, provide instruction about making introductions, then later about giving directions, and so on. Instruction should probably be more direct and more systematic than for the average child. Most

instruction would be with small groups or with individuals. Proceed from the easy to the more difficult. For example, when teaching manuscript, the letters o and c might be presented first, followed by l, i, and v; then b and f; and then g and j; and so on.

6. Expectations should be consistent with what children can realistically produce: for example, only five new spelling words per week for some children.

7. There must be frequent provision for practice and review.

8. Attention should be given to seating (in terms of the chalkboard, the teacher's position, and lighting).

9. Special tables, desks, and other work areas may be required for some physically impaired children.

10. Thoughtful consideration must be given to the learning problems of each child. For example, if poor motor coordination is affecting a child's handwriting ability, he should be encouraged to produce large handwriting; and in severe cases, it may be well for the child to use manuscript only. Due to the distinctness of the separate letter forms, manuscript style may also be most advantageous for the pupil with defective vision. For the brain-injured child, however, cursive writing is generally recommended by authorities.[10]

IDEAS FOR CORRECTIVE INSTRUCTION

There are pupils in almost every average classroom who are in need of special corrective or remedial instruction in the language arts; and this need becomes particularly apparent during the intermediate school years. Much has been written about such corrective work in the field of reading. Considerably less attention has been devoted to the other language arts.

Analytical testing

Providing materials and procedures for children in need of special instruction is considered a basic part of the regular classroom program. The first major step toward individualization of instruction would be the administration of a survey-of-language-arts test to all pupils in the class. This survey might be the language arts subtest of

---

10. Articles of the following nature are extremely valuable to teachers of special children: Anna McElravy, "Handwriting and the Slow Learner," *Elementary English* 41 (December 1964): 865–868; E. A. Enstrom, "Handwriting for the Retarded," *Exceptional Children* 32 (February 1966): 385–388; and Joseph Mullins et al., "A Handwriting Model for Children with Learning Disabilities," *Journal of Learning Disabilities* 5 (May 1972): 58–63.

any standardized test. The survey test should probably not be given until the third or fourth week of school in the fall. The results of the survey test should be examined in detail by the children. In individual conferences with the teacher, an effort should be made to determine why the overall score is low and why individual items on the test have caused difficulty.

After this analysis, the teacher could say, "Perhaps the results were not so good for several reasons. For example, you might have missed something in your earlier study. I have some other tests that may help in locating your difficulties more specifically." The teacher would have a number of tests dealing with specific skills, like listening, capitalization, punctuation, usage, vocabulary, spelling, and handwriting. A sample set of questions from a test dealing with punctuation is provided below. It can be seen that the items being tested involve the use of the period (1) at the end of a sentence, (2) after an abbreviation of the title of a person, (3) after an abbreviation of the name of a business organization, and (4) after the initials in a proper name.

These are exercises dealing with the period. Each sentence illustrates one usage of the period. Insert the needed period(s) for each sentence.
1. Bill is at his desk
2. Dr Jones is out of his office.
3. The Baker Co is located in Columbus, Ohio.
4. B F Brown is absent today.

Then, the teacher might say, "There are a number of these tests. You may start with any one, but as it is likely that you will want to take all or most of them, I suggest that you begin with the one on punctuation. Remember, you are taking these tests to find out what is causing your difficulty, so do your best, follow the instructions, and try each item, but do not spend too much time on any one item." At a later time, items missed on any test would be discussed with the pupil until the pupil is aware of his difficulty.

Follow-up materials

For each test, there would be a package of follow-up materials and exercises. In introducing them to the children, the teacher might say, "These special worksheets may help you to get a better start in punctuation. Look them over and see whether you wish to work on some of them instead of the regular work." (These worksheets may come from workbooks, other textbooks, programmed materials, or teacher-made materials.)

This procedure of specialized tests and sets of follow-up materials need not be used continuously, but can be interspersed with regularly scheduled times for providing special help. In whatever manner, the effort must be made to create a situation whereby pupils realize their deficiencies and are willing to make a serious effort to study some of the topics again. Some of the special study projects are carried out during the regular period and are, of course, used only with the few who volunteer and are weakest in achievement.

A sample of the type of exercise used on the worksheets is presented on page 460.

Additional resources

For those interested in further study of diagnostic and remedial teaching, with particular emphasis on the area of language arts, five additional reference sources are cited.

Blair, Glenn Myers. *Diagnostic and Remedial Teaching*. Rev. ed. (New York: Macmillan, 1956). See chapter 10, "Remedial Spelling"; chapter 11, "Remedial Handwriting"; and chapter 12, "Remedial Work in Fundamentals of English."

Brueckner, Leo J., and Bond, Guy L. *The Diagnosis and Treatment of Learning Difficulties* (New York: Appleton-Century-Crofts, 1955). See chapter 10, "Language"; chapter 11, "Spelling"; and chapter 12, "Handwriting."

Greene, Harry A., and Petty, Walter T. *Developing Language Skills in the Elementary Schools*. 4th ed. (Boston: Allyn and Bacon, 1971). See page 229 for speech; pages 274–277 for written expression; page 332 for usage; pages 425–427 for spelling; and pages 451–461 for handwriting.

Otto, Wayne, et al. *Corrective and Remedial Teaching*. 2d ed. (Boston: Houghton Mifflin, 1973). See chapter 10, "Spelling"; chapter 13, "Handwriting"; and chapter 14, "Written and Oral Expression."

————, and Koenke, Karl. *Remedial Teaching: Research and Comment* (Boston: Houghton Mifflin, 1969).

Corrective Worksheet: Punctuation (The Period)

Doing this exercise may give you a new look at the uses of the period. The questions are not difficult, but read each one carefully and think about what is called for before you mark or write.

1. Study each sentence below. Notice each circled period and try to figure out why it is used in each case.
   a.   John is not at home⊙
   b.   Mr⊙ Brown is a very busy person.
   c.   The Book Supply Co⊙ is located in a large city.
   d.   His name is R⊙ T⊙ Jones.

2. Is the period used in 1,a at the end of a sentence? Place periods correctly in each of the following sentences.
   a.   The skaters danced gracefully
   b.   Cats like fish
   c.   Bill is a good football player

3. Read aloud the sentences in 2. Did your voice drop at the end? Is that where you put a period?

4. Is the period used in 1,b after an abbreviation of a person's title? Place periods correctly in each of the following sentences.
   a.   Dr Jones is out of town.
   b.   Mrs Brooks lives next door to us.
   c.   The parade was led by Mr Davis.

5. Is the period used in 1,c after an abbreviation of the name of a business organization? Place periods correctly in each of the following sentences.
   a.   The Randolph Co makes many toys.
   b.   Le Grand, Inc is the name of a large firm.
   c.   Jim wrote a letter to Baxter Co for some materials.

6. Is the period used in 1,d after initials in a proper name? Place periods correctly in each of these.
   a.   G L Meers is our class president.
   b.   Billy C Stone took a trip to Chicago.
   c.   The book was written by T Robert Smith.

7. Place periods correctly in each sentence below.
   a.   We saw some squirrels in the park
   b.   The squirrels were eating nuts It was fun to watch them

8. Write four sentences to show the four uses of periods studied on this worksheet.

9. Find examples of these four uses of periods in your reading material.

10. If you would like more work with using the period, see your language arts textbook, page ____ .

LEARNING CENTERS AND SOME ADDITIONAL MATERIALS

Throughout this book, ideas for language arts learning centers have been proposed. Many language arts experiences lend themselves to a learning center concept where children may do specific activities related to some concept or skill reinforcement through activity cards or worksheets.

The worksheet below suggests how such an arrangement might be established at a language arts learning center for practice with filling in order forms.

Worksheet: Order Forms

To order something from a catalog, you must fill out an order form. Order forms ask for the following information:
1. Name and address
2. Catalog number
3. Name of article
4. Quantity desired
5. Size and color
6. Price of article
7. Shipping cost
8. Total price

Task:
1. Take a dittoed order form and a catalog.
2. Select a few things to order and fill in the order form.
3. Put the completed order form in your folder.

The more the teacher gears his thoughts toward providing part of the instruction through the learning center approach, the more ideas he can call to mind. The learning center concept is another valuable instructional procedure for helping to individualize instruction; it focuses upon the individual (or small group) and his needs in terms of ability, mode of learning, and rate of learning. It provides opportunities for incorporation of some of the better features of the exploratory approach to facilitate important learnings—motivation, responsibility, and true inquiry.

One excellent reference for the interested reader is Joyce F.

Glasser, *Elementary School Learning Center for Independent Study.*[11] Some commercially prepared learning center packages are available. For example: Instructo Corp., Paoli, Pa. 19301 (capitalization, abbreviations, letter writing, creative writing, contractions, punctuation, and homonyms).

Many suggestions of materials, helpful in meeting the needs of the varying range of pupils within the classroom, have been made in the preceding chapters. The following listing suggests still other materials.

Oral Composition

Plays for Echo Reading. New York: Harcourt Brace Jovanovich. (books and records, primary level)

Story Plays. New York: Harcourt Brace Jovanovich.

Talkstarters. Chicago: Scott Foresman. (primary)

Tell Again Story Cards. Levels I and II. Manchester, Mo.: McGraw-Hill.

Tell the Whole Story Series. Santa Monica, Calif.: Bailey Films Associates, Educational Media Co. (super 8 silent filmloops for primary-elementary)

Written Composition

Capitalization and Punctuation. Baldwin, N.Y.: Barnell Loft. (sets A–1 or grades 1–9)

Letter-writing. Paoli, Pa.: Instructo Corp. (series of four transparencies, intermediate)

Elementary English Filmstrips. New York: Collier-Macmillan School and Library Services. (six filmstrips for grades 3–6)

Thirty Lessons in Outlining. Wellesley, Mass.: Curriculum Associates.

Writing Can Be Fun. Minneapolis: S. Amidon and Associates. (ten audiotapes, grades 4–6)

Spelling

Spelling Demons I and II. Chicago: Central Scientific. (levels 4–7)

Spelling Progress Laboratory. Tulsa: Educational Progress Corp. (grades 2–6)

Word Growth Program. Wellesley, Mass.: Curriculum Associates. (spelling for grades 2–6)

---

11. Joyce F. Glasser, *Elementary School Learning Center for Independent Study* (Englewood Cliffs, N.J.: Prentice-Hall, 1971).

Handwriting

Alphabet 68. Forest Hill, N.Y.: Numark Publications. (grades 3 and above)

Handwriting for Beginners: Manuscript and *Improve Your Handwriting.* Chicago: Coronet Films.

SELECTED REFERENCES

General Professional

Greene, Harry A., and Petty, Walter T. *Developing Language Skills in the Elementary Schools.* 4th ed. Boston: Allyn and Bacon, 1971, chapter 4.

Smith, James A. *Adventures in Communication: Language Arts Methods.* Boston: Allyn and Bacon, 1972, chapter 13.

Strickland, Ruth. *The Language Arts in the Elementary School.* 3rd ed. Lexington, Mass.: D. C. Heath, 1969, chapter 9.

Specialized

Birch, Jack W., and McWilliams, Earl M. *Challenging Gifted Children.* Bloomington, Ill.: Public School Publishing, 1955.

Bureau of Curriculum Development. *Language Arts Games.* New York: City of New York: Board of Education, 1971.

Burns, Paul C. *Diagnostic Teaching of the Language Arts.* Itasca, Ill.: Peacock Publishers, 1974.

Courts, Ann. *Teaching Language Arts Creatively.* Minneapolis: T. S. Denison and Co., 1965.

Cutts, Norman E., and Moseley, Nicholas, eds. *Providing for Individual Differences in the Elementary School.* Englewood Cliffs, N.J.: Prentice-Hall, 1960.

Drewes, Ruth H., et al. *Practical Plans for Teaching English in Elementary Schools.* Dubuque, Iowa: William C. Brown, 1965.

Gerbrandt, Gary L. *An Idea Book for Acting Out and Writing Language, K –8.* Urbana, Ill.: National Council of Teachers of English, 1974.

Glaus, Marlene. *From Thoughts to Words.* Urbana, Ill.: National Council of Teachers of English, 1965.

Henry, Nelson B., ed. *Individualizing Instruction.* 61st Yearbook, part 1. Chicago: National Society for the Study of Education, 1962.

Hopkins, Lee Bennett. *Let Them Be Themselves: Language Arts Enrichment for Disadvantaged Children in Elementary Schools.* New York: Scholastic Book Services, 1969.

Hurwitz, Abraham B., and Goddard, Arthur. *Games to Improve Your Child's English.* New York: Simon & Schuster, 1970.

Joyce, William W., and Banks, James A. *Teaching the Language Arts to Culturally Different Children.* Reading, Mass.: Addison-Wesley, 1971.

Kaplan, Sandra, et al. *Change for Children*. Pacific Palisades, Calif.: Good-year, 1973.

Knight, Lester N. *Language Arts for the Exceptional: The Gifted and Linguistically Different*. Itasca, Ill.: Peacock Publishers, 1974.

Platts, Mary E., et al. *Spice*. Stevensville, Mich.: Educational Service, 1960.

Thomas, Janet K. *How to Teach and Administer Classes for Mentally Retarded Children*. Minneapolis: T. S. Denison and Co., 1968.

Thomas, Robert M., and Thomas, Shirley. *Individual Differences in the Classroom*. New York: McKay, 1965.

Torrance, E. Paul. *Rewarding Creative Behavior*. Englewood Cliffs, N.J.: Prentice-Hall, 1965.

Wagner, Guy, et al. *Language Games: Strengthening Language Skills with Instructional Games*. Darien, Conn.: Teachers Publishing, 1963.

Classroom Organization and Management

CLASSROOM ORGANIZATION
AND MANAGEMENT

OBJECTIVES	PERFORMANCE RESPONSES
1. To examine reasons for alternate organizational plans	1. Talk to at least two teachers at different levels to determine how they organize their class during formal language arts instruction. If possible, find out *why* they use the plan.
2. To compare and contrast different organizational plans	2. In small groups, discuss the advantages/disadvantages of the proposed organizational plans. Try to sketch the physical layout of a classroom of your choice.
3. To become acquainted with one method of classroom management	3. Prepare an outline of seven steps for behavioral reinforcement for one language arts concept or topic.
4. To identify various ways to explain a language arts program to parents	4. Prepare a letter or bulletin to parents on one of the suggested topics. (See page 480.)
5. To explain the role of the paraprofessional in the language arts classroom	5. Talk with a paraprofessional about his role in the language arts program. Share findings with members of the class.

The authors of this book have frequently taken the position that learning the language arts is an individual process dependent upon the interaction of the learner and the teacher or material. The first section of this chapter describes some alternative ways of organizing a class for effective learning. The plans described are used in classrooms throughout the country. The second major section of this chapter provides an example of behavior modification for one language arts component. Discussion of how paraprofessionals (both trained aides and volunteer parents and tutors) can best be utilized in the language arts program is offered in the third section of this chapter.

ALTERNATE PLANS

There are a number of reasons for offering alternative organizational plans in the seventies:

1. New technology has freed teachers to serve in new roles.
2. Systematic instruction based on objectives and individual needs has gained momentum.
3. Conventional organization (whole class or achievement—high, average, low) has not worked well for many children.
4. Numerous self-directing materials are now available, allowing pupils to move at their own rate and in their own style.
5. Interest in techniques of programming and reinforcement has received renewed interest.
6. Some vocal critics of the schools have reported that boring, mindless activities are taking place in the classroom.

The following organizational plans will be explored: individualized; partially individualized; like and unlike ability pairs; groups—intraclass, interclass, interest; nongraded/ungraded; and team.

Totally individualized

An individualized classroom would be represented by all pupils working on individual assignments, much like the Individually Prescribed Instruction (IPI) program for spelling.[1] IPI was begun in Pittsburgh in the mid-sixties in an attempt to prepare an individualized program of instruction for each child. This is an expensive

---

1. Philadelphia: Research for Better Schools, Inc., in cooperation with the Learning and Development Center, University of Pittsburgh.

approach, involving preliminary evaluation of performance and diagnosis of specific needs of pupils in terms of abilities and skills. The steps in the program involve:

placement test $\longrightarrow$ unit pretest $\longrightarrow$ prescription $\longrightarrow$ instructional activities $\longrightarrow$ scoring of work $\longrightarrow$ unit posttest $\longrightarrow$ demonstration of mastery $\longrightarrow$ next unit pretest

The instructional units are arranged in convenient skills boxes. These boxes contain student skill booklets, answer keys, and teacher packages containing testing materials and a guide. This individualized program relies on self-help and self-corrective instructional materials. Programmed materials provide one avenue for individualization.

Even though the ideal of totally individualized instruction (each child working alone and at his own rate and ability) is appealing, the reality of providing such instruction is generally overwhelming to many teachers.

Partially individualized

With partially individualized instruction, basic experiences are provided for the class or group, but individual follow-up and practice materials are also provided. By using several copies of workbooks, teachers can have a ready supply of practice material. Selected exercises may be mounted on cardboard and used repeatedly if covered with transparent contact paper on which answers may be written with a grease pencil. Such materials should be as self-instructional and self-checking as possible (answer key on back of card or at a checking station). Films, filmstrips, filmloops, records, tapes, and other devices may be part of the package of materials. Learning centers are another possible avenue toward individualization.

Commercial materials, like the "kits" or "laboratories" mentioned in the listening, spelling, and handwriting chapters, provide additional opportunities for individualization. Records and other supplementary material from basic textbook publishers are helpful in providing certain oral language experiences. Motivational writing centers and writing activity cards bolster the written composition program. Transparencies are available for capitalization and punctuation skills. Dictionary skills can be programmed.

Other opportunities for individualization already mentioned include bulletin boards, the language arts table, library or trade books, summary and review sessions, use of several different textbooks, activity cards, and corrective or remedial worksheets.

Even though the ideal of totally individualized instruction is appealing, the reality of providing such instruction is generally overwhelming to many teachers.

Ideas for differentiated instruction presented in chapter 12 lend themselves more easily perhaps to the partially individualized plan just described. Chapter 12 presents two basic complementary types of work: (1) whole-class work for common language experiences (conversation, storytelling, dramatization, etc.), followed by flexible grouping for specific instructional practices; and (2) special corrective or follow-up materials and exercises, largely for small-group and individual work. It is assumed that the teacher has a comprehensive view of the major language arts objectives and some preliminary evaluation of class and individual performance (by checklists, anecdotal records, etc.).

Like and unlike ability pairs

Several preceding chapters have recommended use of pupil pairs or teams working cooperatively. Pupil pairs or teams can work on special projects while the rest of the class is doing something else. While working relationships between individuals need supervision, results to date are encouraging.

Grouping

• *Intraclass* Placing children in "reading groups" based on ability (high, average, and low) is an almost universal practice in our schools, but the same grouping for the other language arts is far less frequent. Subgroups within the classroom have not truly met the different needs of children; most often pupils remain rigidly in their assigned groups and the same material is used with each member of the group, even though there is undoubtedly a diversity of abilities within any one group.

• *Interclass* Cross-class grouping necessitates parallel scheduling of language arts periods among several sections of one or several grades. Pupils go to different rooms (or spots within an "open classroom") according to their abilities. Thus, one teacher provides instruction for the high ability group, another teacher works with the average ability level, and so on. The assumption is that the range of abilities is reduced for each teacher, although the evidence is that differences in abilities in such situations is not appreciably lessened. (For grouping to be more truly "homogeneous," many criteria are needed for group formation: achievement, intelligence, interests, learning modality, and motivation.)

**Pupil pairs or partners
increase productivity by
providing mutual aid in
skill-development
activities. Moreover,
pairing of pupils permits
the teacher to become
a roving consultant and
facilitator.**

Interclass grouping ignores age and maturity by combining pupils from several different grade levels; it also often separates one content area from all others, somewhat lessening its overall effectiveness.

• *Interest*   All sorts of dynamic forces tend to create subgroups. The degree to which a group develops the ability to work together determines its learning of the tasks at hand. In the following illustration, Shaw and Shaw allowed second graders to choose their own groups for spelling study.

Some of the children formed groups that quickly developed cooperative work habits and learned more spelling words.

Other groups wasted time in arguments and nonwork activities and did not learn very much. In time, the weak groups developed more compatability and began to learn more effectively.[2]

This suggests that by assigning pupils to groups, they often lack common goals, and, as a result, learning is inhibited. Interest grouping (on the basis of friendship, common concerns, age, and the like) might be recommended for certain language arts activities (for example, projects involving creative writing, producing a class newspaper, or study exercises). Skills instruction for children of similar abilities can still be presented at other times.

The nongraded and ungraded classrooms

A nongraded class is one with a wide age span regardless of academic performance. Sometimes this plan is called "multiple-graded," "leveled," or "continuous progress." In such a situation, individual differences are often not much greater than in a single-grade situation. Again, it is possible to carry on different language experiences simultaneously and then to direct concentrated effort on specific abilities and skills according to maturity and needs. Differentiated exercises can be handled in small groups or on an individual basis. Nongraded classes can provide for differing rates of growth, but this can be obtained in any classroom by individualizing instruction and materials.

The ungraded plan emphasizes informal grouping by achievement levels. Pupils sometimes may continue with the same teacher for several years. This plan tends to encourage the child to progress at his own rate and often serves to direct the teacher toward individualization of instruction more than the ordinary classroom setting.

Team teaching

The team teaching arrangement involves two or three classes combined in one large area with a staff of several teachers. One teacher may instruct the entire class or a group in an area of his particular specialty, while other teachers work with different groups or individuals. Whether there are advantages in terms of greater recognition of individual differences is yet to be proven, but this has not

---

2. Marvin E. Shaw and Lilly May Shaw, "Some Effects of Sociometric Grouping Upon Learning in the Second Grade Classroom," *Journal of Social Psychology* 57 (August 1962): 453–458.

As a result of group efforts, team or cooperative teaching can identify individual pupil learning needs.

deterred a trend in this direction. "Open" classrooms (three or four sections of children in a large undivided area) are becoming more and more prevalent.

Comments

Obviously, organizational plans have a bearing on instruction, but the authors of this book feel that a competent teacher, not the structure, is really what makes the difference. Too often, new patterns are proposed without much consideration of teachers, available instructional materials, and in-service preparation. There are strengths and weaknesses in each of the organizational plans suggested in the foregoing discussion. Teachers must work toward an organizational system with which they are comfortable. Just as there is no one best way to teach the language arts, there is no one best way to organize a class that will suit the needs of every teacher or pupil.

A MANAGEMENT PROCEDURE

Several methods of classroom management are currently proposed for consideration. One popular procedure is termed *behavior modi-*

fication. Seven steps in this procedure are illustrated in the following example.

> "... Don't you want to be good spellers?"
> "Not me," says Sam, "I'm dumb and I don't even care."

A hypothetical case, Sam, is considered for a brief behavior modification program.

1. *Identify the behavior to change.* The teacher would want to alter Sam's attitude toward spelling, his self-concept ("I'm dumb and I don't care,"), and increase his spelling performance. The teacher would probably consider this a log-jam effect (several interrelated areas that could be worked on) and pick one area to attempt to modify, hoping the modification of it would take care of the others. Probably if the teacher could modify Sam's spelling performance, it would prove to him that he can spell and that he is not dumb, and this would help improve his self-concept. His "don't-care" attitude is probably a self-defense mechanism.

2. *Identify the terminal goal.* In order to realistically set a goal, the teacher will need to consult a prerequisite skills sequence checklist, diagnostic tests, and observation checklists to determine Sam's level of spelling. He might conclude that Sam has a good grasp of the prerequisite skills, but that he doesn't have an interest in learning to spell and has not had an opportunity for contextual use of spelling words. These are to be provided in the modification program.

Now the goal may be stated: "After a period of four weeks, in which the pupil (Sam) is permitted to keep a list of words (ten words per week) that he finds difficult and needs to learn to spell, he will demonstrate his increased spelling word performance by spelling, on a written test with 90 percent accuracy, ten randomly selected words from his list."

3. *Select the criterion level.* The criterion level, as stated in the terminal goal, is to spell with 90 percent accuracy ten randomly selected words from his list.

4. *Select a behavioral procedure.* The procedure, as stated in the terminal objective, is to *increase* his spelling performance.

5. *Specify contingencies (or reinforcements).*
Intervention Phase I: Each week, for two weeks, Sam

will be given a piece of candy for each of the ten words from his list that he spells correctly on a weekly written test.

Intervention Phase II: For the third week, Sam will be given five minutes free time for every word he spells correctly on his weekly spelling test.

Intervention Phase III: If Sam reaches his terminal goal, he will be permitted a leadership role, such as tutoring a younger child in spelling or another chosen area.

6. *Provide a favorable environment.* Changing to an individual spelling word list made by Sam, instead of a textbook list, should provide a more conducive situation to learning.

7. *Carry out the procedure.* Before anything is done or said to Sam regarding the modification program, his spelling performance would be observed for about one month to obtain a baseline. The program would then begin, graphing the data.

The desired behavior—improved spelling performance —was exhibited, but it cannot definitely be stated that the reinforcement was solely responsible. Sam's behavior might have changed simply because the method of assigning spelling words was changed. To determine if there is a relationship between the behavior and the reinforcement, a probe may be used. In the hypothetical case, reinforcement of the desired behavior (Intervention Phase IV) is stopped. A relationship could probably be inferred if there were a drop in the desired behavior with a return of it when the reinforcement was reinstated (Intervention Phase V).

A sample hypothetical behavior pattern is graphed in figure 13.1.

Students must learn to accept delayed reinforcement. Therefore, fading, by using delayed reinforcement or perhaps by pairing praise or social approval with the reinforcer being used until it generalizes, should be programmed into the behavior modification procedure.

Significant advantages of behavior modification in the schools include:

a. Effectiveness in dealing with motivational and instructional problems

FIGURE 13.1: Sam's Behavior Pattern During Behavior Modification

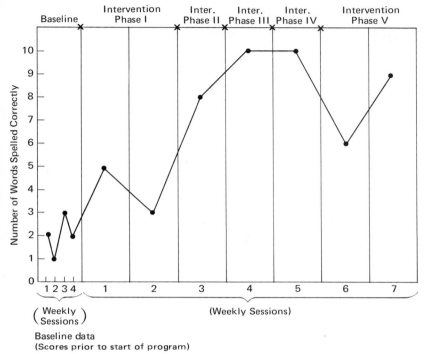

b. A pragmatic, problem-oriented approach
c. A built-in evaluation system

Behavior modification has much to offer in certain areas; in others, its application is not relevant. It is particularly relevant to questions related to motivation and to the organization and presentation of instruction, but it is not relevant to the instructional content. Behavior modification does have limitations in scope and approach. It may be helpful with individuals, but may not be the best approach for groups. Although the philosophy of educating children as individuals is a prevalent attitude among today's educators, there are times when it may be more practical to make group predictions and decisions.

Contingency contracting is another method of behavior modification. This is a means of specifying terminal behavior and the roles played by all individuals concerned with the program. The contract is drawn up so that it explicitly states the terminal behavior and the consequences to be applied to specific behaviors, as well as the stipulations mutually acceptable to the pupil, teacher, and parents. Contracting is sometimes used to avoid ethical problems regarding reinforcement.[3]

(Note: Many items affect the child's reaction to instruction. Two important factors are materials and teaching approaches used for instruction. A review of materials and teaching approaches, treated in chapter 1, may be beneficial. Moreover, the need for greater attention to the affective educational objectives, also presented in chapter 1, is closely related to the topic of classroom management. See also "Evaluation of Oral Expression" in chapter 5 and "Evaluating Handwriting" in chapter 11.)

PARENTS AND PARAPROFESSIONALS

Parents

Among the traditional methods of communication between teachers and parents are newsletters (carefully written letters and bulletins to keep the parents informed about happenings at school); school booklets (including rules and regulations and helpful information that parents need to know before and after sending their child to school); Parent-Teacher Association meetings; written reports in the form of a personal letter or checklist; telephone calls; social or covered-dish suppers; home visits (which give the parents and teacher a chance to discuss a particular problem and acquaint the teacher with the home environment of the child); and Open House (a day when the parents visit in the classroom—with or without the presence of the children—to familiarize themselves with the materials, schedules, and routines of the school day). For years, schools have utilized these methods to foster communication between school and home.

Many avenues are open to the language arts teacher who wishes to communicate with parents. For example, he can suggest general and specific activities for the children to do at home; he can hold conferences about reporting devices, tests, and homework; and he can send out letters or bulletins to keep parents informed of what is going on at school.

---

3. Beth Sulzer and G. Roy Mayer, *Behavior Modification Procedures for School Personnel* (Hinsdale, Ill.: Dryden Press, 1972).

• *Home activities*   Language has been initiated long before the child has his first encounter with the school. Parents are usually the first and most long-term teachers of their children. They talk with their children, sincerely listen to them, introduce them to the world and broaden their horizons, point out signs and labels, help them to perceive relationships, and read to them. All of these activities lay the foundation for success in the language arts program. Since not all children have had the benefit of these activities, a concerted effort should be made to help all parents develop this type of home program. For this to occur, parents must be considered allies in education; their help should be sought and welcomed. Most parents want to help but may need assistance and information about how to go about it. Such information can be disseminated through home visits, parent-teacher conferences, study groups, or other means. Some ideas of the sort of things appropriate for such instruction are described in the following paragraphs.

Parents should be helped to understand that talking with their youngsters provides a backlog of information that is basic to the language arts program. Children learn many words through conversations with their parents. As parents listen to children, they are con-

When adults read to children, children develop language skills essential to becoming readers.

veying the idea that the child has something worthwhile to say, which encourages him to speak more often and more freely. It is not necessary for parents to make special preparation or provide structured content as they talk with their children; rather, they should share some of the everyday things like time, seasons, special holidays, animals, food, transportation, and weather. Answering children's questions and explaining the meanings of new words comes naturally when chilren are enjoying an experience with their parents. Experiences could include going to the grocery store, dime store, drugstore, bank, service station, airport; taking a walk; or taking a more special trip, like a visit to the museum, zoo, bakery, dairy farm, or bottling company. Longer trips provide even more talk about roads, rivers, mountains, etc. A camping trip, for example, offers many opportunities for vocabulary development, as suggested below.

> *Bedding:* air mattress, bag liner, cot, mosquito net, sleeping bag
> *Kitchen equipment:* aluminum foil, charcoal, cooler, dutch oven, grill, propane, spatula, tongs
> *Personal equipment and shelter:* first aid kit, ground canvas, insect repellent, stakes, wash basin
> *Tools:* axe, compass, lantern, pliers, portable radio, saw, screwdriver, shovel

In addition to a shared, enjoyable experience, many valuable by-products accrue when parents read to children. Facility in the use of oral language is developed. As the child asks questions, describes pictures, repeats favorite parts, and retells the story, he is getting an excellent foundation in essential language arts skills. The child's listening and speaking vocabularies are increased as he learns the usage and meanings of words through pictures, context, and parent definitions. Children are able to experience vicariously, storing valuable background information to be drawn on later for interpretative purposes. Moreover, children come to see the connecting link between speech and printed symbols. A part of reading to a child would certainly involve making maximum use of the public library, seeing that the child has his own library card, and taking him to the library often to check out books that fit his interests and level of development.

Some topics for parent-teacher discussions might include the following:

1. What we know about how children learn language
2. The importance of self-concept in language learning
3. The use of learning games in the language arts

4. Using mass media for enhancing language learning
5. Parents as pacesetters for the language arts program

• *Reports, tests, and homework*   The report card is a report to parents and children about the child's performance in school. There are additional facts, however, that teachers want parents to know about their children and the school program that are not included on a report card.

To prepare an individual report or to hold a parent-teacher conference, the teacher needs a folder of work samples. In addition to the child's work samples, classroom charts giving information on weekly test scores or other achievement records should be kept.

With regard to parent-teacher conferences, many schools schedule three conferences per year—around the last week of November, the first week of February, and the second week of May. Frequently, a standard form is utilized at this conference, where comments about the child's personal and social growth and his academic progress in the various subjects are to be filled in. A record may be maintained of main points discussed with parents, conclusions reached, and recommendations by the teacher and the parents.

At the November conference, the language arts materials used in school may be presented to the parents, as well as an explanation of the language arts experiences and abilities and skills to be emphasized that particular year. Some explanation may be given about how the language arts program is organized and the general approaches the teacher uses. At this time, some idea of what (if anything) will be required of the child in terms of homework may be suggested, as well as what to do when the child requests help.

In an early parent meeting, the teacher also might suggest supporting materials, such as language arts games (homemade or commercially produced) and trade books that present language arts concepts. (See chapter 2, pages 56–57.)

The February conference may consist of sharing children's work and test results (textbook, teacher, standardized). When a standardized language arts test has been administered, it is generally a good idea to report the results to parents. The range, the median score of the class, and the individual pupil's score are considered to be essential information to give to the parents. In parent-teacher conferences, test results provide some tangible information for discussion. Furthermore, this type of information is relatively free of teacher bias and therefore lends itself well to discussion of problems. In these parent-teacher conferences, teachers should attempt, just as in discussion with pupils, to give parents a true picture of the test results and their implications.

The teacher should explain why and how he is attempting to help when particular difficulties of the child are brought up in discussion. Interested parents may request additional ideas to use with their child for reinforcement purposes.

The final conference is often more of an evaluation session. Again, the child's progress since the last conference is reported, along with possible ideas and suggestions for summer activities. Parents should have the opportunity to ask questions and to find ways they can be of help.

Homework certainly involves the entire family. When homework assignments are made, they should be carefully planned, with the pupils motivated to complete the assignment. Most homework should be of an informal nature, supplementing formal preparation in the classroom, and should only be made after children understand the concepts and ideas sufficiently to do the homework unaided. Hopefully, most homework assignments should be personalized—with little or no regularly assigned, drill-type homework for the entire class.

• *Letters and bulletins*   Teachers should recognize that the report card or the teacher-parent conference are still only two means of interpreting the child's interaction with the school language arts program. Another means is a simple progress report, containing news the children bring home in their own handwriting. For example: "Everyone in the first grade can write the figures to 10." A school or district-wide pamphlet on "Our Language Arts Program" may meet a common need and be more efficient than a teacher's individual efforts. Some teachers provide a letter with each report. On page 481 is a sample letter sent from one classroom.

Some topics suitable for bulletins or letters include the following:

1. How parents can help in building language arts concepts prior to school entrance
2. How new language arts experiences are introduced in the classroom
3. An illustrative lesson taught in the classroom
4. Explanation of various modern procedures
5. How fast and slow learners are managed in the language arts classroom

• *Concluding comments*   The following general suggestions for parents may be of help.

Hawthorne School
Springfield, Missouri
October 18, 1975

Dear Parents,

Many of the children in the class are working on their listening skills. I would like to tell you what we are doing and to ask your help, if you wish.

We are working each day with a new listening center. The children are listening to tapes I have prepared for the tape recorder. They are listening to different sounds, trying to identify each one. These are everyday sounds at home and school. This may help the children to learn to be more attentive to sounds around them. They are also listening to tapes that give them certain directions to follow. This helps them to listen carefully. Other tapes have stories on them. The children listen and then answer questions about the story. This may help them to remember things they hear. I want you to know about these activities so that you will be aware of things your child may be talking about at home. If you would like to visit our listening center and see how we use it, please come in and see us.

At school, your child is a part of a group much of the time, but at home, you have the opportunity to spend some time with him alone. This provides an excellent opportunity for talking and listening. When you read to him, this involves listening he can enjoy and it helps him to concentrate on a particular thing for a longer period of time. Talk with him, if you like, about sounds made by various things: natural sounds, mechanical sounds, people sounds. You might like the idea of playing sound games with your child. For example, you can fill bottles or glasses with different amounts of water and strike them with a spoon. Ask the child which makes the highest sound and which the lowest sound. Or play the "quiet game." Have everyone be very quiet for five minutes. Then see how many sounds heard during the quiet period can be identified and named.

Children usually enjoy following directions. Tell the child to do one thing, such as "Turn around." When he can follow simple directions, make them harder, such as "Turn around and walk upstairs." The directions can be made as difficult as the child can handle at the time.

A record player and records are also useful. Children enjoy listening to stories and music on records. This may help them to learn to listen for more sustained periods of time.

Finally, take as much time as possible to talk with your child, listening to his ideas and the things he tells you about his school day. This may be the single most important thing you can do to help your child's listening skill.

Sincerely,

Ms. Stein

1. Work from the beginning to keep in touch with your child's language arts program. Read his textbook.
2. Have your youngster explain his language arts program to you. Play the role of the patient listener and curious questioner.

3. Attempt to learn some of the technical vocabulary of the "new" language arts.
4. Encourage your child to complete assignments, read books, think independently, and be curious about language arts ideas.
5. Help him to study by providing him with the space, the time, and the tools he needs.
6. If your child has a natural talent for the language arts, be sure to capitalize on this potential. Encourage him to participate in language arts fairs or to complete optional projects for language arts classes.
7. If your child is having difficulty with any part of the language program, try to give him help at an early date.
8. To promote independent thinking, use good judgment in giving help with homework. Express interest when questions are asked and try to ask questions that will help your child find the answer himself rather than answering the questions directly.

Paraprofessionals

There is a growing use of adults as paid or volunteer assistants to the teacher. Programs involving adult assistance take many forms: working with an individual or small groups while the teacher conducts a lesson for the rest of the class; tutoring after school hours; and helping with clerical work, marking workbooks, making displays or other audiovisual materials, and many other of the tasks inherent in the operation of the classroom.

Many teachers have reacted positively to this new source of assistance. When aides are used to assist in instruction, it is apparent that they need some professional training in how to relate to children positively, how to teach a simple skill, and how to judge pupil progress. Under the best conditions, the role of the paraprofessional in the language arts classroom can be that of an instructional aide as well as a clerical aide. Basically, the classroom teacher is responsible for the activities the aide performs, as well as preparing the aide to carry out assigned activities. Supervision of the aide is mandatory, and the teacher again assumes the major responsibility of this supervision. Assuming the paraprofessional is a capable and responsible person, the following items suggest some areas where he may be of assistance within the classroom.

1. Score teacher-made tests or worksheets.
2. Work with small groups or individuals on particular language arts skills.
3. Read to large or small groups.
4. Set up and use audio-visual materials (transparencies, charts, posters, tape recorders, projectors, etc.).
5. Prepare instructional materials, such as word files, skills boxes, etc.
6. Arrange for guests to speak to the class.
7. Assist in planning and supervising field trips.
8. Work with small groups in instructional games.
9. Assist children in the use of reference materials.
10. Set up displays and bulletin boards.
11. Develop and set up learning center activities.
12. Assist in maintaining records that evaluate pupil progress.

In addition, student aides or tutors (older students helping younger students) have been used during the past decade with varying degrees of success. Where most successful, extensive preplanning has been involved, there is special attention given to attitude and

Paraprofessionals, like teacher aides, can help the classroom become more child-centered, providing more individualized planning and instruction, more personal attention, and an enriched variety of activities designed to meet the needs of individual children.

approach, orientation to the program and materials, a clear-cut plan of organizational structure and supervision, and record-keeping procedures.

There are a number of books available on the general topic of paraprofessionals and tutors. Most of these sources relate directly to reading instruction, but ideas may be gleaned from them that may be adapted to other areas of the curriculum.

Brigham Young University Press. *Structured Tutoring*. Provo, Utah: Brigham Young University Press, 1970.

Brotherson, Mary Lou, and Johnson, Mary Ann. *Teacher Aide Handbook*. Danville, Ill.: Interstate, 1971.

Gartner, Alan, et al. *Children Teach Children: Learning by Teaching*. New York: Harper & Row, 1971.

Rauch, Sidney. *Handbook for the Volunteer Tutor*. Newark, Del.: International Reading Association, 1969.

Sleisenger, Lenore. *Guidebook for the Volunteer Reading Teacher*. New York: Teachers College Press, Columbia University, 1965.

Tutor-Student System. Kansas City, Mo.: National Tutoring Institute, n.d.

Wright, Betty Atwell. *Teacher Aides to the Rescue: Program Guidelines to Better Home-School-Community Partnerships*. New York: John Day, 1969.

Information about school volunteer programs is available from:

National Center for Voluntary Action, Paramount Building, 1735 Eye St., N.W., Washington, D.C. 20006 (newsletter: *Voluntary Action*).

National School Volunteer Program, Inc., 16 Arlington St., Boston, Mass. 02116.

Project Print, Washington Technical Institute, 4100 Connecticut Ave., N.W., Washington, D.C. 20006 (newsletter: *Volunteer Viewpoints*).

SELECTED REFERENCES

General Professional

Boyd, Gertrude. *Teaching Communication Skills in the Elementary School*. New York: Van Nostrand Reinhold, 1970, chapter 2.

Corcoran, Gertrude B. *Language Arts in Elementary School: A Modern Linguistic Approach*. New York: Ronald, 1970, chapter 3.

Reading

READING

OBJECTIVES	PERFORMANCE RESPONSES
1. To identify and describe reading readiness factors	1. a. Prepare a written critique of a set of commercial reading readiness materials. b. Prepare a file of suggestions for promoting some aspect of reading readiness.
2. To gain insight into features of basal reading materials	2. Compare two basal reading programs. Summarize findings in a short report.
3. To be able to design a Directed Reading Approach (D.R.A.)	3. Develop a Directed Reading Approach lesson plan for use with a child or group of children.
4. To be able to design a Directed Reading-Thinking Activity (D.R.T.A.)	4. Develop a Directed Reading-Thinking Activity lesson plan for use with a child or group of children.
5. To become familiar with major features of the language-experience approach	5. Observe a teacher using the language-experience approach. Discuss with the teacher the strategies used for vocabulary development (word banks), skills development (decoding), and record-keeping.
6. To become acquainted with major features of individualized reading	6. Observe a teacher using this approach. Discuss with the teacher the materials used, the conference, and record-keeping for evaluation.
7. To gain insight into other approaches to reading	7. Give an oral report to peers on one of the other reading approaches (linguistic, phonics, changed alphabet, or systems).
8. To identify important phonic, syllabication, or accent generalizations	8. a. Prepare a list of phonic, syllabication, or accent generalizations presented in one set of basal reading materials. b. Present knowledge of generalizations by completing the exercises in the Hull or Wilson references. (See Selected References.)
9. To become aware of some strategies for promoting basic reading skills	9. Develop a card file of ideas (or prepare teacher-made devices) for enhancing word

recognition, comprehension, or vocabulary development at one age/grade level of your preference.

10.	To illustrate the hierarchy of questioning techniques on reading materials	10.	Develop a set of written questions (as categorized by Sanders) for a story to be used with a child or a group of children.
11.	To demonstrate ability to use a readability formula	11.	Apply a readability formula to a basal reader and to a content-area book (at an age/grade level of your preference).
12.	To know some strategies for promoting content reading	12.	Prepare a set of teaching ideas for content reading.
13.	To identify and describe features of standardized reading tests	13.	Secure a copy (and teacher's manual) of a standardized reading test. After study, report to your peers about it.
14.	To become acquainted with ways to assess reading performance in informal ways (like determining three levels for a child and his reading attitudes and interests)	14.	Prepare and administer as many informal inventory suggestions as possible to a child. Write a report summarizing the results.

Reading (the interaction between a reader and written language through which the reader tries to reconstruct the writer's message) is a language process. The previous chapters focusing on listening, speaking, and writing are a necessary foundation for the special language arts experience termed *reading* in this chapter.[1] For example, the language experiences for children five and under are part of the growth process leading toward reading. (See chapter 3.) A special relationship exists between listening and reading. (See chapter 4.) Oral expression has been called the "warp and woof" of the language arts curriculum, basic to extending meanings to all of

---

1. Reading deserves a more detailed consideration than can be given here, but the major ideas cited herein may provide a guide for study of textbooks devoted exclusively to the teaching of reading. (See Selected References.) One advantage of a chapter of this nature is the opportunity it provides for highlighting the many interrelationships within the total language arts curriculum.

its facets. (See chapter 5.) Chapter 6 on literature developed one of the major purposes for providing the child with reading tools. One means of relating early writing experiences with reading (language-experience approach) is described in chapter 7. In chapter 8, the notion of developing and expanding concepts is explored; encoding skills (vis-à-vis decoding skills) are presented in chapter 10 ("Spelling"); and the idea of providing for individual differences—recognition of cultural differences and the importance of attitudes toward "special" children—certainly applies to children as readers.[2]

The English language is replete with figures of speech. One common type is the simile. Children need experiences with figurative language, for it can be a barrier for some children in understanding the intended meaning.

2. For example, see Thomas D. Horn, ed., *Reading for the Disadvantaged: Problems of Linguistically Different Learners* (New York: Harcourt Brace Jovanovich, 1970).

OVERVIEW

In a general way, the reading program for the elementary school years may be divided into four closely related and overlapping periods or stages, as follows.

1. The period of preparing the child for beginning reading, sometimes called the period of reading readiness
2. The period of instruction in beginning reading, with emphasis upon the rudiments of word identification and word recognition and upon reading for meaning
3. The period of stimulating rapid growth in reading power, particularly in those skills essential to the development of independence in word identification and to effective word recognition, in the attitude of demanding meaning, and in those understandings and skills which constitute the beginning of independence in coping with meaning difficulties
4. The period of establishing reading power, with emphasis upon the achievement of independence in word identification, of a high degree of skill in word recognition, of the attitude of demanding meaning, and of independence in coping with meaning difficulties[3]

Flexibility, ingenuity, and creativity are essential on the part of the teacher.

For the fruition of the more mature "fourth" level reader, sound principles of instruction are a necessity in the instructional program. Following are some of these principles.

1. Since reading is a language process, reading instruction is built upon past and present language experiences.
2. Reading instruction is a part of the language activities in other curricular areas.
3. Reading instruction focuses upon meaning—at all stages of instruction. Reading is more than a mechanical process, even though some skills are an essential part of the process.
4. Reading instruction demands a variety of approaches, since any procedure is likely to work better with some children than with others. Authorities agree that there is no one best method or set of materials for teaching reading. For this reason, flexibility, ingenuity, and creativity are essential on the part of the teacher.
5. Reading instruction should be diagnostic in the sense that it is appropriate for each child's weaknesses and strengths.

---

3. Paul McKee, *The Teaching of Reading in the Elementary School* (Boston: Houghton Mifflin, 1948), p. 138. Reprinted by permission of the publisher.

In this way, emphasis is placed on early detection and correction of reading difficulties in order to prevent deterioration into reading failure.

6. Reading instruction must be systematically pursued throughout the elementary school and beyond since it is a long-term, developmental process.

READINESS

Ausubel defines readiness as "the adequacy of existing capacity in relation to the demands of a given learning task."[4] Readiness is a factor at all reading levels, though most frequently associated with beginning or first-grade reading: that is, the gradual development from nonreading to beginning reading. Even though readiness has been achieved at one level of experience, it does not necessarily follow that readiness is present at a higher level (for example, reading of content area textbooks). Readiness is an important concept for any reading experience at any level.

Factors influencing beginning reading instruction and their implications for teaching are noted in chart 14.1.

As noted in chart 14.1, the language experiences suggested in chapters 3, 5, and 6 are some which the teacher can arrange so that prereading skills will be developed. The relationship between language development and reading readiness factors is easily identified in such recommended activities as conversing, listening to records or to the teacher read or tell a story, planning an excursion or a party, distinguishing sounds, and the like. With such activities, the opportunities for building vocabulary and listening and speaking skills are quite obvious. Other activities (such as drawing, painting, rhythm, and play) are also related to reading in terms of color differentiation, eye-hand coordination, and attention. Both types of activities are bound together with language—developing and extending concepts. Reading is an extension of this process.

The readiness activities will vary from classroom to classroom; some activities are suitable for some children but not for others. The length of time to continue the readiness activities will vary from child to child; they cannot be arbitrarily ended by a certain calendar date.

Ideas of some specific criteria, which may be kept in mind by the teacher in the assessment of a child's readiness for reading, are

---

4. David P. Ausubel, "Viewpoints from Related Disciplines: Human Growth and Development," *Teachers College Record* 60 (February 1959): 246.

CHART 14.1: Reading Readiness Factors and Related Implications

Factors	*Implications*
1. Background of experience	1. Implementation of ideas like those presented in chapter 3 (experiences, opportunities, materials)
2. Language facility	2. Implementation of ideas like those presented in chapters 3 and 5
3. Interest in reading	3. Implementation of ideas like those presented in chapter 6
4. Social and emotional development	4. Individual and group communication and participation; experiences structured so the child feels accepted and secure and develops desirable attitudes toward himself and others (Language is a prime catalyst in social and emotional development.)
5. Physical development	5. Other than good general health, vision and hearing acuity are most important. Auditory discrimination of speech sounds suggests ideas like rhyming words and initial sounds in words. The child's need to make fine visual discriminations is obvious, suggesting early activities with forms and shapes, like those presented in chapter 3, and later involving letter recognition, words beginning or ending alike, etc.
6. Intelligence	6. Data attest to the importance of mental age, but do not establish a particular point on the mental age-continuum as the point below which children will not achieve success in reading. Prereading activities, socioeconomic factors, teachers, methods, and materials must be considered in each individual situation.

cited on pages 87–88. A representative commercial readiness program, which includes an excellent set of activities for growing into and beginning reading (as well as a set of assessment ideas), is *Language and How to Use It, Beginning Levels*, by Marion Monroe.[5]

An issue often raised is: "Should formal reading instruction begin in the kindergarten?" The authors of this book feel that any time a child is eager for help in this area, he should be encouraged with materials and time. The idea of introducing reading to children who meet the criteria of readiness has merit. But there are many other important functions at the kindergarten level, one of which is attention to language facility (experience stories, oral speaking activities, dramatic play, etc.). It is virtually impossible to overemphasize the relationship that exists between a child's language facility and learning to read. Reading is related to all language functions, and learning to read is built upon past language experiences. In brief, all kindergarten children should be challenged and aided to grow toward learning to read, but not necessarily toward reading itself in a formal program of reading instruction.

For parents who are interested in learning about the prereading stage (birth to sometime in grade 1), several references are footnoted.[6]

MAJOR APPROACHES TO READING INSTRUCTION

While some major approaches to reading instruction are presented separately in this section, one approach does not necessarily exclude practices which may be highlights of other instructional approaches. Differences—teachers, circumstances, pupil needs—militate against the idea of a single method as the "best" way to teach reading to all children. Poor practices can flourish under any label and are not necessarily inherent in the set of materials or methods.

Basal

For many years, basal reader series (coordinated sets of textbooks, teaching guides, and supplementary materials) have served

---

5. Marion Monroe, *Language and How to Use It, Beginning Levels* (Glenview, Ill.: Scott Foresman, 1970). For the role of boys in the reading program, see David Austin et al., *Reading Rights for Boys: Sex Role and Development in Language Experiences* (New York: Appleton-Century-Crofts, 1971).

6. A. Sterl Artley, *Your Child Learns to Read* (Chicago: Scott Foresman, 1953); James L. Hymes, *Before the Child Reads* (Evanston, Ill.: Row, Peterson, 1958); Doris M. Lee and Richard V. Allen, *Learning to Read Through Experience* (New York: Appleton-Century-Crofts, 1963); and Marion Monroe, *Growing into Reading: How Readiness for Reading Develops at Home and at School* (Chicago: Scott Foresman, 1951).

as some of the chief instructional materials in the elementary school for teaching reading. Basal materials are of an eclectic nature; the authors and publishers attempt to meet the needs of all children by providing for the various developmental levels with interesting reading materials, carefully sequenced skill development plans, and a variety of related teaching materials, equipment, and activities. Following is a list of typical basal reading materials.

1. A sequential set of pupil reading materials
    For example, Houghton Mifflin readers include the following:

Level 1	*Getting a Head Start*	(prereading)
Level 2	*Getting Ready to Read*	(prereading)
Level 3A	*Tigers*	(preprimer)
Level 3B	*Lions*	(preprimer)
Level 3C	*Dinosaurs*	(preprimer)
Level 4	*Rainbows*	(primer)
Level 5	*Signposts*	(1st reader)
Level 6	*Secrets*	(2^1 reader)
Level 7	*Rewards*	(2^2 reader)
Level 8	*Panorama*	(3^1 reader)
Level 9	*Fiesta*	(3^2 reader)
Level 10	*Kaleidoscope*	(4th reader)
Level 11	*Images*	(5th reader)
Level 12	*Galaxies*	(6th reader)

2. Teacher manuals or editions (These contain suggestions for use of the reading materials at each reading level.)
3. Supplementary materials (These are to be used in conjunction with the regular series, even at the primary level. Some reinforce the regular basal texts; others are designed for the less and more advanced readers.)
    For example, the Scott Foresman Reading Systems offer these other components:

    teaching/learning materials
        read-aloud collections (literature to read to pupils)
        pupils' books (stories, poems, articles, riddles, and other selections)
    Magneboard, Magnepiece File, and Magnepieces (display boards for sentences, words, letters, and pictures)
    studybooks (skills development exercises)
    independent practice pads (available also in duplicating masters)
    take-home books (reprints of selected pupils' books)

classroom management materials
    tests (for each level)
    class record books (to note progress of children)
    pupils' cumulative record cards (maintenance of records)
    teachers' professional library (softbound reference books)
    informal reading inventory
additional components
    special practice books (extra reading needs)
    special practice kits (multi-sensory learning aids)
    overhead visual (additional practice on skills)
    match-and-check, choose-and-check, read-and-check (manipulative activities)
    alphabet cards
    word, context, and dictionary puzzles

Providing a well-balanced and skill-sequenced program with an economy of the teacher's time is one of the virtues of basal readers, along with the advantage of the availability of excellent teacher's guides and supplementary materials. On the other hand, the concern for controlling the introduction of new words hampers the construction, content, and variety of reading materials, particularly at the beginning levels. Some school systems adopt several different basal reader series to be used by different pupils within the schools.

• *D.R.A.*   Many basal readers have specific lesson plans often referred to as D.R.A.—Directed Reading Approach. They often include steps like those suggested in chart 14.2.

A sample second grade reading lesson will suggest more specifically the manner used in one basal reader to present a directed reading activity. This lesson uses the story, "Bascombe, the Fastest Hound Alive," from *Rewards*, the second level reader for the second grade in a basal series.[7]

STEPS IN A D.R.A. LESSON

1. Building readiness: After the teacher tells the children that the first story they are going to read in this book is about a basset hound called Bascombe, he asks if anyone can tell anything about a basset hound. The teacher develops the information (supplying it if necessary) that a basset

7. William K. Durr, *Rewards* (Boston: Houghton Mifflin, 1971), pp. 45–46.

CHART 14.2: Lesson Plan for D.R.A.

I. PREPARATION FOR READING
building an experience background, introducing new concepts and vocabulary, and setting up purposes for reading

II. FIRST READING
reading silently to get the sense of the story

III. CHECKING COMPREHENSION
answering questions; clearing up confusions through retelling; noting main ideas, details, and inferences; and relating to real experiences

IV. SECOND READING
reading orally all or parts of the story as a means of diagnosis, checking on specific skills, developing expression before an audience, and enjoying the story

V. RELATED SKILLS/ABILITIES
practicing skills: word recognition, comprehension, and vocabulary development

VI. EXTENSION
reading supplementary materials, viewing films/filmstrips, listening to records, participating in activities related to the story

---

hound is an unusual looking, slow-moving dog with short legs, a heavy body, and long, drooping ears.

2. Introducing new vocabulary: The teacher prints *Bascombe* on the chalkboard and tells the children that this is the name of the basset hound. He prints *Mr. Winston* on the chalkboard and tells the children that this is the name of Bascombe's owner. The teacher prints *Herbert* and *Sam* on the chalkboard. He tells the children that these are the names of two other characters in the story and asks if anyone can read their names. (For slower groups, the teacher may also introduce the words *country, droop, tiny, sigh,* and *caught.* Suggestions for doing this are found in the teacher's guide and in the Word Introduction Book for Level 7.)

3. Setting purposes for reading: The teacher asks the pupil to read the title of the story. He asks the children to consider why Bascombe might be called "the fastest hound alive." He asks them to find Bascombe in the pictures on pages 8 and 9 and to note what Bascombe is doing about

the caterpillar on his nose. The teacher tells them to read pages 7 through 11 to themselves to find out why Bascombe is feeling so sad. He suggests that they use what they know about the sounds that letters stand for and the sense of the other words to help figure out any new words.

4. Discussing the content read: The teacher asks different children some of the following questions:

> Why was Bascombe feeling sad?
> Why was Mr. Winston going to sell Bascombe?
> What did Bascombe say when they asked if he was sad?
> What word did Bascombe use instead of *yes?*

5. Reading to answer specific questions: The teacher tells the children to find on page 10 what Bascombe said when asked if he was sad. He encourages a child to try to make his voice show how Bascombe felt. In the same manner, he asks for sentences to be read that tell where Bascombe lived, the paragraph that describes Bascombe, the paragraph that tells what Bascombe did during the day and at night, and what Bascombe did if anyone called him.

In a manner similar to that described above, the teacher has the pupils read the remainder of the story. In a subsequent daily lesson, attention is given to the reading skills suggested in the teacher's guide as appropriate for the unit and for pupil needs.

• *D.R.T.A.*   The D.R.T.A. (Directed Reading-Thinking Activity) has been proposed as an alternate general plan, suitable not only for basal reading but also for content area reading.[8] In the sample lesson below, the teacher uses a story, "The Notable Thomas Jefferson," from *Bold Journeys*, the fifth level reader for the fifth grade in a basal series.[9]

1. Making predictions and setting purposes from title clues only:
   a. Instruct pupils to turn to the table of contents to locate the title of the story.
   b. After the title is located and read, the prediction and

---

8. Russell G. Stauffer and Ronald Cramer, *Teaching Critical Reading at the Primary Level* (Newark, Del.: International Reading Association, 1968).

9. M. Gartler et al., *Bold Journeys* (New York: Macmillan, 1967), pp. 250–251.

purpose-setting session can be initiated with open-ended questions like "What do you think the story will be about?" "What do you think will happen in this story?"

   c. Adequate time should be given to the children for thinking and reflecting during the prediction and purpose-setting session. The teacher should try to involve each child during this initial discussion.

   d. The teacher does not give any of his own ideas and judgments during the discussion. It is essential that the teacher accept all ideas the children mention, no matter how ridiculous they may seem to him.

2. Reading of text:

   a. Children are directed to open their books to pages 250–251. They read silently for the purposes established earlier and decide whether they are right.

   b. The teacher is available during silent reading to give help and to encourage pupils to check out their predictions.

   c. Since there are five subheadings in this story, children read only to the first one on page 251.

3. Appraisal of predictions and purposes—adjustments, extension, refinement, or rejection of original purposes and predictions:

   a. As the children finish silent reading, they close their books with a marker in the place. After all have finished, the teacher initiates the discussion by asking questions such as "Who was right?"

   b. If some children think they were right, they are asked why they think so. In some cases children may need to reread the story. Some children can tell why their prediction was wrong. Each child is checked to see how he dealt with his original prediction.

   c. The children who think they were right are asked to read orally that portion of the text proving they are right. Other children listen with their books closed.

   d. On the basis of information gained during reading these two pages, students are given an opportunity to adjust their predictions and purposes for what is going to happen in the next section. They also consider the second subtitle, "Like Father, Like Son."

4. The above plan is repeated with each of the remaining four sections until the story is completed.

Many types of flexible grouping for reading are necessary if children's needs are to be met—for example, achievement grouping, special needs grouping, partner grouping, tutorial grouping, interest grouping, and research grouping.

The preceding lesson may have follow-up activities, such as word recognition, vocabulary meanings, or related projects. What is done will vary according to the instructional needs of the group.

• *Grouping*   While the three-grouping plan (high, average, low) is associated with basal reading materials, grouping is not restricted to this approach.

There are no magic formulas for classroom organization, as suggested in chapter 13; some work better for some teachers and children than others. Since there are so many possible arrangements—ability, interest, social preference, pupil teams, etc.—flexibility should be a keynote of any classroom plan.

Language-experience approach

An introduction to experience chart writing and the language-experience approach was presented in chapter 7, focusing first upon its potential for written composition and then relating it to a beginning reading procedure. There are several advantages to the language-experience approach: it is based on active involvement of the children; it provides for the greatly divergent needs of children; it avoids ability grouping as such in the classroom; the materials used are relatively inexpensive; and it has strong motivational or remedial applications for many children. Most importantly, with this approach, learning to read is conceived of as a part of the process of language development, where the close relationship among reading, speaking, writing, and listening is recognized. On the other hand, it has been criticized as promoting an incidental attitude toward teaching and learning the basic reading skills.

In a classroom using the language-experience approach, many devices are used to encourage the children: picture dictionaries, labels on classroom objects, lists of interest or topical words, and charts of all kinds which help pupils extend their reading and writing vocabularies. Various beginning readers, easy-to-read trade books, and other materials are available to the class as resource materials.

Phonics instruction is developed on a "say it, see it" basis, the child gradually learning how to represent by letters the sounds he wishes to record on paper. Small group or individual help may be provided for various decoding tasks (structural analysis or contextual analysis) as children need them in writing and reading their own and other children's materials. Vocabulary is developed through individual "word banks" maintained by each child. The deposits in the "word bank" are the words marked in the child's dictated story as a known (recognized at sight) word, printed on small cards, and filed in a container. The "bank" serves as a valuable source for development of many skills.

Many teachers who are not too familiar with this approach have found the following guide helpful, particularly for the areas of record keeping, skills development, and evaluation: Roach Van Allen and Claryce Allen, *Language Experiences in Reading: Teacher's Source Book* (Chicago: Encyclopaedia Britannica Press, 1966). The interested reader may also wish to refer to the books cited in the Selected References at the conclusion of this chapter (especially the ones by Hall and Stauffer).

Individualized

With the individualized approach, reading is viewed as a personal involvement of pupils. While there is no universal definition for "individualized reading," there are a number of practices associated with it:

1. Self-selection of materials by pupils, according to interest and reading level
2. Self-pacing
3. Individual pupil conferences (perhaps five to ten minutes per child, one to three times per week)
4. Diagnostic record keeping and follow-up instruction

Such an approach necessarily requires a wide variety of materials (trade books, magazines, newspapers, reference books, pamphlet files, reading "games," and the like). One to three hundred books, representing a variety of interests and readability levels, are suggested for the classroom library.

Teacher guidance is needed along the way. Some of the guidance comes through detecting, broadening, and supporting the child's reading interests. (See chapter 6, "Literature.")[10] Further guidance is needed in the individual conference, where the child expresses himself on the story or book, stimulated by the teacher's thought-provoking questions. The questions usually range from those that probe into the child's interests ("Who is your favorite character?" "Why?") to comprehension ("How does the setting relate to the story?") to audience reading ("Which part would you like to read aloud to me?") to skills ("What is the meaning of the word *set* as used in this sentence?").

As the teacher listens to the child, he notes skills acquired and needed by the individual, later organizing some groups for skills teaching based on the analysis. Many teachers have found checklists helpful for skills analysis, such as the ones provided by Barbe.[11] Otto and Smith have constructed a scope and sequence chart of reading skills that can be helpful to teachers, both in familiarizing them with the skills and in improving their diagnostic abilities. Their chart of reading skills and objectives for the elementary level follows. The teacher using an individualized approach must be familiar with the reading skills, as well as with activities and materials that can develop them. The interested reader may also note the Veatch reference at the conclusion of this chapter.

---

10. Informal interest and personality inventories can be particularly helpful. For example, see Albert J. Harris, *How to Increase Reading Ability*, 5th ed. (New York: McKay, 1970).

11. Walter B. Barbe, *Educator's Guide to Personalized Reading Instruction* (Englewood Cliffs, N.J.: Prentice-Hall, 1961).

CHART 14.3: Statement of Skills and Objectives for Elementary Reading

Level C: Grade 2

I. Word Attack
  A. Has a sight word vocabulary of 100–170 words
    Objective: Given a maximum two-second exposure per word, the child is able to recognize 133 preprimer, primer, and first-grade words selected from the Dolch Basic Vocabulary List of 220 words.
  B. Has phonic analysis skills
    1. Consonants and their variant sounds
      Objective: The child recognizes the variant sounds of *s, c,* and *g* in words like *sit, three, sure, picnic, circus, giant, good, drag, cage, cake, city.* (The child matches words that have similar sounds of *s, c,* and *g.*) Note: The following consonants have more than one sound—*c, g, s, q, d, x, t, z,* but the variant sounds of *s, c, g* are commonest at this level.
    2. Consonant blends
      Objectives: When directed to a list for the first two sounds— i.e., *st, sk, sm, sp, sw, sn*—in a word pronounced by the teacher, the child is able to (a) identify words that begin with the same two sounds and (b) identify the two letters that make the initial sounds. The child is able to pronounce nonsense words that contain the following blends: *st, sk, sm, sp, sw, sn.*
    3. Vowel sounds
      a. Long vowel sounds
        Objectives: The child is able to pronounce real words and nonsense words with a single long vowel sound and to identify the vowel (e.g., *nose, brile, cheese, seat, labe*). The child is able to designate the letter that makes the single vowel sound in a word and indicate whether the sound is long or short.
      b. Vowel plus *r*
        Objectives: The child is able to pronounce words with *r*-controlled vowels. The child is able to name the vowel before *r* in nonsense words pronounced by the teacher (e.g., *darl, mur, der, forn*). Note: Because *er, ir,* and *ur* have the same sound, *e, i,* or *u* is the appropriate response in *er, ir,* and *ur* words.
      c. *A* plus *l*
        Objectives: The child is able to pronounce words in which there is an *al* combination (e.g., *ball, halt*). The child is able to name the vowel and the subsequent letter in *al* nonsense words pronounced by the teacher.

    d. *A* plus *w*
    Objectives: The child is able to pronounce words in which there is an *aw* combination (e.g., *draw, lawn, saw*). The child is able to name the vowel and the subsequent letter in *aw* nonsense words pronounced by the teacher.

    e. Diphthongs *oi, oy, ou, ow, ew*
    Objectives: The child is able to pronounce words in which there is an *oi, oy, ou, ow, ew* combination (e.g., *house, boy, soil, cow, new*). The child is able to identify the two vowels in *oi, oy, ou, ow, ew* nonsense words pronounced by the teacher. (Given an explanation that two vowels sometimes have a single sound, the child indicates when words pronounced by the teacher have such a vowel team and names the vowels in the team.) Note: Either *oi* or *oy* and *ou* or *ow* may be an acceptable response for certain words (e.g., *soil, soy, house, cow*).

    f. Long and short *oo*
    Objectives: The child is able to pronounce words in which there is an *oo* combination (e.g., *look, book, choose*). The child is able to indicate when the *oo* in key words has the long *oo (choose)* or the short *oo (book)* sound.

4. Vowel rules
    a. Short vowel generalization
    Objective: Given a real or nonsense word in which there is a single vowel and a final consonant, the child gives the vowel its short sound (e.g., *egg, bag, is, at, gum*), with exceptions known as sight words (e.g., *cold, bold, sight, fight*).

    b. Silent *e* rule
    Objective: Given a real or nonsense word that has two vowels, one of which is a final *e* separated from the first vowel by a consonant, the child first attempts pronunciation by making the initial vowel long and the final vowel silent (e.g., *cake, tube, mape, jome*), with exceptions known as sight words (e.g., *come, have, prove*).

    c. Two vowels together
    Objective: Given a real or nonsense word that has two consecutive vowels, the child first attempts pronunciation by making the first vowel long and the second vowel silent (e.g., *boat, meet, bait, each*) except when the two vowels are known diphthongs (i.e., *oi, oy, ou, ow, ew*) or when the word is a known exception (e.g., *bread, true, August*).

    d. Final vowel
    Objective: Given a real or nonsense word in which the only vowel is at the end, the child gives the vowel its long

sound (e.g., *go, she, me, he*). Note: Application of the vowel rules is best assessed individually and informally.

5. Common consonant digraphs (two letters with a single sound)
Objective: The child is able to name the letters in the common two-consonant combinations *(ch, th, sh, wh, nk, ng)* that result in a single new sound. (The child is asked to identify the digraphs in real and nonsense words enunciated by the teacher (e.g., *sink, frink, wharl, gling, chorf, thunk*).

C. Has structural analysis skills
1. Base words with prefixes and suffixes
Objective: The child demonstrates his understanding of how base (root) words are modified by prefixes and suffixes. Given a root word, the child adds affixes to complete a sentence [e.g., *An umbrella is (use) on a rainy day.*].
2. More difficult plural forms
Objective: The child is able to select singular and plural forms of words (e.g., *mice, lady, children, dresses, circus*).

D. Distinguishes among homonyms, synonyms, and antonyms
1. Homonyms
Objective: The child is able to choose between homonyms, given a sentence context [e.g., Mother bought some _____ for dinner *(meet, meat).*].
2. Synonyms and antonyms
Objective: The child is able to tell when the words in a pair have the same, opposite, or simply different meanings.

E. Has independent and varied word attack skills
Objective: In both self-directed and teacher-directed reading, the child uses a variety of skills (e.g., picture clues, context clues, structural analysis, sound/symbol analysis, comparison of new to known words) in attacking unknown words. (In the oral reading of an expository passage at his instructional level of difficulty, the child uses a variety of skills to attack unknown words.) Note: The objective can be assessed through the administration of an informal reading inventory.

F. Chooses the appropriate meaning of multiple-meaning words
Objective: Given a multiple-meaning word in varied contexts, the child is able to choose the meaning appropriate to the context. (The child chooses the appropriate given definition of *spring* for each of the following contexts: The lion was about to *spring*. We had a drink at the *spring*. The violets bloom in the *spring*.)

II. Comprehension
A. Is able to gain meaning from:
1. Words
Objective: The child demonstrates his understanding of individual words in connected text by responding correctly to

specific questions with a single-word focus [e.g., questions concerned essentially with word meaning (vocabulary)].

2. Sentences

Objective: The child demonstrates his understanding of specific sentences by responding correctly to specific questions regarding the literal content of these sentences.

3. Paragraphs

Objective: The child demonstrates his understanding of paragraphs by responding correctly and appropriately to questions regarding the literal meaning and the implied meaning of whole paragraphs.

4. Whole selections

Objective: The child demonstrates his understanding of a coherent passage of connected text by responding correctly and appropriately to questions regarding the literal meaning and the implied meaning of entire selections. Note: The materials used in assessing the four preceding objectives may be written at a level of difficulty appropriate for the child's grade placement, instructional level, or independent level.

B. Reads in meaningful phrases

Objective: In any oral reading situation, the child reads familiar material with phrasing appropriate to logical units of thought. Note: This objective is best assessed informally.

III. Study Skills

A. Uses picture dictionaries to find new words

Objective: The child is sufficiently familiar with a picture dictionary to locate newly introduced words. Note: This objective is best assessed through informal observation.

B. Groups words by initial letters

Objective: The child is able to put words that begin with different letters into alphabetical order.

C. Explores the library as a research center

Objective: The child actively seeks out library or learning center resources that are appropriate for completing an assigned task. Note: This objective must be assessed by observing the child's response to a number of assignments over a period of time.

D. Shows increasing independence in work

1. Reads and follows directions by himself

Objective: Given a series of four to eight written directions, the child is able to read and follow the directions with no guidance from the teacher.

2. Uses a table of contents without being reminded to do so

Objective: The child, without teacher direction, turns to a table of contents to gain general familiarity with new books, look

for information, and find specifically assigned sections or chapters.
  E. Begins to read maps
      Objective: Given a simple picture map, the child is able to answer questions regarding locations and relative distances.
 IV. Self-Directed Reading
  A. Broadens skills
      1. Cares for books properly
      2. Is aware of sequential order of books
      3. Begins to show initiative in selecting picture books
      4. Begins to apply independent word study skills
      5. Is able to find answers to questions independently
      6. Begins to do recreational reading
      7. Begins to select suitable reading materials independently
  B. Develops increasing fluency

  V. Interpretive Skills
  A. Recognizes implied ideas
  B. Identifies character traits
  C. Begins to make judgments
  D. Begins to draw conclusions

 VI. Creative Skills
  A. Shows initiative in large-group activities
  B. Uses voice intonation creatively
  C. Writes original stories

Source: Wayne Otto and Richard J. Smith, *Administering the School Reading Program* (Boston: Houghton Mifflin, 1970), pp. 47–69. This statement of skills and objectives for elementary reading was published as a project of the Wisconsin Research and Development Center for Cognitive Learning at the University of Wisconsin, Madison.

Other approaches

Other approaches to reading instruction include linguistic, phonics, changed alphabet, and systems. Some materials containing linguistic principles are:

Bloomfield, Leonard, and Barnhart, C. L. *Let's Read: A Linguistic Approach.* Detroit, Mich.: Wayne State University Press, 1961.
Fries, Charles, et al. *Linguistic Reading Program.* Columbus, Ohio: Merrill, 1975.
Rasmussen, Donald, and Goldberg, Lynn. *Basic Reading Series.* Chicago: Science Research Associates, 1970.

Smith, Henry L., et al. *Linguistic Readers*. Beverly Hills, Calif.: Benziger Press, 1970.
Stern, Catherine. *Structural Reading Series*. New York: L. W. Singer, 1963.

Programs that emphasize letter sounds or a decoding procedure have been labeled as "phonics." They include:

Gattegno, Caleb. *Words in Color*. Chicago: Encyclopaedia Britannica Press, 1962.
McCracken, Glenn, and Walcutt, Charles C. *Basic Reading Series*. Philadelphia: Lippincott, 1963–65.
Trace, Arthur, et al. *Open Court Basic Readers*. LaSalle, Ill.: Open Court Publishing, 1970.

Various proposals have been made for changing the alphabet (and spelling) in hopes of simplifying the task of initial reading and writing: for example, D. M. S. (Diacritical Marking System) and i/t/a or i.t.a. (Initial Teaching Alphabet). For D. M. S. information, see Edward Fry, "A Diacritical Marking System," *Elementary English* 41 (May 1964): 527–528. Descriptive literature about i/t/a may be secured from The Initial Teaching Alphabet Publications, Inc., 20 E. 46th St., New York, N.Y. 10017.

Systems materials are based on the theories of operant conditioning, as exemplified by programmed instruction involving reinforcement of learning, active participation of the learner, self-pacing, and a detailed analysis of the desired performance of the learner in terms of behavioral objectives. They frequently involve use of computers, talking typewriters or teletypewriters, and cassettes. A representative systems program is *Programmed Reading* by Sullivan Associates (New York: McGraw-Hill, 1965). Computer Assisted Instruction (Stanford University) and the program *Listen, Look, Learn* by Educational Development Laboratories (New York: McGraw-Hill, 1967) are other examples of "systems" material.

Some schools rely heavily upon the use of high interest-low vocabulary readers. The well-known works of Dr. Seuss fit this description as exemplified by his *Beginner Books* (New York: Random House). Other series are *Dan Frontier* Series (Chicago: Benefic Press); and the *Jim Forest Readers* and the *Morgan Bay Mystery Stories* (San Francisco: Harr Wagner). Other publishers of high interest-low vocabulary books include:

Children's Book Center, 150 Kensington Church St., London W 8
    England.
Follett Publishing Company, 1010 W. Washington Blvd., Chicago,
    Ill. 60607.
Garrard Publishing Co., 1607 N. Market St., Champaign, Ill. 61820.
E. M. Hale and Co., 1201 S. Hastings Way, Eau Claire, Wis. 54701.
Harper & Row Publishers, Inc., 10 E. 53rd St., New York, N.Y. 10022.
D. C. Heath and Co., 125 Spring St., Lexington, Mass. 02173.
Webster Division of McGraw-Hill Book Co., 1221 Ave. of Americas,
    New York, N.Y. 10020.

BASIC READING SKILLS

Four important basic reading skills are word recognition, vocabulary
development, comprehension, and audience reading.

Word recognition

Word recognition skills are the techniques used by the reader to
identify, pronounce, recall, and thus read each word. Children use
several techniques in this skill. For example, an accompanying picture would give a clue to the meaning of the unknown word. Other
words may be recognized by their pattern or shape, like *left*.
Labeled objects in the classroom, picture-word cards, and experience
charts are other ways for using clues to words.

• *Sight*   Gradually the child builds what is termed a "sight
vocabulary," meaning instant recognition. For example, one of the
first sight words for many children is their own name.

To illustrate how a sight word may first be introduced to a six-
year-old, one basal reader has a picture of animals living in the
jungle, with the question, "What animals live here?" (The word to
be introduced is *live*.) Following is an excerpt from the teacher's
edition.

Before Reading
    Look at the picture on this page. In what kind of environ-
ment do these animals live? How has the artist who painted

this picture helped you to know? (Use of tropical colors; no open spaces, suggesting dense vegetation; the kinds and shapes of plants indicating a hot, wet environment.)

You will see the word *live* on this page. Who can read the question?

After Reading

What animals do live here? Where on the chart should they be listed? Why do you think these animals would like to live in a jungle? Why would they not like living there?[12]

Later pages pose the same questions for animals living in the desert and in other places, providing additional exposure to the word *live*.

The Dolch Word List contains 220 basic sight words. According to Dolch, the list contains 70 percent of the running words in first-grade reading materials, 65 percent in the second grade, and 60 percent in the fourth through sixth grades.[13] A similar list of sight words are the first 220 words of the Kucera-Francis corpus, which follows. The list may be used to suggest important words for children to learn. Dolch has also compiled a list of useful nouns that are most common in primary reading.[14] There are other important lists of sight words, such as the one by Edward Fry.[15]

CHART 14.4: The 220 Most Frequent Words in the Kucera-Francis Corpus

Rank	Word	Rank	Word	Rank	Word
1.	the	6.	in	11.	for
2.	of	7.	that	12.	it
3.	and	8.	is	13.	with
4.	to	9.	was	14.	as
5.	a	10.	he	15.	his

12. From *Teacher's Edition, May I Come In?* by Theodore Clymer and Nita M. Wyatt, of the READING 360 series, © Copyright, 1969, by Ginn and Company. Used with permission.

13. The Dolch word list may be found in Edward W. Dolch, *A Manual for Remedial Reading* (Champaign, Ill.: Garrard Publishing, 1945), p. 29.

14. Edward W. Dolch, "95 Nouns Common to Three Word Lists," *Teaching Primary Reading* (Champaign, Ill.: Garrard Publishing, 1950), p. 269.

15. Edward Fry, *Instant Words* (Sunland, Calif.: Learning Through Seeing). The list appears in *Elementary English* 34 (November 1957): 456–458.

16.	on	62.	only	108.	how
17.	be	63.	other	109.	too
18.	at	64.	new	110.	little
19.	by	65.	some	111.	state
20.	I	66.	could	112.	good
21.	this	67.	time	113.	very
22.	had	68.	these	114.	make
23.	not	69.	two	115.	would
24.	are	70.	may	116.	still
25.	but	71.	then	117.	own
26.	from	72.	do	118.	see
27.	or	73.	first	119.	men
28.	have	74.	any	120.	work
29.	an	75.	my	121.	long
30.	they	76.	now	122.	get
31.	which	77.	such	123.	here
32.	one	78.	like	124.	between
33.	you	79.	our	125.	both
34.	were	80.	over	126.	life
35.	her	81.	man	127.	being
36.	all	82.	me	128.	under
37.	she	83.	even	129.	never
38.	there	84.	most	130.	day
39.	would	85.	made	131.	same
40.	their	86.	after	132.	another
41.	we	87.	also	133.	know
42.	him	88.	did	134.	while
43.	been	89.	many	135.	last
44.	has	90.	before	136.	might
45.	when	91.	must	137.	us
46.	who	92.	through	138.	great
47.	will	93.	back	139.	old
48.	more	94.	years	140.	year
49.	no	95.	where	141.	off
50.	if	96.	much	142.	come
51.	out	97.	your	143.	since
52.	so	98.	may	144.	against
53.	said	99.	well	145.	go
54.	what	100.	down	146.	came
55.	up	101.	should	147.	right
56.	its	102.	because	148.	used
57.	about	103.	each	149.	take
58.	into	104.	just	150.	three
59.	than	105.	those	151.	states
60.	them	106.	people	152.	himself
61.	can	107.	Mr.	153.	few

154.	house	177.	don't	200.	took
155.	use	178.	does	201.	head
156.	during	179.	got	202.	yet
157.	without	180.	united	203.	government
158.	again	181.	left	204.	system
159.	place	182.	number	205.	better
160.	American	183.	course	206.	set
161.	around	184.	war	207.	told
162.	however	185.	until	208.	nothing
163.	home	186.	always	209.	night
164.	small	187.	away	210.	end
165.	found	188.	something	211.	why
166.	Mrs.	189.	fact	212.	called
167.	thought	190.	though	213.	didn't
168.	went	191.	water	214.	eyes
169.	say	192.	less	215.	find
170.	part	193.	public	216.	going
171.	once	194.	put	217.	look
172.	general	195.	thing	218.	asked
173.	high	196.	almost	219.	later
174.	upon	197.	hand	220.	knew
175.	school	198.	enough		
176.	every	199.	far		

Source: Dale D. Johnson, "The Dolch List Reexamined." *The Reading Teacher* 24 (February 1971): 455–456. Reprinted with permission of Dale D. Johnson and the International Reading Association.

A variety of supplementary exercises can be used to help pupils learn to recognize instantly on sight the words that have been presented in their reading materials. Some examples are:

1. Choosing a picture or the object itself that a word represents
2. Distinguishing look-alike words; pointing out their differences
3. Placing needed practice words in new sentence arrangements
4. Choosing the correct word from a list of two to four others given for a blank in the sentence
5. Finding the same word as it appears throughout a paragraph
6. Selecting the named word from a list of words
7. Playing word games, such as "fishing" or "wordo" (bingo)

Most of the practice on a word needing attention should be given in exercises that present the word in context; and the exercises

Reading games can provide interesting practice and should always pertain to the specific needs of the participating children.

should be adjusted to meet individual needs. (The Ekwall book (see Selected References) has an excellent collection of games and activities for teaching sight words.)

• *Context*   Training in contextual analysis is part of the program in word recognition. A number of types of contextual clues are classified on page 299. They suggest the kinds of context situations faced by children; they provide a clear implication and need for constructing, studying, and discussing sentences with these kinds of situations. One of the most important things for the reader to do when he encounters an unknown word is to keep reading. There may be clues before an unknown word or after it. "What word would make sense?" should be a frequently asked question. This encourages the child to listen to his pronunciation and try to match it with some word stored in his oral vocabulary bank. Some procedures for providing practice with context clues are:

1. Encourage children to supply a missing word while a sentence, rhyme, or story is read to them, discussing reasons for word selection.
2. Question children on meanings of new words presented in a story, discussing reasons for the meanings.
3. Use the cloze technique, supplying reading material with every tenth word omitted, and encourage the children to insert the missing words and defend their selections. Accept synonyms or close guesses. Vary the procedure by playing a tape recording with key words omitted, providing a copy of the script to the pupil and having him fill in blanks as he listens to the tape.
4. Insert several nonsense words in place of certain nouns or verbs in a paragraph, asking children to infer the words intended and to explain their selection.
5. Vary the idea in 4 above by supplying the correct beginning letters only, the length of the word, or only the beginning and ending letters of the missing word.

As children gain experience, similar types of exercises may be made more difficult by using selections from textbooks in other content areas.

Some commercially available materials for supplementary work with context clues include:

Boning, Richard. *Using the Context, Book D*. Specific Skill Series. Baldwin, N.Y.: Barnell Loft, 1973.

Durr, William K., and Hillerick, Robert L. *Overcoming Meaning Difficulties, Book B*, Level 1 and *Reading Skills Laboratory, Book A*, Level 2. Boston: Houghton Mifflin, 1968.

Liddle, William. *Reading for Concepts, Books A–H*. New York: McGraw-Hill, 1970.

Loretan, Joseph O., and Umans, Shelley. *Building Reading Power*. (Fifteen sequential programmed units in three series: "Context Clues," "Structural Analysis," and "Comprehension Skills.") Columbus, Ohio: Merrill, 1964.

Niles, Olive Stafford, et al. *Tactics in Reading I and II*. Glenview, Ill.: Scott Foresman, 1965.

• *Phonic analysis*   Chart 10.1 on pages 364–365 provides some valuable information about the consonant and vowel phonemes, key symbols, other graphemes representing the sound, and other phonemes represented by the grapheme. But the teacher needs to know a great deal more about phonics than can be presented in this book. Attention should be given to the Selected References section at the conclusion of this chapter, particularly the books by Hull and Wilson, which can be independently studied for background information.

Heilman has proposed sequential steps in which phonics may be introduced.

1. Auditory-visual discrimination
2. Teaching consonant sounds
   a. Initial consonants
   b. Consonant digraphs (e.g., *sh, wh, th, ch*)[16]
   c. Consonant blends *(br, cl, str)*[17]
   d. Substituting initial consonant sounds
   e. Sounding consonants at the ends of words
   f. Consonant digraphs *(nk, ng, ck, qu)*
   g. Consonant irregularities
   h. Silent consonants
   i. Sight-word list—nonphonetic spellings
   j. Contractions
3. Teaching vowel sounds
   a. Short vowel sounds
   b. Long vowel sounds
   c. Teaching long and short sounds together
   d. Exceptions to vowel rules taught
   e. Diphthongs[18]
   f. Sounds of $\bar{oo}$ and $\breve{oo}$
4. Syllabication
   a. Rules
   b. Prefixes and suffixes
   c. Compound words
   d. Doubling final consonants
   e. Accent[19]

---

16. *Digraph:* A grapheme composed of two letters that represent one speech sound (phoneme)—*ch* is a consonant digraph in *cheek;* oo is a vowel digraph in the word *foot.*

17. *Blend:* A combination of two or more consonant phonemes blended together.

18. *Diphthong:* Two vowel sounds combined, beginning with the first and gliding smoothly into the next (e.g., *coin, cow*).

19. Arthur W. Heilman, *Phonics in Proper Perspective* (Columbus, Ohio: Merrill, 1964), pp. 19–20. Reprinted with permission of the publisher.

Examples of how initial consonants (2a) and short vowel sounds (3a) are presented through phonetic analysis are provided below.

LETTER-SOUND RELATIONSHIP: b /b/

1. Use pictures to introduce.

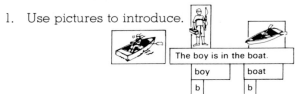

Guidance: Read the sentence aloud for the pupils (*The boy is in the boat.*). Have the class repeat these two words: *boy, boat.* (Point to the words.) Ask the pupils:

What is the first letter in the word *boy?*

What is the first letter in the word *boat?*

Do the words *boy* and *boat* begin with the same letter?

Let's say the words again—*boy, boat.* Do both words begin with the same sound?

Ask the pupils to read the sentence again.

Ask the pupils to identify objects around the room that begin with the letter *b* and the /b/ sound. List them on the chalkboard. Read the list, having the pupils say the word with you.

2. Use the Studybook pages to provide additional practice in associating *b* and /b/. Pupils can use picture cues to identify written and spoken words that begin with *b* and /b/.

3. Provide further step-by-step guidance for children who do not seem to grasp the relationship as they complete copies of masters. (This serves as independent work for those who understand the relationship between *b* and /b/.)[20]

DECODING ACTIVITY: /a/ o

Specific Objectives

Phonemic analysis: Introducing the correspondence /a/ o
                        as in *not*

NOTE: In certain geographic areas the letter o may stand

---

20. Adapted from Scott, Foresman Reading Systems, Teacher's Manual, Level 2. Copyright © 1971 by Scott, Foresman and Company.

for the sound /ɔ/ in some or all of the words used here.

On the chalkboard write *hot* and have it read. Tell the class that they have heard the vowel sound of *hot* many times in other words. Illustrate by writing the familiar words *got*, *hot*, *hop*, *top*, and *stop*, and ask someone to read them. Be sure the children note that the vowel sound is the same in all the words.

Briefly pronounce the sound /a/ as in *not*, and have the children repeat it. Establish the point that this sound may be represented by the letter o as in the words listed on the chalkboard.

Now lead the pupils to recall that in words of the CVC or VC spelling patterns the vowel sound is usually unglided. If necessary, list words containing unglided vowel sounds /ae/, /e/, or /i/ under corresponding headings *Pat*, *met*, *hit*. Lead the children to conclude that the vowel letter o between two consonants can stand for the unglided vowel sound /a/ as in *hot*.

Let the group read the following words, some of which are known.

cop	hop	lot	got
cod	hot	lop	not
mop	hod	pot	top
	rot	pop	sop

If the correspondence /a/ o is quickly mastered, you may continue with substitution of consonant digraphs and consonant clusters, using the following words: *stop, stock, chop, shop, smock, trot.*[21]

In each of the above examples, note the orderly manner of procedures:

1. Helping the child to hear the sound accurately
2. Helping the child to see that in the words a certain letter stands for a certain sound
3. Helping the child apply the letter-sound relationship in reading

21. From *Teacher's Edition, Seven Is Magic*, by Theodore Clymer and Virginia W. Jones, of READING 360 series, © Copyright, 1969, by Ginn and Company. Used with permission.

Note further that most basal readers present phonic analysis in an *analytic* manner, rather than a *synthetic* manner. With an analytic manner, sounds are presented as integral parts of words ("This new word begins with the same sound as in the beginning of the word *dog*."). With the synthetic manner, attention is given to isolated letters ("This new word begins with *d-duh*.")

From such introductory work, generalizations develop about phonics, syllabication, and accent. With different sets of materials, there is a variation of grade level of introduction, emphasis, and phrasing of such generalizations. For example, the idea that "When there is one e in a word that ends in a consonant *(get)*, the e usually has a short sound," may be recommended for the preprimer level, while "Words having a double e *(seem)* usually have the long e sound," may be assigned to the first-grade level in some materials but not in others.

Several studies have attempted to find out what generalizations have a "reasonable" degree of application to words commonly encountered in primary or intermediate grade materials.[22] By dividing the number of words that follow the generalization by the total number of words to which the generalization could be expected to apply, a "percentage of utility" may be computed. A general statement of the findings may be summarized:

1. Certain generalizations apply to large numbers of words and are rather constant in providing the correct pronunciation. (For example, "When two consonants are side by side, only one is heard.")
2. Other generalizations seem to work, but apply only to a few words. (For example, "When a is followed by r and final e, we expect to hear the sound heard in *care*.")
3. Many generalizations have a low percentage of utility; they fail to work even half of the time. (For example, "When there are two vowels side by side, the long sound of the first one is heard and the second is usually silent.")

How should the teacher decide which generalizations to present and to which children? One guide is to follow the Clymer study (cited in footnote 22) in this manner:

---

22. For example, see Mildred Hart Bailey, "The Utility of Phonic Generalizations in Grades One through Six," *The Reading Teacher* 20 (February 1967): 413–420; Theodore Clymer, "The Utility of Phonic Generalizations in the Primary Grades," *The Reading Teacher* 16 (January 1963): 252–258; Robert Emans, "The Usefulness of Phonic Generalizations Above the Primary Grades," *The Reading Teacher* 20 (February 1967): 419–425; and Carol K. Winkley, "The Applicability of Accent Generalizations," *Academic Therapy Quarterly* (Fall 1966): 2–9.

1. Low ability children: Generalizations of a high percentage of utility—90 to 100 percent
2. Average ability children: Generalizations of 75 to 100 percentage of utility
3. High ability children: Generalizations of 50 to 100 percentage of utility

Some supplementary materials for phonics instruction are footnoted.[23]

• **Structural analysis**   Structural analysis includes the ideas of

1. Inflectional endings (like *-s, -es, -ed, -ing, -er, -est, -ly*)
2. Prefixes and suffixes (like *ex-, re-, dis-, pre-, un-, -ment, -less*)
3. Compound words (like *snowman, farmyard, playground*)
4. Possessives and contractions (like *John's hat; didn't*)
5. Syllabication and accent

Inductive development is appropriate for common inflectional endings and affixes. Following initial instruction, skills may be presented and practiced in the following ways:

THE *SHIP* SUFFIX

Write the following sentences on the chalkboard and have volunteers take turns reading the sentences and identifying the underlined words. Provide assistance where necessary.

His <u>friendship</u> means a lot to me.
It was a <u>hardship</u> to go out that day.
The men argued about the <u>ownership</u> of the plane.
The boss has a good <u>relationship</u> with his men.

Then erase the chalkboard except for the underlined words and ask someone to name the common factor in the list of words. With a slash mark separate each base word from its suffix and have volunteers use both the base and derivative in sentences to demonstrate usage and meaning. Finally, lead the children to generalize that the suffix *ship* can be added to some words to form a new word that shows a quality of the base word.

---

23. *Ginn Word Enrichment Program* (Boston: Ginn); Mary Meighen and Marjorie Pratt, *Phonics We Use* (Chicago: Lyons and Carnahan); and Don H. Parker, *Reading Laboratory I: Word Games* (Chicago: Science Research Associates).

Ask children if the suffix *ship* forms a separate syllable in the words above, leading them to the understanding that, as with most suffixes, the suffix forms an additional, unstressed syllable.[24]

LEARNING STATION: PREFIXES AND SUFFIXES

1. Read the paragraph at the learning center. List all the words you can find made up of a prefix and a root (base) word. Underline the prefixes.
2. Now list all the words you can find made up of a suffix and a root word. Underline the suffixes.
3. Take the answer sheet from the answer-sheet folder. Check your answers.
4. Choose five of the prefixes you found. Add a different root word for each than you found in the paragraph.
5. Choose five of the suffixes you found. Add a different root word for each than you found in the paragraph.
6. Ask a friend to check your words for 4 and 5.
7. Make a word puzzle for a different partner. You do this by writing one of your words in 4 and 5 on a three-by-five-inch index card. Leave space between the prefix (or suffix) and the root word. Cut between the prefix (or suffix) and the root word. Do this for each of your words. Mix them up and put them in an envelope with your name on it. Ask your partner if he can make ten words by matching the twenty pieces. If he has any questions, he may ask you.

Strategies for presenting and practicing compound words, possessives, and contractions may be located in the teacher's manual of a basal reading program.

Knowing both the phonic and structural features of words leads to the ability to study syllabication and accent. Note the use of affixes in dividing a word like *re-turn-able* into syllables. When generalizations about syllabication and accent are to be taught, children should be provided with a number of examples and then led to see for themselves what happens. Teaching accent and stress is one of the later stages in word analysis, since the learner must be able to use a dic-

---

24. From *Level 8*, pages 175–176, of The Young America Basic Reading Program by Leo Fay and others. Produced by Lyons and Carnahan. © 1974 by Rand McNally and Company.

tionary and note primary and secondary accent marks. Memorization of a set of rules to apply in determining accent is probably not defensible, since there are numerous exceptions to most such rules. However, this does not negate the value of pupil observations as they apply to a set of words.

Comprehension

Getting the meaning out of the material demands a grasp of many language features already discussed in this book: vocabulary, multiple-meaning words, synonyms, homonyms, figurative language, etc.

One classification or ordering of reading comprehension skills has been prepared by Barrett.

1.0 Literal Comprehension
   Recognition or recall of:
   1.1 details
   1.2 main ideas
   1.3 sequence
   1.4 comparisons
   1.5 cause-and-effect relationships
   1.6 character traits
2.0 Inferential Comprehension
   Inferring
   2.1 details
   2.2 main ideas
   2.3 sequence
   2.4 comparisons
   2.5 cause-and-effect relationships
   2.6 character traits
   2.7 predicting outcomes
   2.8 figurative language
3.0 Evaluation
   Judgments of
   3.1 reality or fantasy
   3.2 fact or opinion
   3.3 adequacy or validity
   3.4 appropriateness
   3.5 worth, desirability, or acceptability

    4.0 Appreciation
        4.1 emotional response to the content
        4.2 identification with characters and incidents
        4.3 reactions to the author's use of language
        4.4 imagery[25]

Comprehension is influenced by many factors, but probably questioning and vocabulary development are the keys to teaching comprehension, especially the higher level (critical/creative) comprehension skills.[26] The child is quite likely to base his reading on the type of questions the teacher will ask. If the questions are limited in scope or depth, thinking (comprehension) tends to be superficial and stereotyped.

Taba has suggested the following hierarchy of questions:

1. Concrete or literal
2. Explanatory
3. Analytical/synthetical
4. Evaluative[27]

Taba's sequence may be implemented by using the types of questions suggested by Sanders.

1. Memory (recognizing information given: facts, definitions, generalizations, or values)
2. Translations (expressing ideas in a different form: "What kind of a drawing could you make to illustrate that part of the story?")
3. Interpretation (seeing relationships among facts, generalizations, and values: "Compare Jim with the boy in our previous story," or "What does Betty's behavior tell us about her?" or "Why did _____ happen?")
4. Application (solving a problem that requires the use of facts, generalizations, and values: "How was it shown that the steel mill should be at this location?")
5. Analysis (applying rules of logic to the solution of a problem:

---

25. Thomas C. Barrett, "Taxonomy of Reading Comprehension," unpublished paper, used with permission of the author. A more complete discussion of the taxonomy may be found in Richard J. Smith and Thomas C. Barrett, *Teaching Reading in the Middle Grades*, Reading, Mass.: Addison-Wesley, 1974.

26. A distinction can be made between the terms *critical* and *creative*. *Critical* implies approaching materials with an inquiring, analytic attitude. *Creative* means adding (from experience) to the printed page to arrive at some original analyses.

27. Hilda Taba, "The Teaching of Thinking," *Elementary English* 42 (May 1965): 534–542.

"Discuss this statement from the story—'A boy can drive a car better than a girl.'")
6. Synthesis (using original, creative thinking to solve a problem: "What other ending can you think of for this story?")
7. Evaluation (making judgments based on clearly defined standards: "Did you approve of Sam's actions?" "Why or why not?")[28]

When questions of this nature are asked ("What do you think will happen next?" "Why was _____ admired?" "What similar illustration of your own can you give?" "Can you suggest reasons why this might be the case?" or "Were both sides of the issue given fair treatment?"), the child is being asked to read for implied and inferred meanings, sense hidden meanings, call sensory imagery into play, and read with sensitivity and appreciation of the situation.[29]

Audience reading

Some "first" or sight reading is used for diagnostic purposes—to check word recognition, phrasing, word-attack skills, and the like—but generally the child is not asked to read aloud until he has read the passage silently first. Oral or audience reading often occurs as the child reads statements that answer specific questions or clarify a point. Often the child shares some part of a story, as is done in oral book reporting. "Round robin" reading (where each member of a group is given a turn to read a part of the story sequentially) can rarely be justified. Choral reading and other aspects of drama often involve prepared oral reading. And, as was pointed out in the literature chapter, the child often reads a poem or story to his peers. An effective strategy for improving oral reading ability is to tape or record the child's oral reading so that he may evaluate his performance. Another effective way to develop good oral reading is for the teacher to provide an excellent oral model through the reading he does aloud for the group.

28. Norris M. Sanders, *Classroom Questions: What Kinds?* (New York: Harper & Row, 1966). Sanders' questions follow the categories devised by Benjamin Bloom in *Taxonomy of Educational Objectives: The Classified Educational Goals—Handbook 1: The Cognitive Domain* (New York: McKay, 1956).

29. Some commercially available material for supplementary work with comprehension skills include: Richard Boning et al., Specific Skill Reading Series, (Baldwin, N.Y.: Barnell Loft, 1962); Lee Deighton et al., Macmillan Spectrum Books (New York: Macmillan, 1964); and New Reading Skill Builder Series (Pleasantville, N.Y.: Readers' Digest Services, 1966).

CONTENT AREA READING

The majority of content area reading in the elementary school is done in the fields of literature, mathematics, social studies, and science. Such material is difficult, since the ideas are complex, vocabulary is introduced rapidly, unrelated facts must be organized, and wide reading is demanded from a variety of sources. Since reading levels will vary considerably within a classroom, a single textbook will rarely be appropriate for all children. An informal test early in the school year will give some evidence as to how well the child can read a particular textbook. This test can be a silent reading of five or six pages, followed by printed questions on the passage. To account for reading differences, many kinds of supplementary materials will be required: easier textbooks, multiple-track plans, paperbacks, booklets, trade books, and materials especially prepared for poorer readers.

Readability

Since the readability level of supplementary materials may not be as obvious as that in the regular program, many teachers have found a need for estimating the reading level of the material they use. A number of readability formulas are available.[30] The one presented in chart 14.5 is perhaps the quickest to apply—and is reasonably accurate.

Learning and study

• *Teacher*   For content reading, it is important to prepare the pupils for reading a selection. (Appropriate follow-up activities are also important.) This preparation could entail discussion of the topic, explanation of important concepts (often supported by the use of audio-visual materials or oral reading of background information to the children), and attention to the technical vocabulary. Supplying the pupils with a set of guide questions for an assigned reading may also be of help.

• *Pupil*   As a way of studying content material, the five steps of the Robinson SQ3R (Survey, Question, Read, Recite, and Review)

---

30. For primary level materials, see the formula by Spache found in George D. Spache, *Good Reading for Poor Readers*, 2d ed. (Champaign, Ill.: Garrard Publishing, 1970), pp. 200–211. For intermediate level materials, see Edgar Dale and Jeanne S. Chall, "A Formula for Predicting Readability," *Education Research Bulletin* 27 (Jan. 21 and Feb. 18, 1948).

CHART 14.5: Fog Index of Readability

STEP I

Take a sample of 100 words. Get as close to 100 words as possible, but stop at the end of a sentence. Divide the number of sentences into the number of words.   _____

STEP II

Count the number of three-or-more-syllable words in the sample passage with the following exceptions:

(a) Do not count proper names
(b) Compound words
(c) Any verb forms   _____

STEP III

Get the following percentage of the three-syllable words obtained by the following formula:

Take the number of words divided into the number of three-syllable words, to three places. This will give you a factor.   (1) _____

Use the average sentence length found in Step I, and this will give you a second factor.   (2) _____

STEP IV

Add the factors and then multiply by the constant .4, which will give you a grade level.   (3) _____

          $\times$ .4

_____

NOTE:

When counting the three-or more syllables words, count the words each time they appear, even if they appear several times in the selection.

SOURCE: The Fog Index is reprinted with written permission of the copyright owner, Robert Gunning, author of *The Technique of Clear Writing* (New York: McGraw-Hill, 1968).

should result in the reader's selecting the more important points of a passage and fixing them in his mind.[31] More specifically, this systematic approach to study involves:

Survey: Survey the passage to obtain the general impression and to set purposes for the reading.

Question: Formulate questions that the selection might answer —often revealed by the headings.

---

31. Francis P. Robinson, *Effective Study* (New York: Harper & Row, 1961), chapter 2, pp. 28–33.

> *Read:* Read the selection carefully, keeping the purposes in mind.
>
> *Recite:* Recite, either to yourself or to another person, what has been learned without looking at the material.
>
> *Review:* Reread and review the selection to fix the main ideas and details firmly in mind, making brief notes, cue phrases, or an outline of the main points and subpoints.

Specific skills and techniques

The reading process itself seems to remain stable in passages from the various content areas, suggesting that the same general strategies may be used for all content areas. One of the major differences in content area reading involves vocabulary particular to the field of study.

Elementary school mathematics can serve to illustrate certain reading skills that appear applicable to verbal (word) problems, apart from general reading skills.

1. *Grammar:* The meaning of numerals, symbols used to represent numbers, includes many aspects of place value. To understand the grammar aspects of mathematics word problems, prerequisite work would involve certain aspects of identifying, describing, comparing, and classifying sets; counting and ordering; the meaning or idea of *number;* and differences between *number* and *numeral.* The idea of different numerals for the same number and the reading of notation systems, such as the Roman system or bases other than 10, are also a part of the grammar of mathematics. Symbols also include those for the operations, number relations (ordering), and others associated with fractions, ratios, decimals, percents, integers, geometry, and measures.

2. *Vocabulary:* There are many words of a technical or specialized nature in mathematics problems. Abbreviations for these technical terms are also very important to check, as well as terms of measures, such as *acre.*

A sample systematic lesson plan for technical terms is provided on page 525.

LESSON PLAN: Mathematical Vocabulary

Performance Objective:

Given technical words found in mathematics, the learner indicates his understanding of the meaning of the word by (1) giving a synonym for the word, (2) using it in an appropriate context, (3) defining it in his own words, or (4) performing a physical operation indicative of the meaning.

Diagnostic Pretest:

A pretest situation might occur in a mathematics class when technical words are encountered. Here it is appropriate to ask the learner what the words mean and to elicit from him an appropriate response in at least two of the four techniques suggested above. Criterion for mastery is 100 percent. Records of words missed should be kept for later instructional activities.

Teaching Suggestions:

1. Use multiple experiences to develop concepts of the word.
2. Audio-visual materials (slides, filmstrips, illustrated math trade books) can be used to reinforce the idea.
3. A well-planned dictionary activity can be used to pinpoint a specific word.

Posttest:

The suggestions provided for the pretest should be adapted and used for the posttest.

Reteaching Suggestions:

1. Take time for occasional word drills, calling upon the learner to demonstrate his understanding of a technical word in one or more of the suggested ways.
2. Encourage pupils to keep individual notebooks of mathematics terms and their definitions. Have pupils check each other at times.
3. Teach words through vocabulary games. (Rules can be the same as for common card games.)
4. Use both oral and written exercises in which words are replaced with synonyms or phrases that mean about the same thing.
5. Teach common prefixes and suffixes as techniques for gaining meaning to words: for example, *peri-meter.*

---

3. *Graphic figures:* Much interpretation of graphic figures is required in reading mathematics materials, such as number lines, arrays, geometric figures, graphs, charts, tables, and coordinate planes.

4. *Analysis:* Though questions are extensively used as an aid in analyzing word problems, there is no generally

recognized best list of such questions. Following are some suggested questions.

> Do you understand all the words?
> Do you understand the setting or situation?
> What data are given?
> What other data are needed?
> What computation is required?
> What is a good estimate of the answer?
> How would you set up the problem for solution?
> How does your answer compare to the estimate?

Such analysis may be considered an adaptation of the SQ3R method. In fact, a more specific technique might be labeled, SQRQCQ, meaning:

S   Survey (Read rapidly for the main idea.)
Q   Question (What is the problem?)
R   Read (Reread for details and interrelationships.)
Q   Question (What operation or operations should be used?)
C   Compute
Q   Question (Is the answer correct?)

5. *Quantitative relationship:* One important skill, of the many complex reading skills involved in the solution of verbal problems, is the ability to grasp quantitative relationships. It is more advantageous to spend time thinking and talking about the basic ideas of a relatively small number of problems than to simply assign a long list of problems to be solved. Several procedures may be utilized to check insight into quantitative relationships: (a) dramatization, (b) restatement or analogy, or (c) estimation.

6. *Comprehension:* Six important comprehension skills in interpreting verbal word problems are:

a.   Operation (identifying the operation necessary to perform for solution)
b.   Main idea (restating the main idea of the problem)
c.   Details (noting main details by identifying relevant and needed data)
d.   Integration of details (formulating a verbal problem in one's own words)
e.   Directions (making a drawing or diagram to represent the problem situation)
f.   Inference (telling how the problem would be solved)

Each content area deserves the same close attention. There are many science terms that require "life and meaning"; and the density of concepts often found in a single paragraph of a social studies textbook poses an awesome instructional responsibility. An excellent text on content area reading has been prepared by Herber. (See Selected References.)

Some commercial material for intermediate level pupils that directs attention to reading in the content areas is the Harper & Row *Study Skills Readers*[32] and *Skills for School Reading* published by Harcourt Brace Jovanovich.[33]

EVALUATION OF PUPIL PROGRESS

More measurement and evaluation instruments are available for the reading program than for any other area of the school curriculum.

Standardized tests

If feasible, students of reading should examine personally the types of standardized instruments available and observe their administration to a child or group of children. Following this observation, learning would be increased by having the opportunity to administer a standardized test to a child and interpret the results. A *group* test may be administered to a number of persons at the same time by one examiner. An *individual* test is one that can be administered to only one person at a time. A *survey* test measures general achievement in a given area. A *diagnostic* test is used to "diagnose" or analyze, locating specific areas of strengths and weaknesses and possibly suggesting their cause.

Following is a list of some standardized reading tests.

Readiness
Murphy, Helen, and Durrell, Donald. *Murphy-Durrell Reading Readiness Analysis.* New York: Harcourt Brace Jovanovich. (For beginning first grade. Includes subtests on visual discrimination, auditory discrimination, letter names, and learning rate.)

Oral
Gilmore, John V. *Gilmore Oral Reading Test.* New York: Harcourt Brace Jovanovich. (For grades 1–8. An individual test.)

---

32. Byron H. Van Roekel and Mary J. Kluive, *Study Skills Readers* (New York: Harper & Row, 1966).
33. Day Ann McClenathan, *Skills for School Reading* (New York: Harcourt Brace Jovanovich, 1971).

Through administration
of an appropriate
reading test to a child,
the teacher may assess
areas of strengths and
weaknesses as a basis
for follow-up instruction.

Gray, William S. *Gray Standardized Oral Reading Check Tests*. Indianapolis, Ind.: Bobbs-Merrill. (For grades 1–10. Individually
administered.)

Word Attack Skills
Rosewall, Florence, and Chall, Jeanne. *Rosewall-Chall Diagnostic
Reading Test*. New York: Essay Press.
McKee, Paul. *McKee Inventory of Phonetic Skill*. Boston: Houghton
Mifflin.

Silent

Tiegs, Ernest W., and Clark, Willis. *California Reading Tests*. Monterey, Calif.: California Test Bureau. [For lower primary (1–2); primary (3–4); elementary (4–6); junior high school (7–9). Checks vocabulary and comprehension.]

Gates, Arthur, and MacGinitie, Walter. *Gates-MacGinitie Reading Tests*. New York: Teachers College Press, Columbia University. [For primary A (1); primary B (2); primary C (3); survey D (4–6); survey E (7–9). Checks vocabulary and comprehension.]

Diagnostic

Spache, George D. *Diagnostic Reading Scales*. Monterey, Calif.: California Test Bureau.

Kelley, Truman L., et al. *Stanford Diagnostic Reading Tests*. New York: Harcourt Brace Jovanovich. [Level I (2.5–4.5); level II (4.5–8.5). Group tests with separate measures of comprehension, vocabulary, syllabication, auditory skills, phonic analysis, and rate.]

Work-Study Skills

Hieronymous, A. N., et al. *Iowa Tests of Basic Skills: Work-Study Skills*. Boston: Houghton Mifflin.

Kelley, Truman L., et al. *Stanford Achievement Tests: Reading-Study Skills*. New York: Harcourt Brace Jovanovich.

Scores on standardized tests identify the range of differences in reading performance within the class but not necessarily the precise achievement level of each class member. This caution is needed, since a test may have been standardized on a sample population that is significantly different from the pupils being tested; and most tests are timed, which may affect individual pupil performance.

It cannot be assumed that a standardized test score and classroom performance level are comparable. A single test score on a standardized reading test frequently reflects the child's frustration level rather than the level at which he should receive instruction. In other words, a child who achieved a fourth-grade score on a test may be unable to perform satisfactorily with a fourth-year reader or with fourth-grade content materials. This is particularly true of the readers at the upper and lower ends of the distribution of scores.

Moreover, a general survey reading achievement test does not identify the specific reading strengths and weaknesses of the reader. More specific diagnostic reading tests must be used to provide a classification of the types of skills with which the child may be having difficulty. Oscar K. Buros' latest *Mental Measurements Yearbook* (Highland Park, N.J.: The Gryphon Press), which is a collection of reviews of reading tests, would be good supplementary reading for this section.

Informal inventories

There are various ways to obtain evidence about the child's reading performance: observation, informal tests, inventories, and checklists in readers and manuals are only a few.[34]

• *Interest, personality, and attitude factors*   Teachers need to know the kinds of materials the child likes to read, the books he has read and enjoyed, the amount of time he spends in out-of-school reading, the use which he makes of the public library, the books he owns, and other facts. In addition, teachers should concern themselves with discovering ways in which a pupil spends his spare time, clubs to which he belongs, games he plays, favorite radio and television programs, travel experiences, and the like. A teacher-made interest inventory, developed from such items as those suggested above, can provide valuable information concerning the interests that may be utilized in promoting reading effort.

Further information may be secured by encouraging pupils to talk or write about their feelings regarding reading and the values (or lack of them) found in reading. An informal reading personality check has been proposed by Boning and Boning.[35]

The importance of attitudes was stressed in chapter 1, pages 18–22, and the several ways of measuring language arts attitudes can easily be modified to direct attention to basic reading instruction. Two additional helpful references are footnoted.[36]

Some of the more powerful attitude motivators are cited in the literature chapter: oral reading by the teacher, oral reading by pupils to one another, using tapes/records to expose students to literature, using filmstrips/films to stimulate reading, and sharing of literature. Upon pupil response, ideas as suggested in the section of this chapter

---

34. This section contains many of the ideas originally presented in the following source: Paul C. Burns and Robert W. Ridgway, "Diagnosing Reading Difficulties through Classroom Procedures," *Contributions in Reading* no. 30 (Boston: Ginn, 1962).

35. Thomas Boning and Richard Boning, "I'd Rather Read Than . . . ," *The Reading Teacher* 10 (April 1957): 197.

36. Ronald C. Filler and J. Estill Alexander, "Constructing Informal Attitude Scales," *Tennessee Reading Teacher* 1 (Spring 1973) 16–18. See also T. H. Estes, "A Scale To Measure Attitudes Toward Reading," *Journal of Reading* 15 (November 1971): 135–138.

entitled "Individualized Reading" (self-selection, time to read, and pupil-teacher conferences) provide activities that will promote positive attitudes toward reading.

• *Sight vocabulary and word recognition techniques*   An informal check for sight vocabulary (word recognition within five seconds) may be developed by the teacher from a list of basic words like the Dolch 220 Words or the words listed in chart 14.4, pages 508–510. The levels may be established as:

1. One-third of the words known—grade 1
2. One-half of the words known—middle of grade 2
3. All words known—middle of grade 3

Another way to make a word recognition inventory is to compose a list of words from the back of the basal readers (about twenty words randomly chosen from each level, preprimer through sixth reader). Each word is written on a three-by-five-inch file card, and the cards are flashed for a quarter of a second to the child. When frustration occurs, a second presentation (about five seconds per word) is made, stopping when about 50 percent or more of the words are missed. In both situations, the alert teacher notes and jots down information relative to responses to:

initial and final consonants	consonant sounds
initial and final blends	vowel sounds
syllables	prefixes and suffixes
compound words	possessives
inflectional endings	contractions

In any oral reading situation, the teacher may note the way the pupil handles picture clues, word-form clues, and various context clues. If needed, a short, teacher-made test on the child's ability to apply word analysis skills can be made from the list of skills taught during a particular period of time. For example, if pupils have received instruction with a word like *hill* and beginning consonant sounds like *b, f, k, j, t,* and *w*, sentences could be composed containing such new words as *Bill, fill, kill, Jill, till,* and *will*. The child's ability to attack these words will be noted.

Numerous clues are given daily to the teacher. If a pupil is missing words like *there, what,* and *were*, more help with difficult sight words may be indicated. If words like *car, hard,* and *burn* are missed, perhaps more attention needs to be given to developing the principle of the vowel sound when followed by *r*.

• *Levels of performance (oral and silent)*   Perhaps the single, most valuable approach to help the teacher define his work with specific groups and individuals would be to provide some time to check each pupil's reading individually in order to establish his *instructional level* (the reading level to be used for instruction under teacher guidance) and his *independent reading level* (reading "on his own").

This procedure requires that a pupil read short passages (30 to 200 words depending on level) orally from sets of unfamiliar basal readers while the teacher is listening, supplying help on words that make the child hesitate for more than five seconds.[37] The pupil reads at successively higher levels of readability until his *frustration level* is located. The child should be started at a level or so below his probable, or suspected, reading level. This level is determined from achievement test results, sampling from a basic sight-word list, or about one level below the place of his first error on a word recognition inventory test from the basal readers as described above.

The *independent level* of reading would be indicated when the pupil can read the material, free from the tension signs, correctly pronouncing 98 in 100 running words (98 percent correct) and correctly responds to 90 percent of the questions put to him (answers 9 of 10 questions). When the pupil reaches the highest level where he correctly pronounces on his own some 85 percent of the words (grades 1 and 2) to 95 percent of the words (grade 3 and above)—that is, 15 errors per 100 words for grade 1–2 children to 5 errors per 100 words for grade 3–6 children—and comprehends approximately 75 percent of the questions put to him, he has achieved his *instructional level*.

If a pupil needs help on more than 1 out of 10 running words (90 percent) or comprehends less than 50 percent of the questions on the material, he may have reached his *frustration level* (too advanced).

After the level of frustration has been reached, the teacher may read higher levels of material to the child until he finds the highest reading level at which the child can comprehend 75 percent of the material read to him. At this point, the child has reached his probable *capacity* (reading potential) *level*. On page 533 is a summary of the different reading levels.

Many teachers have found it helpful to use a simple system of marking on the teacher's copy of the reading material the oral reading errors of pupils. For example:

---

37. That is, preprimer, 30 words; primer, 50 words; book (grade) 1, 75 words; book 2, 100 words; book 3, 125 words; book 4, 150 words; book 5, 175 words; and book 6, 200 words.

LEVEL	WORD RECOGNITION	COMPREHENSION
independent	98 percent	90 percent
instructional	85 percent (grades 1–2)	75 percent
	95 percent (grade 3 and above)	
frustration	90 percent	50 percent
capacity		75 percent

unknown word supplied (𝒫)

words, or parts of words,
   mispronounced (underlined)
omitted words or parts
   of words (circled)
insertions (caret ∧)

reversals (ᴎ)

This is (a) story of a dog
who was playing with a

ball one day. He did many funny

tricks. Bob smiled as . . . .

Repetitions, punctuation omissions, and spontaneous corrections may be marked, but some authorities suggest that they not be scored as errors. Proper names and dialect differences are also not counted as errors. Some teachers have found the tape recorder effective for pupil oral reading, replaying the tapes to note the errors.

In day-to-day oral reading situations, the teacher may note left-to-right orientation, eye-voice span, number of regressions, types of eye movements, phrasing, expression, and varying the voice to indicate changes of meaning. In addition, the quality of voice, pitch, juncture, stress, poise, posture, and freedom from tension can be detected.

To develop questions to check the comprehension power of the child, the questioning strategies cited earlier are of help. Each passage should be checked with sets of questions, at least one of each of the following kinds: main idea, detail, vocabulary, sequence, and inference.

The teacher may choose to make his own booklet for checking the instructional level by cutting out sample passages from graded readers and developing comprehension questions about them. For the use of the teacher in marking oral reading errors, each reading selection should be dittoed.

Smith has eased considerably the teacher's work in this type of assessment by collecting and arranging selections that allow the teacher to measure levels in basal materials.[38] She has structured the follow-up materials so that a check may be made of comprehension, phonic and structural attack, and word recognition. Many basal reading programs also include an I.R.I. (Informal Reading Inventory).

If the teacher uses the following pattern, there is opportunity to note many facets of the pupil's reading habits and skills.

1. Oral sight reading, with comprehension questions
2. Silent reading of a page or two (30 to 200 words), with comprehension questions
3. Oral rereading of the material read silently (to compare with sight reading)

• *Speed*   If the teacher times the silent reading suggested in (2) above, some indication of words-per-minute is given. With a silent reading situation, questions that help the teacher check the progress of pupils in speed of reading include:

What are the pupils' rates of speed in reading for various purposes?
Is the speed appropriate to purpose and content?
Does the pupil vary the rate according to the material?
Above all, does he insist upon comprehension of what he reads?

• *Content*   As with basic reading materials, the pupil's appropriate reading level of content subjects may be found by having him read sample sets of passages and answer comprehension and vocabulary questions. Study skills, such as use of a table of contents and an index, location and use of basic reference materials, map and globe reading, use of a dictionary, reading of tables, charts, and graphs, may be diagnosed directly in situations in which such skills are being used. Examination of pupils' oral and written reports help to reveal strengths and weaknesses in power of organization, summarizing, outlining, and note-taking. Informal teacher-made tests, which require the child to use the actual reference sources, could well be used to supplement observations.

---

38. Nila B. Smith, *Graded Selections for Informal Reading Diagnosis, 1–3*, 1959; *4–6*, 1962 (New York: New York University Press). See also Marjorie S. Johnson and Roy A. Kress, "Individual Reading Inventories," *Sociological and Psychological Factors in Reading*, 21st Annual Reading Institute (Philadelphia: Temple University, 1964), pp. 47–60.

• *Remarks*   No pupil reveals all there is to know about his reading in any one sample of his reading performance. When informal procedures are continuous, patterns of strengths and weaknesses become more apparent. Something can be learned each time the child reads aloud, each time he attempts to use worksheets independently, each time he reads silently for a given purpose, each time

CHART 14.6: Informal Analysis Sheet

Name_____ Age_____ Grade_____ Date_____	
Major interests	Reading levels Independent _____ Instructional _____ Frustration _____ Capacity _____

Sight vocabulary level
                   ¼ sec.   5 sec.
Dolch Word List   _____   _____
  (or other basic
  word list)
Recognition inventory _____   _____
	Feelings toward reading

Main types of word recognition errors Unknown words _____ Mispronunciations _____ Omissions _____ Insertions _____ Reversals _____	Speed
Observations: Word recognition: Comprehension:	

he makes a trip to the library. Chart 14.6 provides a suggested form for recording pertinent data about the child's reading performance as revealed through informal inventories.

All this information is useless, however, unless it is used as a blueprint for instruction. And instruction is more effective if teachers are familiar with the skills of reading and activities and materials that can be used to strengthen noted weaknesses. The Hafner-Jolly book provides a comprehensive listing of commercial reading materials—kits, audiovisual equipment, games, workbooks. (See Selected References.) An excellent description of "homemade reading kits" can be found in Hap Gilliland, *Materials for Remedial Reading and Their Uses* (Billings, Mont.: Eastern Montana College, 1965), pp. 97–103.

Finally, the teacher needs to be aware that there may be some children in the classroom who have reading difficulties that require corrective (classroom teacher) or remedial (specialist) assistance. Books by the following authors provide a beginning place for such study: Ekwall, Gallant, Harris, Kennedy, and Wilson. (See Selected References.)

SELECTED REFERENCES

General Professional

Anderson, Paul S. *Language Skills in Elementary Education.* 2d ed. New York: Macmillan, 1972, chapter 5.

Boyd, Gertrude. *Teaching Communication Skills in the Elementary School.* New York: Van Nostrand Reinhold, 1970, chapter 15.

Burrows, Alvina T.; Monson, Diane L.; and Stauffer, Russell G. *New Horizons in Language Arts.* New York: Harper & Row, 1972, chapters 3, 5, and 7.

Corcoran, Gertrude B. *Language Arts in Elementary School: A Modern Linguistic Approach.* New York: Ronald, 1970, chapter 7.

Dallmann, Martha. *Teaching the Language Arts in the Elementary School.* 2d ed. Dubuque, Iowa: William C. Brown, 1971, chapters 9 and 10.

Greene, Harry A., and Petty, Walter T. *Developing Language Skills in the Elementary Schools.* 4th ed. Boston: Allyn and Bacon, 1971, chapter 14.

Smith, James A. *Adventures in Communication: Language Arts Methods.* Boston: Allyn and Bacon, 1972, chapter 7.

Strickland, Ruth. *The Language Arts in the Elementary School.* 3rd ed. Lexington, Mass.: D. C. Heath, 1969, chapters 11 and 12.

Specialized

Aukerman, Robert C. *Approaches to Beginning Reading.* New York: Wiley, 1971.

Austin, David, et al. *Reading Rights for Boys: Sex Role and Development in Language Experiences.* New York: Appleton-Century-Crofts, 1971.

Barbe, Walter B. *Educator's Guide to Personalized Reading Instruction*. Englewood Cliffs, N.J.: Prentice-Hall, 1961.

Dallmann, Martha, et al. *The Teaching of Reading*. 4th ed. New York: Holt, Rinehart and Winston, 1974.

Durkin, Delores. *Phonics, Linguistics, and Reading*. New York: Teachers College Press, Columbia University, 1973.

————. *Teaching Them to Read*. 2d ed. Boston: Allyn and Bacon, 1974.

Ekwall, Eldon. *Locating and Correcting Reading Difficulties*. Columbus, Ohio: Merrill, 1970.

Gallant, Ruth. *Handbook in Corrective Reading*. Columbus, Ohio: Merrill, 1970.

Goodman, Kenneth S., et al. *Choosing Materials to Teach Reading*. Detroit: Wayne State University Press, 1967.

Gray, William S. *On Their Own in Reading: How to Give Children Independence in Analyzing New Words*. Rev. ed. Chicago: Scott Foresman, 1960.

Hafner, Lawrence, and Jolly, Hayden B. *Patterns of Teaching Reading in the Elementary School*. New York: Macmillan, 1972.

Hall, Mary Anne. *Teaching Reading as a Language Experience*. Columbus, Ohio: Merrill, 1970.

Harris, Albert J. *How to Increase Reading Ability*. 5th ed. New York: McKay, 1970.

Harris, L. *Reading Instruction Through Diagnostic Teaching*. New York: Holt, Rinehart and Winston, 1972.

Heilman, Arthur W. *Principles and Practices of Teaching Reading*. 3rd ed. Columbus, Ohio: Merrill, 1972.

————. *Phonics in Proper Perspective*. 2d ed. Columbus, Ohio: Merrill, 1968.

Herber, Harold L. *Teaching Reading in the Content Areas*. Englewood Cliffs, N.J.: Prentice-Hall, 1970.

Horn, Thomas D., ed. *Reading for the Disadvantaged*. New York: Harcourt Brace Jovanovich, 1970.

Hull, Marion A. *Phonics for the Teacher of Reading: Problems of Linguistically Different Learners*. New York: Harcourt Brace Jovanovich, 1970.

Kennedy, Eddie C. *Classroom Approaches to Remedial Reading*. Itasca, Ill.: Peacock Publishers, 1971.

Lee, Dorris M., and Allen, Richard V. *Learning to Read Through Experience*. New York: Appleton-Century-Crofts, 1963.

Miller, W. H. *The First R: Elementary Reading Today*. New York: Holt, Rinehart and Winston, 1972.

Monroe, Marion, and Rogers, Bernice. *Foundations for Reading: Informal Pre-Reading Procedures*. Chicago: Scott Foresman, 1964.

Russell, David H., and Karr, Eta E. *Reading Aids Through the Grades*. New York: Teachers College Press, Columbia University, 1951.

Schell, Leo M., and Burns, Paul C., eds. *Remedial Reading: Classroom and Clinic*. 2d ed. Boston: Allyn and Bacon, 1972.

Smith, Nila B. *Reading Instruction for Today's Children*. Englewood Cliffs, N.J.: Prentice-Hall, 1963.

Spache, Evelyn B. *Reading Activities for Child Involvement.* Boston: Allyn and Bacon, 1972.

Spache, George D. *Reading in the Elementary School.* Edited by Evelyn Spache. 3rd ed. Boston: Allyn and Bacon, 1973.

Stauffer, Russell G. *The Language Experience Approach to the Teaching of Reading.* New York: Harper & Row, 1970.

――――. *Teaching Reading as a Thinking Process.* New York: Harper & Row, 1968.

Veatch, Jeannette, and Acinapuro, Philip J. *Reading in the Elementary School.* New York: Ronald, 1966.

――――, et al. *Key Words to Reading: The Language Experience Approach Begins.* Columbus, Ohio: Merrill, 1973.

Wallen, Carl. *Word Attack Skills in Reading.* Columbus, Ohio: Merrill, 1969.

Wilson, Robert M. *Diagnostic and Remedial Reading for Classroom and Clinic.* 2d ed. Columbus, Ohio: Merrill, 1972.

Wilson, Robert, and Hall, Mary Anne. *Programmed Word Attack for Teachers.* Columbus, Ohio: Merrill, 1968.

Zintz, Miles V. *The Reading Process: The Teacher and the Learner.* Dubuque, Iowa: William C. Brown, 1970.

Index